THE ANN LOVEJOY
HANDBOOK OF NORTHWEST GARDENING

THE ANN LOVEJOY
HANDBOOK OF NORTHWEST GARDENING

NATURAL:SUSTAINABLE:ORGANIC

PHOTOGRAPHS BY JANET LOUGHREY

SASQUATCH BOOKS
SEATTLE

Printed in China
Published by Sasquatch Books
Distributed by Publishers Group West
10 09 08 07 06 05 04 03   6 5 4 3 2 1

Cover & interior design: Rowan Moore/doublemranch.com
Cover & interior photographs: Janet Loughrey
Interior illustrations: Bill Evans
Copy editor: Rebecca Pepper

Library of Congress Cataloging in Publication Data
Lovejoy, Ann, 1951-
      The Ann Lovejoy handbook of Northwest gardening :
Natural : Sustainable : Organic
      p.   cm.
      ISBN 1-57061-198-X
      1. Natural landscaping—Northwest, Pacific. 2. Organic
gardening—Northwest, Pacific.
      I. Title: Handbook of Northwest gardening. II. Title.

      SB439.24.N673L68 2003
      635'.0484'09795—dc21   2003045608

Sasquatch Books
119 South Main Street, Suite 400
Seattle, WA 98104
206/467-4300
www.sasquatchbooks.com
books@sasquatchbooks.com

CONTENTS

To all compost lovers, everywhere.

INTRODUCTION

For many years, gardening was America's favorite leisure activity. Many of us found it relaxing to do a little weeding and watering in the cool of the evening after work. Early risers might put in an hour or two of garden puttering before the family was ready for breakfast. We happily spent our weekends on lawn care and in grooming beds and borders. Today gardening still ranks high on many Americans' to-do lists, but something has changed.

Despite the modern conveniences at our disposal, our lives are busier than ever. We spend our days rushing from meeting to workshop, or from soccer practice to the dentist. The busier we get, the more we need relaxation. Gardening can be relaxing, but it can also be a competitive sport, pursued with the same intensity we bring to our work. Years ago most folks were content to have a nice lawn surrounded by pretty shrubs, a tree or two, and some colorful flowers. Today we want beauty, elegance, and style, right now. Unfortunately, most of us take our cues from high-maintenance models that eat time.

Busy people don't need needy gardens. Busy people need green havens, lovely places where they can be gracefully enveloped in the natural without stressing about weeds. By gardening naturally, following the principles of sustainable design, we can have year-round gardens that provide beauty, style, and elegance with a modicum of work. What does it mean to garden naturally? Natural care is a way of gardening in cooperation with natural patterns, from weather and soil type to the size and shape of plants.

In contrast, many standard gardening practices are aimed at controlling nature; these do not work well or for long. Those who have made gardens with high hopes only to find themselves slaves to an endless stream of chores already know this: Nearly all traditional gardens require more work from the gardener with each passing year, and they often deliver less and less satisfaction. In addition, gardens made using classic techniques are decidedly not sustainable. Leave most gardens alone for a few weeks in July and you will come home either to a rampant jungle (if somebody watered for you) or a bone-dry desert.

What's the alternative? Happily, it's not artificial turf and plastic flowers, but a handsome, thriving landscape full of regionally appropriate plants that appreciate the natural conditions we can offer them. Sustainable design allows us to create flexible, adaptable gardens that grow less needy each year. Most of the work comes up front, when we make beautiful soil and simplify the shapes and flow patterns within the garden. Applying the concepts of sustainable design helps us to reduce or eliminate many repetitive chores likes weeding, fertilizing, and watering. Once the garden is established, annual chores consist largely of mulching and grooming. Seasonal chores still include some fertilizing, dividing, watering, and weeding, but a well-designed, well-planted garden of up to an acre can be kept in tip-top condition with an average of only two chore hours a week.

Successful gardening depends on many factors, only a few of which we can change. The Pacific Northwest can be one of the world's best places to garden. However, our region also has challenging native soils that can be difficult to improve, interesting weather, and little summer rain. Fortunately, thousands of attractive and useful plants will grow well here, given the proper start and follow-up care. But to take full advantage of our regional riches, we need to rethink a great deal of standard garden advice, in terms of care and culture and design.

A very high percentage of North American garden books are written primarily for the Eastern seaboard. Although the Northwest is sometimes called "little England" by the envious, the advice offered in imported English books does not always apply directly on this side of the water. Even books that are supposed to be specifically for the Northwest may have a California bias. (The largest market share generally gets the greatest attention.) The goal of this particular handbook is to make it very easy to be a happy and satisfied gardener in the maritime regions of the Pacific Northwest, which we refer to as Cascadia.

In geologists' terms, Cascadia is the stretch of land west of the Cascade Mountains, starting in southern British Columbia and reaching into Northern California. This same region is also the natural range of the salmonberry and the glittering rufous hummingbird that feeds on salmonberry nectar. The famous Northwest native flora has won awards from horticulture societies all over the world. These plants, our several types of native soils, and

Our Northwestern native flora is well-adapted to our typical dry summers and wet winters. Thus, durable native beauties like fragrant, evergreen Mahonia aquifolium *earn their way into gardens of all sizes.*

all the various attributes of our modified Mediterranean climate are what make gardening here different—sometimes just a little, sometimes a lot. Our gardens are most lastingly successful when we take these differences into account.

If we try to garden as people do back East or even in England, sooner or later we'll run into problems. When we take our cues from the plants around us, we can adapt our gardens to take advantage of the natural strengths of our region. Naturally, we can't grow everything in the world, but we can grow a huge range of plants very well indeed. Our own rich and varied native flora is an obvious place to start looking for plants adapted to our regional weather cycle of wet winters and dry summers. (This cyclical pattern is what classifies our climate as a modified Mediterranean type.) Certainly, we do not need to limit our garden plantings to natives, but our exceptional flora does make an excellent basis for a relatively independent matrix of garden plants.

I often use a palette of what I call "natives and allies," combining Northwest natives and their relatives from similar parts of the world, along with natural allies or companion plants and their relatives. This simple formula provides a large, varied, and adaptable selection of plants that settle in quickly and need relatively little care once established. When we stick to the thousands of plants, natives and not, that love the conditions we can offer them, we reduce pest and disease problems dramatically. That's because plants that are happy to be here are generally healthy. With nature on their side, gardeners in the maritime Northwest can make gardens that are as good as any in the world.

Fascinating as plants are, this handbook covers a lot more than what to grow and how to grow it. My intent is to help you make a garden that becomes easier to care for with each passing season. I'll take you through the all-important transition period in which you wean the garden off "drugs"—common agrichemical toxins. I'll explore ways to improve garden soils, promote plant health, and simplify garden care. I'll also discuss critter controls of many kinds, dealing with pests from aphids to antelopes (well, okay, deer). I'll look at design techniques that help you to reduce or minimize repetitive garden chores. Whether you garden for flowers, food, or fun (or all three), you'll find important information and ideas that will help you to rethink the way you garden. The goal is to do less and less hard work and more and more work that gives you pleasure.

Flip through these pages and you'll notice a great many topics. Some, like garden design, are conceptual, intended to help you decide how you want your garden to look. For instance, I prefer a style I call Northwest naturalistic, reflecting native Northwestern planting patterns. Design such as this, with a regional bias, uses local or regional materials and echoes regional architectural patterns, helping to give gardens a decided sense of place. In the Northwest we can also "garden where we are" by incorporating places to be in the garden during the long rainy season, when the weather is often mild enough to make outdoor meals or tea-taking a pleasure despite the rain.

A further point to consider is that much, if not most, garden maintenance is designed in. In other words, poor design creates a lot of work for the gardener. Thus the design concepts and techniques you will find here don't always match standard advice. Instead you'll learn simple organizing principles that let you make gardens in any style you like without creating an unwanted burden of care. Follow-up sections on bed making, hardscape (paths, patios, pergolas, and so on), and plant placement will help you turn your personal garden vision into a functional, beautiful reality.

Most garden themes, from shade gardening to edible landscaping, are best approached with a combination of expansive vision and earthy practicality. When we simply mimic an idea seen in a magazine or book, the result is often less than satisfactory. When we know both why and how we want to use a certain kind of design effect, we can implement it both thoughtfully and efficiently. In every case, both overviews and specific details are geared for this particular part of the world, taking into account everything from native plants and habitats to soil types and weather patterns. By working your way through the sections that apply to your site and interests, you'll learn how to create easygoing and lastingly satisfying gardens, whether edible or ornamental or both.

Practical sections on lawn care, foundation plantings, routine garden chores, and annual maintenance will help you avoid many typical chores and maintenance problems from the outset. If poor design creates work, sensible design can reduce or eliminate a lot of repetitive tasks. You can adapt the practical design ideas presented here to reflect any style you prefer, knowing the result will be easier to care for than traditional models.

Sections on common pests and problems stress prevention while also offering the least toxic ways to manage difficulties. It is my experience that most of these common problems are healed out of existence once we exchange the old chemical fixes for healthy, natural methods of gardening. Healthy soil makes for healthy plants. Well-chosen plants that like where they are will rarely be troubled by pests and disease. Once the toxic chain is broken, the healing of soil and plants begins almost immediately. Within a single season, you will begin to reap the benefits of benign natural care. I like to call this "guilt-free gardening," because these techniques are good for the earth and are so easy to implement that the gardener has time to savor the garden.

Lists of plants that are high performers in the long term will help you make good choices when you want to plant a tree, make a hedge, or enjoy winter flowers. Plants of all kinds are ranked for their overall contributions through the seasons, as well as for adaptability and ease of care. Both these selective lists and the various sample designs are intended to reduce or eliminate repetitive garden chores such as mowing, shearing, and weeding as much as possible.

Given the choice, most of us would prefer to be enthralled by our garden instead of being in thrall to its workload. After all, the point of having a garden is to enjoy it. You will learn here not how to "maintain" or hold your garden at a certain state—a sure road to obsolescence—but how to garden toward the future. When each garden task is carried out with thought for its long-term effects, we can create more sustainable, self-sufficient gardens.

If sustainable horticulture is a recent concept, sustainable agriculture is of longer standing. When we seek environmentally benign ways to work with soil and water, plants and pests, we don't need to reinvent the wheel. Our brothers and sisters in the fields are ready to share a mother lode of solid, proven information as well as practical and philosophical guidance. In this handbook, you'll find many tips and techniques gleaned from organic farmers and growers who are happy to share their experiences and observations.

Finally, it is my personal hope that this handbook will help you to relax and enjoy making and caring for a healthy, sustainable, easy-growing garden that pleases you to the ground.

Many repetitive chores like mowing, edging, trimming, watering, and feeding can be reduced or eliminated by sustainable design techniques. My ¼-acre garden can be kept attractive year-round with an average of two hours of weekly maintenance.

ONE: SUSTAINABLE GARDEN DESIGN

Eliminate mowing, edging, and reseeding by replacing lawn with paved or graveled areas where plants can relax over the edge without harming turf.

Sustainable garden design is all about creating gardens that become easier to care for with each passing year. We achieve this noble goal by editing the garden carefully, reducing or eliminating unwanted chores through thoughtful design.

As with any design process, we begin creating a sustainable design by examining the site, locating important features and access points. We look at physical realities such as soil type, drainage patterns, and the way the sun and wind move across the land. We also take into account our own patterns of living, how we want to be in the garden, and what we want the garden to do for us. The difference between a sustainable design and a traditional one is what we do with the information we gather.

Sustainable design is totally practical. It can also be more attractive than many traditional designs. When influenced by the naturalistic planting patterns seen in nature, sustainable designs have an elegant simplicity that makes them visually and emotionally pleasing even before a single plant is placed. It is usually possible to incorporate almost any design feature a gardener desires into a sustainable design, but every feature, from path to pergola, is

PRINCIPLES OF SUSTAINABLE DESIGN

Here are the main guidelines that inform all sustainable garden designs:

1. Begin with access and flow patterns. The goal is to get in and out of the garden as well as through it gracefully and with ease, even if you are pushing a heavy garden cart or are in a wheelchair.

2. Use bold, simple shapes. Make paths and beds as large as possible. Use soft, generous curves instead of straight lines, and eliminate fussy details such as narrow strips of grass between beds and a sidewalk.

3. Keep plants off the house, garage, and all wooden structures. Keep a plant-free strip at least 18 inches wide and 6 inches deep between a building wall and foundation plants. Even at maturity, foundation plants should never enter this plant-free strip.

4. Reduce or eliminate lawn areas to minimize chore time and water use. Eliminate edging by making mounded beds and using ground covers where soil meets paths.

placed where it makes the most sense in terms of the realities of the site and how it will be maintained. By addressing garden care at the design stage, we can reduce or eliminate high-maintenance areas and plant types that require ungratifying amounts of work.

Sustainable design is also deeply rooted in reality. If an area is boggy, instead of trying to drain it and make a lawn, we'll turn the boggy area into a bog garden filled with plants that love moisture, or we'll excavate a bit and create a pond. Surrounding planting beds will be bermed or mounded to give plant roots more air. When a site is dry and windy, we'll create flat or even slightly sunken beds that retain moisture, and we'll seek out dryland plants that thrive without seasonal watering.

When working toward a sustainable design, it is important to have the plants you want to grow in mind when you begin shaping the garden as a whole. When we deliberately create planting areas that will suit specific kinds of plants, we increase our chances of having a healthy, productive garden that thrives without much intervention.

This chapter addresses the basics of designing a sustainable garden. Each piece is examined in turn and is explained in ways that will help you make good decisions about how you want to shape and plant your garden. When you put all the pieces together, you'll find that the whole is synergistic, greater than the sum of its parts.

GARDENING BY DESIGN

Garden design seems mysterious to many gardeners who struggle to make and keep their yards attractive. In garden terms, design simply means making places to be, places to plant, and ways to reach them. We can do this well, in ways that make garden care easy and promote plant health, or we can do it the hard way, making a muddle of shapes, impeding flow with undersized paths, using path materials that require constant maintenance (such as turf), and building planting beds where many plants can't thrive (for example, in dry, rooty shade).

The difference between a terrific garden and a frustrating one often lies in the overall design. Garden design primarily involves space, not plants. Good design makes it easy to get to the garden and pleasant to be there. Good design creates planting spaces that are easily kept healthy and attractive. It offers paths that entice us into the garden and reward us with destination places along the way. Good gardens include places to sit and dream, places to play, and places to party, as well as places to keep our tools and to carry out seasonal chores.

Perhaps most important, good design makes it easy to move through the garden, whether you are pushing a wheelbarrow or a stroller, using a walker, or sitting in a wheelchair. Good design means using safe surfacing for paths and patios, keeping steps wide and uniformly level, and using code-approved riser heights. Good design means that our gardens are usable in all weather, for gardeners of all ages. Accessibility separates a lot of pretty but impractical gardens from truly livable ones. Good design also makes it easy to take care of our plants and to keep plant-free surfaces clean and usable. Good design is visually attractive all year-round.

That's quite a list, yet all these goals are surprisingly easy to accomplish when we follow the prime directive of garden design: Keep it simple. Clean lines and generous, uncluttered spaces allow plenty of elbow room for plants and people alike. As a rule of thumb, it's always better to have one wide path and one or two large beds than many small ones. Even in a tiny yard, wide paths and the largest beds possible will look most attractive because they relate in scale to the house, the street, mature trees, and the neighborhood as a whole.

Simple, big spaces are also extremely practical. Indoors or out, generous, uncluttered spaces are far easier to use and to keep tidy than small, crowded ones. Undersized paths, beds, and borders tend to look fussy and are a pain in the neck to maintain. For example, one of my projects was to redesign a small (12- by 35-foot) front yard. Originally, it was packed with many small beds surrounded by narrow grass paths. The gardener spent most of each weekend mowing, edging, and weeding the front yard. She admitted sadly that it never looked very attractive, even with her endless work. Not only was the design confusing to look at and walk through, but the beds were too small for anything but perennials. Thus the main entry to the house looked empty for half the year.

We replaced the complicated design with a wide gravel path that skirted the house. Overgrown old foundation plants that were touching the wooden house walls (inviting insects in to feast on damp siding) were removed. The

5. Use natural attributes like boggy areas or dry, windy places to advantage by matching them with plants that appreciate those conditions.

6. Develop a palette of native plants and allies that thrive in wet winters and dry summers. This can include many plants from the Mediterranean, such as lavender, rosemary, and sage; from the South African cape, such as cape fuchsias (*Phygelius* species); from Australia and New Zealand, such as hebes and copper carex; and from temperate parts of South America, such as hardy fuchsias.

7. Choose woody plants (trees and shrubs, including hedging) with an eye to their mature sizes and shapes in order to reduce or eliminate annual pruning and shaping. Since well-chosen, well-placed woody garden plants are far less needy than annuals and perennials, make sure that at least half the garden's plants are woody.

Continued on page 5

flurry of small beds were combined into one large, curving one along the sidewalk that was 8 feet wide at the deepest point. We gently mounded this bed to give the streetside plantings some extra height. The depth of this single bed gave us enough room to make a handsome privacy planting that layered down from small trees and backbone shrubs to a border of colorful plants for every season. With no lawn, there's no longer any mowing or edging. The mulched beds are nearly weed-free. The new front garden can be cared for in an hour a week or less, and the small, private seating area we tucked in gets more use than the weeding tools.

Over the years I've made gardens all over the country. Along the way, I've made every mistake you can imagine and some especially clever ones that few other folks have thought of. For many years, I gardened at least six hours or more a day and carried on the work all year-round. Today I'm both older and smarter than I used to be, and I've learned how to make gardens that don't need me very

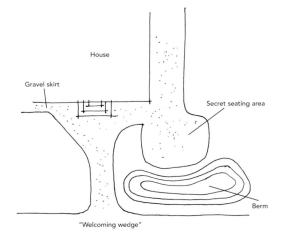

A small, cluttered yard became a serene daily retreat once we simplified the design. A generous gravel path now invites visitors in with a "welcoming wedge," a flaring shape repeated at the front door to create plenty of room for guests, kids, dogs, and baby strollers. The new bermed bed is about 8 feet wide at the deepest point, and holds a selection of compact evergreen shrubs that screen the tucked-in seating area from the sidewalk. An 18-inch wide gravel skirt lines the entire house and all wooden structures, acting as a plant-free zone and reducing insect access to the house.

House

Gravel skirt

Secret seating area

Berm

"Welcoming wedge"

much. My present gardens are large and well filled with a wide variety of plants. The abundantly planted beds and borders are easily cared for in just a couple of hours a week, though they cover more than half an acre. I still put in a few hours a week all year-round, but I enjoy the work (or play) enormously. My gardens look attractive in every season, yet I rarely water or feed the plants, and I spend very little time weeding. Most of my chore time is spent redesigning my container plantings, grooming or dividing plants, making compost, and spreading composted dairy manure and compost as mulch over every bed.

I consider my gardens sustainable because they can be kept healthy largely by recycling the plant wastes removed by grooming into the compost that nourishes the beds. The first year I made the gardens, I did quite a bit of weeding, watering, and feeding. As the soil improved and the mulches grew deeper, I fed and watered and weeded less each month. Now the gardens always look handsome yet need very little attention, and I prune, water, and feed just a few times a year.

I learned how to make gardens more sustainable by questioning every established design principle I knew, asking myself if the old rules and techniques really made sense today. Do I really need to double or triple dig each bed? (No. Layering amendments works fine and is far less work.) Must I divide and reset the perennial beds every three years or so? (Yes, so I no longer make traditional perennial beds.)

I came to realize that the old ways worked well when a garden owner could count on a large, well-trained, and inexpensive staff of willing workers. Today most of us do the garden work ourselves, with perhaps some part-time help (usually unskilled and quite expensive). As I grew older and accumulated various kinds of bodily damage, I began to wonder whether there wasn't a simpler, easier way to achieve my desired goals.

I wanted a garden that was wonderful to look at and to be in all year-round yet could be cared for easily and without putting in too much time. To have that, I needed to reevaluate everything I knew about garden design and maintenance. I like experimenting, so I began making many kinds of beds, applying ideas I had learned about sustainable agriculture and organic farming to the garden. Over time, I developed a method of bed making that has proved both attractive and long-lastingly effective. I also developed a palette of plants that were well adapted to the conditions in my garden and in the maritime Northwest in general. Finally, I hit on a system of natural care that proved to be highly efficient and quite simple. The resulting system pleases me very much, especially because it is so flexible that it can be adapted to suit any style of garden you might want.

8. Place key woody evergreens for privacy and visual screening, then create evergreen island groupings of smaller shrubs throughout the beds and borders to keep the garden looking furnished all year long. Always place these plants where their ultimate size and shape will fit properly and be a design asset.

9. Cluster plants with similar needs, placing them in sites and situations where most of their needs will be met naturally. Always put shade lovers in shade and sun lovers in sunny places. Give bog plants soggy spots, and put dryland plants where drainage is good.

10. Select color spot plants with care, choosing well-mannered plants that won't outgrow their position too quickly, seldom need division, and thrive in moderate conditions. Don't go all out for spring or summer effects, but divide your allotted color space between the seasons, making sure there are flowers and colorful features such as berries and bark all year long.

COMMON THREADS OF GOOD DESIGN

I do a great deal of garden consultation, a fascinating and informative pursuit. While the site and size and setting of each garden can differ enormously, it's interesting to note how frequently certain issues arise. One string of very different kinds of gardens I saw had similar difficulties.

Although the styles of the gardens varied, all had a high percentage of high-maintenance perennial beds that demanded a lot of work. All had overly narrow paths that were hard to use companionably and that made it impossible to push a wheelbarrow along without causing damage to the plants. All had beds with awkward shapes that made access challenging, encouraged weeds, and were difficult to keep attractive. All had starved soil and unhealthy, stressed plants that did not properly fill their allotted spaces. All had significant problems with weed control. Every one of the gardens had some lovely features, and all gave their owners pleasure. However, that pleasure was rapidly becoming tempered with annoyance as the endless chores mounted.

At the last garden I visited, we discussed the many factors that were causing so much work for the gardener. I then offered suggestions for implementing control measures to alleviate the problems. The owner listened and nodded appreciatively as I recounted the list of chores created by poor design. However, her friend, who was not a gardener, was baffled.

"This garden looks just like the magazine ones," he pointed out. "How can so much be wrong with it?" In many ways, it did look like a magazine picture. Indeed, with a little cleanup and some restructuring, it could be featured in a magazine. There were even a couple of potential cover shots.

So what was wrong? Clearly, a lot is right with a garden that still looks pretty good even when it's edging out of control. What's wrong in design terms might not even matter to the homeowner, who may not much care (especially if he or she finds endless chores meditative). However, addressing these very common design flaws will greatly improve the ease of garden care and reduce the need for many of the annoyingly repetitive chores created by poor design.

The main design issues in a garden are usually the same few things, all of which were exemplified in this particular garden. Here's how to avoid them:

1. **Garden to scale.** Gardens that are in scale with the overall setting are always as generously proportioned as possible. Even when the site is small, it is most effective and practical to work boldly. Bigger beds and wider paths simplify access and make it easier to keep the garden tidy. Beds planted to scale will have a high proportion of woody plants, which have presence all year-round and need far less maintenance (if properly chosen) than perennials. When gardens are designed without paying attention to scale, they invariably have

overly narrow paths and undersized beds that look wimpy and insignificant in the overall setting. Here in the Northwest, our soaring trees and endless vistas make bitty little gardens look trivial.

Easy access and unbroken flow make gardens comfortable to use in all seasons. Always allow extra room at entryways and where paths cross.

2. **Use strong, simple shapes.** Clean lines and simple shapes make for powerful, satisfying design. They also make for easily kept gardens that clean up quickly. Avoid fussy designs cluttered with lots of small beds and unnecessary curves and wiggles; these are visually distracting and hard to maintain attractively.

3. **Design a clean, clear structure.** Structure helps to define the garden space and delineate areas of use. Structure may come from hardscape, such as paths,

patios, arbors, walls, and fences. It can also be created with powerful plants, particularly trees and shrubs that have potent natural architecture. Gardens that lack structure usually look insignificant and may be visually confusing. Often, such gardens vanish entirely in winter.

4. **Plan for access.** Start your design at the front entry and be bold; make your entry path as wide as possible (6 to 8 feet is ideal). This will look generous and inviting and provide adequate space for several people to approach at once. Make sure you can get to the garden easily from inside the house as well as from the main entry and the garage. Gardens you can't reach easily are seldom used.

5. **Create flow.** Garden paths direct the eye and the foot, guiding us through the available space. Make sure your paths are wide and well surfaced and that they take visitors where you want them to go. Whenever possible, use gentle curves rather than straight lines, which hurry us along and have a rigid, unnatural look. The garden design should reflect the natural environment, not the shape of the house. Naturalistic curves not only look more relaxed and inviting but are easier to keep tidy than rectilinear patterns.

6. **Screen for privacy.** Much yard space goes unused because it feels too exposed or overlooked to be comfortable. Simple privacy screening can create garden rooms and seating areas that are cozy and inviting. However, be careful not to overscreen by using plants that are too tall or wide. As they grow, you will be forced into a chain-saw relationship with them and constantly be battling for space. What's more, excessive screening robs the garden of light and air. If space is limited, screen with fence or fence sections or trellis panels draped with vines rather than with hedge plants.

7. **Plant for year-round interest.** Most amateur gardens suffer from either an excess of structural plants with little or no seasonal flow or an overemphasis on spring and summer plants that disappear in the cooler months. Ideally, you should create a balanced blend of evergreen structural plants and seasonal color, including plenty of fall and winter interest.

8. **Reduce lawn to reduce work.** No ground cover, perennial, or shrub needs to be watered, fed, edged, and mowed as often as a lawn. To reduce chore time, minimize the lawn size or eliminate it altogether. Replace lawns with gravel paths and seating areas that can be kept clean with a flame weeder. Fill the beds and borders with appropriate drought-tolerant plants, including trees, shrubs, perennials, ground covers, and sheets of seasonal bulbs. Such areas can be kept attractive with an annual feeding mulch and a few hours of tidying each year.

9. **Include a reality check.** Before planning the garden or planting anything (especially trees), look up. Then look down. What are you looking for? Power lines, sewer and water lines, and cable and telephone connections, for starters. If you are not on a sewer system, be sure to identify where the septic field is, and keep it free of large, deep-rooted plants and water hogs. It is also important to learn where natural pathways lie, because no matter how pretty your design is, it won't work if it doesn't address natural flow patterns.

10. **Mulch, mulch, mulch.** A good mulch reduces garden chores, builds healthy soil, and reduces plant needs. Compost is my favorite mulch; this weed-free substance conserves soil moisture, regulates soil temperature, discourages weeds, and feeds plants, all at the same time. What's more, it looks far more attractive than water-shedding bark, which also competes with your plants for nitrogen, which it needs to break down properly.

NATURALISTIC DESIGN

Naturalistic garden design borrows its bones from natural environments. The layering that occurs in unspoiled habitat consists of the treeline or canopy, high and low understory, the furnishing layer, and the ground cover layer. Mixed in with these are vines that link the higher and lower layers, and seasonal plants, from perennials and annuals to bulbs, that come and go. Naturalistic garden designers layer plants in the garden in ways that evoke natural environments. Putting plants into their proper ecological niches gives them a visually appropriate context, so that the size and shape they have by nature fits the garden's design. Proper selection and placement of plants also eliminates much of the "chain-saw relationship" between the gardener and the garden. Naturalistic designers seek to work cooperatively with the environment and the plants they choose, rather than imposing arbitrary rules or patterns.

ORGANIC DESIGN

Frank Lloyd Wright wrote about "organic architecture," a school of design that works with the relationships between people, place, and buildings. Similarly, organic garden design builds on the intimate relationships between people, place, and plants. This type of design is sometimes called "gardening where you live," meaning that you pay attention to local and regional patterns of many kinds. Soil types, weather, ecosystems, and history can influence an organic garden design. Like naturalistic design, organic garden design is essentially a cooperative, intuitive process that emphasizes links to natural environments. In both types of design, natural, asymmetrical forms replace geometrical, domination-based patterns.

ADAPTING TRADITIONAL DESIGNS

Traditional garden designs can create a great deal of work for the gardener. When we impose artificial forms on plants and places, we set up an endless cycle of maintenance intended to keep those chosen shapes intact. When instead we make designs based on natural shapes and forms, much of this automatic maintenance is reduced or eliminated. Many simple techniques can be applied to gardens of any kind or style with equally satisfactory results.

This does not mean you shouldn't make a Japanese Zen garden or try to reproduce an English garden, if that is where your heart calls you. However, if you choose to work with those styles, you can reduce the enormous workload implicit in both by making sensible, informed choices about the plants you use and where you put them.

Indeed, it may be easier to make a mossy Zen garden in the Northwest than to struggle with an unhappy lawn. When you let the lush native mosses replace grass (as they are often longing to do), the velvety carpet can be set with bold rocks and stone lanterns, evergreen ferns and compact rhododendrons, and choice Asian woodlanders like toad lilies and Japanese anemones. You'll spend far less

time encouraging the moss and its compatible companions than you did trying to get grass to grow where it was
deeply unhappy.

If the billowy English border look grabs you, be aware
that a great deal of control work is in store for you,
notably staking, trimming, shearing, and shaping. You
can eliminate a lot of it by choosing plants with care. For
instance, when you edge your beds with true miniature
boxwood, you reduce clipping from a chore needing to be
done four to six times a year to one annual session. Select
plants that don't flop, and staking is minimized. Give
preference to plants with more than one season of beauty,
and your garden will have less visually dull down time.
(Historically, many English gardens have been summer
oriented, with little of interest for the remaining eight
months of the year. Hmm.)

SOFTEN THE EDGES

In any kind of garden, replacing hard-edged geometry
with soft, simple curves can reduce maintenance immediately. Many people bristle when I say this and insist that
using curves can't possibly make any practical difference.
However, it does. For one thing, graceful curves are easier
to edge and much faster to mow than right-angled
straight lines. Soft curves are also more forgiving, since
minor imperfections don't shout at you the way they do
when sharp angles and geometrical shapes aren't edged or
trimmed just so.

If you want to increase your hammock lounging time,
try this: Whether in the paths, the lawns, or the beds,
eliminate any fussy wiggles, awkward corners, or sharp
angles. Eliminate narrow strips of lawn or border by
making the paths or beds wider. Eliminate edging by
bringing your paths right up to the bed edges, with no
grass between them. If you aren't convinced that these
changes will matter, keep track of where you spend your
yard care time over the next few weeks. It's also interesting to note that the places that eat chore time are rarely
the ones that reward the eye. Simplify those places and
prepare to have free time on your hands.

REDUCE WEEDING

Weeding is another huge job that can be almost eradicated
by good design and proper planting. Start by simplifying

the shape of any space that is hard to work in or that requires more time than it is visually worth. Next, start planting the places that insist on being weedy. Nature clearly wants a plant there, so why not choose your own? Gravel walkways and drives are an exception; where gravel insists on being weedy, you probably need more gravel. A depth of 4 to 6 inches is minimal (more is better), and annual top-dressing of 1 to 2 inches is advisable for heavily used areas where gravel can wear thin quickly. Quarterly flame-weeding sessions (February, April, October, and December) can keep deep gravel completely weed-free.

In the garden beds and borders, mulching is the appropriate next step. The right mulch (compost is usually the best choice) makes healthier soil that in turn supports healthy plants. Mulch reduces weeds, conserves moisture, and looks better than bare earth, which is an invitation to weeds anyway.

GARDEN REDESIGN

Whether you are beginning a brand-new garden or remodeling a mature or frustrating one, it makes sense to start the design process with two vital questions: Where do you want to be in the garden, and what do you want to do there? Do you want a meditative retreat, a place to read and rest, a convivial place to eat with family and friends, a place to cut flowers, grow vegetables, play with the baby? As you refine it, this wish list will guide the size and shapes of the places your garden will include.

Next, determine the simplest, safest way to get to the places that will house your chosen activities. Three of the most important design concepts—entry, access and flow—develop naturally when you make easy and efficient ways to get about in the garden. The closer form and function are related, the more elegant the design solutions.

Here you will find simple step-by-step instructions for developing your own garden design. Use the before and after examples from our sample garden remodel as a guideline, aided by the questions and comments for each section. Follow along with the examples, altering the questions and features to reflect the realities of your own site and situation. By the time you finish this chapter, you will have a workable site map and a clear list of garden design goals.

An important part of creating a sustainable garden design is addressing the physical realities of your site. I often refer to this approach as design by problem solving: By designing in solutions to the problems we encounter, we reduce or eliminate that potential or actual problem for the future garden.

To clarify each step, I'll use one of my garden designs as a guide. This garden site originally included nearly all of the classic disasters. Each time we identified a problem, we tweaked the design to eradicate or mitigate the difficulty. In the rest of this section, you'll learn how this key concept of designing by problem solving turned an awkward, unattractive yard with lots of wasted space into a serene, beautiful environment flexible enough to provide safe play spaces for kids and pets and offer the gardener a lovely green haven. All this was accomplished in just a few work sessions (with the help of a skilled garden tractor operator and a fencing crew) and on a modest budget.

ASSESSING THE PROPERTY

The irregularly shaped lot lies at the end of a quiet cul-de-sac in a suburban neighborhood. The site occupies about a third of an acre, which will seem tiny to some readers and huge to others. In general, gardens are getting smaller as land costs rise and building lots shrink. However, the size issue is relatively unimportant, since the same principles apply to all sites, and design elements can be scaled both up and down.

The garden redesign begins with an overall property assessment. In design terms, this means examining the site in terms of assets and liabilities, as well as the owner's needs and desires. Her wish list started with a safe place for children and pets to play, necessitating secure enclosure. She wanted to replace her hard-to-mow, ratty lawn with rugged, easy-care plants. She needed a better drainage plan for neighborhood runoff that accumulated on her property. She prefers native plants and wanted to make them the basis for the garden, starting with a shrubby grove where birds could shelter and feed. She also wanted to retain some roses she had planted in memory of her mother and to salvage a number of elderly rhododendrons that were scattered about the yard.

The next step is to assess the lot for usability. It's fairly easy to see how a site can be used as it stands. It often

This oddly shaped lot was full of poorly placed trees and shrubs and a jumble of mixed fencing styles. Access from front to back was limited with overgrown paths, and the back was awkwardly graded.

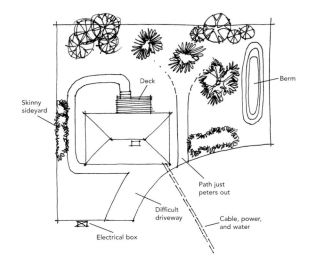

KNOW YOUR GARDEN

To develop a workable overall design for your garden, break the design process down into logical steps, starting with information gathering. Here's what to do and why you should do it:

1. **Make a map.** The site plan shown in our example is very simple, but it showed us everything we needed to know about the site. You can do the same thing for your own site in just a few minutes. You don't have to be an artist; just trust in graph paper. Here are some important features to locate on your map:

- Overhead power lines. No planting trees under power lines, please.

- Underground pipes and wires. No planting trees or shrubs over the sewer or water line, unless you want to support the Roto-Rooter guy.

- Existing features. Record trees and shrubs, sidewalks and stairways, decks, arbors, and so forth. Decide later which to keep, reshape, or remove.

2. **Evaluate the site.** What do you have to work with? What kind of feeling do you

takes training to see how hidden possibilities might be developed. The owner wanted an open yard with play space, a sheltered seating area outside her bedroom with access from the house, and a layered greenbelt to attract and support birds. What she had was a cluttered yard with indirect paths, random planting beds, abrupt changes of grade, and areas of high use that were not readily accessible from the house or each other.

Well-made paths would improve access between these high-use areas and open up unused spaces. With many near neighbors, establishing some privacy screening would change the nature of several neglected spaces, making them more attractive and comfortable without shutting out the neighbors entirely. Adding French doors to the master bedroom would create access to the new seating area, and more selective privacy screening would provide restful views from within both house and garden.

The lot had never been landscaped and included several abrupt and arbitrary changes of grade. Correcting the grading doubled the usable space in the garden, making room for several new seating areas. The goal was not just to flatten out pockets for seating, but also to take advantage of the changes in grade, creating wide stone steps and some berms to add drama and interest to the garden's topography. We also reserved space for a rocky water feature to be incorporated as the owner's budget allows.

LOCATING UTILITIES

Before beginning any earth-moving work, contact a professional utility locating service to find and mark all underground telephone and television cables and water mains. Also note where overhead electrical wires require the repositioning of young trees. These steps are extremely important and not to be neglected. Designs that do not take these vital factors into account are guaranteed not to be sustainable in any sense of the word. Ignoring them leads to thirsty hedges being planted too close to a water line, trees placed under power lines, cable lines being cut by an enthusiastic shovel, and much, much more (none of it good).

TAKING INVENTORY

The next step is to make a list of all physical features, including existing plants. The resulting inventory list included a row of bird's nest spruce and various dwarf conifers that the owner did not like. There were also several badly placed young cherry trees and half a dozen young filbert trees, as well as roses and rhododendrons, bamboo, and ferns. Most of the lot was covered in rough grass. Several groups of tall firs remained from the original clear-cut, joined by younger conifers added by the original homebuilder over the years. Ivy and blackberries required removal, as did several sapling alders.

On the initial map, identify every important object and plant that is already in place. Because sustainable design principles insist that all large plants be placed where their eventual size will be appropriate and attractive, almost every tree and shrub (except the mature firs) had to be removed or repositioned. By clustering the trees and shrubs into groves and replacing them near the property lines, we could free up room for beds, paths, seating areas, and play space.

Clustering trees and shrubs is sometimes called layering. The idea is to re-create the layers we see in a natural environment. If you look across a field at a woodland, you'll notice the treeline or canopy line against the sky. Below it, high and low understory shrubs make visual ladders that step the eye up to those treetops and back down. Below these is the furnishing layer, a blend of low-growing shrubs, perennials, annuals, bulbs, and grasses,

get in different parts of the property? One area may feel private and secluded, suggesting a secret getaway, while another place feels open and convivial. What kind of soil do you have? Is it the same everywhere? Some sites offer both acid sand and acid clay. New construction sites may combine deep hardpan with a light coating of imported topsoil. Determine your sun, shade, and wind patterns. This is best done over the course of a full year, to learn how seasonal changes affect the immediate environment. Discover present or seasonal drainage issues by examining soil erosion patterns. Where native vegetation has not been removed, wetland plants like reed grass and hard hack (Spiraea douglasii) are also tipoffs that you have seeps, boggy spots, seasonal streams, or localized runoff. The rainy season is the time to find this out for sure.

3. **Assess use patterns.** How is the yard space used now? The best-looking design can fail if it does not take real-life use patterns into account. Consider which use patterns are probably

Continued on page 16

permanent and which might be altered with new path and bed shaping. Consider access for the meter reader, the family dog, kids, and so on. Also assess how the garden relates to the house and to the neighborhood. Are existing access areas and entryways obvious, functional, safe, and attractive?

4. **Determine assets and liabilities**. What are the best features of the site? What makes it difficult to use well? Assets might include:

- Terrific views (even if partial)

- Good mix of sun and shade

- Shelter from wind

- Mature trees that can be centerpieces or backdrops

- Great neighborhood trees you can "borrow" visually

- Attractive, sound fencing

- Good flow of space

as well as a final carpet of ground cover plants. In a naturalistically designed garden, we layer down from the tallest trees (which may be next door or down the street) with shrubs and then create a furnishing layer of garden plants to bring things to human scale.

In this case, we needed to move quite a few good-sized shrubs and small trees. Fortunately, we were able to enlist the services of a small John Deere tractor-dozer and make many changes efficiently and quickly. We began by establishing a holding bed in an out-of-the-way corner, which we filled with compost. Simply moving inappropriately placed young trees, shrubs, and bushes to the holding bed revealed the true shape and size of formerly cluttered spaces more clearly. Uncluttering the garden this way can trigger an imaginative rethinking about potential uses for each space.

DESIGN BY PROBLEM SOLVING

As our map suggests, this garden site had more potential assets than existing ones. We did identify some mature garden and neighborhood trees, a sturdy back porch and deck, good storage space in the garage, and enough potentially available space to make some simple home remodeling a great choice.

Liabilities included awkward, ill-defined entryways to both house and garden; a big garage that overwhelmed the house, making it hard to find the front door; lots of wasted space; unhealthy plants; tired soil; poor drainage; excess seasonal runoff; lack of visual privacy; street noise; and unattractive views. In addition, there were seven different kinds of fencing on the property, including a long

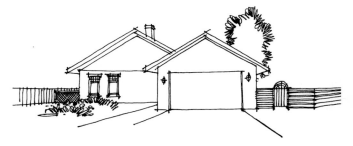

The front door was almost hidden and hard to find, and the entry was dominated by a gaping garage. Sideyards were difficult to access through old, mismatched gates and fence sections. The small front yard was cluttered with little beds and lacked a clear pathway.

section of chain-link fencing owned by a neighbor. The property was badly graded, and an abrupt dry ditch marked an area where excavation had left scars. A large and sagging berm was full of rotting stumps, logs, and construction rubble.

This probably sounds dismal, but that long list of liabilities created clear goals that guided each step of the continuing design process. Here's how we solved each problem, leading to a good, sustainable design.

Problem: The front entry was almost hidden, the garage was too obtrusive, and side entries were awkward and wasted a lot of space.

Solution: A new design for the front yard and entry solved several problems simultaneously. To create a unifying look for the house and garden, we moved the front-yard fence sections forward and built matching arbors and entry gates on both sides of the house. A matching roof detail over the double garage door blended the garage into the house. The house gained visual importance, the garage became less dominant, house and garden access was clearly defined, and the property has a new sense of welcome.

Problem: Unmatched fence sections looked funky and did not adequately secure the yard for children and pets.

Solution: We created an attractive, secure enclosure. Fencing is generally the best enclosure choice for small lots, offering several advantages over a hedge. It offers immediate, secure enclosure and provides instant visual screening for seating and dining areas. A well-constructed, unpainted cedar fence needs little or no maintenance and never outgrows its position or needs pruning.

- Functional, adequate storage and practical space for composting, keeping tools dry, potting up, and so on
- Wide, well-surfaced paths
- Structurally sound decks, sheds, arches, trellises, or gazebos

Common problems include:

- Lack of visual privacy
- Street noise
- Poor drainage
- Poor-quality soil
- Awkward changes of grade
- Narrow, inefficient, or unsafe paths and steps
- Excess shade or sun
- Overgrown hedges (including those that may belong to a neighbor)
- Lack of usable garden space

Matching trellis-paneled sideyard entry gates united the look of the front, as did an add-on trellis "eyebrow" that softened the front of the garage. A wide gravel path and large entryway pots now create a strong sense of entry at the front door.

Problem: The deck and yard were underused because they lacked privacy screening. We needed to create a visual barrier that blocked sound and dust without sacrificing sunlight and air flow. Overscreening is a common response to privacy problems, but using plants that will get too large only makes matters worse.

Solution: We reshaped the moldering old berm and planted it with low (8- to 15-foot-tall) screening plants. Existing young hazelnut trees were clustered into a small grove that baffles sidewalk views into the garden. Since the new berm will be in active use (the kids and dogs both like it), we didn't use any finesse plants here. Instead, the hazelnuts (to 15 feet) were joined by medium-sized shrubs, including native wild roses (*Rosa woodsii,* to 5 feet), flowering currant (*Ribes sanguineum,* to 6 feet), and snowberries (*Symphoricarpos* species, to 4 feet). All provide food and shelter for birds, bees, and butterflies. They are also hardy and tough enough to take playful children in stride.

To clean up the hodgepodge look of the backyard, one simple fence style that could incorporate most of the old wood was chosen. The neighbor's chainlink fence was covered (with permission) with honeysuckle, clematis, and roses. As part of the backyard regrade, a low ditch in front of the fence was backfilled with rubble (to keep the fence from being pushed over), then covered with soil and planted with bird-attracting shrubs like viburnums and native red currants.

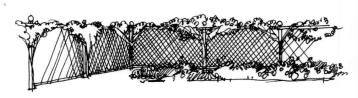

Problem: The chain-link fence belonged to a neighbor and offered unattractive views.

Solution: We removed ivy and weeds from the fence and replanted (with permission), using climbing roses and honeysuckles for summer fragrance and bird-attracting fruit in fall. A lusty Chinese evergreen vine (*Clematis armandii*) and two climbing evergreen hydrangeas (*Hydrangea seemanii* and *H. integrifolia,* both to 15 feet) fill in the shady section, providing winter and summer blossoms and year-round screening. The newly clothed fence will become part of the program to attract birds to the garden. As the plants mature, the fence will also provide more screening. We could also have mounted large, V-shaped trellises on stout posts set along the fence line to create areas of higher screening where visual privacy is important (dining and seating areas).

Problem: Seasonal drainage was eroding a channel through the backyard, and there was significant puddling after rain in several areas.

Solution: We reshaped the driveway with a lip to guide neighborhood runoff into the storm drain. Deep (6- to 8-inch) crushed-gravel paths were added to act like French drains, pulling water away from the house and redirecting it into the garden beds. All beds were gently mounded with a base of sandy loam to improve drainage. During the renovation, we discovered that the puddling was caused by black plastic left under large sections of path and bed. When we removed the plastic, the soil began to percolate better.

Problem: The foundation plants touched the house walls, creating mold and damp wood and inviting insects into the house.

Solution: We surrounded the house, garage, and deck with an 18-inch-wide skirt of ¾-inch crushed gravel, 4 to 6 inches deep. This plant-free zone keeps carpenter ants and other bugs away from the house and outbuildings and allows people to put up shutters or paint the house without having to prune back plants. Outside of that gravel band, we built mounded beds that ranged from 3 to 5 feet wide. We then selected foundation plants that would not grow any taller than the windowsills nor any wider than the beds. These were set into the middle of these beds, so branches will never touch the house. Our foundation shrub mix included evergreen herbs like rosemary, sage, and lavender on the sunny sides. The shady sides got a mix of compact rhododendrons, heavenly bamboo *(Nandina domestica),* and native *Leucothoe axillaris,* a handsome evergreen shrub with great seasonal color.

Problem: The garden was accessible only from the front and back of the house. The owner wanted to be able to reach the garden as well as see it clearly from her bedroom.

Solution: We replaced a small window with a generous pair of French doors that connect the main bedroom with the garden. To ensure visual privacy, several large rhododendrons were repositioned, along with some small fruit trees. Now the main bedroom opens into a sunny, graveled seating area cupped within a protective grove of trees and shrubs.

Problem: The existing lawn was hard to mow and unhealthy and grew unevenly.

Solution: We replaced all turf with 4- to 5-foot-wide curving paths and larger, rounded seating areas of crushed gravel. Everything that was not a path or seating area became a bed or border or play space. Crushed gravel is a splendid material for paths and seating areas because it drains well, is relatively inexpensive, and can be kept weed-free with an eco-cool flame weeder. It can also be compacted readily, providing a firm, safe surface for trikes and strollers as well as wheelchairs. Note that this is *not* true of pea gravel or rounded river rock. (For other ideas about lawn renovations, see Chapter 4.)

Problem: Abrupt grading created a hazard and wasted space. A narrow, dry ditch ran immediately beside the neighbor's chain-link fence.

Solution: To modify the slope without pushing over the fence, we used scavenged broken concrete to create a small retaining wall alongside the metal fence. This wall now holds the weight of the soil we used to backfill the little ditch or gully that made that part of the yard unusable. The old lawn and excess soil removed from other areas of the site nearly filled the gully. We filled in the rest with sandy loam, creating a "river" of sand for the kids to enjoy. Later, when the yard is ready to become more of a garden, this will make an excellent, fast-draining base for better topsoil.

Problem: Unhealthy fir trees showed signs of stress. An unhappy cherry tree displayed small, sparse foliage.

Solution: We removed almost 2 feet of soil left piled over the root zones of the fir trees during construction. Even though this had happened some fifteen years ago, the trees showed signs of recovery almost immediately. The suffering cherry tree had been planted too deeply and was reset at the proper height. Trees must be planted so that the gentle swelling just above the branching root system is aboveground. This swelling is called the collar or neck, and all trees have at least some form of it. Trees planted too deeply are always stressed.

Problem: The soil was tired and compacted, producing unhealthy, slow-growing plants.

Solution: All new beds were given a 4- to 6-inch base of sandy loam to improve drainage. An additional 6 to 8 inches of organic topsoil was mounded gently over the sandy loam. Most so-called topsoils are simply a mixture of sand and compost or shredded bark, often with some native soil blended in. We found a local supplier who mixes sandy soil with compost, creating a well-balanced soil that drains well yet retains enough moisture and nutrients to make plants very happy. This layering is called sandwiching, since the layers are not tilled up but simply left in place. To top it off, we added a final 3- to 4-inch layer of composted organic dairy manure. This final layer keeps weeds at bay, insulates the soil, conserves moisture, and looks terrific. New and old plants alike responded to the new beds with gusto.

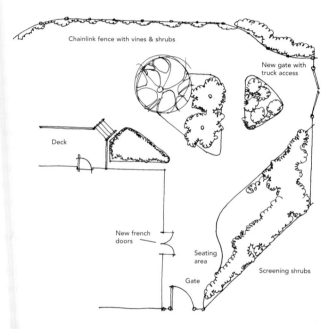

Chainlink fence with vines & shrubs

New gate with truck access

Deck

New french doors

Seating area

Gate

Screening shrubs

The new backyard design offers wide paths, plenty of play space, and well-prepared beds for planting. Shrubs and trees are now clustered where they provide screening and can grow up without impeding access or flow through the garden.

NOW YOU DO IT

To start your own sustainable design and problem-solving process, assess your yard using the guidelines given in the previous section, and record your findings in your garden journal. This can be a plain notebook with places to paste in photos, maps, and sketches. Gather as much information as you can about the yard, locating everything underground and overhead. If you aren't sure where the underground items may be, call the utility locator service in your area. This is usually a toll-free number and a free service. The company will send somebody to your property within a few days to mark the location and direction of underground cables, water mains, sewer lines, and so on.

Once you have collected all your specific information, transfer it to a simple map. Often a simple site map will be included with the papers you got when you purchased your home. If your home is new construction, the drawings submitted to the planning department will include a very detailed map for the septic system and drainage retention plan. Make a copy (that original needs to remain intact), and then use correction fluid to remove details you don't need. Copy it again and you have a usable, accurate map ready for your information gathering. If you can't find a ready-made map, just make a simple sketch showing the relative position of the house and other buildings, as well as hardscape items like sidewalks, paths, fences, decks, arbors, and so on. Also note the location of any trees and shrubs.

Now make multiple copies of your map, blowing it up to the largest workable size. This way, you and anybody else who is interested can play around with various ideas. Where will you put the vegetables, the kids' play area, the dog? How do you want people to move through the space? Plan paths that work realistically with established use patterns.

Here's the initial thought process for our sample garden. First we identified high-use areas, using loose bubbles to show where people spent a lot of time. We also identified where people enter the garden and how they might move through it to get to points of high use.

We then marked places where paths might intersect. Always make these points of intersection as large as possible to assist flow and to allow for seating or placing large ornamental containers. Squeezing such intersections into narrow spaces or trapping them in fussy plantings is a very common design flaw that impedes traffic flow in many gardens.

Once that first sketch was done, we could pick places for some of the owner's favorite projects. In a shady corner near the deck, removing a rotting shed made room for the bird sanctuary. Here we decided to plant a witch hazel (*Hamamelis mollis* 'Pallida'), a handsomely tiered shrub (to 15 feet) with enticingly fragrant winter flowers. Clusters of wild plum and cherry trees will bring in the birds and help screen the neighbor's long chain-link fence.

LAWNS

Sustainable design guidelines help us to eliminate or reduce repetitive chores wherever possible. Unless you have managed to create a very high-maintenance garden indeed, no part of the yard will require as much work as the lawn. In addition, here in the maritime Northwest, there are many areas where traditional lawns are challenging to grow well, thanks to a great deal of shade and heavy clay soils.

In my own gardens, there are no lawns. Instead, everything that isn't a path, seating area, or access or storage space gets planted with a matrix of easygoing, site-appropriate plants that don't need much fertilizing, pruning, or watering. Where babies need play space or pets need exercise, however, lawn may be a good choice. For information on how to install a regionally appropriate, low-maintenance lawn or renovate a tired lawn, see Chapter 4.

PROPER PATHS ARE THE KEY

One of the goals of sustainable design is to build paths that will remain serviceable and easy to keep clean for many years. In our sample garden, this goal led to broad new paths that immediately defined the flow of access for both foot and eye and defined the future planting areas. The new front entry gates dictated where main entry paths would run. We then made logical and attractive extensions of these paths, letting them balloon out at intersections and where we wanted to create seating areas. All paths and seating areas were generously proportioned to ensure ease of use, even when the surrounding beds are spilling over with plants.

Because the owner wanted a natural-looking garden, she chose to use gently curved paths, to help relate the garden space to the layered, natural tree line around the property and to the interior plantings. As you can see on page 21, the main entry paths vary in width. At important entrance and access points like front and back doors, the deck, and the gateways, the paths are 6 to 8 feet wide. Where they pass between raised beds, they are 4 to 6 feet wide.

At first this seems too wide to many people, but these are generally appropriate widths. Generous paths look more graceful than skinny ones because they are in scale with the overall property. Wide paths are much easier to use when pushing a loaded garden cart or carrying groceries.

They also allow two people to walk companionably side by side.

Where expanded seating areas were wanted, near the deck and outside the new French doors installed in the bedroom wall, we made the paths balloon out into rounded or oval patios. Because both of these areas had long-standing seasonal drainage problems, we made the crushed gravel paths 6 inches deep so they would act as French drains, pulling excess water off the site. In such cases, it is important to use fast-draining crushed gravel (never pea gravel) instead of hard paving or other impermeable path surfaces.

GRAVEL PATHS

Both driveway and paths can be made with a 6-inch-deep layer of any crushed local rock (I usually use local basalt). The best all-purpose size for driveways, paths, and seating areas is a ¾ minus mixture (this means the largest pieces are ¾ inch across, with the "smalls" or fine-textured pieces included). This mixture compacts into a firm base that drains quickly. Depending on how much use a driveway gets, it should be top-dressed every few years with 1 to 2 inches of clean ¾-inch gravel (without smalls), which looks nice and tidy and resists weed growth. Weedy driveways and paths are the direct result of inadequate gravel coverage.

Gravel is a terrific starter path surface, practical and inexpensive. As your budget allows, you can dress up plain gravel by adding flat flagstones of slate, granite, or whatever landscaping rock you prefer. The same kind of flat flagstones can easily be mortared over concrete slabs, patios, porches, and even steps to dress up a plain Jane setting. Local slate also comes in boxes of thin tiles that can easily be cut with a water-cooled tile cutter and mortared over concrete steps and slabs in simple or intricate patterns to give a more artful appearance to your home's entry.

DEALING WITH DRAINAGE

Throughout the Northwest, drainage is a common seasonal issue. Many gardens are like our example, which definitely needed a design that maximized absorption of water on the site and minimized runoff for neighbors below the property. If we want our design to be sustainable, we most definitely need to include a comprehensive drainage plan. When we are gardening on certain kinds of clay, we need to go further, treating the undersoil as if it were concrete and creating positive drainage for every planting bed. Too often, beds excavated into clay become bathtubs in which innocent plants are placed to drown.

In general, the best way to deal with drainage is to direct all runoff water away from the house and then give it somewhere appropriate to go (the neighbor's yard is usually not an acceptable destination). Bio-sponge plantings of natives that enjoy lots of water in winter and can tolerate summer drought are terrific drainage buffers.

To channel seasonal runoff through the sample garden, we built deep paths of crushed native basalt gravel in a mixture of ¾ minus. These paths are at least 6 inches deep and a minimum of 4 to 6 feet wide. The deep gravel paths help pull water out of the mounded beds that line the paths on both sides. In some situations, it may be necessary to place larger infiltrator drains under the paths to

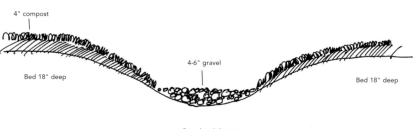

4" compost

4-6" gravel

Bed 18" deep

Bed 18" deep

Gravel path between
raised beds

carry the water away from rooftops and storage tanks. These large drains are buried in 2- or 3-inch rocks, at the proper depth for their size (which varies), and then covered with a minimum of 6 inches of crushed gravel.

Often a drainage plan will require an aboveground holding pond that remains empty most of the year. These areas can be planted with natives that don't mind being underwater in winter but can also tolerate dry summers. Redtwig dogwood *(Cornus stolonifera,* also called *C. sanguinea),* hard hack *(Spiraea douglasii),* dwarf arctic willow *(Salix glauca* 'Nana'), and various reed grasses *(Juncus* species) are good choices for such spots.

Where holding ponds are not required, French drains can be fingered out at the ends. Instead of ending in a

Self-leveling gravel paths are easy to install, easy to change (just add soil and plant), and easy to keep clean with a flame weeder. Soil doesn't wash into the gravel because the compost mulch holds up to 300 times its weight in moisture (also helping to reduce the need for frequent watering).

plastic pipe that concentrates runoff and dumps it on neighboring property, we create long "fingers" of crushed gravel that divide the water stream and carry it off in several directions. Generally, these long fingers can end up under plantings beds, where plant roots will happily draw up the extra moisture. We can also direct the water to an area planted with the moisture lovers just mentioned, all of which tolerate being quite dry in summer once established.

SAVVY SEATING AREAS

Why is seating worth its own section? Many gardeners rarely sit in their own gardens, but the goal of sustainable garden design is to put you happily on the garden bench or into the hammock. When we minimize garden chore time, we increase garden relaxation time. Instead of spending chore time on your knees, you can revel in the rich variety of sights and scents that the healthy, well-planted garden offers. If you aren't yet in the habit of sitting in the garden, read on; you'll find many ideas that may help you to create satisfying and beautiful seating areas of your own.

Practical seating is a significant issue in a rainy climate, where many materials can rot or mold when exposed to wet weather. The guidelines of sustainable design suggest using materials that are regionally appropriate and minimizing choices that can't take local weather conditions in stride. Sustainable design also involves creating seating areas that will be usable in every season. This is especially important here in the maritime Northwest, where we really can actively enjoy and be in our gardens every month of the year if we so choose.

Sustainability also implies fulfilling basic needs for both plants and people. No matter where we live, even if we dwell in the heart of the city, it is important to make places where we can renew our connectedness with the natural world and its cycles. Well-placed garden seating can help us to exchange the bustle of the city for the peace and quiet of nature. Layered, naturalistic plantings help us to feel comfortable and peaceful in the garden. If we are to enjoy them fully, our garden seating must fulfill our often hidden needs for psychological comfort as well as the more obvious requirement that the seat feel comfortable to our bodies.

You may have noticed that in most garden books, when

GUIDELINES FOR ESTABLISHING PATHS AND SEATING AREAS

In creating a sustainable garden design, always start by deciding where the paths go. Establishing the path and seating areas instantly defines the planting areas and guides the entire design. Once the path lines are established, it usually becomes obvious where to build the planting beds in order to provide visual screening for high-use areas. Here are some guidelines for developing paths and seating areas.

- Main entry paths to the house and front garden should be a minimum of 6 to 8 feet wide.

- Side paths should be a minimum of 4 to 5 feet wide.

- Seating areas should be a minimum of 6 feet wide to accommodate one chair. To accommodate several people, 8 to 12 feet is a minimal size.

- Path and entry surface material should drain quickly and provide safe footing in every season.

Continued on page 28

we see lovely benches in the garden, they are always empty. That's because seats used chiefly as decoration are often not attractive in terms of use. When we are outside, we want to feel secure. Our genetic heritage makes us prefer "safe" places where we don't feel threatened. This is why a bench placed in the open with nothing behind it will rarely be used. Seats placed with a wall or hedge behind them will always be preferred. We like feeling that our vulnerable backs are covered.

Most people also enjoy the combination of enclosure with a territorial view. If we can create a place where we can sit in semi-shelter, with a wall to our backs and evergreens growing on each side, and look out at an expansive view, that place will be the most popular part of the garden—as long as it is also a sunny spot.

Our most powerful preference for seating is always for sun. If you often pass by a public park, take notice of where people are sitting, which benches are usually in use,

and which are usually empty. Except in very hot weather, the sunny benches will be almost constantly in use, while those in shade will be neglected. When you start looking for places to put year-round seating, seek out the sunniest places, the natural basking spots where everybody wants to be. Backed by a wall or building, your seats will receive reflected heat and light. This is the place where you will

Seats nested in gravel are usable in all seasons and don't need to be moved or hand-edged each time you mow. Seating is most inviting when backed with shrubs or a wall and offers an intriguing, open view.

spend the most time and receive the most enjoyment. This is also where you'll find your pets; cats and dogs have a terrific instinct for finding just the spot to bask. Where little sun is available, consider selectively limbing any large trees to let in more light. If shade is cast by apartment buildings, garden mirrors can reflect and redouble what light comes your way.

Shady spots are seasonally attractive, in use during the summer only. If your yard is mainly sunny, you may want to figure out where to sling a hammock in the shade or arrange for some summery seating beneath a shade tree. Be aware, however, that in this part of the world, there are usually only a few days each year when it is unpleasantly hot in the sun. In the early morning and in the cooler evening, you will certainly prefer to sit where you can revel in the slanting sunlight. Winter seating definitely needs to be in a sunny place. South-facing spots with shelter from wind are ideal during those months when full sun is rare and fleeting.

FOCAL POINTS FOR SEATING AREAS

We humans like to see something when we sit. In public places, benches that let us see the action—watching passersby or children at play—will get the most use. In our own gardens, we generally prefer to enjoy an interior or distant view rather than to look out at the street. If we can find even a glimpse of distant mountains or forests or water, this view can be framed with plants and made the focal point of a seating area. If no such luxury is available, we can create interior views. Perhaps the easiest way to do this is by creating a water feature. It may be as simple as a water jar or a birdbath or as complex as a pool with a cascading waterfall. Garden art or sculpture also serves as a focal point for seating areas.

These features will be most effective if they are used as a slightly distant view, something to be seen from the seating area. The relative positioning of both the bench and the object of interest can make a great deal of difference in the impact of the scene. As I mentioned earlier, people especially like to look from a position of semi-enclosure out to a more open situation. Therefore, the view will be most satisfying when we place the sculpture or water feature in a more open part of the garden and then place the bench in a more sheltered spot so that we see the focal point through a layered framework of plants.

- Dark-colored gravel or stone produces less glare in summer than light-colored materials, which can be painfully reflective.

- Night lighting increases safety for visitors of all ages.

- Planting beds should be a minimum of 3 to 4 feet wide. Plantings that include trees and shrubs should be a minimum of 8 to 10 feet deep. (For more on building beds, see Chapter 3.)

- Curving lines create naturalistic settings where plants look at home and visually link the garden to any natural surroundings.

- Angular lines reflect the formal, artificial shape of the house and do not relate to the shapes of garden plants.

COMFORT BEFORE STYLE

When choosing garden seating, comfort comes first. Style is all very well, but it's amazing how many stylish seats are not comfortable to use. Before you buy, spend time sitting or lounging in many kinds of seats. Take a book to the store with you and read for a while. Most seats feel okay for a few minutes. Only time and use reveals their hidden drawbacks.

In general, simple seats are more comfortable than intricate ones. Wrought iron can be lovely to look at but often feels painful to the human back and bottom. Cushions can add a lot of comfort but are apt to rot, mold, or mildew in damp climates. To avoid this, provide dry winter storage where mice won't wreak havoc on soft, stuffed cushions.

Wooden seats are more comfortable, but poorly designed ones feel stiff and unyielding or have backs set at awkward angles. Seats that are slightly scooped often feel better than flat ones, and seat backs that are gently angled feel more supportive than straight backs. Oversized seats are generally more comfortable than smaller ones. The best seats allow room to sprawl out with a pillow, a book, a friend, or a cat. Overbuilt pieces hold up to use better than delicate furniture, which may last only a season or two.

Rattan, wicker, and bentwood seats are often comfortable but may be very short-lived. Many natural materials are not really weatherproof, and furniture made from them must be sheltered from winter damp. Unless you have plenty of storage space (wide, covered porches are perfect), rustic twig garden furnishings are often not really practical. (You may also need another set of furniture for the off-season, which doubles your expense.) The obvious exception is sturdy cedar furniture, which weathers beautifully and can last twenty years or more without shelter or protection.

If your sunniest spot is the deck or porch, consider widening the steps. Steps can provide terrific informal seating if they are built wide enough. Broad, shallow steps leading from a deck to the garden can be beautiful as well as practical, offering spaces for containers as well as for people.

RAIN VIEWING SHELTERS

To qualify as sustainable, a design should take seasonal weather patterns into consideration. I've always thought it strange that so few garden designers create snug places to be in the garden during the rainy season, which is lengthy here. Since the autumn rains can begin anytime after mid-September and continue through May (or July), rain is clearly a constant in our garden design equation. It therefore seems as logical to include places to be in the garden during the rainy season as it does to have sunny seating areas. By making places where we can enjoy the garden despite the rain, we don't need to be stuck indoors for months on end.

A lot of folks who suffer from seasonal affective disorder (SAD) are light deprived. Even on a rainy day, there is far more light outside than inside. Rainy days lose their dreariness when we spend even a small part of them outdoors. Adding a covered area of some kind can extend the way we use the garden greatly. A covered porch can be a place to drink morning tea, grill salmon on the hibachi, and enjoy a simple meal outside even during the winter.

Covered porches are part of many cultural design traditions. A visit to the home design section at the library will yield intriguing examples of covered indoor-outdoor areas from all over the world. One unifying feature that successful porches share is adequate width. When such porches are seldom used, it is generally because they are too small to be comfortable.

Several researchers have found that covered porches are rarely used unless they are at least 6 feet deep and wide. Smaller spaces may appear visually attractive, looking at first glance like a cozy nook. In practice, however, narrow porches tend to be shunned (except perhaps by small children). Adults need enough elbow room to move about freely. In many older homes, the porches are about 8 feet wide. This much space invites use by offering plenty of room for furniture and movement.

Deep, covered porches make terrific rain shelters and allow us to observe the winter garden closely. If we plant winter-fragrant plants, such as winter honeysuckle (*Lonicera fragrantissima),* sweet box (*Sarcococca* species), and winter-blooming daphnes and viburnums, we can also breathe in the garden's fragrances in comfort.

If your rainy-day retreat needs to be big enough for only

one, almost any porch will do. An unused side porch can become a place to enjoy rain very simply, as long as there is room for a single chair or bench. To make any spot more cozy in winter, place the seats well back against the house so they remain dry.

If the porch is open to the wind, consider creating a wind baffle that can be moved from side to side as needed. Wind baffles can be solid panels made from wood or lightweight screens of stretched canvas on a simple frame. These can be fastened in place with hooks or lightly nailed into position. More elaborate screens can be made with old windows (some of which are quite handsome) set into wooden frames. The point is not to make the spot completely impervious to weather but simply to avoid getting rain splash or wet wind in the face.

A garden gazebo can be converted into a rainy-day shelter by closing off the windiest sides with trellis panels backed with glass or plastic sheeting. Mounted between two trellis sections, the glass or plastic is almost invisible, but it works well to cut down on wind. Deep-sided tea huts can be made usable in winter by placing the trellis panels during the windy season. If the panels are positioned so that the prevailing winds blow from behind the

Rain shelters allow us to experience the garden in all seasons and every kind of weather. An open-sided tea hut like Vancouver Island artist Robin Hopper's works fine if arranged to block wind and rain in winter, yet allows lovely views.

structure, it remains dry and cozy even in rain or snow.

To be really useful, rainy-day shelters must provide an intriguing view. This may be a very intimate one of the garden itself. If so, it's a good idea to bolster the overlooked area with plants that bloom or have special beauties in winter. Evergreens of many kinds are obvious candidates, from rhododendrons to dwarf conifers. Other possibilities include Christmas and Lenten roses (hellebores), cream striped evergreen iris (*Iris foetidissima* 'Variegata'), and beautyberry (*Callicarpa* species), upright or spreading shrubs that carry bright purple berries all winter. Winter nursery visits will help you locate other great choices.

If you are fortunate enough to have territorial views of water or woods or mountains, the rainy-day retreat should certainly encompass those if at all possible. Few winter pleasures beat that of watching a storm rolling in across the water. Seeing snow fall on an orchard or in deep woods is also delightful, as is looking at the way wind ruffles through open fields. Once shelter is achieved, it is deeply satisfying to look at and listen to the rain or snow while sipping a steaming cup of tea. Observing nature closely without being at the mercy of the elements is part of the charm of the situation.

Many gardens offer places that might be used very differently if some seasonal shelter were provided. Part of a patio or terrace might be covered, or a small porch might be extended and given a roof and sheltering sides. If you have a hot tub, consider adding a trellis top that could serve as an arbor for grapes in summer. In winter, a sliding panel could convert the "roof" into a solid, rain-shedding surface. Canvas roofing is also very attractive. Like Japanese shoji screens, oiled canvas is translucent and flexible but still works to keep out rain and wind.

I know many gardens that hold moon viewing benches and platforms, but very few that offer rain viewing places. Since these can be as simple as a covered porch or as elaborate as a tea house or hut, it's possible to find an appropriate model for any garden, no matter the size or style. When gray skies are so much a part of our life, it's important to the spirit that we not allow weather to cut us off from the experience and enjoyment of connection with the natural.

When we spend wet winters shut away indoors, we feel

dull and sad. Rainy-day shelters bring us out into the light. Once there, we begin to see unsuspected beauties in the shimmering raindrops quivering on each branch tip, in the sheeting rain streaming past our hidden retreat, and in the soft, lazy clouds of snow that drift down with silent grace. Once you discover the pleasures to be found in our own soggy backyards, I predict that you'll find yourself using your new retreat on a daily basis.

SUSTAINABLE DESIGN AND PRIVACY SCREENING

Screening can make or break a garden. If we take time to do it properly, our screening plantings may last for decades without needing more than annual feeding and mulching and occasional shaping or pruning of dead-wood. Before planting anything, take time to clarify your goals and decide where screening will be lastingly effective. It makes sense to start by screening out views you don't want, such as the busy roadway and the neighbor's house. You'll also want to frame any views you want to preserve, whether of lovely trees across the road, a glimpse of distant mountains, territorial views of rolling hills, or a water vista.

The best way to determine the screening needs of your particular yard and garden is to perform a simple partner exercise. First find a friend, preferably somebody who is taller or shorter than you are to give you a broader perspective. Now assemble a handful of stakes, some file cards, and a marking pen. Start by standing and sitting in visually important places on your site to discover where you need screening and how much is enough. Inside the house, begin with doorways and key windows. Outside, start with decks and seating areas.

Consider as well the views from unused spaces that might become more appealing with some privacy screening. Many a front yard is visited only at chore time, even though quite often it's the sunniest part of the lot. A little screening and a new bed or two could convert that wasted patch of lawn into a sunny herb garden where you can relax and enjoy your own handiwork for a change.

To determine screening needs, one person acts as the viewer and the other becomes a stick holder. The viewer stands in a key spot and then directs the stick holder into position. Each key view stick is placed in the ground and numbered, and the viewer creates a file card corresponding to each stick. On each card, you jot down all relevant specifics and ideas, which might read something like this:

Stick #1: Need a 6-foot-tall shrub to block view of busy street. Plant should not be wider than 4 to 6 feet because of pathway. Soil drains badly there, and the spot is very shady. Clump of heavenly bamboo? (Maybe soil is too poor and wet?) Substitute a vertical trellis-over-plywood panel framed with 2-by-4s, painted midnight blue or deep green?

These cards help you define your screening problems, which in turn helps you develop appropriate solutions. Take the cards to the nursery when you shop and show them to the staff. Guaranteed, you'll come home with better choices than when you buy impulsively.

SCREENING FOR ENCLOSURE

It is often said (by Europeans) that North American gardens lack enclosure and structure. Structure can refer to the hardscape or man-made things in the garden. It can also mean the enclosure of garden space with fences, walls, or hedges. Enclosure provides visual boundaries, but it also provokes subconscious emotional responses that strongly affect the way we use our garden space.

In many yards, a great deal of space is wasted because the overall design does not invite us to use it. Open space can feel particularly unappealing when neighbors or passersby on the street look into it. Because of this, the average front yard is literally never used except when yard maintenance chores are being performed. Many a backyard remains empty as well, particularly those that are open to view from other houses. One time-proven way to make such a yard more attractive (in the sense of drawing us in) is by creating smaller, enclosed areas within the greater space.

Very often this is done by creating garden rooms, which are best described as fully or partially enclosed areas within the yard. These may vary greatly in style and character, but they are united in feeling like a place to be, a destination spot within the garden. Making these places usually will require the addition of fencing, hedging, or trelliswork that is best put in place before the garden beds are planted.

The most common gardening screening error is to overscreen, creating problems for the future by using plants that are too big for the available space when mature. To gather ideas about how screening plants behave over time, stroll around an older neighborhood in your area. Make note of the various ways in which others have attempted to solve similar screening needs. Visit the library for how-to books on screens and fencing. Look for minimalist solutions that don't do more than you need them to.

You will soon discover that overscreening is a very common design flaw. It is not unusual to see huge old hedges of English laurel eating small city yards. Replacing that fat hedge with a slim privacy fence can often double the effective size of the garden.

Privacy screening need not involve straight hedgerows, fences, or walls. Softly layered green "walls" of shrubs block or frame views beautifully, creating a more naturalistic ambience. Such green architecture needs little shaping, pruning, or clipping to maintain its proper appearance.

FENCES

Fencing is an excellent screening option, particularly in small yards where the width of a mature hedge (typically 12 to 15 feet) robs us of valuable space. Long-lasting cedar fences don't need painting and soon weather to a lovely silvery gray. Where partial plantings exist, spot screening with a freestanding fence section may provide plenty of privacy.

Covenants can restrict both fence and hedge height but may not apply to fence caps or screening panels with ornamental details that can provide a little extra elevation or privacy just where you need it. Check out the local rules and regulations first. Build or plant too high and you risk paying fines, having your hedge butchered, or losing your new fence.

HEDGES

Hedging is rarely the best solution. New hedges take time to grow up, so it may be years before they fill in enough to provide the privacy you want. Faster-growing plants usually get far too large and don't magically stop growing when you want them to. Although hedges seem to cost less up front, hidden costs (fertilizing, watering, constant pruning and shearing, replacement of dying plants) add up over time. What's more, many common hedging plants are simply unsuitable for use in small yards.

When you wander through that older neighborhood, observe the legacy of poor hedge plant choices. You'll find huge, bulky laurel hedges taking up most of a small yard. You'll see thinning, poorly clothed Lawson or Leyland cypress with bare or dead patches. You'll see a "root shadow" of impoverished soil where nothing grows well.

It is sad to see new hedges being made with totally inappropriate plants that promise nothing but trouble for the well-intentioned owners. Unless your lot is big, planting a hedge of Leyland cypress, *Photinia fraseris,* or English or Portuguese laurel is not a wise move. These trees will all do their best to achieve 20 feet or more in height and over half that in girth. Where space permits that kind of growth, they can really be exciting screening plants. However, only folks with ample acres should use trees for hedging. Similarly, bulky traditional hedges require constant shearing, and the resulting dense growth can make them tough to water.

These difficulties can be eliminated by selecting small hedge plants that won't ever outgrow their position. Many compact evergreens mature at 8 or 10 feet, which is often the desired ultimate height for screening. To reduce maintenance, look for plants that like the conditions you can offer them. The idea is to enclose your seating area and any other parts of the garden where you want visual privacy, not to grow an urban forest. By limiting the ultimate height of your plants, you avoid losing light and air as those hedge plants mature.

If you want a formal-looking hedge without clipping, choose slender, columnar shrubs with naturally regular shapes, such as Irish and Italian junipers. In very tight situations, ultra-slim 'Skyrocket' junipers make a tidy 2-foot-wide hedge that won't ever require clipping. Where you can spare 5 to 6 feet of width, consider an upright, flat-topped Hick's yew (*Taxus media* 'Hicksii'), the closest thing in nature to a rectangular shrub. Both yews and junipers appreciate sunny settings and prefer relatively dry soils.

In a damp, shady yard, think about a hedge of native redtwig dogwoods (*Cornus stolonifera* and forms), which reach 6 to 8 feet or more. Exotic twiggy dogwoods such as 'Midwinter Fire' offer even more dramatic stem colors and are less tasty to deer. Where a lower hedge will do, try dwarf arctic willows (*Salix purpurea* 'Nana'), with fine-textured, blue-green foliage and dark, whippy stems that get 3 to 5 feet tall.

If dry shade makes growing things challenging, consider container hedges. A row of compact 'Little Gem' magnolias will make a delightful evergreen privacy screen and will grow happily in large containers where space is truly limited. So will dwarf fruit trees, which can also be espaliered on a homely chain-link fence to soften its outline with flowers and foliage. Grown in containers, any of these small trees will remain at about 10 to 12 feet for a long time. For more on sustainable hedging, including lists of plants for various needs and situations, see Chapter 9, Shrubs in the Garden.

PRIVACY SCREENING AND BERMS

Privacy berms are long mounds of soil planted with low shrubs that buffer street noise and help screen out unwanted views. Berms can be almost any size, though a huge berm can look a bit odd on a small, flat lot. On small lots, a modest berm of soil can often screen out the road and neighboring homes very effectively.

To find the right size berm for your setting, consider what will be most practical and serviceable as well as what will look most attractive (or least peculiar). If you will be building your berm with a shovel and a wheelbarrow, a smaller one will certainly be more attractive.

Usually a privacy berm will be of most use when placed along the length of the street side of the property or along the driveway. On small lots, a low mound about 2 feet high provides ample protection. In some situations, privacy berms can be very large indeed, but this is rare and probably not a do-it-yourself option.

PRIVACY PLANTINGS

When choosing and placing privacy screening plants, keep the cardinal rules of sustainable design clearly in mind.

- Don't use trees and shrubs that will quickly outgrow available space.

- Figure out how much screening you actually need, and choose plants that will deliver that much privacy at maturity.

- In most situations, screening plants that mature at 8 to 12 feet provide plenty of privacy for seating areas and important house windows.

- Place screening plants where they will perform their intended function without intruding into neighbors' yards or over public sidewalks, even at maturity.

- Where space is limited, use a short section of fence, a trellis, or a bamboo screen to block unwanted views.

NATURALISTIC LAYERING WITH BACKBONE PLANTINGS

Layering is a way of integrating the garden into its setting and of combining plants of all kinds, from trees to ground covers, in a meaningful and attractive context. Layering gives us a way to place plants intelligently, using the larger ones around the perimeter of a property and stepping down gently to the level of garden plants like peonies and roses. Layering also makes plants look comfortable, since they are placed within their appropriate ecological niche of canopy, high and low understory, furnishing layer, or ground cover. By layering our plants, we can also create soft green walls to frame our homes and a wide, shallow bowl of sunlight where we place our private garden and seating areas.

Backbone plantings are the intermediate shrubs that create transitional layers between the surrounding canopy or tree line and the smaller garden plants. These backbone layering plants can be considered as visual ladders that carry the eye from ground level up to the tree canopy and back down to ground level again. Like screening plants, transitional plantings can block unwanted views or frame desirable ones. They also help to link the garden to its setting, which means both the actual site and the neighborhood trees that lie beyond the property lines.

CAPTURING VIEWS

Transitional plants can help integrate the garden with any borrowed view that may present itself. Borrowed views can include nearby majestic trees or more distant territorial vistas such as forested hillsides, a faraway mountain, or a glimpse of the sea. By carrying the eye up to those views, the transitional layers subtly suggest that those distant scenes are somehow part of the garden's setting. Framing partial views with layered plants makes them more defined and more visually important. Even tiny views that seem too small to be worth framing can gain surprising impact when carefully captured with plants.

Indeed, in many garden styles, from Zen to Italian baroque, partial views are considered to be more lastingly powerful than panoramic ones. Humans are paradoxically fascinated by huge, sweeping views yet quickly bored by them. Smaller, barely glimpsed views retain their ability to tantalize indefinitely, seeming fresh each time we see them.

In one famous Florentine garden, a tremendous overview of the city is all but blocked out by hedges and trees. The most breathtaking city view is seen through a large keyhole set in an iron gate. In Zen gardens, the most telling views of mountains and ocean are framed to be seen obliquely and only from certain angles. This way, they always come as a surprise and never lose their power to move us.

HIGHLIGHTING ORNAMENTAL PLANTINGS

Within the garden, transitional layering creates a frame or backdrop for ornamental plantings. Flowery beds of roses or perennials rarely have much impact alone. Indeed, English and European designers are always telling us that we need to bring more structure into the garden.

Structure can, of course, be thought of in terms of Elizabethan stone walls and three-hundred-year-old hedges. Where these are in short supply (as in a typical Northwestern neighborhood), we can quickly create living structure instead.

We do this initially by careful placement of our key specimen trees and backbone shrubs. To keep our design sustainable, we choose plants that will be lastingly appropriate in size and shape. We also create living structure by layering our transitional shrubs to connect the large-scale trees with the more intimate scale of our flowery garden plantings.

Transitional plantings act like a picture frame to give ornamental plantings more visual importance. Many a sumptuous landscape painting owes much of its impact to a wide and impressive frame. Remove the frame and the picture has less obvious boundaries. Without the firm lines of the frame, the picture loses focus and importance.

The same is true in our gardens, which is why flowery gardens without much else going on tend to look "cute" or "sweet" rather than awesome. Back those beds with evergreen shrubs and our intended composition snaps into focus. The backdrop plantings provide a visual full stop that shows off the contents of bed and border just as a picture frame would.

CHOOSING BACKDROP SHRUBS

Like good screening plants, sustainable backdrop shrubs are selected from plants that will not quickly outgrow their position or need frequent pruning to keep them the desired size. To avoid creating ongoing chores such as clipping, shearing, and pruning, we look for plants that will mature to the height and bulk that suit both our design and the size of our yard.

In the maritime Northwest, whether our site is urban, suburban, or rural, we are often lucky enough to garden against an established backdrop of mature trees and shrubs. In such a situation, we'll probably do more editing and thinning than bringing in new backdrop plants.

In mature gardens where the backdrop plants have grown into trees, we may need to reestablish some lower layers. By renewing the intermediate plantings, we will bring those green walls back down to human scale. Where a small yard is packed with large plants, selective removal and thinning of overgrown plants will allow us to introduce better choices.

More commonly, however, we are gardening without much context at all. We may have enclosure, in the form of walls, fences, or hedges, but nothing to carry the eye from the lawn to the big tree down the block. As with key trees, small lots require smaller-scale backbone plants.

In shady yards, wonderful backdrop plants will be found among the rhododendron clan. Look for compact forms that rise just as high as you want them and stop there. Heavenly bamboos *(Nandina* species) make great transitional layer plants and are reliably evergreen. Unlike true bamboo, nandinas do not run away with the yard. These dignified shrubs are slow growers that spread moderately over time. Compact viburnums and taller daphnes are also good choices, as are twiggy dogwoods and smaller forms of elderberry.

In sunny spots, consider compact conifers, which come in a stimulating variety of forms, textures, and colors as well as shapes and sizes. You may also want to look at compact California lilacs *(Ceanothus* species), taller rock-roses *(Cistus* species), purple smoke bush *(Cotinus coggygria* 'Atropurpureus' and others), and Mexican orange *(Choisya ternata).*

To get more ideas, visit lots of gardens and nurseries and stroll through well-planted neighborhoods. By looking at mature plants, you can learn how and where to plant backdrop plants so that they remain lastingly attractive and useful. Chapters 8 and 9 also provide lists of trees and shrubs for layering.

ASSESSING YOUR DESIGN FOR SUSTAINABILITY

After thinking through the considerations discussed in this chapter, it's time to do some reassessment of the garden you are living with or are designing. How practical and sustainable is the design? How much work does the existing design require? How much time would it take to implement a new design and to maintain it? How much time do you really want to spend working in the garden?

If you are gardening from scratch, you can scrap a dozen designs before settling on the one you like best. One great way to try out a design is to use spray paint (you can buy special cans that spray downward for marking grass or dirt). Mark out your proposed paths and live with them for a while. You can edit your lines by cutting the grass or scuffing out lines marked on soil with your shoe. Now see how it feels to use the garden as it would be shaped according to your plan.

The best way to increase the sustainability of an existing design is slowly, area by area, project by project. Start by reworking the areas that take the most time to keep attractive, or renovate the place that annoys you the most. After implementing whatever initial changes seem best to you, live with the garden for a season or so before making any further alterations. Once you've had a chance to grow into the first phase of your design, you can make a thoughtful assessment of its merits and identify any remaining difficulties.

The best time to evaluate any garden design is in winter, when you can readily assess how well it works without the distraction of summery flowers and lush foliage. This evaluation is not just about how the garden looks, though winter is a great time to discover where you have gaps in privacy screening or areas of high use and low plant interest. For a sustainable design analysis, you'll mainly be looking at patterns of flow and form.

Earlier, you learned to make a garden map that included physical features such as trees and shrubs, sidewalks and stairways, decks and arbors, sheds and garage, and so forth. As you change the garden, the relative importance of these things can also change. When it's time to reassess, you may decide to keep, edit, or remove some of those features.

To do this, get out your original map and compare how your site looked when you began the design process with how it looks now. Are your improvements functional and attractive? If not, will the plants involved just need a little more time to do their intended job well? If so, might an interim structural solution such as visual screens or baffles be in order?

You also listed your site's assets and liabilities, including everything from privacy to practical paths and usable spaces. Now you can take a good look at the way these factors may have changed. To reevaluate your site's characteristics, pull out that initial list and go over it again, step by step. Each point can be assessed in terms of how well your design has solved problems or made the most of assets.

Here are the major points to consider:

• Privacy and screening: Is there enough? Does it work year-round?

• Places to be in the garden: Are seating areas functional and attractive? Do you need a handy kitchen garden, ornamental borders, play space, or places for pets?

• Flow—getting to and from those places: Are path widths and surfaces appropriate? Is it easy to move around in the garden? Does it offer pleasing sight lines?

- Editing: Do you need to prune hedges, remove problem plants, add specimens?

- Ease of use: Do the paths work well? Are the activity spaces conveniently arranged? How much time does your garden require to look great and be fun to use?

A good design celebrates entry by welcoming us into both the home and the garden. It also establishes clear connections between the garden and the house. Both involve choosing lastingly appropriate foundation plantings as well as creating hardscape (paving, arbors, arches, and so forth) that is in a pleasing proportion and scale to the overall setting. To assess these points, you will need to look at your site from various places, including from across the street, from neighboring homes, and so forth.

Check to see whether foundation plantings are placed properly. There should be a band of clean gravel 12 to 18 inches wide around the house. This is a plant-free zone. The foundation beds should be built out and away from the house walls and beyond the eaves and gutter line. They should be at least as wide as the chosen plants will be at maturity.

Foundation plants should be placed in the center of these beds, not at the back. At maturity, the plants should leave the plant-free gravel zone empty. The plants should be set so that at maturity, they will just touch each other without crowding. Unless you bought large plants, there may be a fair amount of empty space in the beds. For now, annuals and perennials can fill in the blanks. If your plants are spaced too closely, this is a great time to move them.

You can also evaluate the layering of beds and borders in terms of proportion. Are the beds large enough for the overall site? Are the plants in scale to the setting, or will they be when they grow up?

Evaluating your plant choices also means asking whether you are making work for yourself or reducing the chore load. Looking ahead to the future, are there plants in place that will soon outgrow their position? Can they be exchanged for more lastingly practical choices that won't require constant intervention?

If you have made a berm, evaluate whether it is the right size and shape for the site and for its purpose. If the berm looks too small or awkward and clunky, would another load of soil allow you to reshape it more naturally? If it is too large, would making several mounded beds around the berm create a more attractive transition to the rest of the garden?

Plant health is another point to consider. If you have done your soil work well, your plants should be flourishing. Even in the first year, you should see signs that your plants are settling in nicely. It's natural for many plants to spend the first year putting on root growth instead of new top growth. However, if a plant looks unchanged since you put it in the ground, dig it up and take a look at its roots and at the surrounding soil. If the plant roots have not grown out from the original rootball, odds are good that the soil was not adequately prepared.

If the roots appear to be rotting instead of growing well, check for waterlogging. The hole you removed the plant from may be filling up with water even as you watch. This means you really do need mounded beds, and you will definitely benefit from bringing in an underlayer of sandy loam to provide better drainage. If you can't do that, you will need to do some research to find plants that live naturally in boggy areas.

Many native plants, such as twiggy dogwoods, native crab apple, Douglas spiraea, most willows, and cedars, are quite comfortable with wet feet in winter and dry soil in summer. By choosing a matrix of wetland natives and their allies (relatives and companion plants) from all around the world, you can make a thriving garden even on poorly drained soil. Plants that are happily at home in a soggy site in the wild will also do well in gardens with less than ideal drainage.

Winter assessment will reveal places where you can bring in new plants to create more winter interest, where your privacy screening needs bolstering, and where crowding will soon be a problem. Without the distraction of bright flowers and dense foliage, you can see the developing bones of the garden. If the overall look is skimpy, take time to measure the spaces between your plants and refresh your memory of their mature sizes. If you planted properly, they will grow up in right relationship to one another.

If you have indeed underplanted, that's great. Now you have room for some new plants. Once the key screening plants are in place, you can take your time about choosing plants for less strategic spots. It can be very pleasurable to work slowly, pacing your purchases and efforts according to your own budget of time and money.

It's important to remember that the desired result is the garden of your dreams, the place where you feel at peace and lapped in the natural. Happily, the garden path is long and never ending. There is no timeline for garden making but the one we choose for ourselves. Our gardens may never be "done" or "perfect," but they don't need to be. Plants are not furniture, and gardens are a living community.

The garden is where people and plants come together. For gardeners, that core relationship is endlessly renewing, endlessly refreshing, and endlessly rewarding. This is one place where good enough is just fine. If your garden suits you, if it makes you happy to participate in it, you have succeeded. If not, just keep on paying attention. That is really the secret to making a great garden.

The beauty of natural gardening is that it can yield stunning results with a minimum of human intervention.

The ideas behind gardening naturally are very simple. The first principle (a very old one) is to feed the soil and let the soil feed our plants. Instead of pouring on artificial fertilizers (many of which can harm or kill soil-dwelling bacteria and other beneficial micro-critters), we feed our soil with organic materials such as compost, composted manures, alfalfa meal, kelp, and other natural nutrients. Healthy, well-fed soil provides all or most of the nutriments most plants require.

This is made obvious when we visit natural environments such as magnificent mountain meadows full of wildflowers, shrubs, and trees. In such places nobody weeds, waters, deadheads, or fertilizes, yet month after month, year after year, the endless cycle of plant growth and regrowth can continue for millennia without human intervention.

We can use this observation as a model for our gardens: If we combine the right plants in the right ways, we can enjoy a similarly steady stream of color and interest all year long without working very hard. The biggest difference is that in natural environments, nothing is taken away from the ecosystem. When browsing animals graze plants, they leave manure behind. When fire sweeps through, the ashes contain nutrients that recycle back into the soil for the next generation of plants to use.

In garden settings, we tidy up after each seasonal wave of color. Removing spent leaves and stems takes nutrients from the system. To replace those nutrients, we need to recycle our garden gleanings into compost, which is then used to feed the soil and suppress weeds.

Natural gardening is based on many concepts of this kind, all designed to promote the overall health of the garden as a system. For instance, instead of attacking a minor problem with an arsenal of chemical weapons, we seek to support the real solution, which is a healthy garden ecosystem. We avoid short-term chemotherapy

Aerobically brewed compost teas inoculate soil and plant foliage with beneficial biota, helping plants outgrow pathogens. Here, a "sock" full of high-quality compost is lowered into a brewing tank at Territorial Seed Company in Lorane, Oregon.

"solutions" that leave soil dead or depleted and can devastate beneficial insects. Instead, we do everything in our power to increase the overall health and well-being of the garden, from feeding the soil to choosing appropriate plants.

To avoid or minimize potential problems, we also use new technology, such as machines for brewing aerobic compost tea, to provide the garden with as diverse a selection of beneficial soil biota as possible. Boosting beneficial biotic diversity is like bolstering the immune system of the whole garden. When a broad range of beneficial biota flourish, plants have less trouble outgrowing the ever-present pathogens that can plague stressed plants.

When challenging problems arrive, we treat them with the least toxic technique or substance possible. Should fungus appear, we spray the affected plants and surrounding soil with freshly brewed compost tea to inoculate the soil and foliage with beneficial biota and help the plants outgrow the pathogens. For black spot on roses, we might add mycorrhizae to the soil in addition to monthly tea spraying of foliage and soil. Powdery mildew on favorite plants might call for a spray of neem oil to smother the mildew pathogens. For red thread on lawns, we could use a combination of fresh compost tea and a pelletized form of microbial soil conditioner that will inoculate the soil as well as the turf with the beneficial organisms that will be of most use in fending off fungal disorders.

Should weeds invade our paths, we'll burn them off with flame weeders or safer steam weeding devices. Instead of endlessly weeding, we blanket our beds and borders with a healthy mulch of compost that keeps the soil moist, evenly warm, and weed-free.

Rather than struggling to grow fusspot border beauties that dislike our changeable climate, we give preference to the hundreds of easygoing plants, natives and exotics alike, that enjoy the conditions we can offer them. If we garden on clay soil, we grow a generous assortment of plants, from primroses to cedars, that prefer retentive soils. If our garden is sandy, we grow beach roses and shrubs like lavender that demand fast drainage.

If our yard is too shady and full of tree roots to support a lawn, we make moss gardens, rich with rhododendrons, evergreen ferns, handsome grasses, and shade-loving flowers that appear in sequence all through the year. If we live in an open, sunny spot, our garden features hardy herbs, prairie flowers, and border queens that need plenty of light and air.

Instead of spending every weekend clipping and shearing and pruning, we hedge our garden with plants that mature at the height we need to give us the privacy we want. Our house is lapped in low-growing plants that never block the windows or touch the house walls, inviting in pests and wood-rotting diseases.

Whatever the reason we are drawn to natural care, we are all faced with a learning curve about new techniques, less-toxic products, and alternative care management practices. If we have relied on toxic weed killers to keep our gardens, lawns, and driveways weed-free, we must find alternatives that do less damage to the web of life.

The more we learn about the abundance of life forms found in healthy soil and within a healthy garden, the more protective we become. Instead of using broad-spectrum chemicals that destroy many kinds of insects, we seek out specific treatments for the precise pest we want to eliminate. In some cases, we learn to modify our a versions, deciding that slight imperfections in our plants are more tolerable than using drastic "cures" that endanger soil (or our own) health. Most often, we work to create the most healthy environment possible, assisting plants and beneficial soil organisms to simply outperform the pathogens. Thus, the core of gardening naturally and employing natural care techniques lies in working toward a simple, elegant solution—a healthy, vigorous garden—instead of spending our energy fighting a host of particular problems.

BASIC PRINCIPLES OF NATURAL CARE

Cooperate, don't compete. Cooperative gardening means working with natural forces such as weather cycles and soil types and relying on a base matrix of native plants and their natural allies from similar bioregions. Its opposite, control-based gardening, seeks to impose human will on everything from a plant's shape to the way nature fills empty spaces or niches of opportunity in the garden. Fighting nature in this way makes extra work.

Build healthy soil. Clean, healthy soil is the single most important key to gardening success. Here in the maritime Northwest, most native soils are sandy and acid or

Recycling garden wastes into compost helps close the garden bio-cycle loop by feeding nutrients stored in foliage and stems back into the soil. Spread compost as mulch rather than tilling it in (an outmoded, destructive practice) for maximum benefits.

clay-based and acid. Most native soils are very low in humus (organic matter), which plants need in order to access soil nutrients. A regular program of soil amendment leads to healthy soil, which in turn creates healthy, sturdy plants. This takes some time to accomplish, and during the transition period from chemical care to natural care, both soil and plants will need to be fed supplementally.

Feed the soil, not the plant. Healthy soil is the backbone of natural care. When our soil is in good heart, well-chosen, well-placed plants can thrive with little intervention from us. Once a garden has made the transition from chemicals to natural care, fertilizing becomes less necessary, because healthy soil can supply all or most of our plants' needs. In a garden setting, certain plants that are gross feeders (notably roses and clematis), container plantings, and annual vegetables will need some supplemental fertilizer each season, yet the amounts will be far less than what is required when gardens with chemically damaged or depleted soil are fed with artificial fertilizers.

Recycle everything possible to close the nutrient loop. In nature, nobody feeds the forest trees or meadow flowers, yet they persist for centuries. This is because nothing is removed from the ecosystem. Whenever we harvest plants from the garden, rake away fallen leaves, or remove lawn clippings, we are taking stored nutrients away from the garden. The garden's ecosystem is a bit like a nutritional bank account: Soil and plants become depleted after we make too many withdrawals and not enough deposits. To keep valuable nutrients in the loop, we need to return them to the garden in the form of compost or shredded plant material.

Compost everywhere, always. Returning nutrients to the garden in the form of compost is the most efficient way to replenish both soil and plants. Spread as mulch, mature compost continues to break down slowly, releasing stored nutrients to the soil over time. The tiny living creatures called soil biota turn compost into nutritional ingredients that plants can use readily. The best way to keep a maritime Northwestern garden in good nutritional balance is to add a 3- to 4-inch layer of compost to every bed and border at least once a year, and preferably twice a year (in early spring and fall). In bioregions where the native soils have higher natural levels of humus (more than the 1½ to 2 percent typical of our maritime soils), a 1- to 3-inch layer of compost will be sufficient.

Diversity is the key to a healthy garden ecosystem. In gardens, as in agriculture, monocrops like hay fields or rose gardens create attractive targets for pests and diseases. The fewer kinds of plants you grow, the more likely you are to experience pest problems. The more diverse our gardens are in terms of kinds and quantities of plants, the more flexible and adaptable the ecosystem we build becomes. The more ingredients we blend into our composts, the more nutrients are available to nourish soil biota. In nature, monocultures are extremely rare; all natural environments, from deserts and prairies to river meadows and mountain forests, are rich with a diverse assortment of plants. Here in the Northwest, some four thousand kinds of plants occur naturally in various communities and groupings. Even our native soils have terrific diversity; more than twenty thousand kinds of soil bacteria can be found in our own backyards.

Find the right plant for the right place. The best way to reduce pests and health problems is to offer plants the conditions they prefer. Plants that are well placed and properly planted are more independent than those that must struggle to grow under inappropriate conditions. When we put shade lovers in sunny spots or grow bog plants in a dry setting, we are creating work for ourselves and stress for the plants. Grouping plants with similar cultural needs also reduces chore time dramatically.

Support the solution, don't attack the problem. When problems occur, try to figure out where the weakness in the system lies. Molds, mildews, root rots, and fungal problems often indicate poor drainage or bad air circulation.

Pests and diseases often attack plants that have root damage or were improperly planted. With all pests and diseases, start your care program by trying a probiotic soil drench and/or foliar spray of freshly brewed compost tea (see Chapter 3). Inoculating soil with beneficial biota and improving soil conditions often help the plant to outcompete the pest or pathogens that are creating the problem.

Provide consistent and timely care. Many plant problems arise when we garden erratically. If you can, try to spend a few hours a week in the garden instead of working in fits and starts. When we make a point of spending at least a little time in the garden each week, we can catch potential problems before they become big ones. We can also see and appreciate the subtle seasonal changes that inform the garden year. Over the year, your weekly average may be two or three hours a week. This may mean that in winter, you spend a few hours a month mulching beds and flame-weeding unwanted seedlings, while in spring or high summer, you may spend four or five hours each week planting or grooming.

THE TROUBLE WITH CHEMICALS

There really is nothing new about natural care. Since the very beginning of agriculture, humans have gardened naturally. For millennia, people all over the world built good soil in the most efficient ways they could in order to grow better crops. Our most ancient agricultural records tell us that even thousands of years ago, gardeners and farmers added all kinds of natural amendments to their soil, from fish scraps to composts of manures and plant wastes.

On the other hand, gardening and farming with chemicals is comparatively new. Although we've used agricultural chemicals for only a few generations, those massive advertising campaigns have made it seem like the intelligent, easy way to garden. In fact, most people aren't even aware that chemical-free gardening is possible, even though a few moments' thought will show you that this very idea is impossible. Why aren't there huge ad campaigns for natural gardening? Because there is far less money to be made from a natural system that doesn't require lots of purchases.

Chemical ads scare us by insisting that "the only good bug is a dead bug." In fact, if we manage to kill off all the bugs, we will shortly die from starvation, since most of the food we eat must be pollinated by insects of some kind. One chemical company boosts its main product by proclaiming that it "kills over a hundred kinds of bugs." However, most of the insects in the world are beneficial and only a small percentage (less than 5 percent) are serious pests. Many regions of our country, including the maritime Northwest, don't even have a hundred insect pests. A healthy garden anywhere in the country might be home to as many as two thousand kinds of insects, nearly all of which are either good for the garden or do it no harm. When we use broad-spectrum killers, we kill or damage beneficial insects like bees and butterflies as well as the intended target.

Given the rate and scale of environmental damage attributable to agricultural chemicals, you might well be wondering how on earth we got into this mess in the first place. During the early part of the twentieth century, experiments with chemical fertilizers, pesticides, and herbicides promised to boost food production for a rapidly growing world population. Only after World War II did large-scale agribusiness develop internationally. At first the so-called "green revolution" seemed like the answer to many problems; crops were larger and pests were reduced quickly.

In just a few decades, however, disquieting signs of ecological disruption appeared, telling the watchful that all was not rosy. Crops began to dwindle as soil quality became impaired. The nutritional quality of food grown in the United States has diminished by more than 20 percent in the past forty years. When soil quality falls, food quality falls too, and more and more chemical fertilizers are needed to keep struggling plants alive. When excess nitrogen and other fertilizers are added to soils, they damage the living creatures, from worms to bacteria, that bring soil to life.

For thousands of years, farmers used cover crops or "green manures" such as field peas, vetch, and clover to boost soil nitrogen. When the plant residues are shallowly tilled into the soil, they add invaluable humus. With the chemical revolution, farmers stopped planting cover crops and left fields empty during the winter, often spraying with herbicides to "clean up" remaining plants. As a result, as much as 10 percent of our topsoil is lost to erosion each year (far more in some situations).

Very soon, many pests and diseases began to develop

WHEN TROUBLE WON'T GO AWAY

No matter how well you care for your garden, troubles may arise that common sense and simple organic remedies can't eliminate. When serious, persistent trouble plagues your garden, seek help from your local Master Gardener organization. This excellent program is run through county agricultural extension service agents. The program consists of well-trained problem solvers who can offer a wide range of solutions specific to your region, including organic and least toxic alternatives to chemical quick fixes.

This program began in Washington and Oregon in the late 1970s and is now operating in every state in the union. Master Gardeners are volunteers who use their extensive training for community service. It's a terrific resource for gardeners everywhere, whether we have problems or questions or are simply looking for some great ideas. In fact, once your naturalistic layered borders are in place, you may find yourself with a lot of time on your hands. When

Continued on page 54

you've enjoyed your garden to the fullest for a few seasons, perhaps you will feel drawn to return some of the joy to the community. If so, please consider joining a Master Gardener program yourself. You will find the work of helping others to discover the secrets of having a healthy, abundant garden every bit as rewarding as reveling in your own.

immunity to the most popular pesticides and herbicides. The industry response was to boost the strength and quantities of the chemicals. Many common agrichemicals are systemic, taken up into every part of the plant. As humans inadvertently ate larger and more frequent doses of agricultural chemicals (as well as hormones, antibiotics, and steroids in meats), various government agencies began attempting to monitor and regulate the residues. However, in nearly every instance, when it became impossible to control problems with low levels of chemicals, the Food and Drug Administration approved ever-increasing residual levels as being fit for human consumption. Now, as the incidence of cancers, Parkinson's disease, and other health problems rises annually, medical research shows clearly that exposure to agricultural chemicals is harmful to humans as well as the environment.

Science advisers to the Canadian government recently called the increasing use of agricultural chemicals and the early approval of genetic modifications and engineering for plants "the most dangerous experiment in the history of mankind." Concerned scientists have spoken out continually almost from the very beginning of the chemical era. Rachel Carson's landmark book *Silent Spring,* published in 1962, focused the world's attention on the danger to humans and the destruction of birds, insects, fish, and other living creatures caused by indiscriminate use of fertilizers, herbicides, and pesticides. Sadly, Carson was attacked and threatened by powerful chemical companies that sought to diffuse and discount her message.

Over the past few decades, Carson's warnings have proved all too true. Every day the news is full of stories of environmental damage all over the world. No natural system remains pristine; pollutants are found from Antarctica to remote rain forests. In the year 2002, every significant natural waterway in Washington State was polluted enough by pesticides to harm fish and other wildlife. Although most people believe that industry creates the bulk of environmental pollution, home gardeners contribute an increasingly large share. Most of the water pollution in these waterways comes in runoff water from lawns treated with weed-and-feed products designed to kill crane fly larvae, a European pest whose grubs disfigure the lawns of suburbia.

Today Washington State has listed almost a dozen

species of salmon as endangered or threatened, largely because of water contamination, much of it coming from runoff from home gardens. Not only fish, but frogs, salamanders, birds, and a host of other living creatures are harmed by the polluted water. Clearly, if we want our children and our children's children to be able to walk in the woods, fish and swim in clean water, and have gardens of their own, we need to change both the way we garden and the way we relate to the natural world.

All of this sounds horribly depressing yet, fortunately, there are many easy, simple ways we can contribute to the health and well-being of our gardens and the earth. The most effective way to simplify gardening is by practicing natural care techniques and adopting the principles of sustainable garden design.

GETTING THE GARDEN OFF CHEMICALS

Natural care is both the oldest way of gardening and the most modern. When we choose to garden naturally, we are not doomed to the endless hard work that our ancestors faced. Today, we have at our disposal a wide range of tools and techniques that make gardening easier than ever. Indeed, the basic premise of natural care is that by gardening cooperatively with nature, we can make gardens that become easier to care for with each passing year. That is not at all the way it works with traditional gardening, as you probably know from experience. With natural care, we reduce the workload by using sustainable design techniques to minimize or eliminate repetitive chores. As we build ever-healthier soil and make more appropriate plant choices, our gardens grow more sturdily independent each season.

Exciting new soil research shows that many plant diseases can be minimized or avoided by using probiotics, a rapidly growing class of care products that boost soil health and thus improve plant health (see Chapter 3). Probiotic products work by creating or encouraging the soil conditions needed by various kinds of beneficial soil biota. In doing so, they help to increase or maintain the biotic diversity of our garden soils by enhancing the living soil environment. As every organic farmer and gardener will tell you, healthier soil makes for healthier plants.

Today savvy producers of topsoil and potting soil are adding beneficial bacteria and other biota, including mycorrhizae, to their soils. Mycorrhizae are living soil biota that work symbiotically with plant roots, helping plants take up soil nutrients and water more efficiently and develop increased disease resistance. Some probiotics, like aerobically brewed compost teas, are alive and need to be used the day you make or buy them. Others are stable and can be used as you need them (most have a very long shelf life).

Natural care products and techniques are not the quick fix that chemicals seem to be, yet they don't have dangerous hidden downsides, like harming soil quality or killing worms and beneficial insects. Although natural care techniques take a little longer to produce results, the results are longer lasting than with chemical fixes. As we improve the health of our gardens, we notice that the plants become better able to fend for themselves. Building great soil really is like bolstering the immune system of the garden as a whole. In well-fed soil, our plants need less water because their root systems are stronger and penetrate deeper into the soil. When the soil is more nutritious, the plants are better able to resist pests and problems. Thus, we feed and water our plants less and groom them less. These reductions add up to more time to enjoy the garden and find in it the refreshment and relaxation we naturally crave.

GETTING STARTED WITH ORGANICS

We gardeners find the question of when and how to feed our plants quite absorbing. It can be hard to select wisely from the dozens of commercial fertilizers that clamor for our attention on nursery shelves and in the pages of glossy garden magazines. However, it is important to remember that most plants share the same general needs. While a few, like roses, peonies, and clematis, are gross feeders that need a real boost to perform well, most ornamental plants are content with a fairly simple and straightforward nutritional regimen. Most vegetables grow best when given excellent soil, well amended with compost, and a quick booster of nitrogen-releasing alfalfa meal or pellets. Herbs do fine with a light (1- to 2-inch) mulch of compost and little or no summer water. Many woodland plants (such as epimedium and Jack-in-the-pulpit) are almost as sensitive to chemical fertilizers as they are to herbicides and pesticides. We can damage or kill them as quickly by overfeeding as we can by carelessly hitting them with pest sprays. Indeed, if given good soil and annual compost mulch, most woodlanders prefer a regimen of benign neglect to fussing.

Compost mulches provide most of the nutrition in a naturalistically planted, sustainable garden. Mulches are spread in fall and winter. By mid-May, there should be no mulched earth showing, so the compost is hidden by spreading foliage.

When do we need to feed? For ornamental plants, including trees and shrubs, spring and fall are the traditional feeding times. Spring feeds are generally fast acting, offering rapidly growing plants the nitrogen and other nutrients they need for a strong summer performance. A feeding mulch of compost can be fortified with fast-acting alfalfa, which will release more nitrogen if used in combination with composted manures. Alfalfa comes in meal or pellets. I like the big pellets used to feed goats, which are easy to spread and are available without added medication.

In fall, most plants stop producing fresh top growth, even though our Northwestern winters are generally mild. Fall is a good time to feed roots, which continue to stretch and grow underground despite low temperatures. Adding whole fish meal to your compost feeding mulch will fortify growing roots with phosphorus. Whole fish meals contain the same nutrients as bone meals, but because they are created from wild fish (fishing industry wastes), they are not likely to contain diseases such as mad cow disease.

Summer feeding is chiefly a concern for annuals and container plantings. Annuals live in the fast lane and need lots of food immediately to keep up their tremendous floral production. Container plantings are completely dependent on us, for they can't access nutrients in the ground. Thus, both annuals and container plantings need steady supplies of fast-releasing nutrients. For both, we can turn to commercial fertilizers that release nutrients quickly. Even so, both will benefit from a light mulch of compost, which will help maintain soil moisture and prevent weed seeds from germinating, as well as conditioning the soil for these needy plants. Chapter 5 gives more information on when and how to feed plants of various types.

In my own garden, I rarely feed plants directly, preferring to feed the soil with what are called "feeding mulches," made of materials such as compost, seed meals, kelp, and fish meals. I give recipes for the feeding mulches I use in Chapter 3. These homemade fertilizers have several advantages over commercial ones. They are relatively cheap to make in bulk and can be designed to promote slow, steady growth instead of dazzling but overly lush growth that rarely ages well. Concentrated commercial fertilizers can badly burn or even kill young or winter-stressed plants, while mild homemade ones are safe even for convalescents. What's more, organically based homemade mulches condition and enrich our lean Northwestern soils, while many commercial, artificial fertilizers can damage or kill soil biota (including worms).

Although some chemical plant foods are sold in time-release form, few people realize that the release does not begin to occur until soil temperatures reach the 70s. Where springs are slow and cool, plants aren't getting any good from those little capsules until July. Often, too, after a slow, cool start, we get a sudden string of hot days that can cause "dumping" in time-release fertilizers. This effect is more common in the cooler maritime regions of the Northwest than inland or in warm southern regions.

To broaden the range of available nutrients, we can blend our compost mulch with substances such as bat and bird guano that are rich in beneficial fungal soil biota. A good range of trace elements and minerals are found in kelp meal, another common feeding mulch ingredient. Whole fish meal, seed meals, and corn gluten all contribute trace minerals as well as varying forms and amounts of protein, potassium, and phosphorus. Combining various kinds of aged and composted animal manures brings more nutritional variety as well.

In the maritime Northwest, many gardeners modify the native soils' acidity with dolomite or agricultural lime as well as neutralizing compost. East of the mountains, folks who garden on alkaline hardpan will also benefit from adding plenty of buffering compost, but they will want to use gypsum (which can come from old wallboard) to encourage heavy soils to develop a finer grain and to boost the naturally low levels of calcium and sulfur. Some soil specialists suggest that it is better for the soil to use composts that have been fortified with these ingredients, rather than introducing them directly into soils. The idea is that nutrients blended with compost are less "shocking" to the natural soil balance and more readily integrated into the soil food web.

THREE : DELICIOUS DIRT

The best investment you'll ever make is in soil building. The secret ingredient is compost, compost, compost.

Good gardens begin with great soil. In the maritime Northwest, great soil is rare. Clearly, then, soil improvement ranks pretty high on the list of things to do in the garden. Indeed, before we begin planting anything, we need to consider what kind of soil we have and what to do about it. Dirt work must come first here; unless we do our soil amending, our plants are not going to thrive without a lot of attention and assistance. If we do our homework, our plants can indeed prosper into independence.

Here in the Northwest, we lose more plants to winter rots than to cold. Poor drainage takes its toll on the soil, which becomes waterlogged and anaerobic (low in oxygen) in winter. Waterlogging causes soil to lose its structure so that it lacks healthy tilth and texture in summer. These problems are compounded when we till or deeply dig the beds, bringing lean sand or heavy undersoil up to the surface level and burying the living topsoil underground.

Modern soil science is teaching us a new way to understand soil life. We now know that most of the active creatures that make soil alive live in the top few inches of soil. When we disturb the soil layers through tilling and double digging, we actually destroy healthy colonies of soil biota. However, many of the soils we gardeners meet up with are not in very good shape. Native maritime Northwestern soils are generally quite lean and low in humus. Whether sand- or clay-based, they tend to have plenty of minerals and nutrients present, but often not in forms that are readily available to our plants. When we are dealing with typical poor garden soils, it is wise to invest in a significant but one-time effort in soil building that will give us a solid base to work with for many seasons to come.

HUMUS: THE LIVING SPONGE

The key to unlocking the potential nutrients in our soils is compost, which provides humus. Humus is the Wonder bread of soil building, functioning in many important ways. It is almost as squishy, too. Indeed, just as its amazing compressibility makes Wonder bread the savvy kid's spitball material of choice, humus gives non-clay-based soils cling, the capacity to hold a shape. This pleasant textural quality, also called tilth, is what experienced gardeners are looking for when they pick up and squeeze a handful of dirt.

Humus is organic plant food, but organic in the original sense; it's the carbon-based leftovers from both animal and vegetable life forms. Mostly it comes from decaying vegetation. The materials that are commonly called humus are really its precursors: Sawdust and manure, grass clippings and chopped hay, leaves and shredded bark are all potential humus because as they decompose, the breakdown process floods the soil with raw nutrients.

Before plants can use these nutrients, they need to be further processed by soil microbes, just as our food is broken down into nutritional building blocks through digestion. The living bacteria and microbes that perform this service also eat humus, but they need different bits of it than the plants do. Just as trees take up carbon dioxide and give off oxygen at night, soil biota and plants have evolved a mutually beneficial digestive relationship with humus.

Besides feeding the soil, humus also holds an exceptional amount of water, acting as a living sponge. Tired, humus-poor soil can take up only relatively minor amounts of water; about 20 percent of the soil's own dry weight is a typical carrying capacity for unimproved urban or suburban dirt. In contrast, woodland duff, the deep soil found in undisturbed woods, can absorb and hold up to 500 percent of its own weight in water.

LEARNING FROM SOILS

Before soil testing was widely available, farmers felt, smelled, and even tasted their soil to learn about its qualities. They also found visual cues about its history by looking at the land and the plants on it. Get to know your soil by digging a few test holes around the garden site. Examine the soil visually: Is it a pale gray or yellow or a rich brown? Pale-colored soils are usually low in humus

Even a spoonful of healthy soil contains billions of minuscule biota that help plants build stronger root systems and fend off pathogen attacks. Compost mulch feeds the biota that bring soil to life.

WHO LIVES IN YOUR SOIL?

Soil biota are the microscopic beings that bring life to the mix of humus (rotting organic materials) and minerals that make up the nonliving portion of soil. They come in many forms, from bacteria to nematodes and fungi. Some biota help build healthy soil and support healthy plants, and these are considered to be beneficial. Others can cause many problems for gardeners, from root rots to blights, molds, and mildews. These critters are considered to be pathogenic. Both have a legitimate and important place in the growth and decay cycles of the natural world. In garden settings and on farms, we prefer to boost the growth of our beneficial organisms and suppress as many pathogens as we can.

All soils contain both bacteria and other kinds of biota, notably fungi, in varying proportions. Soils that are bacterially dominated are best suited for growing lawns, most annuals and perennials, and most vegetables. Soils that are fungally dominated are best for woody plants (trees and shrubs).

Continued on page 64

Here's a brief introduction to the cast of critters that create the soil food web and make soil come alive.

Bacteria. Our native soils are full of bacteria, both beneficial and pathogenic. A spoonful of ordinary backyard soil may contain billions of bacteria of thousands of different kinds, many of them specific to this region. Nitrogen-fixing bacteria dine on particles of humus, creating waste products (bacteria manure) that add new forms of organic content to the soil. Many plants absorb nutrients through this bacterial waste product, so the better the bacterial balance, the better the soil quality for plants. Bacteria (and their waste products) are eaten in turn by fellow soil dwellers of many kinds. Thus, beneficial bacteria help retain the nutrients and organic matter they eat in the soil. Bacterially dominated soils are best for lawns, flower beds, and most vegetables.

Earthworms. Worms are among the most beneficial of soil dwellers. Sadly, they are harmed or killed by exposure to many pesticides and herbicides, including some common weed-and-feed products. Most gardeners cherish their earthworms, knowing that these

and need lots of organic material as a primary amendment. Dark brown soils may be peat based and thus rich in humus yet very low in nutrients. Smell the soil as well: Acid soils often smell sour or have the pronounced stink of organic decay. Neutral soils smell "woodsy" and clean. Sandy soils may have a mineral smell. Squeeze some in your hand: Is it sandy or crumbly or does it tend to form a tight ball? Sandy soils will need enrichment with humus. Crumbly soils may be well balanced, while those that make firm balls have a high clay content. With clay, as with sand, it is important to add plenty of compost and other humus builders.

Like farmers, experienced gardeners can learn a great deal about a site's soil and overall conditions by looking at the native plants and weeds that grow there. Chickweed, for instance, indicates good garden soil that has been improved with organic material. Gardens with lots of chickweed are usually fertile and fairly well drained. Horsetail indicates an acid clay soil with poor drainage. Hardpan and subsoil may be covered with morning glory, mosses, and liverworts. Dry, sandy soils may support little besides wild peas and vetch.

We can also make educated guesses about soil by watching how it drains. Sandy soil drains fast and tends to be nutritionally lean. In areas with high annual rainfall, many nutrients will be washed out of light, sandy soils before plants can access them. This will be especially true of nutrients provided by chemical fertilizers, which persist for only a short time in any case. Sandy soils make a very good base for dryland plant gardens. Many of the hardy herbs, from rosemary and sage to lavender and thyme, do well in sandy soils. So do penstemons and many other plants that hail from dry regions, few of which thrive in heavy clays.

If water drains very slowly or not at all, you are working with clay-based soil. Clay soils are often fairly nutritious and moisture retentive, yet they frequently harbor the pathogens that promote root rots. Clay soils also tend to be acidic for a number of reasons. Natural soil acidity is amplified by compaction and poor drainage (common flaws in clay soils), both of which conditions may lead to low soil oxygen levels. Seasonal standing water also increases acidity, as can excessive nitrogen from imbalanced fertilizing programs.

With a long-established garden, we can learn a lot about

what has or has not happened by reading the visual clues offered by plants. Where most plants look healthy, we can assume that the soil has been tended and amended regularly. Where the majority of plants look stressed, we can assume that the soil has been neglected and will need remedial assistance. If the garden looked fine when you bought the house but looks sad the following year, you can assume that the fleeting good looks were due to chemical assistance.

New construction sites are much harder to read, since most are stripped of all native soil, leaving mainly subsoil with just an inch or two of imported topsoil for top-dressing. It can be difficult to tell what the real prevailing conditions are (or were) until poor plant performance, failing lawns, and patches of bad drainage reveal the underlying patterns.

The best way to create a more sustainable garden environment is to start a soil-building program. Within a few seasons, the improved soil will have your plants looking healthy again, and this time they will be better able to maintain their health over time with less help from you.

BUILDING HEALTHY SOIL

Organic farmers and gardeners have a saying: "Feed the soil and the plants will feed themselves." The idea is that when we build healthy soil, plants of all kinds can be well nourished without the use of artificial fertilizers or pesticides. For years, traditional agriculturalists laughed at this idea, considering it unscientific, if not outright kooky.

Now, thanks to research carried out by soil scientists across the country, we are learning that the old saying is true. Soil is alive, and when we feed it properly, we encourage a healthy biosystem that can indeed nourish our plants and fend off many plant pests and pathogens naturally.

The new knowledge about the nature of soil life helps us to understand what our garden soils really need from us. Most people think of dirt as inert, but healthy soil teems with life. A gram (about a teaspoon) of good garden soil contains organic material as well as minerals. It also contains what's called soil biota, the tiny creatures that bring dirt to life.

A spoonful of average garden soil may contain several hundred thousand soil bacteria. Well over twenty thousand different kinds of soil bacteria have been identified

hard workers are the soil builder's best friend. Worms do the mixing for us when we layer amendments onto garden soil. Worm tunnels open heavy soil to let air get down to plant roots. Worm castings promote sturdy root growth and feed many soil dwellers. It would be hard to have too many worms, but soils suffer quickly when worms are in short supply.

Fungi. Most gardeners assume that soil fungus must be bad, but this is far from the truth. Fungi are vitally important to soil health, and beneficial forms are found in virtually every kind of soil on earth. Like bacteria, fungal hyphae (mycelia) break down organic matter by digesting and excreting humus and recycling nutrients through the soil food chain. Healthy woodland soils are fungally dominated, meaning that there are more fungal creatures than bacteria. To keep woodland soils healthy, we need to maintain the fungal balance by restoring the nutrients stored in fallen foliage that has been removed for the sake of visual tidiness. To restore the lost nutrients easily, simply shred the leaves and replace them as light mulch. Since woody plants grow best in a fungally dominated soil, "parking out"

Continued on page 66

woodlands by replacing under-story shrubs with grass usually results in stressed trees.

Microarthropods. These tiny insects such as springtails are recyclers that feed on bacteria and fungi as well as plant parti-cles, making nitrogen and other nutrients more readily available to plants and other soil biota.

Nematodes. Nematodes, like fungi, are usually assumed to be pathogens, but beneficial nematodes abound. All good garden soil contains an ample supply of beneficial nema-todes, which feed on many other creatures, from bacteria and protozoa to other nema-todes (including the patho-gens). These support root growth, passing vital nutrients along to plants through their manure. Pathogenic nema-todes eat live plant tissue, harming roots rather than pro-moting healthy root growth. In healthy soil, beneficial nema-todes help keep their patho-genic cousins under control.

Protozoa. Soil-dwelling proto-zoa eat bacteria and produce a manure rich in available nitro-gen. They are a favored food for nematodes and other soil fauna, which release nitrogen and other nutrients back into the soil as they excrete in turn.

to date, many of them regionally adapted to feed (and feed off) the local flora. These bacteria eat decaying organic matter, which they then excrete, often in forms that plant roots can absorb.

Soil that's rich in humus is generally also rich in soil life, while leaner soils may be extremely impoverished. Well-amended soil with a high humus content may contain millions of beneficial bacteria and other active biota per teaspoon. Exhausted or degraded soils (the kinds most urban gardeners contend with) may hold only a few hun-dred bacteria and very few other life forms per teaspoon. As a rule, the livelier the soil, the healthier the plants that soil supports.

To find out what is living in your own soil, you can have a biotic count performed by a qualified lab (see "Testing Our Own Backyards," later in this section). Biotic counts track the kinds and relative quantities of creatures, both beneficial and pathogenic, that inhabit our garden soil. Although many kinds of biota populate all soils, the relative proportions will change according to several factors. For instance, in grasslands, meadows, lawns, and most garden settings, the soil is bacterially dominated, which means it hosts a higher percentage of bacteria than fungal biota.

Healthy woodland soil is predominantly based on fungi (microscopic mushroom relatives), which are critical to the long-term health of trees and shrubs. The presence of soil fungi is measured in meters. One teaspoon of good wood-land garden soil may hold sixty thousand meters of benefi-cial fungi, which help to break down the toughest forms of carbon to digest, such as chunks of bark and tree limbs.

That same spoonful of soil may also be home to some one hundred thousand protozoa, single-celled critters that eat bacteria as well as each other. There are many kinds of protozoa, including amoebae, flagellates, and ciliates. Since some of these single-celled (or acellular) creatures can cause serious health problems to humans, it's tempting to think they don't belong in garden soil. However, like bacteria, protozoa can be beneficial or pathogenic. Also like bacteria, protozoa excrete nitrogen in forms that are accessible to plant roots. Beneficial protozoa provide as much as 80 percent of the plant-available nitrogen in our soils, so their presence is clearly desirable.

Nematodes are also generally considered to be bad, since they can damage or kill plants. However, our little soil sample may contain up to five hundred beneficial nematodes that eat bacteria, fungi, and other pesky nematode cousins, once again releasing nitrogen to plants. Pathogenic or harmful nematodes eat living plant roots, making these creatures less welcome guests. Since they favor tight, acid soils that are low in oxygen, we can reduce pathogen populations by improving soil texture to bring in more oxygen and adding pH neutralizers such as compost. (As compost matures, it is buffered by the decay process, no matter how acidic the components. Thus, most compost is roughly neutral in pH.)

Healthy soils may also hold mycorrhizae, symbiotic mycelia that colonize the fine root hairs of plants, enabling the host plant to take up nitrogen and other nutrients more efficiently. Soil tests that measure VAM are counting vascular arbuscular mycorrhizae, microscopic fungal hyphae that dwell among the roots of herbaceous plants such as vegetables and perennials. Ecto tests count their cousins, the ectomycorrhizae, which occur on the roots of trees and shrubs. Both are still quite newly recognized as being valuable soil components and have very recently become available to gardeners as a probiotic soil amendment or plant food supplement.

Certain plants (chiefly natives) with a reputation for being tricky to transplant are limited by these mycorrhizal relationships. Unless the right kind of mycorrhizae are present in the soil, the host plants die, because they can't process nutrients well without their soil-based companions, and the new soil lacks the proper mycorrhizae to support them. In some cases, degraded soils that resisted standard improvement techniques have responded with a healthy crop of biota when VAM inoculants were added. VAM inoculants may encourage the establishment of native plants better than ordinary soil amendments.

All these tiny creatures chase each other through the soil, competing for food and feeding plants in the process. Most of this intense activity takes place in the top few inches of soil, where oxygen flow is good and there is a regular supply of moisture from dew and rain as well as gardeners.

Dr. Elaine Ingham of Oregon State University in Corvallis talks about these complex relationships in terms of the "soil food web," stressing the interrelatedness of both participants and ingredients. She notes that our understanding of the soil-building process is still developing. Thanks to

WHAT'S pH?

When soil is called sweet or sour or base, the terms refer to what scientists call its pH balance. Simple pH testing kits are available at most nurseries and garden centers and are quite easy to use. You can also get more refined soil tests through your county cooperative extension agency (they also run the Master Gardener programs). Soils are rated on a scale that runs from 0 to 14. Soil chemists use the pH scale to describe where soils fall in the acid-to-alkaline spectrum. This spectrum identifies the relative proportions of hydrogen and hydroxyl in a given soil. Soils (or water, or anything else) with more hydrogen ions are what we call acid, while those with more hydroxyls are described as alkaline.

A low score (a pH of less than 6.5) on your soil test indicates that your soil is acid. A high score (above 7) tells you that your soil is alkaline. In a few favored places, the soil is neutral (between 6.5 and 7). These neutral soils are called sweet, while low-ranking or acid soils are called sour and alkaline or high-ranking soils are called base.

Since our culture prizes sweet things, it's easy to assume that

Continued on page 68

the patient research (imagine counting all those little things) of Dr. Ingham and others, we know that productive soils of many types boast impressive quantities of soil biota, while degraded soils may have mere hundreds instead of bountiful thousands. For Dr. Ingham, the good news is that "We don't always know why soils degrade, but we are beginning to understand how to get them back into a healthy balance."

These days, scientific studies are determining the optimal biota numbers for soils all over the world. In time, Dr. Ingham and her co-workers hope to be able to determine what healthy soil food webs should look like for every kind of soil, according to factors such as climate and type of crop or plant community.

TAKE A LOOK UNDERFOOT

To get started on our journey of change, we need to take a closer look at the soil that lies underfoot. Most of us start out with lots of questions. Reading only brings in more possibilities, as dozens of books and articles present us with choices. Should we bring in topsoil and make mounded or raised beds? Should we simply add soil amendments? If so, which are right for our area? How much is enough? Can you add too much manure or compost?

As any expert worth her salt will tell you, "That depends." The right answer for one situation may cause more problems elsewhere. To decide how best to amend your soil, you need to know what's wrong with it. Take a look around the yard. If you see flourishing plants with glossy foliage and well-filled branch structure, and those great plants have been in place for at least five years, your soil is probably pretty good. In this case, all you will need to do is provide an annual mulch of 3 to 4 inches of compost to keep the soil in good heart. A top-dressing of another 1 to 2 inches of aged dairy manure will help keep your soil happy and keep weeds out as well.

However, if you see yellowing rhododendrons, skimpy perennials, scrawny trees, and a patchy lawn, you have some work to do. Start with soil tests.

A simple pH test will identify your soil as acid (sour), alkaline (base), or closer to neutral (sweet). Since most vegetables prefer soils that are near neutral, standard advice is to amend soils with neutralizers such as lime or gypsum. However, it's helpful to know what pH range is

sweet soils are good and sour or base ones must be bad. However, when we consider that most maritime Northwestern soils are acid or sour and that most soils in Eastern Washington and Oregon are base, and we then look at the amazing flora both kinds of soils can support in their natural state, we can figure out pretty quickly that sour and base soils can't be all bad. Here in the Northwest, soils with a pH range of 6 to 5 are not uncommon. Such soils will please acid lovers like azaleas and blueberries but must be neutralized with compost to make most vegetables and many garden flowers grow well.

Although pH progression looks quite straightforward on paper, soil pH is less simple. When hydrogen and hydroxyl are in balance in a given soil, the soil is considered to be neutral. When they aren't in balance, each successive pH level is ten times greater than the last one. Thus, soil with a pH of 5 is ten times more acid than one with a pH of 6 and a hundred times more acid than one with a pH of 7. Clearly, changing soil pH even half a step takes a lot of work.

The pH concept is especially important if we want to grow vegetables, since most typical for your region before acting on your results. In much of the maritime Northwest, acid soils are the norm. Rather than trying to change that acid soil, gardeners in our region can seek out the many plants that prefer it that way, from azaleas and rhododendrons to blueberries and heathers. We can also explore our outstanding regional flora, which includes many gardenworthy natives.

There are also other ways to determine the kind and quality of the soil you have to work with. Tests called soil assays can tell you the relative amounts of minerals, such as phosphorus, calcium, and magnesium, in your soil. Nitrogen is not a mineral, but it is an important nutrient whose presence can be determined in several ways (colometric tests are the most common). However, because soil is much more than a mass of lifeless minerals, a microbial assay will give you a more complete picture of what's going on in your soil.

TESTING OUR OWN BACKYARDS

A microbial assay is basically a creature count for your soil. It consists of tests that measure active bacterial biomass, protozoa counts, and VAM. Such tests are not expensive (most run between $10 and $50), but they can be difficult to interpret. Even when you know your active bacterial biomass, what are you supposed to do about it?

The most helpful test is a very complete one. It is not cheap, but it will provide the best possible picture of what's going on in your soil and will also tell you what to do about it. When you compare such a test with the cost of 10 yards of topsoil or a lengthy expert consultation, it starts to look pretty reasonable.

At Soil Foodweb, Inc., Dr. Ingham offers many single-item assays as well as a Total Foodweb Analysis of all food web groups and their relationships for less than $200, as of this writing. This full-spectrum test includes specific counts of eight different soil organisms, with an interpreted report to help you make sense of the information. (See the Resources section at the end of this book for contact information.)

The idea is to see both what you have in your soil and what you don't have. For instance, you might have plenty of soil bacteria but not enough bacteria predators. Until the bacteria are eaten, they can't release their stored nitrogen. To get our soil back into balance, we need to know which group of critters to feed, and how to do it.

vegetables perform far better in improved soils that approach neutral than in strongly acid or alkaline ones. When maritime Northwestern gardeners work hard to make good soil and feed their plants well, yet find their vegetable garden crops disappointing, the culprit may well be low soil pH. Vegetables are an especially sensitive crop because they are mainly annuals, which need to live their brief lives unchecked by lacks and needs if they are to shine. Any factor that inhibits their rapid, even growth will have a significant effect on their overall performance, since they must cram a productive (and reproductive) lifetime into a mere few months.

In an ornamental garden, where we are chiefly growing longer-lived plants with more flexible survival strategies, pH definitely remains a factor but is less critical in terms of performance. We can still grow a wide range of plants in less-than-optimal conditions, though they may not perform quite as well as they would if every preference were met. Indeed, most pH incompatibilities can be avoided simply by choosing plants that grow well in the type of soil you have to offer.

HOW GOOD SOIL IS BORN

Dr. Michael Holmes, lab director at Soil Foodweb, notes, "There are three important parts to soil building. First, we want to retain nutrients. Second, we want to make them available to plants. Third, we want to suppress pathogens."

He emphasizes that soil building starts with good biota counts. "The bacteria glue tiny soil particles together to make micro-aggregates. The fungi tie those micronutrients together to make bigger chunks, called water-stable macro-aggregates, that are the basis of good soil structure," he explains.

"Plant roots also help to tie all the soil pieces together," Dr. Holmes continues. "So do larger soil organisms like nematodes, microarthropods [tiny insects such as springtails], and earthworms," all of which push soil particles around, mixing them up.

"When you understand how the soil food web works, you can build soil structure, reduce applications of fertilizers, and eliminate the need for pesticides, " Dr. Holmes adds.

To create a healthy soil food web in our own backyards, we must encourage beneficial soil biota. It's fairly easy to provide organic matter to feed those hungry microbes. Composted manures and garden crops can be recycled into beds and borders, adding a nearly neutral source of food for many kinds of soil dwellers. But how do we encourage the right kinds of critters? For one thing, we stop using pesticides and herbicides, both of which are seriously damaging to soil biota.

According to Dr. Ingham, pesticide use drops naturally when soil is in balance, because fewer problems present themselves. As she puts it, "Conditions that favor beneficials are less favorable for most pathogens. When beneficials significantly outnumber pathogens, the bad guys just can't compete effectively."

PROBIOTICS

Another way to encourage soil biota is to use an exciting new group of products known as probiotics. The word "probiotic" essentially means "encouraging biota." The term is used to describe any technique, substance, product, or material that improves conditions for beneficial biota.

Probiotic soil inoculants are becoming more widely available as information about their uses and effects reaches farmers and gardeners. Based on the soil food web concept, these products were initially designed for agricultural use. The first clients were farmers and orchardists who were tired of paying high prices for chemical fertilizers and pesticides that left their land sterile and nearly dead.

Agricultural probiotics are stabilized liquid mixtures of soil nutrients, buffers (pH and salt neutralizers), and flocculants (soil clumpers). They provide immediately usable nutrients to soil biota, promote the rapid growth of beneficial soil biota, and improve soil texture, creating better oxygen flow. All of this accords precisely with Dr. Holmes' three-point program for soil building: retaining nutrients, making them available to plants, and suppressing pathogens.

One such agricultural product is called BLEND. Farmers use BLEND to balance and replenish soils, but gardeners can also take advantage of this remarkable substance. It works like a layer of compost and manure, enriching the microbial content of the soil (or leaf surface) and improving tilth, drainage, and beneficial bacterial counts. Used on a monthly basis, it can open nondraining soils and transform hardpan. In vegetable and ornamental gardens, monthly doses of BLEND will improve the soil as much as or more than applications of heavy, bulky compost and manures. The stuff also buffers the salts that tend to build up in Northwestern soils, binding them into inert or disassociated states. (Clearly, soil particles have as many mood problems as people do.) For information on obtaining BLEND, see the Resources section at the end of this book.

Other probiotic products foster bacterially dominated soils in which lawns, annuals, and many vegetables flourish, while still others encourage the healthy growth of beneficial fungi that promote optimal growth in trees and shrubs.

To use probiotic soil inoculants of any kind, you simply dilute the suggested amount with water (a chart tells you how much, depending on the area you plan to cover). The water and room oxygen activate the stabilized ingredients, so once a batch is mixed, it must be used within a few hours. You spray the diluted solution directly on damp soil (biota need moisture to propagate fast), where it begins colonizing beneficial biota almost immediately.

Woody plants like trees and shrubs, and certain vegetables like corn, all prefer a fungally dominated soil. Probiotic stimulants like LASE can help fungal soil biota thrive even in disturbed, depleted, or poor soils.

Probiotic soil inoculants can also be used as foliar feeds. Spray some on a few sad plants and observe what happens. You can often see marked improvement within a day or two. Like soil, plant foliage harbors many kinds of microscopic biota that need proper food to thrive. By filling the bacterial slots on each leaf with healthy biota, we can reduce or eliminate many common plant problems, from black spot to botrytis. In my experience, when probiotic sprays are used promptly at the first sign of trouble, they can halt many diseases, from fungal infections to powdery mildew, that are already in progress. For more information on using probiotics as foliar sprays, see "Plant Diseases" in Chapter 6.

One new class of probiotics includes mycorrhizae, a large group of beneficial fungal biota that form symbiotic relationships with plant roots and soil biota. The presence of beneficial mycorrhizae helps plants access soil nutrients, including water. Probiotic products containing mycorrhizae come in a number of stabilized forms, as concentrated liquid solutions that are activated by air and water and as dry powders and prilled (pelletized) products.

A number of companies are also now producing potting soils, mulches, and fertilizers that combine mycorrhizae with beneficial bacteria. Whitney Farms has created a specific blend they call Life Link, which adds the probiotic element to their line of soil amendments and fertilizers. A company called Organica has a line of probiotic lawn care products, including a microbial soil conditioner that introduces beneficial bacteria into depleted lawn soils and a natural dethatcher that inoculates the soil with specific bacteria that break down thatch before it can accumulate.

PROBIOTIC TEAS

In recent years, soil scientists at several major universities have been investigating the value of an ancient, low-tech resource. Teas based on manure and compost have long been used by organic farmers and gardeners to boost the tilth and health of their garden soils. These teas create a healthy bloom of beneficial soil and plant biota.

The biggest problem in making effective teas is the difficulty of getting enough oxygen into the mix. Most of us make manure or compost tea by dumping a shovelful into a bucket of water and letting it steep. This is not very efficient, since teas made by passive steeping don't have very high biotic counts. What's more, teas brewed without ample oxygen can contain many pathogens. That doesn't mean you are harming your soil by adding compost tea, but it does mean that a more efficiently brewed tea will have a far more powerfully beneficial result.

Advanced studies at Oregon State University (and elsewhere) have led to the development of simple yet highly sophisticated aerobic tea brewing machines, so named because they pump oxygen into the tea as it is brewing. These teas can boost soil tilth without the addition of humus, which is helpful for growers of plants such as herbs that prefer lean soils. It's also great news for gardeners who don't really have the option of bringing in yards of composted manure each season. Indeed, spraying with aerobically brewed compost tea is said to be the nutritional and conditioning equivalent of adding 6 inches of compost to your soils. These tea-brewing machines are now being sold commercially, and some nurseries and garden centers have also begun selling freshly brewed tea.

Like probiotic soil inoculants, living teas can have either bacterial or fungal dominance. Woody plants and woodland gardens thrive in soil that is fungally dominated, while leafy vegetables and perennials prefer bacterially dominated soils. Several companies make starter solutions for brewing either kind of tea. Thus, if your Japanese maples are struggling with verticillium, you'll use the fungal tea. To perk up flower beds or increase tilth in the vegetable patch, you'll make bacterial tea. Also like the concentrated probiotic inoculants, aerobic compost teas can be used as a soil drench and as foliar protection from fungal and bacterial diseases.

Another use for the teas is as an accelerant for compost.

Tests carried out by the Seattle Tilth Association demonstrate that adding aerobic compost teas to newly mixed composts can dramatically reduce the time required to achieve a finished product. Time to maturity depends on several factors, including the size and carbon-nitrogen balance of the initial material used.

Two types of aerobic brewing machines are presently available to home gardeners. Despite a sizable price difference, both work very well. Indeed, in recent double-blind tests run by an independent research lab, the two machines produced virtually interchangeable products. Interestingly, no two batches were exactly alike, but all were within the same range of biodiversity.

These machines continually circulate a tankful of water through a bag of mature compost or vermicompost (worm compost). To boost biotic populations, you add a feeder solution based on agricultural-grade (unrefined) or black-strap molasses with several kinds of composts. Other ingredients include a soluble form of kelp, which adds valuable trace elements and feeds many biota. A small amount of soluble rock dust is added to give beneficial fungi a place to grow. (The fungal hyphae can grow properly only when they can attach to tiny mineral chunks.)

As the tea steeps, the brewing machine pumps a constant stream of oxygen into it. That steady supply of oxygen eliminates most pathogens (which prefer anaerobic conditions) while actively encouraging beneficial organisms (which do best with more oxygen). Depending on temperatures, compost mixtures, and other factors, the brew cycle can take anywhere from eighteen hours to three days. The result is a highly concentrated tea that offers many (even hundreds of times) more beneficial biota than are found in normal healthy soil counts. Typical biotic counts are in the millions but can reach the billions under optimal conditions.

Like the probiotic inoculants, these super teas must be used quickly or their potency is lost. They are literally alive with biota that are continuing to multiply. For best results, aerobic teas should be used within about ten hours of decant time. By eighteen hours, the teas are beginning to degrade, since once their artificial food supply is gone, the only remaining food source the biota have is each other. Biotic snacking can quickly reduce the diversity of the remaining soil critters. Twelve hours after being decanted, living teas go on the compost heap, where they actively aid in rapid decomposition.

When faced with the prospect of replacing or manipulating many yards of compost or soil, consider trying a course of probiotics first. After all, whether you plan to grow edibles or ornamentals, natives and their allies or plants from all over the world, there is no greater gift you can offer them than healthy home soil.

Dr. Ingham of Oregon State University has produced an excellent handbook on making and using compost teas. For more information, visit her website at www.soil foodweb.com. See the Resources section at the end of this book for more information on sources of aerobic compost teas and tea brewing machines.

COMPOSTING

In the maritime Northwest, no matter where you garden, the native soils are extremely likely to need improvement. When we want to create a sustainable garden, we need above all to promote healthy soil with good structure and plenty of humus. Historically, Northwestern soils contain as little as 1 to 2 percent humus. Since most plants prefer to live in soils that boast 5 to 8 percent humus, we have our work cut out for us.

The very best substance we can offer our less than optimal soil is a steady infusion of lively, mature compost, preferably homemade. Though compost is not particularly high in nitrogen, compost improves the nutritional value of soils of all kinds by allowing soil biota to access nutrients locked up in our lean soils. Acid soils in particular can be quite nutrient rich, yet unless that invaluable humus is added, the nutrients are not readily available to most plants. As compost breaks down in the beds, it releases not only its own stored nutrients, but also helps (through the interactions of those tiny soil microorganisms) to alter those soil-bound minerals and nutrients into forms more readily available to plant roots.

I always recommend mulching the garden beds and borders with finished, mature compost for several reasons. Like any mulch, compost reduces weeds by covering the seeds (most of which need light and air to germinate). Compost mulch also conserves soil moisture, which helps plants by keeping roots moist and cool. Compost mulch

RECYCLING MANURE

Dairy manure may be the single most useful soil builder around. Modern dairies rinse their barns after each milking, storing the manure in pits. (This is often sold as "pit-washed" dairy manure). After it gets mixed and tumbled through a composting cycle, the manure is light, fluffy, and perfect for garden use. Cows digest their feed so well that weed seeds seldom survive, so dairy manure can be used as sheet compost, as top-dressing, and for soil improvement. Since cows eat alfalfa rather than timothy hay or weed-free grains, you don't need to worry about contamination by clopyralid (an herbicide; see clopyralid sidebar) in dairy manure.

This extremely renewable resource is becoming readily available as counties and towns create manure-recycling programs. To find one in your area, contact your county extension service agent. Local dairies are also good starting points; many will deliver manure for a reasonable price. If no manure-recycling program exists, get one started by enlisting a local garden club, nursery, or recycling group. Manure recycling not only makes great garden soil, it also helps preserve (or improve) local water quality.

also creates an ideal miniclimate for healthy microbial life in the top few inches of soil. A 2- to 3-inch compost blanket forms a bubble of humid air that captures the carbon dioxide that plants take in and convert to oxygen. For plants, having lots of available carbon dioxide is similar to the effects humans feel when they breathe oxygen-rich clean air; it invigorates them and makes them grow more strongly.

This is not a speedy process, but plants are rarely in a hurry. When we mulch soils with compost, the result is a satisfyingly slow but persistent release of plant foods in highly usable forms. Where artificial chemical fertilizers can provoke excessive growth or even burn plants (not to mention killing soil biota), organic supplements like compost and composted manure patiently give of their goodness for months and even years.

RECYCLING THE GARDEN

Historians recognize that since the birth of agriculture, the most productive growing systems have been those that recycled waste nutrients. Ancient horticultural practices from cultures throughout time and all over the world shared what we think of as the modern concept of biosustainability: Everything that comes out of the farm goes back in, one way or another. Everything the farm needs can be supplied from its own abundance.

Homemade compost is especially valuable as a soil amendment because it is teeming with microbial life. A gram (about a teaspoonful) of healthy compost may contain billions of microbes that feed our plants by feeding the soil. When we recycle garden wastes into compost, humus and nutrients that would be lost are returned. Both garden and kitchen scraps are sensible additions to a healthy heap, for the greater the variety of ingredients, the higher-quality the finished product will be, particularly in terms of soil biotic diversity. Thus the better such compost can promote healthy garden soils.

The more varied the raw plant materials we use, the richer the microbial mix in our finished compost. Since perhaps as many as a million species of microbial life forms exist, each favoring certain environments and plants, we can encourage microbial diversity by taking full advantage of each microclimate to grow a rich variety of

CLOPYRALID: A PERSISTENT HERBICIDE

Over the past few years, we have learned that certain pesticides and herbicides may be far more persistent than previously assumed. In 2002, a fair amount of press was given to issues surrounding the commercial use of clopyralid, a persistent herbicide. As it turns out, clopyralid can persist in soil and in compost for as long as two years.

Even at levels as low as 3 parts per billion, this agrichemical can remain active and potent enough to kill or disrupt growth in many plants. One of the most susceptible families is the legumes, a vast clan that includes such diverse members as peas and beans, clovers, broom, and alfalfa. Pea crops seem to be the most susceptible, as nearly all peas are damaged by very low levels of clopyralid contamination.

This makes peas an excellent choice to use for testing soil or compost for clopyralid contamination. In tests conducted at Washington State University, no false-positive results have been found when peas were used in bio-assays for clopyralid. A bio-assay is a standard test that in this case you can try at home.

plants. When we mulch those plants with complex, plant-based composts, we build and nurture both the plants and the soil, which in turn feeds our plants better than chemical fertilizers can.

HOME COMPOSTING

Composting is essentially an extremely simple process: You heap up piles of organic wastes and wait until they rot. In practice, however, there are many things (most of them almost that simple) that we can do to accelerate the process and make the end product more consistent. Here are the most important ones:

- Put your pile where it will be unobtrusive yet easy to use.

- Make it big enough to be serviceable.

- Shred, chop, or mow over all materials before you add them to the pile.

- Layer on equivalent quantities of green (wet) and brown (dry) materials.

Set aside a place with a minimum ground area of 4 square feet, the minimal effective size for a compost heap. You can purchase compost bins in various sizes that are smaller· than this. Cubic bins are far more efficient than freeform heaps. Twin bins will work far better than a single pile. A set of two 4- by 4-foot bins make it possible to be building a new, active pile in the second one while using mature compost from the first bin for the garden. Triple bins are better yet, allowing for a full cycle (three turns of the compost pile) to be completed while new piles are waiting in the wings.

Whatever the size, all bins will be a lot more efficient if you shred all materials except grass clippings before composting. Fine-textured materials like grass clippings or small leaves can be added directly to the compost pile. Big leaves and large stalks and stems need to be reduced in size before they go on the heap. Smaller bits break down much faster than big ones; by creating more surface area, you can significantly speed up the decomposition process.

It is quite easy to do this with a leaf shredder, or by running over mounds of leaves with a lawn mover. It's quite fun to reduce volume by whacking those mounds with a machete or brush-clearing knife. As you slash away at big

To make the test, mix 1 part by weight of compost or potting soil that you want to test with 6 parts of clean soil from your garden or another site you know to be healthy. A successful vegetable garden is an ideal source of soil. If you use 1 pound for each part, you get 7 pounds of soil. Fill pots and label each with the soil or compost type you are testing. Plant at least two peas in each sample. If you are testing several types of compost or potting soil, use the same kind of peas in each sample.

Peas sprout quickly, so you may see the first pair of leaves ("seed leaves") within a week. Clopyralid damage will appear with the second set of leaves (true leaves), which may be distorted, curled, or twisted, pale, or yellowed and usually lacking the normal leaf shape.

If you do this test at home and the peas look just fine, you can be comfortable that your mulch or soil is not contaminated. If you do have a problem, the good news is that you can do something about it. Studies done at Washington State University indicate that activated charcoal can pick up clopyralid and other contaminants from soil and compost

Continued on page 78

and hold them in an inert state indefinitely. The recommended rate of application for activated charcoal is 5 pounds per 100 square feet. (See "Detoxing with Activated Charcoal," later in this chapter, for more details.)

If you don't have a clopyralid contamination problem, the good news is that you are not likely to develop one, as long as you are careful. All commercial compost and mulch makers in Washington and Oregon are now routinely screening for clopyralid contamination and can certify their products as clean.

Because the main vector routes are now well known, it is also possible for home composters to avoid accidental contamination. Here's how:

- Do not use lawn clippings from any lawn that is treated by a non-organic commercial lawn service.

- Do not use straw or hay unless it is certified organic.

- Do not use stable sweepings or manure from horses fed with weed-free grain unless it is certified organic.

- Do not use any animal manure, from rabbits and goats to emus and llamas, unless the animals are fed certified organic feeds.

piles of garden leftovers, those daily stresses and tensions melt away. However you slice it, the result is a more uniform mixture of organic ingredients that can decompose happily together.

What you mix into your compost heap is also important. The traditional rule of thumb is to combine half green and half brown ingredients. That means for every barrowload of fresh grass clippings, you need to add an equivalent quantity of something like dried leaves or chopped straw. The idea is that the nitrogen in the green stuff is balanced by the carbon-rich brown stuff.

Daily kitchen scraps can contribute a splendid variety of micronutrients and biotic organisms, but stick with scraps from fruits and vegetables. Adding fats and proteins from meat, fish, or even dairy leftovers to compost is a standing invitation to rats and raccoons, not to mention wandering dogs. If you find that any food scraps attract pests, put your food processor to work. Each day, grind up your leftovers with water and pour them into the compost. Top the slurry off with a bit of dried grass or leaves and you won't have a pest problem any longer.

You can add garden weeds galore as long as they aren't full of ripe seed, which can create even worse weed problems when you reapply them to the garden. (Most casually made compost does not get hot enough to kill seeds, many of which can withstand temperatures below 150 degrees F.) Some of the obvious exceptions are thuggish weeds that spread rapidly by root and shoot as well as seed. Pests like bindweed (*Convolvulus* species, also called wild morning glory), stinging nettles, brambles, and the running grasses can all cause serious problems in the garden and do not belong in the compost. Bag these and discard them into the trash, or add them to the burn pile. If these options are not available, put the worst weeds on a tarp on the driveway and bake them to a crisp in the sun. On sunless days, fry them with your flame weeder, *then* you can safely add them to your compost.

BUILDING A COMPOST PILE

A well-constructed compost pile can reach temperatures of more than 150 degrees F, hot enough to bake most weed seeds and destroy many fungal diseases and bacterial blights. To get your compost off to a quick start, begin your first pile in even brown-green layers. If you use bottomless bins set right on the ground, begin by scuffing up the soil surface with a hoe or rake. This allows a good interface between the soil and the compost, letting water, air, and beneficial soil microbes pass freely back and forth.

Make your first layer a brown one, using spent materials that are already dried out. Layer on 6 or 8 inches of shredded leaves, grass clippings, and garden leftovers. Top that layer with a similar amount of fresher green stuff. Now add a thinner layer of 1 to 2 inches of good garden soil to bring healthy soil microbes into the mix. You can also add a few twiggy sticks to help make air spaces, especially if all your material is finely shredded. Repeat the process, layering on garden goodies until you run out, ending with a carbon-based brown layer.

If your brown materials are very dry, sprinkle each new layer lightly with water. Ideally, the entire pile should be evenly moist but not sodden, since you also want plenty of air flow in your pile. Damp materials will rot faster and more evenly than dry ones. Cover the pile with a burlap sack, a sheet of heavy plastic, or a piece of tarp to keep the heap moist.

Like people and plants, compost requires air. Made without enough oxygen, the pile will become a breeding ground for pathogens. Compost piles that smell like dead animals, sour milk, rotten eggs, vomit, and other unattractive compounds are not getting enough air to their core. Well-made compost will decompose beneficially and will never smell nasty at any stage.

If after a few days you do not notice a marked rise in heat within your pile, use a long-handled composting tool to get more air to the center. These tools are long rods with folding metal "wings" that collapse against the rod when shoved into a pile of compost, then expand outward when the rod is pulled back out. A day or two after you aerate your pile, you should see signs that your compost has started to heat up. The pile will feel noticeably warm to the hand, and during the cooler months you may notice steam rising from it.

TURNING THE COMPOST PILE

As the pile heats, it begins to shrink. When it has reduced in volume by about a third, the compost usually cools off, having used up all the available oxygen. Unless more air is added, the breakdown process can take months, especially in cold weather. To speed things up, turn the heap, using a round-tined composting fork (square-tined forks work best for breaking up clay soils). Turning ventilates compost and reactivates the heat, just as pumping air into a fire with a bellows increases its temperature. Turning the pile over redistributes both the cooler outside material and the hotter middle.

If you are using a multiple bin system, fork the reduced pile into the next bin. If the compost seems dry, sprinkle on a little more water during the turning, and re-cover the pile when you're done. Once again it will heat up, and again it will reduce in volume. When it cools again, turn it a second time.

It may take anywhere from three to five turns to get finished compost, which may in turn take anywhere from six weeks to six or eight months. If you started with mostly shredded material, the process will go faster and the final result will be quite even textured. If you used a lot of unshredded material, the compost may take longer and the finished compost is likely to have a few lumps.

SIFTING THE COMPOST

To get rid of lumps, wrap coarse hogwire netting over your wheelbarrow and rub the compost through it with the back of a flat shovel. To make fine-textured compost for seed starting, you need a soil sieve or screen. Soil sieves are small pans lined with wire mesh, usually in ½- or ¼-inch screen. Set a sieve over a pot or bucket, scoop in some compost, and rub it through the holes.

Soil screens are larger, flat versions of the same thing. Generally square or rectangular, they are designed to use over a wheelbarrow or cold frame. They are usually of coarser gauge wire than the sieves, with 1-inch or ¾-inch mesh. Toss a few shovelfuls of compost on top, then rub it through the screen with the back of the shovel (again, flat blades work best). Now you have garden-ready compost, fit to dig into bed or border or use as a feeding mulch anywhere in the garden.

Having emptied your compost bin, you are ready to begin the cycle all over again. With a multibin system, you can start building a new pile as soon as any bin gets emptied out. To stockpile raw materials until you are ready to use them, make round hogwire cages to hold garden scraps. Hogwire comes in many sizes, but I find the

4-foot-wide rolls the most useful (this size also makes a great cage for deer-candy shrubs, and two hoops can be stacked to keep browsing deer away from young trees). Cover each hogwire cage with a tarp to keep the materials damp and neatly in place.

PASSIVE, STATIC, OR COOL COMPOSTING

At its simplest, composting is a very slow process that can take several years. Static or passive piles are simply heaps of garden leftovers, combining everything from branches and cornstalks to leaves and grass clippings. Static piles are not turned or mixed but are added to continually, layer by layer, as raw materials present themselves. After a year or so, you can remove the top layer to find that much of the inner heap has decomposed on its own. Remove the more finished compost, screen it (press it through a coarse screen) to give it a more uniform texture, and use the result as a mulch anywhere in the garden. Any coarse bits that didn't make it through the screen get tossed back on the pile to cycle through again.

In yards that have been gardened for a long time, most of the compostable pieces will be fairly small, a factor that accelerates the breakdown process. Where gardens abut woodlands or greenbelts, and in neglected gardens with many older, overgrown plantings, the base materials may be coarser and larger. This makes for slower processing, but can also be used to advantage. If you are working to tame a wild garden, consider creating two different piles, one for faster-rotting materials such as leaves, grass clippings, and fine-textured garden detritus. Larger, coarser materials can be heaped separately in an out-of-the-way corner, where it can become a valuable resource for all kinds of wildlife.

IMPROVING NORTHWESTERN SOILS

Soil altering is important to maritime gardeners, because although a wide range of common garden plants will grow well in moderately alkaline soil, fewer are comfortable in very acid soils. Although many plants are surprisingly adaptable, the majority of common garden plants grow most happily within the fairly narrow pH range between 6 and 7. As always, it makes sense from the start to select plants that naturally prefer the soil conditions you have to offer. If your soil displays very low or very high pH, you may want to contact a native plant society and read up on plants that enjoy your local soils.

That said, it may also make good emotional sense to create a few places where you can enjoy less-adaptable plants. Choose a small area of the garden where you will grow a wider range of plants, and focus your soil pH altering efforts there. This generally requires giving the soil a buffering blanket of compost twice a year to bring it closer to neutral, but certain other amendments such as lime or seed meals may be needed as well.

The most effective way to modify the acidity of native soils in order to grow vegetables and annuals is to add buffering or neutralizing soil amendments such as compost and dolomite or agricultural lime. (Never use industrial quicklime or slaked lime; they are for outhouses.) To boost acid soils about half a step upward on the pH scale, you'll need to add about 50 pounds of lime per 1,000 square feet of soil. It's hard to overlime acid clay soils, which resist change as if they were human. Where winters are wet, you may need to replace lime annually, since heavy rains scour nutrients and lime from the soils.

Alkaline soils (rare in the maritime Northwest) seldom require much modification. Native soils that have a pH of between about 6 and 8 won't need acid/base adjustment unless you plan to grow acid lovers like blueberries, rhododendrons, and azaleas, which can't tolerate alkaline conditions. You won't be able to grow lime lovers like rhodies with ease, but most plants, including vegetables, herbs, and many flowers, will be perfectly content. Adding plenty of compost helps too, and the extra humus will help plants access soil nutrients. If you want to grow acid lovers, you can buffer alkaline soils with pine needles and other acidic amendments. Over time, deep sheet mulching with compost will bring any soil closer to neutral. (Sheet mulching is discussed later in this chapter.)

SOIL AMENDMENTS

In most situations, the most helpful soil amendment will be generous quantities of humus-building organic materials. Manure compost is the best source of organic material because it is the most biologically diverse. Aged animal manures, kelp meal, shredded leaves, well-rotted sawdust, and many similar amendment materials can also be layered over or dug into poor soils to build better tilth and contribute specific nutrients. When using amendments such as sawdust and shredded bark, allow about a month to pass before planting into the newly amended beds. When using mature compost, you can plant immediately after amendment, mixing some of the compost into each planting hole. Use the information that follows to choose the best soil amendments for your situation. Then read the next section on building beds for ideas on how to apply the amendments. Soil supplements, such as bone meal, lime, and seed meals, are discussed in Chapter 6.

Many of our native trees, like madronas, need soil that contains special biota called mycorrhizae. If we disturb the soil grade around a madrona, or place a lawn or garden so the trees receive water in summer from an irrigation system, we can lose our majestic natives.

ALFALFA MEAL AND PELLETS

Alfalfa is an excellent soil conditioner, adding balanced nutrients along with hormones that assist healthy plant growth. Alfalfa lightens heavy soils and adds moisture-retaining tilth to light ones. Spread an inch of alfalfa meal under an inch of compost, or broadcast alfalfa pellets over beds and borders. In the vegetable garden, top-dress with either form a week after planting starts. If you use pelletized alfalfa, usually sold as animal feed, look for non-medicated brands to avoid adding hormones and steroids to your soil.

BIOWASTE

Human biowaste is often composted with green wastes into a highly nutritious material. However, biowaste can contain high levels of heavy metals (a common problem with human waste). Also, the fats in human waste can disguise the presence of fecal contamination, allowing unacceptably high levels of *E. coli* and other pathogens to be present even when the biowaste tests clean by current federal regulation standards. Organic growers do not allow the use of biowastes, and they are certainly not a good choice for the vegetable patch or fruit orchard. However, biowaste compost can be used to boost soil nutrient quality for strictly ornamental plantings.

BUCKWHEAT HULLS

Shredded buckwheat hulls can be added to heavy soils as a long-lasting conditioner. Spread a ½ inch of shredded buckwheat hulls under an inch of compost, which will keep them from blowing away.

COFFEE CHAFF AND GROUNDS

Both coffee chaff and grounds make excellent soil amendments. Layer a ½ inch of chaff under an inch of compost to keep it from blowing away. Coffee grounds can be layered under or over compost. Recent research indicates that coffee contains several substances that promote healthy root growth and combat root rots.

COMPOST

Compost is my favorite soil amendment. In my own gardens, I add it annually as a feeding mulch (see later in this chapter). Compost markedly and quickly improves soil tilth, texture, and nutritional value.

DAIRY MANURE

Washed and composted cow manure is an excellent tilth builder. Use a 1- to 2-inch layer as a weed-free top-dressing for compost and other amendments. Try to find a dairy that does not use steroids or bovine growth hormone, both of which may end up in your soil.

Be aware that steer manure is not the same as dairy manure. Steer manure is collected in stockyards, where salt licks encourage animals to drink a lot of water, thus increasing their weight. It therefore contains a high percentage of salt, which can burn young plants. It will also contain steroids and other medications that have no place in healthy garden soil. (The left ear of a steer contains an ampule of steroids that are released slowly over the animal's lifetime. At slaughter, the left ears are collected separately and taken to high-hazard waste disposal facilities.)

GRASS CLIPPINGS

Half an inch of fresh or dried lawn clippings can be layered under an inch of compost. Large quantities should be composted before being used as an amendment. Don't use clippings from chemically treated lawns.

HAY AND STRAW

Traditional farming methods included recycling rotted or spoiled hay into the midden (manure heap) as well as using it on growing fields. Today, we must be careful to get straw or hay from organic growers, lest we accidentally contaminate our growing beds with persistent herbicides such as clopyralid (see sidebar later in this chapter). To use as a soil conditioner, chop fluffed straw with a machete or run it through a lawn mower. Cover an inch of hay or straw with 2 inches of compost to keep it from blowing away.

LEAVES

Whenever possible, shredded leaves should be replaced under the tree that gave them up. If you collect discarded leaves from neighbors, shred them before layering them over new beds. Cover an inch of shredded leaves with an inch or two of compost. Be wary of leaves collected from lawns treated by chemical lawn services; even small amounts of lawn clippings inadvertently mixed in could introduce persistent herbicides such as clopyralid into your compost.

MANURE

Almost any well-composted animal manure makes a good soil amendment. Be cautious about using manure from animals fed with timothy hay or weed-free grain (notably horses and rabbits), since either may contain long-lasting herbicides that can harm vegetable and ornamental crops. Layer 1 to 2 inches of composted animal manures under an inch or two of mature compost.

MUSHROOM COMPOST

Mushroom compost tends to be free of pesticides and herbicides but may include significant salt residues. Seek out organic growers, and test a batch with vegetable seedlings before using a lot of it. Add 1 or 2 inches to each bed.

NEWSPAPER

In the past, newsprint contained heavy metals and other toxic chemicals, both from the paper-making process and the inks (particularly in color supplements). Check with your local paper to be sure they are using soy-based inks (most will be). Shredded newsprint breaks down quickly but blows away easily. Cover an inch or two of shredded newspaper with 2 inches of compost.

PEAT MOSS

Peat makes no nutritional contribution to the soil but is a fair soil conditioner, though very prone to dry out. Peat grows so slowly that it should not really be considered a renewable resource; improperly harvested peat may take several centuries to replace. In addition, peat bogs are vital, complex wetlands that host a rich variety of wildlife when undisturbed and are difficult to restore once depleted. Peat moss can also cause dangerous respiratory infections, so wear gloves and use a full face mask respirator whenever you handle it, as nursery workers must. For all these reasons, I don't recommend the use of peat moss.

PINE NEEDLES

When alkaline soil needs buffering, add an inch of pine needles to each bed, covered with 2 inches of compost.

SAWDUST

Like wood chips and bark, fresh sawdust quickly depletes soil nitrogen as it rots. Let fresh sawdust age for a year, or add it to a hot compost pile before using it as a soil amendment. If unevenly added, even aged sawdust can create dry, airless pockets where plant roots can't survive. Any sawdust left on the soil surface tends to crust over, shedding water rather than absorbing it. Add 1 inch of well-rotted sawdust covered by 2 inches of compost.

WOOD BY-PRODUCTS

Arborist's chips are a mix of shredded shrub and tree limbs, bark, and leaves. This blend is better balanced in carbon-to-nitrogen ratio than most wood by-products, but is usually quite coarse and not suitable for sheet layering. When tilled in or piled under berms, large quantities can cause eventual ground slumping in areas where lots of chips were mounded together, since the materials will continue to shrink as they compost in the soil.

Bark is only useful as a soil amendment when very finely shredded. It is best used in combination with compost and other ingredients, such as shredded leaves and grass clippings.

BUILDING BEDS

As I stress throughout this book, nothing reduces plant problems like great soil. Organic farmers feed the soil rather than plants; they know that healthy soil makes for happy plants. Our goal in amending the soil is a good balance of drainage and retention. We want soil that lets air and water pass through freely yet retains enough nutrients to support active growth.

There are two main ways to make garden beds that achieve this goal. The most traditional is by digging or tilling in lots of amendments. The second is to create mounded beds in layers with no mixing or tilling. Read the sections on how each system works, and decide which way will work best for your situation.

BALANCING HUMUS AND NITROGEN

In order to do its work well, humus needs to be applied in quantity—between one fourth and one half the total volume of soil in each bed or border to be amended. The amount of humus you need for optimal improvement depends on the soil you start off with. Dry, sandy soil or dusty, compacted, and impoverished soil can use half again as much humus by volume. These are ballpark

LOOKING FOR LEAD

Although lead has long been banned from paint and auto fuel, it may still be present in soil. If you garden in a city or older suburb, along a busy roadway, or beside any kind of older building, your soil may be contaminated with lead. In the most common scenario, garden soils are contaminated by paint peeling from the walls of an older house, which could have occurred many years in the past. Lead may also linger in soil where painted buildings and fences formerly stood. This is obviously hard to know for sure, since wooden structures often vanish completely. Thus, it's important to check garden soil for the presence of lead if there is even a slight possibility that a source may have been present at one time. This means any and all city gardens and any suburban or rural gardens where old buildings and fences might once have stood.

Although all gasoline is now lead-free, soil tests from urban, suburban, and even rural roadside properties often reveal measurable lead content left years ago by car exhaust. Since lead does not leach out of soils, lead tests should be made of sites near current and former roads.

measurements; making good soil isn't like making a soufflé, where miscalculating an ingredient can spell disaster. In most soils, adding practically any organic tilth amendment (humus builder) in almost any quantity will make a positive difference.

Where wood by-products like aged sawdust and shredded bark abound, they often constitute a large proportion of the commercial compost mixes. They can be great tilth makers, but it's important to remember that wood-based humus builders use a lot of nitrogen in the breakdown process. Unless you supply more nitrogen, the end result may be a fluffy, humus-rich soil that is nitrogen poor. Good sources of supplemental nitrogen are the seed meals—cottonseed meal, soy meal, and so forth. (See Chapter 6 for more on seed meals.) Ammonium sulfate also works fine and is easy to find in most nurseries.

You can mix nitrogen directly into the soil amendment, but it isn't easy to blend them well. I find it simpler to apply the supplementary nitrogen when you add humus builders to garden soil. To do this, mark the beds off in 10- by 10-foot grids or the equivalent (100 square feet). Spread out your humus-building amendment on top (the compost, manure, or whatever), and then measure its depth. In most cases, you should have between 4 and 6 inches, but with really poor soil, you could end up using close to a foot of amendment. Next, cover each marked (100-square-foot) area with a pound of nitrogen for every inch of humus builder.

Oh, that math! A lot of us shut the book and take a walk at this point, wondering what this has to do with gardening. Really, it's not that bad: Let's say you used 6 inches of sawdust. You need 6 pounds of nitrogen for each 100-square-foot bed. Okay? And remember, if you are using compost or aged manure, you don't need any extra nitrogen unless your soil test showed a deficit.

DIGGING IN AMENDMENTS

The traditional method is to mix and mingle the whole business into a glorious melange. Dig or till to a depth of at least 1 foot, and keep mixing until the amendments are well incorporated. If you are doing your mixing by hand, a short, square-tined garden fork may be just as efficient and far easier to handle than a shovel, which can get very heavy very fast.

Beds made in this way need this radical renovation done only once. They will then remain vital and healthy for many years if they are maintained with feeding mulches of compost and aged dairy manure. Each season, spread several (3 to 4) inches of compost over your beds, then top-dress with aged dairy manure. Again, spreading 2 to 4 inches of aged dairy manure each spring will feed your soil and also suppress most weeds. If you don't want to till, read on.

LAYERING MOUNDED BEDS

Another way to rectify most common soil problems is by making mounded beds. Mounded beds are built in layers that do not need mixing or tilling. They also do not need wooden sides, as is common with raised beds. The layers are simply put in place, one over the other. As you prepare each planting hole, gently stir up the layers a bit. For initial plantings, you may want to add some compost to each hole. In subsequent years, the layers will be far less noticeable. Even though you keep adding more layers of compost and aged manure each year, the worms mix the layers up so well that there will no longer be any discernible break between your mounds and the native soil. Usually the native soils will show improvement quickly, and within a few seasons even the dense undersoil will become rich with humus and life, from worms to beneficial biota.

I first read about layered beds in the books of Graham Stuart Thomas, a famous English gardener. In several of his writings, he explains that he long ago stopped digging and tilling in amendments. Instead, he simply tosses the amendments (such as compost) in layers over the beds each season. I decided that if Graham Thomas no longer tilled or double dug, that was good enough for me. I started layering my beds immediately, and the results were so good, I never looked back.

My early experiments were bolstered by lessons gleaned from George Shenk, a well-known Northwestern gardener whose works include the classic book on shade gardening and the world's best moss book. Shenk built mounded beds in his woodland garden that combined deep layers of sandy loam and composted leaves. With an annual feeding mulch of leaf-based compost, his well-made beds lasted for over twenty years.

To be safe, have the soil checked in areas where you plan to make a children's play yard and in pet areas as well, because children and small animals are more vulnerable to lead poisoning than adults. Should testing reveal the presence of lead, consider having the contaminated soil mechanically removed (a small tractor can clear the ground far faster than a person with a shovel). Since lead won't migrate through the soil, you can also cover the ground with weed barrier cloth and then bring in fresh soil to make mounded beds.

Mounded beds can be of any shape, with gently sloping sides that do not require hard edges. To eliminate edging and grass trimming, create wide, gently curving beds edged with gravel paths. Since gravity keeps the gravel of the paths in place, there is no need for edging of any kind. When we build shapely, curving mounds with plenty of natural-looking topography, this earth sculpting creates great places to tuck in rocks and character plants and offers strollers new views from every direction.

Raised or mounded beds do not need sides to keep them in place. Build them with a base of sandy loam if your original soil is clay or hardpan. Add a layer of compost or good topsoil (if you can get it). Top it all off with washed dairy manure or compost and you'll have a handsome, easily planted, weed-free environment for your plants.

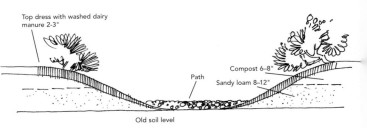

THE FIRST LAYER: SANDY LOAM

Here in the maritime Northwest, our undersoil is often slow-draining clay or impervious hardpan. Some garden books suggest using a metal rod to make drainage holes in the hardpan. That's an interesting idea, but it is not always practical; in my backyard, the hardpan layer extends over 13 feet deep. When making mounded beds over slow-draining undersoil, it's a very good idea to start off with a deep base layer of fast-draining sandy loam. This layer can be anywhere from 6 to 12 inches deep or even more, depending on the site.

Often used in construction, sandy loam holds its shape yet drains well. Because it has a lot of integrity, sandy loam holds any shape you give it. It is easy to sculpt and can be raked into almost any form you prefer. Sandy loam is relatively inexpensive, so it makes a logical base material for large beds and berms. It is not the same as sandbox sand or river sand, but is a type of loamy soil that naturally includes coarse sand. It may be more readily available from construction companies than from topsoil and gravel suppliers. If you can't find sandy loam, plasterer's sand makes a good substitute. However, avoid fine-textured sandbox sand, since it will combine with the underlying clay and create adobe. Unless you plan to re-create the Alamo, adobe is not what you want in your garden beds.

THE SECOND LAYER: ORGANIC TOPSOIL

Over the sandy loam, add a layer of good organic topsoil. If your undersoil is already sandy, skip the sandy loam and begin with the topsoil layer. Many municipalities are now making good organic topsoils and composts by recycling urban yard wastes (not human biowastes). Check with your county agricultural extension service or local Master Gardeners to learn about community compost resources in your area. If you can't find good organic topsoil, just use a thick layer of compost.

Our soils in the maritime Northwest need a lot more compost than most garden books suggest (perhaps because most of these books are based on East Coast garden needs). Around here, a mere inch of compost is practically worthless. Build up your beds with sandy loam, and then add a generous compost layer at least 8 inches deep (though 1 foot or even 18 inches is not too much) and you won't need any topsoil. Not only that, your plants will thank you for years to come.

This depth will look extreme at first, but if you do your shaping well, you can avoid the suspicion that you have planted your dog or father-in-law out there. As the beds settle, they will relax into attractively natural-looking shapes. In general, settling will reduce the bed height by about 20 percent within a few weeks. Some additional settling will occur over time, so make your beds deeper than you think you want them.

TOP-DRESSING WITH DAIRY MANURE

You can finish off the mounds with a layer of compost, but for optimal weed suppression, I prefer to top-dress with organic dairy manure. Unlike steer manure (which is collected in stockyards with salt licks), dairy manure is not salty. Organic dairy manure won't contain steroids or BGH either. Dairy manure is weed-free and sometimes even includes tiny weed seed–eating mites that will help keep things that way for quite a while. Now you are ready to plant.

WHICH WAY IS BEST?

Many organic growers swear by amending beds annually, and they regularly till compost and manure into their soils with fine results. However, when we remember that soil is alive, with most of that life concentrated in the top few inches, burying our biota seems like a less-good plan. An annual layer of compost mulch keeps these beds in good condition for years.

Many ornamental gardeners are moving toward layering techniques because they don't involve frequent plant disturbance. Over time, layering is less labor-intensive than tilling. Indeed, the same amount of spreading must be done for both techniques, but with layering, there is no need to dig or till materials into the soil. Most compost and amendment mulching is done during the off-season (fall to early spring), when other chores are less pressing.

Since most maritime Northwestern soils are lean in humus and low in available nutrients, I believe that mounding makes the best use of imported materials. It is less wasteful to mound good soil and compost than to dilute them by mixing them in with poor native soils. Thus, we make mounded beds and plant entirely into them, not digging down into native soils at all. This means you need to plan on building up a sufficient depth of new soil to plant trees and shrubs as well as young perennials. However, keep in mind that young plants set into good soil will grow better and faster than large plants in poor soil. Thus, you can plant younger, smaller, and less-expensive woody plants into your new beds and see satisfying results in a season or two.

Some growers use a combination of both techniques, tilling in large quantities of organic matter along with mineral supplements such as rock dust, dolomite lime, and cottonseed meal for an initial treatment. In subsequent years, lesser quantities of these materials are added as needed, depending on which crops are being grown.

What is the bottom line here? For the home gardener who is mainly interested in growing some ornamentals and perhaps a few fruits and vegetables, making mounded beds and layering on amendments will prove to be far less work and provide lastingly satisfying results.

RAISED BEDS

Another traditional way to make beds is to create boxes and fill them with soil and/or compost. Where space is very limited, this system can be quite functional. Drawbacks include the fact that wooden sides rot over time and that beds that are too small will dry out quickly come summer. It can be difficult to turn cover crops over in raised beds of this nature, and weeds can lodge in the cracks, resisting the most persistent efforts to dislodge them. Also, slugs and other garden pests love to hide out between the boards, emerging at night to ravage the garden. In design terms, this kind of bed is nearly always of rectilinear design, which may suit urban gardens well but looks very out of place in a more natural setting and with an overall naturalistic design.

If you do elect to make raised beds of this sort, be sure that any wood you use has not been treated with toxic chemicals. Even some of the new, recycled-plastic "woods" can leach chemicals into soils that will end up in your homegrown food and can be carried as contaminants into public or natural water systems.

Fill your raised beds with a base of sandy loam topped by compost or composted dairy manure. Spread the initial layer of sandy loam to a depth of 8 to 12 inches. Unless the garden site is extremely weedy, you need not remove underlying grass. Next, add a thick (6- to 8-inch) layer of compost or aged manure, mounding it smoothly. There is no need to till or mix the beds. Simply prepare each planting hole individually, mixing the loam and compost or manure before placing the new plant.

Top-dress and mulch with dairy manure or compost. A thick blanket of manure conserves moisture, helps keep beds weed-free, and looks tidy. Over time, the worms will incorporate the loam and manure, so add an annual 2- to 3-inch top-dressing of manure or compost mulch.

WHY MULCH?

Mulch is one of the key elements of sustainable gardening and natural care. In general, mulch as a substance can be defined as a protective layer of material (which may or may not be biodegradable) that is spread over the ground. Mulch is intended to serve one or more of the following purposes:

• Reduce soil moisture loss through evaporation.

• Help reduce and suppress weeds.

• Modify or stabilize soil temperature.

• Improve soil tilth.

• Improve soil nutritional quality.

Almost any mulching material, from sawdust to plastic sheeting, can perform the first three functions. Obviously, only biodegradable mulch materials can contribute to the final functions, since nondegradable substances can't improve the nutritional quality of the soil.

MULCHING MATERIALS

There are so many mulch materials that it can be hard to know which to use when and where. Use the list that follows to decide which materials might work best in your garden. Spreadability, availability, and appearance may influence your decisions. You may decide to experiment with several kinds of mulch, seeing which works or looks best in different settings. The vegetable plot is a good place to make a mulch sampler, using as many different kinds as possible. Divide the garden plot into as many sections as you have mulch materials, and give each its own blanket. The patchwork look won't be as distracting in the vegetable bed as it would be in your front yard, and you can easily evaluate the performance of each candidate when the various materials are used side by side.

BIOWASTE

See the earlier "Soil Amendments" section. Biowaste can be used in ornamental plantings, where it makes a very rich feeding mulch.

BUCKWHEAT HULLS

Buckwheat hulls are attractive, lightweight, and very easy to spread. They do tend to sprout, but buckwheat sprouts are a fine addition to the compost pile. Buckwheat hulls are too unstable to be a good choice for mulching slopes or large mounded beds.

COFFEE BEANS, CHAFF, AND GROUNDS

Unless you live in an area where coffee is extremely popular (such as Seattle), you probably won't be able to locate a source of coffee beans or grounds that can supply enough to mulch large areas. However, both make a beautiful mulch, with a handsome color and texture that showcase ornamental plants to perfection. Coffee beans can be used as a deep mulch for beds or pathways. Even when piled thickly (6 to 8 inches deep), the whole beans will not mat or crust over. I once used several hundred pounds of over-roasted coffee beans as a mulch for a short path. It looked stylish, smelled like heaven, and felt terrific underfoot. Even more important, I noticed that a number of generally fussy, difficult plants rooted enthusiastically into the path in preference to the well-prepared bed I had made for them. Some years later, soil scientist Dr. Elaine Ingham explained to me that coffee contains several substances that promote healthy root growth and combat certain pathogens.

Organic farmers have used this information to advantage, mulching beds of tomatoes with an inch of used organic coffee grounds to reduce or prevent late blight. (Layers that are more than an inch or so deep can form an impenetrable crust that keeps water and air from plant roots.) In ornamental beds and borders, a 1-inch layer of coffee grounds can be used to protect plants that are susceptible to root rots and to encourage rapid root growth in slow starters. When you mulch with coffee grounds, you will soon notice a thready, white, moldlike substance that runs through the grounds. This is actually beneficial and can reduce the damage caused by honey fungus, pythium, and other root growth enemies. Coffee grounds can also help keep carrot crops clean of carrot rust maggots, probably because the strong smell of the coffee overrides the attractive smell of the carrots.

Coffee chaff is a lightweight, sand-colored substance that is best added to compost rather than used alone. As a mulch, the fluffy chaff tends to blow around until it is watered. Once wet, it quickly packs down, forming dense mats that prevent air and water from reaching the soil.

COMPOST

Compost is my favorite mulching material and an important ingredient in most feeding mulches, discussed later in this chapter. Use coarse, less-refined compost around shrubs and trees and anywhere that plantings won't be seen from close at hand. Compost improves soil tilth, texture, and nutritional value.

DAIRY MANURE

Cow manure is a delightful substance that is endlessly useful in the garden. If you are lucky enough to live near an organic dairy, consider mulching all your beds with a generous (3- to 4-inch) layer of cow manure each fall. Pit-washed dairy manure is the best for this use, since it has been washed to a fluffy, light consistency that looks like peat moss but has none of peat's drawbacks. Because cows have many-chambered stomachs, dairy manure is weed-free (unlike horse manure, which is often full of weeds). Recent research indicates that cow manure helps suppress several kinds of pathogens and has a beneficial effect on plant root growth. Dairy manure can be used as a deep mulch or as top-dressing or mixed half and half with compost for a feeding mulch. See "Mulching with Manure," later in this chapter, for more on using dairy manure as a mulch.

Avoid steer manure. See the earlier "Soil Amendments" section for more information.

GRASS CLIPPINGS

If you practice natural lawn care and use a mulching mower, grass clippings are not a great compost resource. If you know that your neighbors also practice natural lawn care, don't be shy about gleaning their excess (if any). Do hesitate to use grass clippings that have been treated with herbicides and pesticides, since the residues don't always break down quickly and may contaminate your garden. This is especially true of lawns treated by chemically oriented lawn services, which may still be using clopyralid-based herbicides (see clopyralid sidebar).

If you can find a source of meadow cuttings, they are usually free of chemicals. A thin (1-inch) layer of grass or meadow clippings can be added to beds and borders, but deeper layers can actually harm your plants. Grass clippings heat up quickly as they decompose, and thick layers can burn foliage and roots. They also stink to high heaven because they clump so tightly that air can't penetrate the rotting mass. If you have a lot of grass clippings, compost them with an equal volume of shredded dry leaves, chopped bracken ferns, or other dry material, and then use the resulting compost as mulch.

HAY AND STRAW

In theory, hay consists of stems with grain or seedheads included, while straw is supposed to be the trimmed stalks only. In practice, most straw includes enough seed to create minicrops in your garden beds. It can be disconcerting to find a thrifty crop of wheat grass or young alfalfa growing where you spread a thick blanket of straw. However, both are easily pulled, and both make excellent additions to the compost heap. If you get a really good crop, you might consider opening a wheat-juice bar.

Be aware that wheat straw and any grain straw grown as "weed-free" for horse consumption may carry a hidden burden of persistent herbicides (notably clopyralid), which can contaminate your compost heap indefinitely.

When I was a child, salt-marsh hay was highly prized by gardeners, who used it to winterize shrubs and to protect vegetable plots from winter rains. These days, protective laws forbid mowing salt marshes, which are an important habitat for birds and small animals.

Alfalfa straw works just as well, and each bale covers a lot of ground. A tightly packed bale of alfalfa straw breaks down into compressed flakes that need to be fluffed open with your hands. Each flake will cover as much as a 5- by 5-foot area with a loose, airy mulch. Use coarse alfalfa straw for making paths, at the back of large borders, to protect young plants from frost damage, or to keep new beds clean over the winter. Where you want a finer-textured mulch, chop fluffed alfalfa straw with a machete or run it over with a lawn mower.

LEAVES

If your home is surrounded by trees, you are in luck, because leaves contribute a wide range of nutrients to the compost pile. Fine-textured leaves like birch or willow can be used freely as a mulch when dry, but be wary about using larger leaves like chestnut and bigleaf maples, which can smother small plants. As a rule, large, leathery leaves should be shredded when dry. Light, attractive, and nutritious, shredded leaves of all kinds are a perfect mulch for woodland gardens or ornamental beds. Leaf mulches are especially important in woodland gardens, which rely on the nutrients stored in foliage to keep the soil fungally dominated. Woody fruit crops such as blueberries, grapes, and huckleberries also benefit from leaf mulches. In mixed borders, use leaf-based mulches around roses and other woody plants, spreading it 3 to 4 inches deep. Shredded leaves can also be mixed half and half with compost and used on ornamental beds of all kinds.

MANURE

Most animal manures can be a valuable addition to the compost heap, but very few make a decent mulching material (dairy manure is the exception). All agricultural extension agents recommend that any and all animal manures be hot-composted before use, and this is indeed an excellent idea. To hot-compost any manure, mix it half and half with a hot, nitrogen-rich material such as shredded green garden gleanings, grass, or meadow clippings. Give all manure-based composts three full turns before using. (For more on hot composting methods, see "Home Composting" earlier in this chapter.)

MUSHROOM COMPOST

Mushroom farmers can't use toxic fungicides (think about it), so the bedding they use tends to be clean and attractive. Some growers use bran mixed with dairy manure as a growing medium for mushrooms, while others use composted straw and various kinds of manures. Mushroom compost can hold significant salt residues (probably from steer manure), which can burn tender seedlings. Explore various sources to find a reliable organic grower before buying mushroom compost in bulk, and use it with caution until you know how salty each batch may be.

NEWSPAPER

Make sure any newspaper you use is printed with soy-based inks, to avoid contamination by heavy metals and other chemicals. If so, use newspapers freely (we might as well, since they tend to pile up quickly in most households). Spread flat sheets of newsprint under new paths to prevent weeds and under new beds to smother grass. Stack at least 8 to 10 sheets per layer (a whole section is not too much), then top with fresh soil or mulch.

Shredded newspaper can be added to the compost heap, where it will rot down very nicely. Use it in high summer, when the garden is full of fresh green stuff but dry, carbon-rich materials are not as plentiful.

PEAT MOSS

Once ubiquitous, peat moss is becoming more expensive and less popular. This is good, since it ranks among the very worst materials for mulch or top-dressing. Dry peat sheds water and is very difficult to rewet once dry. See the earlier "Soil Amendments" section for more on peat moss.

PINE NEEDLES

Spiky brown pine needles look great under pine trees. Elsewhere they look silly, and the coarse needles can smother small plants. Spread thickly, pine needles tend to form water-shedding mats that keep the soil bone-dry. Mulches containing pine needles can help buffer excessively alkaline soils. Compost pine needles with garden gleanings, meadow cuttings, and animal manures rather than using them straight.

WEED BARRIER CLOTH

Woven or punctured artificial mulch cloth has become ubiquitous in recent years. Theoretically, these materials let air and water reach plants but keep weed roots at bay. In practice, many succeed in keeping air and water from plants yet letting weeds proliferate. The best results come when we match cloth weight and rating to our particular need. The best grades are called "professional" and are said to block even persistent pests like johnsongrass. A few weed cloths are biodegradable and will decompose over time, especially if exposed to sunlight, though they don't build healthy soil when they do.

Never use these materials in beds that you plan to till (getting them snagged in a machine is a real nightmare). They are often used as a surface mulch, generally topped with several inches of bark. This is both wasteful and inefficient, since weeds will soon appear in the "attractive" bark mulch that covers the ugly mulch. Extremely unattractive, cloth mulches are best used to line permanent pathways.

WOOD BY-PRODUCTS

Here in the Northwest, wood by-products, such as bark, sawdust, and wood shavings, are among the most common mulching materials. Most are inexpensive, readily available, and easy to use. However, they all have significant drawbacks that need to be considered. To a greater or lesser degree, all wood by-products use up stored soil nitrogen as they break down. Fresh sawdust uses the most nitrogen, while coarsely ground bark chips use the least and are the longest lasting as a path mulch. Most wood by-products (particularly bark) shed water rather than absorb it, a trait that is rarely an asset. Wood products can also increase the likelihood of many common root rots and fungal problems, such as honey fungus, particularly in clay soils. Here are some more specific pointers about the main types of wood by-products.

Arborist's chips. See the earlier "Soil Amendments" section. This composite tends to break down much as compost does and can be used around large trees and shrubs without harm.

Bark. Shredded bark comes in several grades of coarseness. Like any wood by-product, bark robs some soil nitrogen as it breaks down, thus competing with your plants for nutrients. Even more importantly, whether shredded or chipped, bark tends to repel water rather than absorb it, which can further stress your plants. Shredded bark can be a useful material for pathways, looking especially at home in wooded settings. A 6- to 8-inch-deep layer of coarsely shredded bark will last for several years without replenishment, and weeds are rarely a problem in bark paths.

Although I personally never use bark as a mulch on planting beds of any kind, many folks do. Bark fans like to say that since forest duff is nutritious and woodland plants grow well in it, it's absurd to suggest that the breakdown of wood products could harm garden plants. However, woodland duff is made up of many components, including leaves, twigs, fungus, lichen, and the droppings of birds and animals. Plain bark chips or sawdust are not even close to the same thing.

That said, very finely shredded bark can be mixed with compost and used as a very effective mulch that will improve soil texture and quality over time. Coarser bark is best used for paths, not around plants. Coarse bark chips and other wood by-products can also be usefully employed as a smother mulch. As I describe more fully in Chapter 6, smother mulches are used to reduce or control bad infestations of noxious weeds. In such cases, depletion of soil nitrogen helps to starve out unwanted plants.

If you must spread bark by hand, use rubber glove liners inside your regular gloves to reduce if not eliminate those nasty splinters.

Sawdust. Once common, sawdust is becoming harder to find and increasingly expensive. It shares some of the drawbacks of wood chips and bark. Fresh sawdust quickly depletes soil nitrogen as it rots and can cause plants mulched with it to turn yellow, showing signs of stress and nitrogen depletion. When you see this, rake away the sawdust and replace it with 2 to 3 inches of compost, aged manure, and alfalfa pellets, and the plants will green right up.

Sawdust also clumps and crusts as it dries, creating dry, airless conditions that do not favor plant root growth. Thick layers crust readily, so water slides away, leaving the soil below it bone-dry. Because sawdust degrades slowly, it makes a fine path material, though it will be more permeable if mixed with coarse bark. Sawdust is a poor mulch choice for beds and borders.

If you have a good supply of sawdust available, run it through the compost pile instead of using it straight. Sawdust, leaves, and grass clippings will make a hot compost that matures quite quickly and can then be used for mulching beds. Well-rotted sawdust that has been composted for at least a full year can be used to mulch blueberries, huckleberries, and raspberries.

Small, fine-textured leaves can be left where they fall to make natural compost in place. Large, coarse-textured leaves like bigleaf maple need to be shredded before you can use them as in-place mulch. Be sure to return at least some of each tree's foliage as mulch to keep their stored nutrients available to the parent tree.

HOW DO WE MULCH?

"Mulch" as a verb means the act of spreading various sub-stances on the ground. How and when we do this is the subject of a great deal of debate. Most of us figure out through experimentation an effective mulching schedule for our climate, crops, soil needs, and so forth. As a rule of thumb, mulches are most usefully applied in late winter or early spring and again in autumn. If you aren't sure how much to use, begin by spreading a fairly thin layer, between 2 and 3 inches deep. (We need to use a lot more humus here in the Northwest than garden books written for Eastern climates suggest.) As you observe the specific results of mulching on your site and for your situation, your garden plants will guide you in refining the timing, amount, and materials you use.

In my own gardens, I spread compost mulches deeply, adding between 4 to 6 inches each year. I came to this fig-ure by observing the amount of natural litter that falls each season in the intact forest around my house. My native soil is lean and low in humus, yet it supports a tremendous array of native plant material in great abun-dance. I decided to try to re-create the natural bio-shed (leaf and litter drop) of the trees and shrubs in the garden and found that a similar quantity of compost helped my garden soil support a similar abundance of plants with lit-tle further intervention.

ANNUAL MULCHES

Annual mulches are generally put on either in early spring or in fall. They are used mainly to suppress weeds and to maintain a healthy soil food web. Established trees and shrubs that don't require a lot of fuss or feeding will respond well to an annual mulch of compost and shredded leaves. In most cases, adding 2 to 4 inches of this mixture each year will keep a well-rooted plant content. When mulching trees and shrubs, begin at the trunk of the plant, using a lesser amount of mulch (1 to 2 inches) to avoid smothering the crown. Work out to the dripline of the plant, mulching more deeply as you go. This helps keep the root zone moist, well fed, and free of weeds.

TOP-DRESSING

English garden books often talk about top-dressing. What is it? After garden plants get tucked in for their winter rest with blankets of humus builders such as compost and aged manure, top mulches are added in thinner blankets, only an inch or two thick. Made of composted manure, very finely shredded bark or chopped leaves, aged sawdust, or (occasionally) gritty gravel, these protective mulches may also improve the tilth and texture of the soil, but that is not their primary purpose.

Top-dressings are used to prevent or reduce soil erosion and excess water runoff in the long, wet winters. They can also be used to keep soil amendments like manure from being washed away by sprinkler systems. In addition, they suppress weeds (which never stop growing in the mild Northwest), insulate tender plants from winter chills, and keep spring flowers from getting mudsplashed. Top-dressing may also consist of a light (1- to 2-inch) layer of an airy mulch such as shredded leaves that prevents deeper mulches of manure or compost from crusting into an impermeable surface under winter rain and snow.

Top-dressings may also serve to conserve soil moisture. During a typical extremely wet winter, it's hard to imagine that this would be a genuine concern, but it may be in a warm, dry autumn. After our usual dry summers, our plants are often stressed by drought. If they go into winter too dry, they are more susceptible to winter damage than plants with adequate water reserves would be. When autumn rains are slow in arriving, we must water the beds and borders deeply before top-dressing.

FEEDING MULCHES

When spring arrives, we can begin to compose still another kind of mulch. As our plants begin to stir and stretch, they need a good breakfast to help them gather energy for their annual performance. Spring feeding mulches provide a steady supply of nutrients for garden plants, combining a quick fix of nitrogen with slower-acting soil builders.

What makes a good feeding mulch? My favorite is compost, which contains both soil-amending humus and a combination of readily available and slow-releasing nutrients. The local soils in much of the Northwest tend to be high in potassium but low in phosphorus. Both bone meal and rock phosphate will increase phosphorus levels—the former immediately, the latter over time—so they are generally used in combination. For soils that are low in nitrogen, we can add seed meals like cotton and soy. I often use a combination of aged manure and alfalfa pellets, both of which are fine tilth boosters as well.

SPRING FEEDING MULCH

This basic feeding mulch of alfalfa, manure, and compost is effective in almost any garden situation. You can scatter it generously through established borders, in shrub beds, over lawns, and around mature trees—all will benefit from the soil conditioners as well as from the boost of nitrogen and other nutrients.

The combination of alfalfa and manure is synergistic, meaning that a greater portion of their nitrogen becomes available to plant roots when they are used in tandem. Heavy feeders like roses and clematis love the immediate gratification this mixture offers them. Rhododendrons and azaleas show their pleasure almost at once, perking up visibly after the winter doldrums. Vegetable starts and soft fruits like strawberries are also visibly appreciative of this simple spring feed.

The following recipe is measured by volume, using a tub or bucket to equal one "part." Mix it up in a wheelbarrow, and then store any leftovers in a tightly closed, waterproof container:

> *2 parts large, unmedicated alfalfa pellets*
> *1 part aged manure (bagged manure is fine)*
> *1 part compost (homemade or commercial)*

Small boxes of alfalfa are comparatively expensive, but some nurseries and most hay and feed stores carry bulk alfalfa or sell the pellets in 50-pound bags for around $10. Choose the large pellets used for feeding calves and goats, but skip the steroids—get the nonmedicated kind. One 50-pound bag is enough (when used in the mulch described above) to feed about 400 square feet of border (spreading the feed an inch deep).

To spread the feeding mulch, scatter it as if you were throwing a Frisbee or feeding chickens. The idea is to distribute a fairly even layer over the entire planting area. Unlike commercial fertilizers, which can be so powerful that they actually burn young plants if used too generously, feeding mulches are mild enough to use in quantity. Don't get too carried away, though; no matter how hungry it is, no plant likes being smothered with lunch. Be sure the crowns of young or small plants can breathe freely.

On new beds or empty vegetable plots, broadcast this feeding mulch generously, covering the surface with 1 to 2 inches of the mixture. In established beds, give each plant a handful or two, depending on size. Roses will appreciate 2 to 4 cups each, as will peonies and clematis. It is perfectly safe to spread a few cups of this feed from the crowns to the dripline of roses and clematis. On clematis, assume a root zone of 2 to 3 feet, depending on the size and age of the vine. For peonies, remember that plants whose eyes are buried too deeply won't bloom—deep planting is the most common cause of failure to flower in peonies. Feather the mulch to the crown, and then add it more thickly (2 to 4 inches) near the dripline.

Under trees and shrubs (particularly rhododendrons), spread 2 to 3 inches of the mixture for 2 feet on both sides of the dripline (the band of mulch will be 4 feet wide). You can also toss this mulch evenly over a winter-weary lawn and rake it in for a refreshing spring pick-me-up.

ALL-PURPOSE PLANT BOOSTER

Humus-based feeding mulches can be added freely in any kind of garden situation, with little worry about overdoing things. Boosters are more concentrated nutrient resources that are lightly scratched into the root zone of each plant.

Careful placement avoids wasting high-nutrient fertilizers, which often end up polluting our waterways rather than feeding our plants. Used carelessly or to excess, chemical fertilizers are a significant source of nonindustrial pollution. Surprisingly, nearly as much water and soil pollution is caused by careless home gardeners as by commercial farmers.

One of my favorite booster recipes originated at the Territorial Seed Company, a mail-order company specializing in regionally appropriate vegetables for gardeners west of the Cascades. The company's founder, Steve Solomon, is an inspired and experimental gardener who is always pushing the gardening envelope. His all-purpose plant booster is quite concentrated and contains both immediate and long-term nutrients. It can be used in ornamental borders or vegetable gardens and is particularly good for new gardens made where old soil is exhausted or raw soil is unimproved.

Like the spring feeding mulch, this plant booster is measured by volume. Use a lightweight scoop or bucket, blending the ingredients in your wheelbarrow. To keep the mixture fresh, store it in a watertight container. (I use small, heavy-gauge plastic garbage cans.) For details about the ingredients used in this booster, see "Soil Supplements" in Chapter 6.

> *4 parts cottonseed meal or soy meal*
> *1 part dolomite or agricultural lime*
> *1 part rock phosphate*
> *½ part kelp meal*

This is not a broadcast mulch; just scatter a small amount around each new plant and gently scratch it into the top inch or two of soil. A small plant, perhaps a transplant from a 4-inch pot, would receive about a tablespoon of plant booster. A gallon-sized plant would need a scant ¼ cup, while a 5-gallon shrub would get ½ cup. A large, mature shrub or tree with an extensive dripline might need a cup or more. In any case, cover the scratched-up soil with a light top mulch of compost or chopped straw to keep weeds down and maintain soil moisture.

NEUTRAL SPRING BORDER BOOSTER

Although the maritime Northwest tends to offer gardeners acid soils, pockets of alkaline soils also exist here.
Thousands of plants will adapt happily to either condition, especially when adequate humus is present (compost! compost!), but many universally popular vegetables
and ornamentals grow best when such soils are buffered
by neutral composts and mulches. The following border
booster is designed to make both natives and exotics
happy. Use it on vegetable plots, mixed borders, and
established shrubberies containing native plants. See the
"Soil Supplements" section in Chapter 6 to find out more
about the ingredients.

> *5 parts compost*
> *4 parts seed meal or soy meal*
> *⅔ part fish bone meal or whole fish meal*
> *½ part kelp meal*

Spread this booster thinly around each plant, extending
it in a circle to the dripline of shrubs. Allow a small handful (about ¼ cup) per plant, adding more (½ to 1 cup) for
larger shrubs. Lightly scratch the booster into the top inch
or two of soil, and cover it with a thin top mulch of compost or shredded leaves.

SHEET MULCHES

Sheet mulching is pretty much what it sounds like: covering an area to be gardened with a sheet of mulch. This
classic technique has many variations, but the main idea is
to cover the ground with enough organic matter to suppress
any underlying turf or weeds. To make a bed with sheet
mulching, mark out the area you want to convert from
lawn or weeds, then cover it to a depth of at least 8 to 12
inches with organic material.

Many gardeners begin by covering the grass or weeds
with a barrier layer to discourage the underlying plants.
This layer might consist of damp cardboard, several thick-
nesses of newspaper, hemp sacking, or burlap. Next
comes a layer of anything that will rot: shredded leaves,
grass clippings, bark dust, sawdust, garden gleanings,
weeds, and so on. The whole bed is covered as evenly as
possible and topped off with a final layer of something
denser, such as straw, hay, raw compost, or manure.

Some gardeners add an additional layer of planting soil

before the final top layer and plant shallow-rooted annuals directly into the bed. These short-lived creatures can carry on as the bed breaks down beneath them. After a season, the entire bed will be plantable to a depth of about 8 inches.

In woodland gardens, make sheet mulches by heaping whatever falls from the trees, together with any weeds or garden groomings, into rough piles that will rot slowly as you decide what you want to do with the space they cover. You can use this simple technique to slowly develop new beds, pathways, and seating areas.

MULCHING WITH MANURE

My favorite mulching material is pit-washed dairy manure, especially when I can get it from a dairy that does not use BGH (bovine growth hormone) or routinely add steroids to the cows' feed. Washed, partially composted, and lumpless, it is lovely stuff. Indeed, few substances can rival the open texture and root-building qualities of this marvelous substance. Incorporated generously into clay or sand, washed dairy manure creates an excellent medium for plant growth. Used as top-dressing, it makes a handsome mulch that keeps soils moist and cool come summer. Naturally, dairy manure must be fully composted before you use it. Any and all animal manures are full of pathogens that could present health problems to plants as well as to people. Composting helps minimize that possibility and also puts the manure in a form that is most palatable to plants.

In dairy country, it's not too hard to find farms (or dairies) that deliver washed, partially composted manure by the truckload for a price. In my area, a 10-yard truckload of washed dairy manure runs between $200 and $300, depending on the distance between you and the cows. Even in the city, the price is usually competitive with that of other mulching materials. Many county extension services offer manure hot lines, where you can call for information on finding local sources of composted manures. Sometimes farm manures are even free for the taking if you have a truck. Some people try to haul manure in cars and vans using tightly closed garbage cans. Let me tell you from experience, this is not a good idea. Even if you manage to get home without losing any cargo, the car will reek for months. If you do have a spill, you will discover that manure spills rival oil spills for long-lasting and unattractive results.

Composted cow manure is in many respects superior to the common run of soil builders and mulches. Unlike shredded bark, it has no splinters. Unlike pine needles, it is not acid but nearly neutral. Unlike sawdust, it carries its own supply of nitrogen in the form of urine, which is pre-mixed with the manure at no extra charge (those kindly cows are always happy to please). Composted dairy manure is the first amendment in all my own gardens.

Indeed, it is sometimes the only one needed to get started on garden making, since it can be used equally well as a soil amendment, top-dressing, and mulch.

While most animal manures are beneficial (carnivorous cat and dog ordure are obvious exceptions), they vary somewhat in quality. Goat or rabbit manure will please plants, but those little pellets take longer to break down. The squeamish may well find themselves shrinking from doing hand work among the bunny droppings. Again, it is imperative to compost manures of any kind before adding them to your garden. If you are doing the composting, be sure to use gloves and wear a mask to minimize exposure to unfriendly bacteria and other pathogens.

Be aware that horse manure can create problems if it is not very thoroughly composted. Well-kept horses are

Sustainably-planted mixed borders need only moderate feeding with low-number fertilizers such as Whitney Farms' 5-5-5 once a year. That and an annual compost mulch will usually provide all needed nutrients.

routinely given worm medications that pass through their digestive systems easily. In garden soil, these medications will kill worms just as well as they do in horses' intestines. Hot composting through four to five turns will break down most if not all of the medication. Mix horse manure half and half with grass clippings and shredded leaves to make a very hot, fast-rotting pile. In addition, horses that have been fed with weed-free grains may pass along the persistent herbicide clopyralid through their manure.

Pig and chicken manure are far too hot to use directly on any kind of garden and should be composted (mix them with grass clippings and shredded leaves) before use. Be sure to take your time and run it through a full three-turn composting cycle, as immature manure compost can burn plants rather than feed them. What's more, both pig and chicken manures smell exactly like their creators for a long, long time. When properly composted, their obtrusive qualities are mellowed without losing their beneficial ones.

HOW MUCH MANURE?

Clearly, the amount of manure you will need will vary with the size of your garden and the state of your soil. In general, one 8- to 10-yard load of composted manure will suffice for a small new garden. A medium-sized garden on a standard city lot might need two or three loads, and a suburban lot larger than 100 by 100 yards could easily require five or six loads. If you are making a really big rural garden, you might want to buy some cows of your own.

Even 10 yards of manure sounds like a lot, looks like a lot, and feels like a lot when you are on the small end of the shovel. However, this is one amendment that is hard to overdo. The only danger is that excess manure can pollute water supplies. To avoid this, build your manure pile where rain won't wash it into the gutter, open streams, ponds, or any waterways.

To safeguard the water further, you can lay down tarps before unloading the manure and surround the pile with plastic silt fences—the kind used to protect construction sites. Secure them in place with straw bales, which will soak up any exudate. When they begin to rot, you can break up the soggy, manure-soaked bales and use the straw as path material. Remember, however, that the straw may have clopyralid in it, so don't add it to your regular compost pile after use. Instead, compost the straw in a separate pile with grass clippings, then do a bio-assay (see the clopyralid sidebar earlier in this chapter) to see if the resulting compost is safe to use on edibles.

HEALING OUR HOME GROUND

Until recently, most garden designers would recommend aggressive treatment for poor soils. Badly drained soils would be trenched, double dug, or laced with French drains. Impervious soil layers (often called hardpan) would be forcibly cracked open with heavy machinery. Many yards of topsoil would be trucked in, giving the site new topography.

There are still situations where such drastic measures make sense. New construction is often graded to hardpan, leaving the gardener with a mere few inches of imported soil to plant. Disturbed sites may contain lead from traffic emissions or chips of old house paint. Former farmland can harbor toxic residues of DDT and other long-lasting poisons, even many years after their use has been banned. Other, similarly toxic chemicals are still in use and may remain actively harmful for months or even years.

Since these toxins can destroy the soil food web, removal of contaminated soil is imperative. New soil must then be brought in, but it is wise to consider how the remaining subsoil may affect the new topsoil. It is often most effective to create a well-drained base layer of 8 to 12 inches of sandy loam (see "Layering Mounded Beds" earlier in this chapter). This creates a well-aerated base layer that drains quickly, reducing habitat for pathogens and making a healthy medium for root growth. The drainage layer is then topped off with an additional 8 to 12 inches of topsoil. Whenever possible, this upper layer should be a certified organic topsoil, especially if you plan to raise edible crops of any kind.

One recent theory that has become popular among gardeners suggests that degraded soil can be improved by sprinkling it with a small amount of healthy soil. The idea is that the good soil will quickly colonize and inoculate the poor soil. Unfortunately, this doesn't work.

As Dr. Ingham of Oregon State University explains, "Soil biota is pretty small and pretty slow. A soil bacterium might move a quarter of an inch in a lifetime. A handful of good soil, or even the probiotic sprays, can affect only the soil they are directly touching." However, Dr. Ingham is an enthusiastic supporter of the new breed of aerobic compost teas (see "Probiotic Teas" earlier in this chapter).

DETOXING WITH ACTIVATED CHARCOAL

On new home sites, the probability of chemical contamination is usually slight. Where gardens have been maintained chemically, the probability of residual chemical contamination is quite high. Those who have chemical sensitivities or who want to grow food organically may decide to treat as much of the site as possible with activated charcoal. This is a standard practice for organic growers who are starting a healing cycle of soil-building crops to reclaim chemically treated soils.

Activated charcoal is simply charcoal in a finely ground form with many binding sites that help to pull toxins out of contaminated soil or compost and hold them in a neutral or nonactive state. Activated charcoal looks like chimney soot and can be tricky to deal with. In wet weather and on wet soils, it is very difficult to handle. Recommended practice is to apply it to fairly dry soil at 5 pounds per 100 square feet and to till it in at least 8 inches deep. It is strongly recommended that you wear a mask and a good respirator when handling or applying activated charcoal. Activated charcoal comes in 40-pound bags and is not widely available as of this writing. See the Resources section at the end of this book for information on obtaining it.

Tests performed at Washington State University showed that tilling in 5 pounds of activated charcoal per 100 square feet was enough to remove persistent herbicides and other chemical toxins from contaminated soils. However, the charcoal must be tilled in as deeply as the chemicals may have migrated. In the WSU test garden (which had been contaminated with the persistent herbicide clopyralid), charcoal was tilled in to a depth of 8 inches. When tomato plant roots grew past that depth, the plants showed symptoms of herbicide damage. But by that time the plants had already set fruit, which ripened well despite the late damage.

WSU researchers also found that they could successfully raise crops in herbicide-contaminated soils by mixing about 1 tablespoon of activated charcoal per cup of mixed compost and soil in the planting hole. Dig this mixture deeply into each planting hole when planting.

Here in the maritime Pacific Northwest, lawn care can be frustrating. In shady gardens, moss often grows more happily than turfgrass. In coastal and woodland regions, native grasses are mainly bog or wetland species. Imported turfgrasses grow fairly well when we can offer them ample sun, good drainage, and a relatively neutral soil. Otherwise we often experience difficulties. One excellent solution is to seek out grass mixtures that are developed specifically for the Northwest. Choosing site-adapted grass seed blends that grow well in cooler or shadier settings can make a pleasant difference to your lawn's looks.

A second consideration is that lawns require a great deal of sustenance and the resources of the Northwest are not infinite. Throughout the region, local government programs now encourage homeowners to learn new ways to plant and manage lawns in a more sustainable manner. We are asked to develop lawns (and landscapes) that require less summer water, create less green waste, and do not introduce chemical toxins into local waterways. Research demonstrates that established lawns can shed water at almost the same rate as a cement sidewalk, turning as much as 85 percent of the water we give them into runoff. Toxic lawn treatments such as weed-and-feed products are carried into local waterways, harming birds, fish, worms, and other soil life every step of the way.

A lot of expertise has gone into developing natural lawn care programs to produce healthy, handsome lawns that are able to thrive with less supplemental water and artificial fertilizer. In large part, these programs work by weaning chemically dependent lawns (which have extremely shallow root systems and are highly susceptible to stress-related problems) off the toxic weed-and-feed cycle. Instead we offer our lawns an environmentally benign natural care program that builds soil health; promotes deep, strong grass roots; and encourages beneficial

Sometimes just a little lawn is plenty. Portland gardener Nancy Goldman keeps her lawn in a box.

soil biota. Working in concert, these factors create relatively independent lawns that can take normal seasonal stresses in stride.

Another key to success is the continuing education of the gardener. Many of us have been taught that lawns should be a monoculture, a smooth carpet woven of a single kind of grass. In nature, however, monocultures do not exist, and nowhere are they easily sustainable. The most adaptable lawns contain several or many components, each of which contributes to the overall good looks and health of the planting. Ecologically balanced lawn mixtures may include clovers to fix natural nitrogen, drought-tolerant creeping herbs, and low-growing wildflowers for seasonal color. The newest all-grass lawn seed mixtures blend several kinds of grass for adaptability. Learning to value a healthy, easily cared for lawn over the seeming perfection of an artificially maintained, unsustainable one is as important to the lawn's health as it is to the gardener's happiness.

Further, we often assume that lawns should be the uniform deep green of Kentucky bluegrass. Unfortunately, bluegrass is intolerant of wet winters. Grasses that grow well in Northwestern conditions (such as perennial ryegrasses and certain fescues) tend to be a lighter green. We can force that rich, dark color for a while by applying nitrogen at dangerously high rates. However, high nitrogen regimes actually damage grass roots as well as the soil biota, creating a cycle of disease and failure to thrive that the increased and ceaseless use of chemicals can mask but cannot truly mend. Fortunately, there are now many ways to create attractive, easily cared for lawns that are not chemically dependent.

WHY NOT USE LAWN CHEMICALS?

Waterways throughout the Northwest are increasingly polluted. Regional studies commonly discover more than twenty-five toxins (all common ingredients in home yard care products) in the great majority of streams, rivers, and ponds. In 1999 a study by King County Hazardous Waste Management revealed that 90 percent of King County neighborhood streams were contaminated with some twenty-three toxins, including Diazinon. A common ingredient in anti-crane fly treatments and some weed-and-feed lawn care products, Diazinon has also become a common ingredient in streams and wetlands throughout the region. Similar tales can be told of numerous common chemicals (including Prozac!), many of which persist in soils and in water for months or even years.

Small wonder our native salmon are endangered. What's more, chemical yard toxins also harm the soil life, from earthworms to beneficial bacteria, that keeps our plants healthy. If you use any pesticides and herbicides, be extremely careful when you use them. Never use more than is needed, and never use any toxin "just in case." If you use poisons, don't spray on windy days, when drift can kill your neighbor's plants as well as bees and other beneficial insects.

Very few people actually follow the directions for using toxins, which require the user to wear a mask, gloves, and protective clothing. Think about it. Toxins that kill birds, bees, and fish as well as pesky bugs can't actually be very good for humans either. Indeed, each year many people become seriously ill from misusing lawn care poisons.

Luckily, there are quite a few less-toxic alternatives to chemical cures. In fact, nontoxic lawn care can even be cheaper and easier than poison-based care. Lawn care experts agree that a healthy lawn is highly resistant to pests and problems, from crane fly larvae to root rots. The best cure is prevention, not poison.

PLANTING A NEW LAWN

Lawns grow best with plenty of sun, good drainage, and nutritious soil. Most lawn care professionals recommend deep-tilling 4 to 6 inches of mature (finished) compost into the proposed lawn area. Mature compost is preferred over topsoil, which is usually a low-quality mixture of native clay, sand, and shredded bark (often with dyes added to give it a dark color). This recommendation holds true for both sandy and clay-based soils. Do not add sand or even fine grit to clay soils; doing so can create an adobelike substance that further impairs drainage.

Top this tilled soil with an additional 2 to 3 inches of mature compost or topsoil mixed with compost before sowing seed or planting sod. If you prefer not to till, simply spread a 4-inch layer of mature compost over the existing lawn area and sow grass seed over that. If you have made mounded planting beds, this will still leave the paths lower than all growing areas, which makes for better drainage and air circulation.

Ideally, lawns are graded to slope slightly away from the house in order to promote rapid drainage (and avoid flooding the basement). A 1 percent slope (a 1-foot fall over 100 running feet) is a suggested minimum, while slopes over 5 percent can present challenges. Slopes greater than 6 percent should be planted with a drought-tolerant, low-maintenance ground cover rather than lawn.

Starting a new lawn from seed is generally less expensive and more successful than using sod. Be aware, however, that inexpensive grass seed mixtures tend to contain a high proportion of annual grasses. These green up fast but die out over the winter, leaving patchy bare spots behind. Sod must be planted quickly and well, and it requires at least as thorough an initial preparation as a seeded lawn. Sod is rarely available as a blend of regionally appropriate grasses and tends to suffer badly in anything less than optimal conditions. Most often, sodded lawns look fine for a year or two but are showing their age by the third season.

An excellent handbook, *Ecologically Sound Lawn Care for the Pacific Northwest*, was published by Seattle Public Utilities in 1999. This 80-page document, available on-line, covers every aspect of lawn care in detail, with reference citations for all presented information. See the Resources section for information on obtaining this publication.

ALTERNATIVES TO TURFGRASS
ECO-LAWNS

Northwestern gardeners are increasingly willing to explore lawn alternatives. Researchers at Oregon State University have developed a line of regionally appropriate eco-lawn seed mixtures for those who want to enjoy their lawns without the burden of frequent care or toxic regimes.

Oregon's Nichols Nursery (see the Resources section) has pioneered the sale of several eco-lawn mixes that need less water, less feeding, and less mowing than ordinary lawns. All contain mixtures of grasses for greater adaptability. Most also include what are often called tapestry ingredients. Tapestry lawns are named after the medieval wall hangings in which surprised-looking maidens coax dim-looking unicorns out of the woods. At the feet of both are lawns studded with small flowers. English daisies, thyme, and chamomile are traditional tapestry lawn flowers. The Oregon State eco-lawn mixtures combine them with regionally adapted bunchgrasses (clumpers rather than runners) and low-growing clovers.

Although most folks assume that clovers are weeds, certain clovers are excellent lawn additions because they can actually improve poor soils by adding nitrogen to them. They do this by taking in atmospheric nitrogen from the air and fixing it into nodules (little white bumps) on their roots that can easily be observed.

Several of the new eco-lawn blends incorporate the classic English lawn daisies, which naturalize freely in the Northwest. Many also include drought-tolerant and fragrant herbs like chamomile and creeping thymes, both of which can stand considerable foot traffic and frequent mowing. A few blend dwarf ryegrasses with taller wildflowers like California poppies (*Eschscholzia* species) and baby blue eyes (*Nemophila* species), giving the turf the look of a low natural meadow. These taller mixtures are most suitable for large areas where tight mowing is unnecessary or undesirable. Such regionally adapted mixtures are ideal for creating wildflower meadows that actually work over time (most seed blends are not well suited for the Northwest). Check local nurseries for versions of eco-lawn seed mixtures, or contact Nichols Nursery (see the Resources section) for more information.

Fall sowing is ideal, allowing the wildflowers and herbs to compete favorably with the grasses and clovers. If these mixes are sown too late in the spring (early April is the cutoff), you will end up with mostly clovers the first year. The best time to sow an eco-lawn is from mid-September through mid-October, when warm days, mild nights, and damp soils encourage seed sprouting and rapid root growth.

Drought-tolerant eco-lawn seed mixtures have been developed to grow well in the Northwest. These blends combine low-growing grasses with herbs and flowering ground covers that create a living tapestry of color and texture.

WALKABLE GROUND COVERS

Where lawns are small or little used, the most practical and attractive alternative may be to replace them with ground covers that can take foot traffic in stride. Creeping chamomile, yarrow *(Achillea millefolium),* and mother-of-thyme *(Thymus serpyllum)* are good choices for sunny, well-drained sites. Though taller in growth than the average lawn, both the chamomile and the yarrow can be closely mowed like a lawn (once or twice a month is sufficient).

Chamomile looks best when given an inch or so of supplemental water once or twice a month in dry summers.

Once well established, yarrow is remarkably drought tolerant and holds its rich green color beautifully, even during prolonged dry spells, without requiring extra water. Mother-of-thyme rarely exceeds an inch or two in height and never needs mowing. This tough evergreen is apt to die out in wet winters unless the site drainage is very good. In all cases, if foot traffic is daily or frequent, stepping-stones will prevent dieback in heavily traveled areas.

In shady settings, evergreen wood sorrel (*Oxalis oregana* 'Wintergreen') makes a lush and effortless ground cover. It can be walked on occasionally but will require stepping-stones for heavy or frequent use. Moss is always an excellent option where native mosses tend to choke out struggling turfgrasses.

NATURAL LAWN CARE

Here in the maritime Northwest, effective lawn care begins with a clear understanding of what grass really needs. Our modified Mediterranean climate has a wet-winter/dry-summer weather pattern. Most years we don't get enough summer rain to keep the grass green. Thus we begin watering and feeding, usually too much and too often. The resulting runoff carries excess fertilizers, pesticides, and herbicides into storm drains and streams. Here's how to break the cycle, simply and painlessly.

1. **Feed the soil as well as the lawn.** Begin by spreading and raking in an inch of compost over the entire lawn surface in spring and again in fall. Each year after that, spread and rake in half an inch of compost over the lawn twice a year, in spring and fall. If you don't make compost, try organic composts, such as those made by Whitney Farms or Seattle's Cedar Grove.

2. **Feed the lawn a balanced meal.** In spring, treat your lawn to the right stuff. The Organica lawn care program is excellent (it includes Lawn Booster, Kelp Booster, Microbial Soil Conditioner, and Natural Dethatcher). Walt's Regular Feed, Whitney Farms Lawn Food, Ringer Lawn Restore, NuLife Lawn Carpet Deluxe, and Webfoot Turf Treet are other good, nutritionally balanced products. Never use more than 1 pound of nitrogen for each 1,000 square feet of lawn.

3. **Mow high.** Set the lawnmower to the highest setting and leave it there. Ideally, lawn grass should be between 3½ and 4 inches tall. Tall turf photosynthesizes more

efficiently than grass that has been cut very short. Longer grass shades its own roots, conserves moisture, and outcompetes many annual weeds. High mowing is more effective than herbicide for eliminating crabgrass.

4. **Mow often.** As with pruning, grass cutting removes valuable resources. Aim to reduce the total length of your lawn by no more than one third each time you mow. This may mean mowing twice a week in high season.

5. **Let the clippings lie.** Short clippings make for a self-mulching lawn. As clippings break down, they release their stored nutrients back into the soil, enriching the lawn just as compost does. This will not lead to thatch problems. By providing earthworms with steady fodder, self-mulching can eliminate thatch buildup in a single season. You can also use Organica's Natural Dethatch to inoculate your soil with beneficial bacteria that degrade thatch as it occurs.

6. **Water wisely.** Most lawns are overwatered, leading to anoxic pathogen buildup. (Most pathogens thrive in low-oxygen environments.) Lawn growing on heavy, clay-based soils may need an inch of water once a week. Lawns growing on sandy soils may need more frequent watering. Since longer grass needs less water than short grass, you'll probably need to reduce your usual watering schedule as you start high mowing.

Do all this and you'll have a healthier lawn that fights off pests and diseases on its own. If this sounds like too much trouble, consider hiring a natural lawn care company that can do it all for you.

CRANE FLY CONTROL

European crane fly larvae—pale, fat, squashy larvae that look like relatives of the Michelin tire man—are the only serious lawn pests in the Northwest. Natural, biological controls for crane fly can be just as effective as the old toxic "cures" like Diazinon (many of which are now outlawed). Most nurseries and garden centers now sell beneficial nematodes that feed on crane fly larvae. Another helpful control is watering lawns deeply (to 2 inches) but less frequently. Since crane fly larvae thrive in moist soils, letting deep-rooted lawns dry out between waterings discourages crane flies.

Crane fly larvae love overwatered lawns. To eliminate larval damage, let your lawn dry out to a depth of at least one inch between waterings (this also encourages deep rooting). Don't water at all after mid-September and most of the larvae will dry up and die.

Spraying lawns with aerobically brewed compost teas monthly can also reduce damage from these larvae to acceptable levels by promoting strong root growth. So will spring applications of a stabilized microbial soil conditioner or probiotic drench. (See Chapter 3 for more about probiotics and compost teas.) Once conditions are improved, the lawn can outgrow most pest and disease damage so quickly that it is hardly even noticeable. Lawns that have had a strong natural care program for a season or two are similarly able to outgrow most pathogens and pests.

CORN GLUTEN: NATURE'S WEED-AND-FEED

When your lawn is looking tired in midsummer, give it a light scattering of corn gluten. This natural by-product of cornmeal manufacturing is nature's own weed-and-feed treatment. Naturally high in nitrogen (it tests at about 10-1-0 for N-P-K, or nitrogen, phosphorus, and potassium), corn gluten feeds lawns better than any chemical, without killing off worms and beneficial bugs.

Corn gluten is also a preemergent, meaning that it kills weed (or any other) seeds by preventing them from sprouting. It must be wet to be activated. When wet, it produces an allelopathic substance that dries out the tiny emerging plant in each seed. When a seedling cracks its sheath open, the corn gluten immediately kills it.

Wetting corn gluten down well also reduces the losses to birds. Like chicken feed, the pellets are amazingly attractive to crows and ducks, so it's best to use the raw or unpelletized form. To reduce losses and get the most benefit from corn gluten, broadcast it over your lawn just before a rain, or scatter it and then water it in well right away.

For lawns, the recommended spread rate is 20 pounds per 1,000 square feet. Do this two or three time a year (in spring and fall, with a summer booster as needed) to keep lawns lush and green without chemical fertilizers or herbicides.

For ongoing weed suppression in existing lawns, apply small amounts of corn gluten directly whenever you remove an unwanted plant. Make a paste of corn gluten and water and apply it when you pull up weeds. This keeps the dormant seeds from sprouting as they reach light and air. Not only will the weeds be vanquished, but the surrounding grass will rebound with vigor.

SPRING OR FALL LAWN RENOVATION

Tired, worn lawns or those that remain soggy all winter will benefit from a lawn renovation technique that transforms poorly drained lawns in about six weeks. Developed by John Caine, staff designer at Joy Creek Nursery in Scappoose, Oregon, this easy, efficient, inexpensive renovation method can be accomplished without professional assistance. Once properly rejuvenated, previously poor lawns will be level, lush, and uniformly green despite heavy foot traffic.

Caine's lawns require less than half the water they formerly required, and they hold their looks for years. Here's his formula for success:

1. Mow the existing grass as short as possible (scalp-mow).

2. Spread 1 inch of clean crushed quarter-ten gravel (I explain what this is below) evenly over the entire lawn surface.

3. Spread 1 inch of compost (I use composted dairy manure with excellent results) over the gravel.

4. Top-seed with a regionally appropriate blend if the lawn is thin and spotty (rake the seed in).

5. Wait 6 to 7 weeks before mowing again.

In six weeks, the grass will grow up through the gravel and compost. Gravel won't be dislodged by the lawnmower, because it will be held firmly in place by healthy grass roots.

It's critical to use the right kind of gravel. Never use pea gravel, which is dangerous underfoot in any garden context and tends to migrate through the soil. Look for clean "quarter-ten"—crushed quarter-inch gravel put through a number 10 screen to remove the fines and smalls (which are then sold as mason's sand). Washed quarter-inch crushed gravel will also work well, because the sand has been rinsed away.

The rough edges of clean crushed gravel help to break water surface tension, promoting excellent water penetration even in dry summers. Quarter-inch gravel with smalls (fine particles) included will lock up the soil, creating an even worse drainage situation. If clean quarter-inch gravel is unobtainable locally, you can substitute a ½-inch by ¼-inch clean gravel.

NATURAL LAWN CARE SERVICES

Throughout the region, alternatives to chemical lawn care are flourishing as homeowners become better educated in appropriate technology. Some natural lawn care companies provide mowing services as well as lawn and landscaping care. Others provide ongoing care but leave the mowing to you (or the neighbor's kid). Most offer free estimates for a range of services.

In the Seattle area, for instance, several lawn care companies offer organic or natural lawn care. In Harmony Organic Based Landscape Services uses a high-tech brewing machine to create aerated compost teas that provide excellent nutrition for both lawns and gardens.

Joeann Goodman of In Harmony says, "We do everything Chemlawn does, but we do it a little differently." In Harmony offers organic lawn fertilization programs, nontoxic insect and weed control, and plant, tree, and shrub care. They also do new and remedial landscaping, as well as pruning for health and beauty.

Continued on page 124

In Harmony is expanding rapidly and recently opened a second branch in Tacoma to serve customers to the south. "People are getting more interested in lawn care that isn't based on poisons," says Goodman.

Another natural care company, Earthguard Incorporated, is also experiencing a steady increase in clients. Owner Sam Macri says, "Basically, we work from ground up, improving soil and providing cultural controls. We also suggest alternatives to lawn, because a lot of people have lawns where lawns really shouldn't be."

Earthguard offers a full program of natural lawn care, including aerating, overseeding, and organic fertilizers. It also provides remedial landscaping, tree and shrub care, and less-toxic approaches to insect and pest control.

"Our goal is to improve existing conditions, creating a naturally healthy lawn and landscape," says Macri. To find out more about these firms, see the Resources section at the end of this book, or check your local listings for lawn care companies.

If mature compost is not available, you can substitute the natural soil amendment called Claybuster (sold by Lilly Miller and Whitney Farms). Simply spread an inch of Claybuster over the gravel and rake it smooth.

Composted dairy manure also makes an excellent top-dressing for lawns. It is among the very best amendments for encouraging healthy root growth. Don't use packaged steer manure, and don't use horse manure or any other kind of manure, unless it has been thoroughly hot-composted first.

There are two main windows of opportunity for lawn refreshment in our region. One occurs in September and October, when grass roots put on a lot of growth. The next prime time is in April and May, when grass growth accelerates again. Caine finds that soggy, badly drained lawns may require several treatments. If your lawn is in really bad shape, you may need to apply this innovative, simple technique twice. Start the first treatment in fall and let the grass grow all winter. The following spring, apply a second treatment in April.

OF LAWNS AND MOSS

Each spring, chemical companies begin heavy promotion of toxic products designed to rid lawns of moss. "It's time to attack!" one ad proclaims. Here in the maritime Northwest, moss can indeed invade lawns. However, we might just as reasonably look at it the other way. Lawn grasses can wreak havoc with our beautiful, thick, cushiony mosses. Lawns, like prairies, are not natural in this part of the world. Moss is.

Lawn lovers often come from the East Coast or the Midwest, places where rolling meadows happen naturally. In the southern parts of Cascadia, past Portland, open savannahs of grass and garry oaks are quite common. In the northernmost parts of the region, there are just a handful of places where native prairie ever existed.

Most of this untouched land is gone now, lost to development. The lawns that accompany most houses cover land that was climax forest not so long ago. Once the trees are gone, the region's natural ecology is changed, perhaps permanently. (Much of Scotland's open moor land was forested until about a thousand years ago, when it was logged to feed a war. The land never recovered, and few people remember the forests that once clothed those bare hills.)

Natural lawn care produces lush, deep-rooted, and drought-tolerant turf that crowds out weeds. Where lawns are mossy, annual over-seeding will reduce the moss, which is simply an opportunist; moss doesn't kill grass, it just inhabits empty spaces.

Replacing lawn under trees and shrubs with ground covers and perennials reduces mowing and edging. This living skirt also protects tree trunks from mower and weed whacker damage—the leading cause of tree disease.

Where the trees are all gone, grass usually does fine (unless the tree roots are still in place). Where many trees remain, lawns are not only impractical, they can endanger the health of the trees and shrubs around them. Traditional lawns need summer watering to stay green. Native and long-established trees and shrubs can develop root rots and other diseases if overwatered in summer.

What's more, lawns need their blankets of tumbling tree leaves to be removed each fall. Soggy leaf piles can rot out grass during the long, wet winter, leaving bald patches next summer. As it happens, however, removing tree leaves from the base of the trees can alter the soil in a vital way. Healthy woodland soil is fungally dominated. Fungally dominated soils are ideal for growing trees and shrubs (including roses) and are also good for certain crops like corn that have woody stalks. Lawn grasses, on the other hand, like annuals, perennials, and most vegetables, favor bacterially dominated soils. Thus, by making the yard tidy and keeping the lawn from smothering, we put the health of our trees and shrubs at risk.

What does all this mean in practical terms? If you have a shady, mossy lawn, consider a novel idea. Instead of poisoning the moss (and, not incidentally, much soil life as well), appreciate it. Bring in some sculptural rocks and set them about at pleasing angles. Plant a few ferns nearby, along with some spilling golden grasses such as the lovely Japanese forest grass *Hakonechloa macra* 'Aureola'.

Add a few compact rhododendrons for contrast, perhaps a shapely little 'Moonstone' and a dusky-leaved 'Northern Starburst'. If you prefer soft colors, look for 'Yaku Angel', a diminutive shrub with fawn felted foliage and white flowers. Pull out those struggling grasses and let the moss prevail. Soon, instead of a frustratingly poor lawn, you'll have an artful Asian-style moss garden.

MAKING MORE MOSS

There are several simple, easy ways to grow moss. With these techniques, you can turn a struggling mossy lawn into a luxuriant, deep green, living carpet. If you need convincing that moss can be beautiful, stop by the library and browse through some books on Asian gardening. Moss gardening is a long-established tradition in Japan, where certain temples are famed for the depth and lushness of their moss.

Where a mossy lawn looks sad, start your improvements by pulling the shabby grass out. Next, spray your moss patches with diluted buttermilk and woodland compost tea. To make this tea, put a shovelful of woodland soil and another shovelful of compost into a bucket. Set it in a sunny place and add warm water to fill the bucket. Stir well, and stir it again every time you walk by it. After a few hours, the garden sun tea mixture will be ready to use.

To make your own powerful moss increaser, mix 1 part of this woodland compost tea with 1 part buttermilk. If you don't have compost or can't make the tea, just use warm water. Apply this blend with a sprayer or watering can to your mossy areas. If you use a sprayer, be sure that it has never been used for any kind of poison. Moss is extremely sensitive to toxins and can be harmed by even trace amounts of herbicides or pesticides.

To accelerate your moss coverage in any bare patches, scrape some pretty mosses off the back steps or the shed roof. If you don't have any mosses, your neighbors surely will. Ask if they can spare a few pieces of moss, and be sure to watch their faces. A laugh like that does the spirit good.

Now crumble the mossy bits in a bowl (rubbing them between your fingers). The pieces should be about the size of a split pea or even finer. When the blend is fairly uniform, pour in enough buttermilk to make a thick slurry. To turn your former lawn into an emerald carpet, spread or spray the buttermilk mixture over the bald patches where the ratty turf once was. (This mixture can also be brushed onto damp clay pots and cement containers to give them that fuzzy green English look.)

To get truly magnificent coverage in very short order, crumble some moss into an old blender and buzz it with buttermilk and water (half and half). This makes a very thin liquid that can be poured through a watering can with a coarse, large-holed rose.

I have a garage sale blender I use for garden concoctions (especially the ones involving slugs and cabbage moth caterpillars). It is not a good idea to mix garden soils or anything containing manure in blenders that are also used for making human food. After each use, soak the garden blender overnight with ammonia and water to avoid spreading disease.

Applied in midspring or early fall (after the rains have

returned), this mixture can have breathtaking results. At these times of the year, mosses are still in active growth and some are blooming (many bloom all winter). You will soon see a film of tender, glowing green infant moss sheeting across the bare earth.

GUIDELINES FOR GREEN WASTE DISPOSAL

From late winter into early fall, gardeners accumulate an ever-increasing supply of grass clippings, leaves, and green "garbage." One place that such green waste should never go is down the side of a bank. Those who garden above cliffs, bluffs, and ravines are often tempted to dump their grass and leaves over the edge where they are conveniently out of sight.

Unfortunately, grass clippings and leaves do not just go away. When we dump green garden gleanings off banks of any kind, we very often create erosion. That's because large quantities of green stuff can smother the native plantings that hold those banks in place.

Although these garden materials will compost over time, even modest heaps can take years to break down. Thus, these heaps act as a smother mulch, killing plants by suffocating them, instead of as compost. This is especially likely when nobody is turning the piles to let in more oxygen.

Anaerobic compost (compost made in piles that lack oxygen) doesn't work well. Anaerobic piles rot slowly and are often home to unfriendly plant and soil pathogens that smell nasty and eat live roots. This is clearly not a great situation to have anywhere in the garden. It is especially dangerous in places where you are counting on plants to hold a slope or bank in place.

Green dumping is so destructive that many communities now fine folks caught tossing grass clippings and garden wastes over slopes or banks. The fines are pretty hefty, and rightly so, so please do not indulge in this destructive practice yourself.

If you have neighbors who do, please show them this section before turning them in (that's the friendly way). If they still persist in illegal dumping, document it and report it to the appropriate city agency or to your state department of ecology. This is not a petty or punitive act: When one piece of bank erodes or slides, it puts everything around it at risk as well.

High bank waterfront properties of any kind are especially vulnerable to sliding and sloughing. Many Northwestern banks and hillsides are extremely fragile ecosystems, and many are inherently unstable. Just about the worst thing one can do to a natural hillside is flatten out a terrace on it and make a lawn that needs a lot of summer water. (Nothing destabilizes a bank faster than excess runoff.)

Dumping near a waterway causes other ill effects as well. Grass clippings and yard waste that have been sprayed or treated with chemical herbicides and pesticides (such as weed-and-feed combos) often introduce dangerous levels of poisons to public waterways. Grass clippings don't have to hit the water to pollute. Rain and yard runoff carry the chemicals to the water's edge, where the real damage is done. Even small traces of many common yard toxins can cause serious harm to plants, fish, and water birds.

If you are lucky enough to live on or near a beach, the very best thing you can do to protect your bank is leave the native vegetation alone. For more guidance, stop by your local city or county engineering department. Throughout the maritime Northwest, waterfront districts offer one or more free handbooks that steer homeowners toward benign practices.

In Washington State, one such booklet is called *Vegetation Management: A Guide for Puget Sound Bluff Property Owners.* It presents clear overviews of site situations and solutions. A companion volume, *Slope Stabilization and Erosion Control Using Vegetation* is subtitled *A Manual of Practice for Coastal Property Owners.* A third title, *Surface Water and Groundwater on Coastal Bluffs,* is invaluable for anybody with runoff and drainage problems. See the Resources section for information on obtaining these publications.

Ideally, gardeners should voluntarily create a buffer zone of native plants between the edge of the bank and their lawn or garden. This buffer should be at least 20 feet deep to protect the slope from runoff. There's no need to let unwanted tree saplings grow up and take away your view, but low growers such as salal, wild roses, twiggy dogwoods, and snowberry should be encouraged.

Once established, such a buffer will be a water-free zone that helps absorb winter rains and summer lawn and garden runoff. The native plant buffer won't want or need any additional watering and won't require much care except an annual thinning. Each fall you can edit your buffer, removing small trees you don't want, along with Euro-trash weeds like English ivy and Scotch broom and the lusty Himalayan blackberries.

The very best way to get rid of excess garden gleanings is by recycling them through municipal green waste composting programs or by composting them at home.

CONVERTING MEADOWS TO LAWNS

Rough meadows can be converted into lawnlike, relatively fine-textured turf through frequent mowing. This is a good solution where a large, open area must be maintained without much work or watering. The resulting turf is good enough to be used as a playing field and stays green with less than half the water needed by lawn grasses. Because frequent mowing selects for fine-textured grasses, mowing the meadow to 3 inches every week or two will alter the mixture of grasses and forbs (nongrasses) in short order. Within a year, a rugged meadow can look surprisingly velvety and will stay tidy when mown twice a month during the growing season (usually March through November).

MAINTAINING MEADOWS

In the maritime Northwest, existing meadows must be mown periodically to prevent incursion by perennial weeds, shrubs, and trees. If a neglected meadow has begun to grow over with pernicious weeds, high-mow it at 3 to 4 inches four to six times the first year to regain control. Edges and perimeters may need to be cleared by hand with machetes or brush cutters. Mature Scotch broom will not resprout when cut, but blackberries certainly will. Once the meadow is cleared, three to four annual mowings will keep most weeds under control. If you can mow only twice a year, make your first cut in early summer, when the first flush of blackberry growth has hardened into mature foliage. By late summer, the second flush of growth will have similarly matured. At these points, your mowing will be most effective in terms of depleting stored nutritional reserves in the plant roots, thus doing the most harm and giving the best control.

FIVE: MAINTAINING THE SUSTAINABLE GARDEN

For many folks, gardening is synonymous with work. The very word "gardening" conjures up an endless round of yard and lawn chores. Most gardeners find at least some of the routine care required by living plants to be pleasurable in itself. (If they didn't, they wouldn't be gardeners.) Weeding can be meditative, keeping us in touch with our plants. Summer watering and autumn mulching can renew our connection to the natural cycles of the year. However, weeding and watering can also feel like out-of-control, ceaseless jobs that get worse rather than better each year. If this is your fear or feeling, take heart. There is a better way.

Part of the problem lies within the very idea of maintenance. To maintain is to hold in place. A garden is never static; it is an ever-changing community of living plants. We cannot freeze it in time, and even to try is to put ourselves at war with Nature herself. This is not a good idea.

It is, however, the basis for much traditional gardening. The essence of garden design is either cooperation or control. Control-based designs may impose artificial shapes on plants, turning bushes into rectangles, cubes, and poodle-balls. Such designs generally rely on geometry, using straight lines and right angles to demonstrate power over the natural world.

To many of us, such designs look neat and tidy. However, keeping a garden that way is a constant battle. When we demand that our plants adapt to artificial shapes or growth patterns, we are making what I call a chain-saw commitment, permanently dedicating time and energy to a struggle that will end only when the plant or the gardener dies.

Control-based designs create work. Traditionally, these designs were made by people who did not actually do the work (which explains a lot). The great gardens of England and Europe have always relied heavily on the presence of a "stawf." On this side of the water, most of us

The key to maintaining sustainable gardens is annual mulching with compost.

garden alone or with minimal help (usually untrained). We have no staff to perform repetitive tasks like clipping, edging, and shearing hedges.

Instead of spending our precious time doing the same tedious chore over and over, we can learn to garden cooperatively. We can choose plants with natural shapes and sizes that suit our design and our site. We can further select plants that like the climate and soil conditions common in the Northwest. We can then put these plants into relationships that echo their natural home positions. Making choices based on these three ideas can eliminate an amazing amount of routine, repetitive work.

Naturalistic, sustainable design replaces straight lines and hard angles with smooth, simple curves. This eliminates hard-to-mow corners and simplifies edging. These designs emulate natural relationships and planting patterns, echoing nature's layering in the garden. Letting plants be what they are eliminates much shearing and clipping and all combat pruning.

Privacy screening is created with small trees and unclipped shrubs that block unwanted views and provide a comforting sense of enclosure. Woody plants are much less demanding than lawn, so yard sections devoted to privacy screening require only a few hours of care each year. Instead of raking leaves, we let them lie and return their stored nutrients to their parent plants. Leaves that land on lawns can be mown over and left in place or shredded and added to the compost.

Naturalistic, sustainable beds and borders are almost as easy to care for. When we fill the garden with plants that like regional conditions, we can reduce feeding and watering to a few sessions each year. When we use a high percentage of border plants with year-round good looks, the usual huge spring and fall cleanup sessions are greatly reduced. Light monthly grooming keeps the garden looking good with just an hour or two of time. Spreading an annual feeding mulch replaces fertilizing and minimizes watering needs. Mulching also reduces weeding, as does thoughtful planting. As a rule, if you have weeds, you don't have enough plants.

Gravel paths and driveways are kept clean of weeds with flame weeders, a meditative, peaceful chore that is ardently embraced by teenaged boys. Natural lawn care recycles grass clippings with mulching mowers or composting. Annual feedings of compost and corn gluten, nature's organic weed-and-feed, eliminate the use of fertilizers and toxic lawn pesticides and herbicides.

What's left to do? Once we break the cycle of endless must-do chores, we get to replace them with easier and more pleasant tasks, such as sitting on the garden bench and drinking in the mingled colors, scents, and sounds the garden offers. And if your garden doesn't offer these things, know that it can.

Best of all, we can do all this in such a way that the garden is relatively independent. Instead of creating a toxic monster that eats time and money and damages the environment, we can make a green haven that shelters humans, birds, butterflies, and other natural creatures without undue use of water and other natural resources. The choice is up to us.

WORKING TOWARD THE NEXT STEP

No matter how hard we work at enjoying the garden, there will always be more to do in it than we can easily find time for. If our goal is to make a sustainable garden, we also need to develop a sustainable attitude toward the garden and its needs. One great way to do this is to practice what I call "working toward." How does it work? Each time we need to deal with a problem or a chore, we begin by looking at the overall goal, not just the next step. If you have ever shifted a stack of lumber or rocks or cement blocks several times in order to get it out of the way of the next project, you will appreciate this concept. This kind of unnecessarily repetitive chore usually recurs when we haven't thought clearly about the various stages of a project. Material reshuffling is even more common when we are multitasking, trying to integrate a series of projects without stopping to ask ourselves how they are or should be related. By making a habit of planning how we will implement our designs, we can spend time lounging in the hammock instead of doing repetitive but avoidable tasks.

The idea of "working toward" also involves breaking down challenging chores to make them less overwhelming. Breaking a big job into a number of smaller ones creates a logical sequence of discrete tasks that can be implemented as we find the time. It is most important that we do this in such a way that we don't lose ground between work sessions. We aren't finished with each piece until we know it will stay as we left it, so when we return to the work, the logical next piece will build on today's achievement. The example that speaks to most of us is that of a weedy bed. If we clear a small section and walk away, by the time we return to that task, the mess is worse than ever and all our efforts are wasted. If we take the time to spread plastic or newspaper or mulch over our work, the bed will still be clean and tidy when we are ready to fill it with vegetables or peonies.

I used to think that the secret to success with any project was to hire somebody else to do it. That does help, but as I learned when my children were small, even ten or fifteen minutes is enough time to achieve something worth doing. During the years when we home-schooled, I saw that just as my kids could learn an amazing amount by doing a bit of work each day, so I could accomplish satisfying garden projects in tiny little chunks of time. All I had to do was keep at it. Day by day, I'd sneak in whatever time I could manage and, amazingly enough, mountains of work got done.

Whenever a big job seems daunting, take the time to see what actually needs to be done and in what order. You might begin the job of clearing a big border of weeds by carrying a stack of newspapers to the border space each time you take out the trash. Every time you hang out the laundry, spend five minutes spreading newspapers over the weeds and weighing them down with rocks or weeds. Well-planned persistence can work small miracles.

Weeding and reweeding the same place over and over can be a heartbreaking chore, but a little strategy can turn a challenge into a slow but simple task. Allow yourself ten or fifteen minutes a day to weed, and use each session's weed harvest to smother the next section. In the garden proper, in meadows, or in the fringes of woodlands, instead of carting the rank weeds off to the distant compost pile, create small compost piles wherever they will help to smother out more weeds, starting with those that are covering the area where you want to work next. When clearing wild areas, making new beds, breaking ground, or weeding trouble spots, make smother mulches your ally. Heap vast quantities—all you can muster—of weeds, wood chips, leaves, or straw on the ground you want to claim, whether for a path or a bed. The more raw material you can come up with, the easier your reclamation will be.

Even if you work slowly, that deep smother mulch will be working for you, slowly clearing the land as it waits for your return.

Even a huge design implementation project can be broken down into many series of smaller tasks. A wonderful musician once described an incredibly complex Bach partita to me as "layer on layer of simplicity." So it is with big projects: Move this rock once, and put it where you'll want it a year from now. Prune that branch. Lift the skirt of that shrub. Mulch this area, create a path there, start a new path over here.

To keep your project pieces manageably small, stay grounded in reality and don't let your imagination carry you away. One of the worst frustrations a gardener can suffer is to open up a huge new bed the size of Kansas, then watch it choke up with weeds because there's no time to plant. The remedy for Kansasitis is to take on any new bed one section at a time. Never develop more of a bed than you can manage, or it will race out of control. Instead of prepping the whole bed at once, do only as much as you can keep mulched. When you have more time and mulching materials, take on a new section. Well-mulched beds won't fill up with weeds, and planting into freshly prepped soil is about as good as it gets.

As your design skills grow, so will your ability to implement them wisely and well. When big projects are designed from the start to be carried out in realistic and fairly small units, everything we do flows into the next piece. The result is practical and pleasant work that feels efficient and almost effortless.

GROOMING WITH OPEN EYES

It's easy to put yourself on autopilot and daydream when grooming, but it's wiser to stay sharp, paying attention to all you see and every plant you handle. While you work through bed and border, look for signs that all is well (or not, as the case may be). Molds and mildews often signal an area where air circulation is poor and some thinning of crowded perennials or pruning of congested shrubs might be in order. A patch of brittle, brown foliage in early summer may mean that a bacterial blight has gained a toehold, while yellowing leaves on broad-leaved evergreens like camellias, bamboos, laurels, and rhododendrons may tell you they are iron deficient. If so, a little liquid iron

will green them right up and send them into winter well protected.

Stunted, puckered, or distorted growth is often a symptom of sucking insects like whiteflies. You can usually tell where aphids are increasing because the nearby leaves will be sticky and often covered with tiny ants that farm aphids and milk them like cows. Leaves that are curled up with fine webbing are being colonized by spider mites. Caught quickly, all these little pests can be hosed off or given a spray of neem oil before they spread through the garden.

Insect damage can be hard to spot in the early stages, but frequent grooming helps us keep on top of these and other problems while they can still be controlled with a quick rinse from the hose, a dose of neem oil, or a squirt of insecticidal soap.

It's important to remember that a few bugs are not an infestation and may not need any intervention at all. Plant diseases are often more serious, since viruses and pathenogenic bacteria can spread more quickly through the garden than little bugs. Most often, plant diseases are telling us that the suffering plant is not in the right place or not getting the treatment it requires. Generally, cutting back affected foliage and refurbishing the soil with compost mulch and brewed compost tea will set things straight quite quickly. Any seriously diseased plants should be put in the trash or burned. Never put diseased plants or foliage on the compost heap, where they might spread the problem to other parts of the garden.

Where you notice a group of plants with smaller-than-average foliage, or plants that are flaccid and floppy, compacted or dry soil may be the culprit (though an excess of shade is another possibility). Like most culturally induced plant growth problems, these can be fixed only by improving the soil, which takes time.

A long list of symptoms such as yellowing, spotted, or browning foliage; stunted growth; and buds that rot before they can open may indicate root growth problems, which may be caused by physical damage to the roots, poor drainage, dry or compacted soil, overcrowding, disease, or poor planting techniques. If so, the solution is to fix the faulty condition, after which the plant will usually fix itself.

If serious or ongoing problems do develop despite your

When one plant in a healthy row fails to thrive, dig it up and look at the roots. Chances are excellent that there is some kind of damage, whether caused by pests or man-made. Injured plants are nearly always the first to be attacked by pests and diseases.

best efforts at containment, your best bet is to dig up the ailing plant. Take a look at the root system, where you may well see the true culprit. Whenever one plant shows stress but its neighbors look fine, root damage of some kind is often the origin of the problem. Plants with root damage have been found to send out hormonal distress signals that attract pests and predators. The mildew or aphids you notice may well be secondary problems that mask the underlying cause of stress, such as poor drainage or physical damage inflicted during planting or by a passing rodent. For more on identifying plant problems and solving them naturally, see Chapter 6.

SELF-COMPOSTING

Over the past few years, I've been doing a lot of research on self-composting in the garden. This is not what it sounds like. I don't mean that I am composting myself (though eventually that's not a bad idea). What it really means is that I let the garden turn itself into compost.

Instead of spending a lot of time in fall tidying up the beds and borders, I just remove anything that looks unhealthy or that might smother a neighbor. Any plant that has enough natural architecture to stand up for itself gets to spend as much of the winter upright as possible. This is very attractive to birds, which love to harvest ripe seeds from perennials and annuals alike.

When plants start to slump or decay, I clean up their act, but not the way I used to. Instead of hauling all the pieces off to the compost pile, I simply clip what's left into small pieces. I use my trusty Felco pruning shears to cut stalks and stems into tidbits. If the plant they come from has a tender new crown emerging, I'll use the old leaves to give it a lightweight winter blanket. If not, I'll scatter the pieces around the border.

In very short order, the bits begin to compost. Since my beds are mulched with aged dairy manure and compost anyway, the new pieces blend in unobtrusively. The immediate beneficiaries of this simple practice are the birds, which love to rootle around in loose duff. They are looking for worms, which they tend to find, since loose, airy layers of decaying plants are primo worm territory.

The scuffling birds mix and remix the raw compost for me, so it cycles into real compost pretty fast. By spring, the clipped bits have become a nutritious breakfast for thousands of tiny soil organisms that in turn feed my plants.

Because not all plants are so cooperative, I still do maintain an active compost heap, as well as many static piles. Active heaps contain roughly equal mixtures of carbon-based materials (such as dried leaves) and nitrogen-rich materials such as grass clippings and salad trimmings.

Static piles are for slow compost. Anything too big to rot fast can be tossed on the slow heap. Over time (we are talking a year or so), the finer things will break down, leaving the bigger bits (such as branches) behind. When you want to use your slow compost, you move it. The big, coarse pieces are the base for the new slow pile, and the finer stuff gets used as compost.

Birds also love slow heaps, since they offer a lot of protection and often a good food supply (worms and bugs) as well. Indeed, many kinds of wildlife benefit from slow heaps, which may house a surprising number of creatures, from bugs, bees, and butterflies to frogs, birds, and snakes. Our native snakes are nonpoisonous, and most eat slugs to boot, so they are very welcome in my garden.

This fall, instead of cleaning up the garden all at once, consider converting to the self-mulching technique. Move slowly, shredding only plants that are starting to slump on their own. By spring, the garden will be tasting the fruits of your slow but steady progress, the beds will look great, and you will have made a lot of birds happy.

THE ROLE OF EDITING

Editing is the process by which we keep the growing garden under control. Editing with a light hand is best, and it is ideally done as frequently as grooming. Indeed, editing is part of the grooming cycle, which can include removal or replacement of whole plants. Editing often means making choices about what stays and what goes in a garden group. Sometimes a combination that has been pleasing for a number of years is suddenly out of whack. One member of the combo may have grown too fast or too slowly, and it's time for some shovel pruning. You may also decide to substitute a new plant for one that seems less exciting than when you first met it.

Sometimes, though, when you do edit in a new choice, that new plant simply won't perform in its new setting. This does not necessarily mean that you did anything wrong; even when we make careful, informed planting

The art of editing lies in maintaining an overall balance. Be sure fast-growing perennials don't overtake the slow-growing woody plants, and give each plant the room it needs to express its natural shape. The O'Byrne garden in Eugene, Oregon, is a sumptuous example of a brilliantly balanced garden.

choices, the specifics of the given site will dictate how those plants behave. Wise gardeners are always ready for some surprises, both serendipitous and not so swell. Sometimes plants we have known and grown elsewhere astonish us by displaying utterly unsuspected manners or attributes in a new setting. Plants said to be timid turn into thugs in our gardens, or plants that are monsters in other situations become kittenish and need coaxing and compost to settle into a new site.

THUGS AND SLACKERS

Thugs are plants that adapt all too well to garden life. Some plants, like golden loose strife *(Lysimachia ciliata)* are rowdy only when given certain conditions, such as damp soil. Others, like bishop's weed *(Aegopodium podagraria)* are capable of penetrating a concrete sidewalk over time, no matter how little they are encouraged. Part of successful editing is removing such plants from choice spots and putting them in more challenging places where their rampant energies may be just what is needed.

On the opposite end of the spectrum are the plants that won't thrive no matter how well you treat them. Whether they be uppity roses or lowly rhubarbs that misbehave, remove and give away or compost all slacker plants that refuse to respond to feeding or extra care.

Both editing and grooming help us to maintain a watchful intervention that keeps the garden growing more or less as it should. Plants are alive and seem to have minds of their own at times. They seldom follow our rules, they don't read labels, and they definitely don't always do what we expect of them. We can't always control our plants, but we can reduce the unhappy surprises by using our own experience and accumulated wisdom to predict what is likely to happen in the garden. For instance, I can predict with certainty that if I don't write a note in my garden journal to stake those tall asters in May, I won't remember to do it until the lanky stems collapse after a brisk June windstorm. Quite often, the time when we spot a potential or present problem is not the right time to solve it. As we groom and make our editing choices, jotting them down in our journal helps to translate plans into action at the proper season.

CHOOSING REPLACEMENTS WISELY AND WELL

It is very easy to lose our heads in nurseries, buying plants we can't use just because they look great. On the other hand, when you see something really special, it is a good idea to grab it rather than resist, since it is likely to be gone by the time you decide several weeks later you really do need it. Balancing these dual concerns is smart, because unless we are both experienced and savvy, buying plants mainly on impulse is usually pretty wasteful.

Instead, keep lists of problem areas in your wallet, along with ideas for plants that might work in each spot. That way, you are buying with a purpose and can make more informed, less sentimental choices. It's also useful to develop lists of plant families you can always make room for. For example, I use a lot of anemones, euphorbias, hebes, meadow rues, and sages in my garden. If I'm shopping to fill gaps, I would feel fine about impulse buys of great-looking plants from any of those families, knowing they will perform reliably for me. With less well-known candidates for refill position, it's important to assess each plant with care. Be judicious when replacing poor choices, since it's silly to replace one problem with another.

That said, go ahead and try new plants that intrigue

you. Unless they belong to known thug families, give unknown beauties a try if you are drawn to them, even if you suspect they may not work out. Why not? Would it really be so awful if a given combination wasn't just right and needed further adjustment, or if our border beauty proved a flop? When our cultural perfectionism drives us to limit ourselves for fear of failure, we lose an important freedom: the right to be wrong. Most people agree that we learn more from mistakes than from easy successes, yet few of us are willing to risk making our mistakes in public. Well, our gardens are our havens, and what better place to do our learning than in the comfort of our own home?

Gardening is an art, not a quantifiable, hard science. There are many ways to be right, and it's hard to go wrong when we are following our tastes and inclinations. Yes, we might easily pick a dud plant or put something in a less than optimal place, but that's what shovels are for. We shovel-prune out the duds and move the almost-winners until we find the place that pleases them and us. Some folks say plants should come with wheels, because some of us move them so often. Again, editing does not imply that you made an error. It may mean that your taste is changing, that your eye is improving, that you are learning new skills or honing old ones. I often say that the best gardeners I know are playful, inventive, and flexible, allowing their plants to drive the design of the garden. When we make a point of trying new plants each year, of actively seeking out new things to try, we help our gardens to stretch and grow along with us. As we gain experience, we slowly refine our skills until our gardens gain the depth and polish that turn raw natural beauty into fine art.

WATERING:
TIMING AND TECHNIQUES

Here in the Northwest, water was long considered to be something we had far too much of. Sure, the summers were dry, but my, oh my, those endless winters surely brought enough to last forever. Today we recognize that clean, safe water is a very precious commodity indeed. In communities of all sizes, water is becoming expensive. Even rural gardeners who irrigate from a well may find that their once-adequate water supply shrinks as new homes appear on all sides.

During hot summer months, when usage is especially

high, water is often in short supply in city and countryside alike. Each spring, government officials warn us that unless we can learn better habits, water rationing may become common instead of rare. Cycles that we used to rely on aren't working as they used to; as global weather patterns shift, even our traditional wet winters are becoming less reliable. As a result, the days of recklessly spraying water galore over lawns and gardens (and usually spilling merrily over sidewalks and streets) are gone forever.

The good news is that watering is simpler and more efficient than ever. Today gardeners have access both to good information about plants' needs and to excellent watering technology. When I started gardening long, long ago, drip irrigation was strictly for nerdy engineer types with math degrees. The first system I tried to install was so frustrating that I hid it in the barn, unwilling to admit that I had spent a lot of money on something so complicated that just trying to read the directions made my mind go numb. Now drip systems have been simplified to the point that anybody willing to spend an hour learning a few easy techniques can master their use. If you are growing vegetables or have a lot of containers and hanging baskets, drip irrigation can save you time, water, and worry and leave you with happy plants.

Drip irrigation systems, especially those with lots of movable parts, are less practical for complex ornamental gardens. Better choices for beds and borders include improving soil, deep mulching with compost, and replacing water hogs with plants that prefer dry summers and wet winters.

As you renovate the beds and replace unworthy plants, consider installing simple soaker hoses, tubes punctuated with tiny holes that release water slowly into the soil. Soaker hoses work by capillary action, webbing the water in sheets sideways through the soil. To do this properly, soaker lines need to be covered with at least 4 inches of mulch, as it says in microscopic print on the back of each label. They are absolutely least efficient when left uncovered on the surface of the soil, where they deliver a very thin band of water instead of a wide sheet.

Made from recycled tires, these inexpensive hoses come in several qualities; the kind sold as "lifetime" soakers are indeed long lasting. Cheaper versions may degrade quickly, especially if exposed to direct sunlight (thus,

CHOOSING HOSES

Not all hoses are created equal. My favorites are hard to kink, even when you're winding your way between pots and planters. Good hoses remain flexible even in cold weather, so you can coil them easily any time of year. The best will keep on flowing even when you accidentally park on top of them.

Before you buy a hose, undo the twist-ties and flip the label over. You may be amazed by what is written on the underside. Many hoses carry a disclaimer on the label that reads, "This hose is not intended for drinking water use. Warning: This product contains a chemical known to the State of California to cause cancer. Warning: This product contains a chemical known to the State of California to cause birth defects or other reproductive harm."

This is your clue that it is *not* a good idea to drink—or to let your kids drink—from this or any other untreated hose. Personally, I would not even fill their kiddy splash pool with this type of hose or use one on the vegetable patch. I buy only hoses that are clearly marked as drinking water quality and are guaranteed to

mulching over them also increases their useful life span). The wise will fasten the hose end cap to the hose with a bit of wire, making sure it won't ever get lost. If the lines are left open when not in use, they become infested with slugs and bugs, making it hard to pass water through properly.

In my own garden, soaker hoses are mainly used with permanent plantings of shrubs and trees. I do water all trees for two or three seasons, and most shrubs get watered through at least two summers. All mixed border plantings are given soaker hoses to get them through their first summer. After that, I rely on the fact that many plants will get by nicely on their own as long as they are well mulched. Just in case, the hoses are left in place, so that should a really hot spell arrive, they are ready to use.

WATER-SMART GARDENS

Visitors are often surprised to hear that my gardens seldom need supplemental water, despite the fact that I live where summer rains are rare. (Typically this particular part of the maritime Northwest receives little measurable rain from mid-May well into October.) The reason the beds and borders don't need much water is that I planned them that way. By making great soil and feeding it well, I can offer my plants good growing conditions. By mulching deeply, I help my soil stay evenly moist. By choosing plants that like both my kind of soil (acid clay) and Northwestern weather (dry summers, wet winters), I can create a matrix of plants that are less needy and more resilient than a random mix of border beauties.

The keys to reducing water needs are threefold:

- Soil preparation
- Plant selection
- Mulching well and at the right time (when the ground is saturated)

When I do need to water the ornamental gardens, I use a combination of soaker lines under deep mulch and overhead sprinklers. It is very true that overhead sprinklers are inefficient, losing water to evaporation. However, today even inexpensive sprinklers are easy to manipulate so that the spray goes exactly where you want it, not all over the neighborhood. We can also now buy spot sprinklers that deliver water evenly to an area as small as 3 by 4 feet. By watering in the morning, rather than at night, we can reduce evaporation losses and avoid health problems that arise when plants face the cooler night temperatures with wet leaves.

These inexpensive, low-tech systems work well for my garden, largely because I water only a few times each summer, if at all. Even within the Pacific Northwest region, climatic variations lead to diverse bioregions, so your garden's needs may be very different. If you find that despite great soil preparation, thoughtful plant selection, and deep mulches of compost, you still need to water once a month or more in summer, visit the library and look for books on xeriscaping. This creative approach to gardening involves using only plants that are reliably drought tolerant in your region. Even so, anything you plant you will need to water for the first season or two, and soil building and compost mulching will still be important. However, once those solidly drought-resistant plants are well established, they will become relatively independent. Flexible, adaptive models such as naturalistic layered gardens and xeriscapes (gardens and landscapes designed not to require supplemental water, even in dry climates) are setting us free from slavery to the hose.

TOO LITTLE, TOO LATE

On the other hand, you may prefer to develop a more efficient watering routine rather than change all your plants. If you aren't sure whether your plants need more water than they are getting, observe them well. If they look fine in the morning, droop during the heat of the day, and then cheer up in the cool of the evening, they are getting enough water. If they look sad and flaccid early and late as well as at midday, they aren't. Until you know your garden's watering needs well, it's better to give each bed an inch of water (enough to fill a tuna can) a week than to hold off until your plants are stressed.

Once the ground is deeply dried out, it can be difficult to get it thoroughly wet again. If you want to cut back on watering, check the soil by digging a few inches down; if it feels damp, wait a week and check again. If it feels dry all the way through the root zone, it's time to water. However, when soil is bone dry, it sheds water. Before you can water effectively, you must soften the surface crust. If you don't, the sidewalk will be full of runoff before you know it. The driveway will be puddled up, but the garden will

remain safe for the hose's lifetime. With reasonably careful use, these high-quality hoses last a long, long time. They cost a little more than bargain hoses, but not much (usually about $5 extra), and in this case, at least, you do get what you pay for.

Where drinking water is not an issue and space is short, I use the new heavyweight coiled hoses. These stretch to 50 or 75 feet but coil up like a slinky toy when not in use. Don't buy narrow, flimsy, lightweight ones with cheap fittings. It's worth spending a little more to get a good-quality, full-sized coiling hose, because it makes watering on decks or boats or in other tight places a pleasure instead of a penance.

be dry again an hour after you finish watering. What's happening is what gardeners call crusting, when the top inch or so of mulch or soil has dried into an almost impenetrable crust. Rather than soaking into the soil, water simply sheets off the crust.

The obvious solution is to add moisture-retaining soil amendments. Sadly, certain common soil amendments actually contribute to crusting. The worst of the bunch is peat moss, which when dry sheets water like oilcloth. In the short term, you can usually get through a crust by sprinkling the whole area for two or three minutes or until the water starts to run off. Stop watering, wait ten minutes, and then sprinkle again. This time you may find you can water for five minutes before runoff begins. Wait ten minutes more, and then sprinkle again. Each time, the water will penetrate a bit further through the crust.

Hand watering is vital for healthy pots. Small pots may need watering several times a day in hot weather, so use the largest pots you can afford, since they are more sustainable and may only need watering every few days or once a week.

To avoid having to do this each time you want to water, renovate your mulch either in fall or spring, when the ground is wet deep down, thanks to natural rainfall. First, top off your beds with a deep mulch (3 to 4 inches) of either compost or composted dairy manure. Add the mulch when the soil is thoroughly wet, usually anytime between October and early May. Having got your soil well moistened, keep it that way. Depending on where you live, this may mean efficient if not frequent watering. Again, soaker lines are ideal, especially the flexible, half-inch hoses that drip evenly along their entire length.

The goal is to keep the top 12 inches of soil moist. Why? Because plants derive more than half of their nutritional needs from the top 12 inches of soil, and for most garden plants, the feeding process works best when soils are moist. Dry soil inhibits root growth and nutrient uptake. Damp soil encourages root growth and enhances nutrient uptake, as well as encouraging healthy soil flora. Unless you are growing bog plants, soggy soil is not desirable, since plants can drown if their roots can't get air. Properly moist soil allows both water and air to reach plant roots. Even moisture levels are especially important for new and young plants.

I never use irrigation systems in gardens, because they invariably overdeliver water, causing waterlogging, breaking down soil texture, and fostering root rots. Unfortunately, it is also possible to overwater with soaker hoses, simply by letting them run too long. Once your soil is properly wet, you may find that it takes as little as ten minutes of soaker hose watering once a week, or even less often, to keep it that way. You'll have to do the digging test to find out (just test once or twice—not every day). Let the top few inches of soil dry out between waterings, but you don't want it to get bone-dry.

Once you figure out how much you need to water, it becomes a routine chore that doesn't take much fussing. When I need to water, I use a small kitchen timer to remind me to change the hoses as needed. When the timer dings, I turn off one hose and turn on the next. To water whole sections at once, you can attach several soaker hoses to solid hoses that connect back to the faucet. If you get bored easily or travel a lot, you can buy timers that attach to the hose bibb. They can be set to run for as little as ten minutes and as seldom as once a week. Wise watering is totally worth the moderate effort required, since it results in less wasted water and much happier plants.

MAINTAINING GARDEN TREES AND SHRUBS

Whether in foundation plantings and hedges or placed about the garden, your trees and shrubs will need regular attention for the first few seasons and an annual checkup after that. If you follow the principles of sustainable design when selecting, placing, and planting your woody plants, you'll find that they return a great deal of beauty, privacy screening, and seasonal effects without taking much of your time. Indeed, well-chosen, well-placed, well-planted trees and shrubs need surprisingly little

GUIDELINES FOR SHRUB CARE

- Apply compost mulches in late winter (February or March) and again in fall (September or October), spreading compost very thinly near the main trunk and more thickly out past the dripline.

- All shrubs will need to be watered regularly for at least two years after being planted. In hot weather, they may need supplemental water once or twice a week. By the third year, established woody plants that are well suited to your site and the Northwestern climate ought to be as self-sufficient in terms of water as your natives.

- If the autumn is dry (unusual, but not unknown), continue watering until the first hard frost. Plants that go into winter with dry roots are more prone to frost damage than properly watered ones.

Continued on page 150

ongoing maintenance. Annual compost mulches keep most woody plants healthy for many years. Apply these mulches in late winter and again in fall, spreading compost thinly at the main trunk and more deeply (3 to 4 inches) to about 2 feet beyond the drip line. If plants look hungry or seem to be growing very slowly, add a mild feeding mulch (see Chapter 3) or use a mild all-purpose fertilizer (such as a 5-5-5; see Chapter 6) in late April or early May. Lightly scratch 1 or 2 cups of this into the compost around each tree or large shrub. Smaller shrubs need only about 1 cup.

- When certain evergreen shrubs turn yellow over the winter, they probably need iron. Camellias, rhododendrons, and bamboo are especially prone to iron deficiency. Add 1 tablespoon of liquid iron to a gallon of water, and water in well. The afflicted plant should green up within a month. If not, take a sample into a nursery for a diagnosis.

ESTABLISHING NATIVE TREES AND SHRUBS

Selecting trees and shrubs with a pleasing natural habit helps eliminate the need for regular pruning and shaping. Here, designer Eamon Hughes has integrated a handsome array of woody plants with perennials, using plant picks and spacing that allow for mature growth without crowding.

Native trees and shrubs are usually self-sufficient once established. However, even highly drought-tolerant plants need help to get established. An established plant is one that is growing strongly, producing sturdy new growth, and demonstrating good drought tolerance. Given our generally wet autumns, it's best to establish woody plants in early fall, thus reducing the need to supplement their water supply.

Mulch native trees and shrubs with compost to help them become established. Keeping a young tree or shrub well mulched for a few years can make a big difference in growth rate and habit. If you like, supplement this mulch with a mild all-purpose fertilizer (5-5-5 is fine) or a feeding mulch of compost and alfalfa (see Chapter 3). This modest investment of time and energy earns you a larger, healthier, and better-looking plant.

Once natives are well established in a natural environment, they will probably need only occasional light pruning to remove damaged limbs or to guide exuberant growth. There is no need to provide mulch, but if you are mingling natives and exotics, mulching the whole planting once a year is both attractive and healthful.

WATERING THIRSTY SHRUBS

Shrubs vary in their need for water, and if our aim is to create a sustainable garden, it is very important to consider which plants prefer damp shade or full sun and dry soil before placing them in the garden. As with larger woody plants, even when we can offer our shrubs conditions they like, they will need to be watered well for their first two years and situationally watered (during dry or hot spells) for another year or so before becoming independent. When watering new shrubs, be sure each one gets at least 5 gallons of water at each watering, directing most of it to the feeder roots, which are concentrated on both sides of each plant's dripline (extending for 1 to 2 feet). Water the roots, not the foliage.

All shrubs and trees, native or not, need at least 5 gallons of water each time you water through the first summer and perhaps the second, as well. Native shrubs like salal are totally drought-tolerant once established, with strong new growth each season.

Some shrubs, such as hydrangeas, will flag sadly in dry years, even when planted in good soil and well mulched. It's worth clustering thirsty shrubs in the garden and winding a soaker hose around their feet. When dry summers make your shrubs look sad, run the soaker once a week until the rains return.

UNSHEARING SHRUBS

Unsheared hedges that are gently shaped instead of constantly clipped tend to be healthier and live longer than overpruned ones. A yard full of bowling balls, gumdrops, and pincushions will look a great deal less contrived if these artificial shapes are allowed to relax into real ones. Gardens that already contain mature sheared hedges and freestanding clipped shrubs can be transitioned into natural ones by a process called unshearing. The term was coined by Cass Turnbull, founder of Plant Amnesty. Turnbull excels at taming unruly plants, and her simple, logical techniques can be applied by anybody, anywhere. Over time, these remedial pruning techniques can restore congested plants to their natural state.

Dense, overly sheared plants are stressed because such tight growth restricts the amount of light and air that can reach the plants' core. Once a plant has been opened up a bit, it can return to its normal, healthy growth patterns. This makes them far more attractive to birds, who shun sheared hedges and plants in favor of loose, open, naturally shaped ones, which offer better cover and more feeding opportunities.

A badly oversheared plant may take several years of partial, step-by-step unpruning to be fully restored to its authentic shape. Most, however, will respond to the initial unshearing session with a flush of healthy new growth that leads to a less artificial appearance in just a few seasons.

Where hedge plants are really too big for the site, you can make them both healthier and less artificial looking by following the unshearing directions given here. Each year, you unshear tight older growth and also reduce bulky new growth. Unshearing helps control the overall size of any unsuitable but already in-place hedge plant. Unsheared plants will need feeding mulches and extra water for a season to make up for the foliage loss (foliage contains both nitrogen-producing chlorophyll and many stored nutrients). Ideally, however, we would replace unsuitable plants with others of more appropriate mature size, rather than perpetuate the endless chore cycle required by oversized hedges.

Even if you decide that you prefer formal, sheared plants at your entryway, you may also decide to let your plants take their own shapes in less public areas. Why not at least create a wild garden in an unused corner of the

yard, layering unsheared shrubs into the ruffled, stair-step shapes that birds find most inviting?

To reduce the resprouting response, it's best to prune trees and shrubs in late winter (mid-February into March) or in midsummer (July and August). Summer pruning (July or August) of suckers on fruit trees or hedge shrubs will trigger less of a replacement response from your tree than spring pruning will.

However, when you unshear hedges or shrubs is less important than how you do it. For starters, always use sharp pruning tools that cut cleanly without tearing bark or mashing stems. Replace anvil pruners with scissor-action or bypass pruners, which are used by arborists and professional pruners. Those clunky old anvil pruners are known in certain circles as "the nurseryman's best friend" because the damage they inflict regularly sends gardeners back to the nursery for replacement trees and shrubs.

MAKING THE CUTS

Clean pruning is critical to success. When you remove twigs and small branches, make clean cuts that leave no stubs. Before making your initial cut, touch the branch and find the collar, a gentle swelling that occurs where each twig comes off a branch and where each branch

To avoid pruning, place shrubs and trees where they can achieve their full size without blocking a path, sidewalk, driveway, entryway, or access point of any kind. To learn how big plants will get, visit mature gardens, parks, and arboretae and take notes. Pieris japonica is an elegant slow grower worth making space for.

comes off the trunk. The stems and branches on most trees and all shrubs with a main trunk and interior branching will have this little collar. Rather than cutting flush with the trunk or branch, start your cut just outside the collar. You'll notice that the branches on a few trees (notably pines) don't have any collar. If you can't find a collar on a given plant's twigs or branches, you can make flush cuts, trimming the stubs flat against the trunk. To find the angle for each cut, imagine that the branch is a hollow tube, and cut straight across it, so the removed piece could stand flat on its new cut if upended.

To avoid ripping bark and scarring trunks, always undercut large branches before removal. To do this, make a small preliminary cut into the underside of a heavy branch, so if it tears instead of breaking cleanly, you won't scar the bark on the tree's trunk. The undercut can be made several inches out from the trunk. When you trim the branch stub, tidy it back to the branch collar.

Begin the cutting process by removing all deadwood. Deadwood does not count against the total of live wood you can remove, so don't include what you remove now in your annual pruning total (you don't want to remove more than 20 to 25 percent of the total plant).

Now do some simple thinning, carefully opening the congested mass of the shrub to make its form airier. Always work from inside the shrub, getting as close as possible to its center. Look at the shrub carefully, observing its natural growth pattern. Next, evaluate the main branches, deciding which are structurally the most important. Note as well which branches lead to crowded outer areas and which might leave big gaps if removed. Remove any obviously damaged branches. Then look for misshapen branches or those that begin growing in one direction and then change course awkwardly. Begin by removing the worst-looking branches. As you work, pause to consider what each branch contributes before removing it. Be conservative; in many cases, taking off every ugly branch will leave you with no branches at all. Work as just described, cutting cleanly and leaving no stubs.

Once the dead and damaged bits are gone, reevaluate the shrub from the outside. The plant will look a great deal nicer now. However, what's left may still be pretty dense. If this is the case, remove all hangers (the downward-curving twigs that grow off the bottom of a large branch). Also remove all water shoots (twigs that sprout straight upward from a larger branch). Stop again and evaluate your work.

Often these few steps remove enough clutter to radically improve the overall look of the shrub. If your plant still looks badly formed or congested, mark the worst areas with colorful surveyors' tape. Significant thinning of a sheared shrub is best done from within, so crawl in as close to the shrub's center as you can get. Look for your marking tape and begin cleaning up those areas by removing dense, twiggy growth that seems to disguise rather than express the plant's natural form. Go slowly at first, and take frequent breaks to check your progress from the outside as well as the core of the plant. Better yet, get a pruning buddy to stand outside while you crawl in. You can gently pull back various branches while the outside partner tells you whether to cut it or not. Sometimes it is simply impossible to tell from inside the shrub how gaping a hole the removal of a given branch will cause. Never remove more than 20 to 25 percent of the foliage in a twelve-month period.

When decisions get tough and you aren't sure what to do next, stop. Give the plant time to recover and yourself time to assess how the plant's new shape looks before taking further steps. This may also be the time to call it quits and admit that a given shrub is simply too damaged to recover its natural good looks. Unless the plant is providing privacy or wind shelter or screening an important view, it may be a candidate for one of Turnbull's favorite techniques: shovel pruning, which involves removing the plant from the ground up, rootball and all.

Where the plant in question is providing an important service, such as privacy screening, consider planting its replacement as close to the old shrub as possible. If you need to prune back the old plant severely on one side to make room for the new, go ahead and cut it back all the way to the trunk. (In England, this is called "the National Trust Hedge cut.") Alternatively, you may decide to replace the old shrub with a freestanding section of fence, a trellis panel, or a bamboo screen to create immediate shelter and privacy until your replacement shrub comes of age.

After remedial pruning, mulch shrubs with compost, extending the carpet beyond the dripline about a foot. Water them well if the season is dry. Unless damage occurs, let shrubs have a year to recover before removing more wood. Badly mispruned plants may need to be patiently reshaped over a period of three to five years.

TURNING SHRUBS INTO TREES

When a freestanding shrub that is an excellent candidate for unshearing is really a small tree (such as English laurel, yew, holly, and certain boxwoods), you may need to make some choices before unleashing each and every sheared plant. Get a few tree and shrub books from the library to help you see what your garden might look like if the sheared plants were returned to natural forms. With these guidelines in mind, you might decide to remove some of them and try to renovate others. In the interest of increased sustainability, you may also choose to get rid of all the butchered plants and replace them with more appropriate choices.

Before you make this decision, consider that large sheared shrubs can sometimes be turned into attractive small trees with careful pruning (and that unsheared shrubs nearly always make this transition successfully). Look carefully at your plant, studying its natural form. Each branch you remove should help reveal that true form. Sheared or not, you begin by thinning and uncluttering the shrub. Like hedges, dense shrubs will benefit greatly from being thinned, since this process allows more light and air to penetrate to the center of the plant.

To figure out whether your shrub can be converted into an attractive small tree, take a look at how it's put together. Cane-growing or thicketing shrubs that toss up many small branches (think of forsythia and weigela) are not good candidates for treehood, because they lack a main trunk. Cane growers can put up with tight shearing for years, but it hopelessly distorts their growth habit. The best way to restore them is to cut them hard, which means back to within a few inches of the ground. These easygoing shrubs will quickly send up new growth from the roots. Thin the new shoots by cutting out the smallest, weakest, and most crowded stems and leaving a sturdy framework of large, healthy canes.

If, however, your sheared shrub has a main trunk (or several) with a lot of interior branching, it may well make a charming small tree. Camellias, privet, and low-growing Japanese maples are good examples of shrubs that can be

Start pruning a shrub by removing all "hangers." This will often lift the skirt of a shrub or a tree limb enough to eliminate the need for further pruning.

elevated to treehood. The process involves gradually lifting the skirts of any bushy shrub that is well branched to the ground. Tidy up the trunk (which may have several leaders or main trunks) by removing small twigs and dead branches, and you have a very small tree.

Naturally, the final canopy level can be as high or as low as you like. There is no "right" height to shoot for; the optimal height for each plant will reflect both the appearance of the newly revealed trunk(s), the bulk of the plant, and the scale of your garden as a whole. Professional pruners refer to this interesting process as "arborizing." Good candidates for arborizing include andromeda (*Pieris* species), rhododendrons, laurels, and boxwoods, among many others.

If you aren't really sure how the plant will look as a tree, but you aren't crazy about how it looks now, why not give arborizing a try?

It's important not to rush this process, so take your time when renovating large shrubs. As with shrub thinning, you start by climbing in and looking round. Generally, it's wise to work with a partner standing outside the shrub who can offer guidance. When you aren't sure which branches to take, wiggle each candidate or lower it a bit (gently, to avoid breakage) so your partner can see how the shrub might look without it. Should you make a mistake and remove a branch that leaves an unsightly gap, remove a few hangers from branches below the gap to lift the lower branches and hide the hole.

Start by removing all branches that touch the ground. With the trunk revealed, evaluate whether the shrub would look best with all its trunks or just one. Mark key branches and trunks that you want to keep with brightly colored plastic surveyor's tape at several points along their length.

Now remove extra trunks or branches, cutting trunks as close to the ground as possible. Undercut large branches to avoid tearing bark should the branches break before you complete your cut.

Next, remove all hangers (the downward-curving twigs that grow off the bottom of a large branch), without leaving any stubs. This alone may elevate the remaining branches to the desired canopy height. Also remove all water shoots (twigs that sprout straight upward from a larger branch), again leaving no stubs; the goal is to be able to run your hand smoothly over a branch without catching on anything.

To adjust the canopy to its final height, continue working from the bottom of the shrub, carefully following the lowest-hanging branches to their source rather than simply cutting branches off starting at the bottom of the shrub. The lowest-hanging branches may well stem from branches that begin high up on the main trunk, and branches that begin lower down may well end up high on the shrub. Before removing any large branch, be sure it does not leave an awkward gap in your desired skirt line.

MAINTAINING TREES

Trees that are properly chosen, carefully placed, and planted with care are rarely needy creatures. Once established, ornamental trees that are well suited to your site and the Northwestern climate ought to be as self-sufficient in terms of care and water as natives.

PRUNING TREES

Well-placed, well-chosen trees will not need routine pruning. Removing the deadwood is generally sufficient to keep trees healthy. Damaged branches broken during winter storms can be removed in late winter, while the plant is dormant.

As your trees expand over the years, however, it may become necessary to edit their size and shape a bit to help them continue to fit well in your gardenscape. Often, simply removing a few lower branches to elevate the canopy of a tree will leave plenty of room for enlarging shrubby neighbors. If not, you may want to consider removing a few of those shrubs instead.

As with shrubs, never remove more than 20 to 25 percent of a tree over the course of a full year or twelve-month period. This means that if you pruned a tree last fall and are having another go at it in the spring, you must include what you removed last fall with what you plan to take away in the spring to get your twelve-month total. Deadwood does not count, but even damaged wood that is clearly past recovery counts to the tree, which may have only recently lost this nutritional resource. Always spread extensive pruning jobs over several years.

Healthy wood should be taken off respectfully and only after spending some time considering alternative approaches. It's also a good idea to consider what this particular type of tree is actually supposed to look like in its natural state. Never top a tree for any reason; tree topping is destructive, ugly, and dangerous. It is far better to remove a troubled or troublesome tree entirely and replace it with a healthy, more appropriately sized substitute. A good arborist will never top a tree.

View corridors can often be opened for your own home or for your neighbors by careful and selective thinning and/or limb removal. Major limb removal must be done properly to avoid creating a wind sail effect that leaves the tree vulnerable in the next big windstorm.

GUIDELINES FOR TREE CARE

- All trees need to be watered regularly for at least two full years after planting. Give each tree at least 5 gallons of water each time you water it.

- In hot weather, newly planted trees may need supplemental water once or twice a week.

- In dry years, continue watering until the first hard frost.

- Mulch trees with compost annually, feathering it out from an inch-deep layer at the trunk to a layer 4 to 6 inches deep near the tree's dripline (and extending at least 2 feet beyond the dripline). This area will clearly get larger as the tree matures.

- Trees planted in grass or ground covers still need a feeding mulch. Keep the mulch layer light enough that it does not smother your ground covers. Two or three inches each spring should be plenty.

Before hiring an arborist, get references and check them out. If there is a branch of Plant Amnesty in your region, call them for recommendations. Even if there isn't, you can get excellent, highly informative pamphlets and booklets about pruning from this determined group. Plant Amnesty also sells an excellent pruning video, which is available in either English or Spanish. Indeed, it is worth joining this group no matter where you live, since members receive monthly newsletters with terrific pruning and tool care tips. See the Resources section at the end of this book for contact information.

MAINTAINING PERENNIALS

Keeping well-chosen, properly placed and planted perennials happy is not difficult. Plants whose essential needs are met remain content with only moderate care. Newly planted perennials must be kept adequately moist for their entire first season. Once established, many are relatively drought tolerant, particularly if given a deep (2- to 4-inch) layer of manure or compost mulch. Renewed each spring and fall, mulch conserves moisture, suppresses weeds, and supplies a measure of protection from frost. If supplemented with alfalfa pellets in spring and seed meal (soy or cotton) in fall, a blend of compost and aged manure becomes a feeding mulch that supplies perennials with all necessary nutrients.

Over the long term, perennials do best with a steady but slowly released supply of nutrients. Plants raised on liquid fertilizers in a nursery may require spot-feeding with commercial fertilizer during their first season. If overfed newcomers dwindle after planting, give them a half-strength dose of liquid or foliar feed. Most will respond immediately, gaining back their lost looks in a few days. Once established, nearly all will be satisfied with a biannual feeding mulch.

Grooming is a constant chore, but the more often it is performed, the lighter the task. The goal is tidiness, not prissy perfection. Daily or weekly, it involves removing spent flowers and damaged or browning foliage. This keeps the garden looking pleasantly kempt and the gardener delightfully aware of its state and subtle changes.

Frequent deadheading (removal of fading flowers) stimulates prolonged and repeated bloom in many perennials. In general, this involves cutting flower stems back to the next set of leaves, where side shoots and buds are often found. As autumn draws near, the need for grooming increases. Messy floppers must be trimmed back, but by allowing upright grasses and statuesque perennials to remain in place, we discover which ones hold their drama into winter.

Be vigilant in observing your perennials, for problems solved quickly remain minor. Yellowing or puckered foliage, stunted growth, and buds that rot before they can open are common symptoms that indicate health problems. Any or all may be caused by crowding, compacted soil, or poor planting techniques. If so, you can correct the problem will by altering the improper condition. If not, discard or burn seriously diseased plants (never put them on the compost heap, where they may spread trouble).

Most insect damage can be controlled with a quick rinse from the hose or a dose of insecticidal soap. If intractable problems develop, dig up the suffering plant and check the roots; when one plant suffers while others thrive, the culprit is often root damage, which invisibly signals distress to potential attackers.

Editing is also a constant job. Keep an eye on your compositions, watching for any loss of balance as proportions alter with time. If certain plants outgrow their partners, remove at least half of the offender to restore the original relationship. Better yet, replace it with another, less rowdy companion. Remove slackers that fail to perform and don't respond to feeding or extra care. Get rid as well of plants that do too well, lest they overrun choicer companions. Be judicious when replacing poor choices, but never hesitate to take a few risks.

STAKING PERENNIALS

When selecting perennials, give preference to sturdy, self-supporting plants, but also learn how and when to use stakes. (Stake plants in early spring, long before the need is obvious.) Even in the best of circumstances, certain plants will need some unobtrusive assistance to stand tall. Where heavy summer rains are common, staking will prevent or minimize the collapse of your prized delphiniums. In exposed, windy gardens, many perennials will be better off for early and ample staking.

There are dozens of ways to keep plants upright, from simple webs of sticks and string to expensive hoops and

GUIDELINES FOR STAKING PLANTS

- For long-stemmed plants like delphiniums, give each blooming stem its own stake.

- Unless the aboveground portion of the stakes is almost as tall as the main stems will be, wind can snap the tops off.

- Place stakes 5 to 6 inches out from the plant crowns to avoid damaging roots.

- Sink stakes at least a foot into the ground (use a rubber mallet).

- As stems grow, secure them to the stakes, tying in every 12 to 18 inches of new growth.

- Tie plants to supports with soft twine, rather than stiff plastic, which can cut delicate stems and foliage.

- A short row of linked stakes will keep heavy plants like tall, arching *Crocosmia* 'Lucifer' in line.

Continued on page 164

linking systems. The goal is always the same: to design effective but nearly invisible support systems.

Many materials work well for plant supports. Thick green or black bamboo wands are sturdy and inconspicuous but short-lived. Plastic stakes are usually ugly colors, and they can bend or break when used on heavy plants. Slim steel rebar is even stronger and lasts forever, and its dull silver soon discolors to a rusty brown that disappears like camouflage into the background. The smallest gauge is called pencil bar. This can be bent very easily and makes great supports for smaller perennials. Quarter-inch rebar must be bent with tools (a pipe bender works very nicely) but makes very sturdy supports that can hold anything from wet peonies to towering monkshoods with aplomb.

Mounding plants like peonies and Oriental poppies splay open when wet, but short-legged border hoops or half-domes of chicken wire will keep them properly in place. Taller tomato cages can be woven with twiggy willow strands to disguise the shiny metal. These will lend support to tall monkshoods and verbascums that look unnaturally stiff if tied to stakes.

WINTER CARE FOR HALF-HARDY PERENNIALS

Many half-hardy or borderline hardy perennials can be overwintered easily in the colder parts of the Northwest. Heat lovers like the Mexican sages, South African honey bush (*Melianthus major*), and New Zealand flaxes often struggle with the combination of cold winds and wet clay soils. Most of these plants will not tolerate standing water in winter, and all will grow best where drainage is brisk. To coax them to stick around, give half-hardy perennials full sun and good garden soil, and be prepared to water them through their first few summers (especially during hot or dry spells).

To come through harsh winters, these semitropical plants require protection from frost; a deep, airy mulch of shredded leaves; and a loose covering of fir boughs.

For insurance take tip, stem, or root cuttings of tender plants (see the next section). In cool regions, protect summer-rooted tip cuttings or autumn root divisions in a frost-free location over the winter.

MAKING MORE PERENNIALS

Most perennials are easy to propagate, and a single mature plant can provide plenty of offspring to fill new beds or trade with friends. Indeed, strong growers require periodic division to stay healthy. For instance daylilies, hostas, and Siberian iris become congested and bloom poorly unless divided regularly. If a mature perennial starts to look unhappy, blooms scantily, or has unusually small foliage, it may be ready to divide. It may also be hungry; plants that seem to be shrinking should be fed rather than divided.

Perennials are usually propagated by making divisions, splitting a large plant into many smaller ones. In proper English borders, fast growers are divided every three or four years, before they become too bulky to handle easily. Slower growers need be divided only when they outgrow their allotted position.

Division is most commonly performed in spring and fall. When possible, work on cool, overcast days to avoid damaging fragile roots. As a rule of thumb, divide early bloomers late and late bloomers early. There are a few basic techniques for division, depending on root type. All begin by digging up the mother plant and shaking off excess soil.

Tall, brittle perennials like delphiniums need staking early, before they reach their full height. To avoid staking, choose stronger stemmed plants like sea hollies or joe pye weed that won't blow over even when wet.

Practice perennial division on easy plants like hostas and grasses. Divide hostas in fall and grasses in spring for best results.

Clumping plants with multiple crowns, such as daylilies and hostas, can be teased apart when young, but older plants must be sliced apart and smaller pieces shaken loose. Border and Siberian iris have plump storage roots called rhizomes that snap into pieces, each with a tuft of foliage. Plants with netted, fibrous roots, like *Coreopsis* 'Moonbeam', can be gently ripped into chunks. In all cases, the woody central bits should be discarded and the younger pieces reset in fresh soil.

ROOT CUTTINGS

To take root cuttings from tender perennials, dig up pieces of the thick storage roots. Cut them in 2-inch pieces and set them, top side up, in pots of sandy soil. Cover these cuttings with muslin or row cover (such as Reemay) to conserve moisture. Water them weekly with willow water (see box), which contains natural rooting hormones. In winter, protect them from frost by putting the pots in a cold frame, an unheated greenhouse, or the garage.

TIP CUTTINGS

Many perennials can be propagated by taking soft tip cuttings in early summer to midsummer (May through early August). Pinch the tips (1- to 2-inch pieces) from the stems of leggy perennials such as asters, phlox, and tall sedums, and stick them in pots of sandy soil. Cover tip cuttings with muslin or row cover (such as Reemay) to conserve moisture. Water them weekly with willow water (see box), which contains natural rooting hormones.

STEM CUTTINGS

Certain perennials, notably slow-growing variegated ones, are best increased by taking stem cuttings. For example, variegated comfrey *(Symphytum* x *uplandicum)* won't come true from root cuttings and resents disturbance. To propagate it, remove a few sturdy side shoots, cut them into 6-inch lengths, and stick them in pots of sandy soil. Cover these cuttings with muslin or row cover (such as Reemay) to conserve moisture. Water them weekly with willow water (see sidebar, next page), which contains natural rooting hormones.

- Shorter plants, like *Gaura* 'Whirling Butterflies', can be given a supportive hoop skirt of pea sticks—stout, twiggy branches (cut from fruit trees, hazel, or alder) that are set firmly into the ground near the crown of flopsy perennials.

- When unstaked plants start to tumble, prevent disaster by weaving cat's cradles of dark string between the stems and anchoring the web to several short but stout stakes.

- After fixing a problem, make a note in your garden journal, writing ahead to the coming spring to remind yourself to stake that plant on time next year.

MAINTAINING GROUND COVERS

Over time, ground cover plantings can exhaust their soil and become tired looking. To replenish a large area of ground covers without ripping up everything, remove hand-sized patches from every foot or so of covered ground. Fill these empty spots in with compost and scatter on some corn gluten to keep weeds out. Within a few weeks, the ground cover will be filling in the blank spots with renewed vigor. The removed plants can be passed on to newer gardeners, composted, or used to start new areas of ground cover.

To keep established ground covers fit and avoid soil exhaustion, give them a mulch of compost (2 to 3 inches) in spring and again in fall. A light scattering of corn gluten pellets (20 pounds per 1,000 square feet) offers plenty of nitrogen and also keeps weed seeds from germinating. This can be done every few months during the growing season.

Most ground covers are quite drought tolerant once established. Deep watering (to at least 1 inch) once a month during prolonged dry spells will help even the hardiest to thrive under stress. Otherwise, well-chosen ground covers should not need regular watering once they are established. In fact, overwatering can rot out established plantings or cause diseases in drought-tolerant plants. If your yard is outfitted with an automatic watering system, shut off the heads that direct water to ground cover areas once the plants have filled in well.

MULCHING BULBS

All bulbs will benefit from a fall mulch of compost and aged manure. (Even bulbs that don't want to be touched by manure-based compost appreciate a top-dressing.) For deeply planted bulbs, you can pile on a thick (3- to 6-inch) layer of mulch. Shallowly planted bulbs such as Madonna lilies, hardy cyclamen, and Guernsey lilies prefer a light (1-inch) mulch.

All bulbs will also benefit from a spring mulch, again composed of compost and aged manure. This will help prevent mud splash from staining your early flowers after spring rains. Again, you can use a thick (3- to 6-inch) mulch above deeply planted bulbs. Shallowly planted bulbs will do better with a light (1-inch) mulch. To boost nitrogen for early bloomers, add a handful of unmedicated alfalfa pellets to each bulb cluster.

WILLOW WATER

To encourage rooting in perennial cuttings or any kind of stem cuttings, make willow water. Cut short (1- to 2-inch) sticks from any kind of willow twigs and place about 2 cupfuls in a bucket of water. After a week, use the water on your cuttings. To make another batch, recut the willow sticks a bit and add more water. Replace your willow twigs every few weeks.

MAINTAINING VINES

Like clematis, most vines are heavy feeders that appreciate an annual feeding mulch (see Chapter 3) as well as fresh compost each spring. March and April are good times to give vines feeding mulches. When you consider the mass of foliage on most vines, it is not surprising that they require a lot of water as well. Give newly planted vines at least 5 gallons of water at planting time and the same amount each time you water during the summer. Established vines are more drought tolerant than new ones, but all perform best when kept adequately moist during dry or hot spells.

Most evergreen vines need only light pruning to clear away deadwood or storm-damaged pieces. Deciduous vines that have a permanent structure (such as Boston ivy) are similarly easy to care for. Deciduous vines that vanish each season (such as hops) can be tidied away in midwinter, when the stems are dry and lightweight. To prune clematis, see Chapter 13.

MAINTAINING ANNUALS

The old saying "Grow flowers hard and vegetables soft" is not always true with annuals, for many of the most popular ones are hard-blooming tropicals that thrive here only when treated royally. Hardy annuals are often troupers that perform well under tough circumstances and flower best without added fertilizers. Most, however, appreciate supplemental water in dry spells and grow best in decent soils. In contrast, tropicals are apt to sulk unless kept in style. Luckily, their needs are modest: adequate warmth, frequent watering, and an occasional moderate feeding will help most annuals perform beautifully.

As a rule, heavy bloomers in sunny settings will appreciate fertilizer more than foliage annuals in shady spots. In warm climates, a single dose of time-release fertilizer gives annuals a good start in spring and carries them through summer. Since most pelletized time-release fertilizers are not active until soil temperatures reach the mid-70s, use liquid feeds in spring when soils are still cool.

Where large quantities of plants need feeding, liquid root or foliar feeds can be delivered either by watering can or by hose. Blend fertilizer concentrate with water in a pail, and use a Y connector to link a short section of siphon hose from the pail to the hose. When you water, diluted fertilizer is delivered to your plants.

Use a long-necked wand to extend your reach when watering plants in containers (especially hanging baskets). Hard-to-reach baskets and containers can also be fertilized with fertilizer sticks intended for houseplants. Press the sticks (which last about 60 days) into the soil beside each annual at planting time. Each watering washes a small amount of fertilizer into the soil. The sticks are easy to replace and dissolve well in cool weather. When water-shedding foliage makes water run off, leaving potting soil parched, try a turkey baster. It's easy to poke the slender tip past the leaves, and all the water reaches the thirsty roots.

GROOMING ANNUALS FOR PROLONGED BLOOM

Improved selections have brought us a wide range of long-blooming annuals that need relatively little care. Even so, most will perform better if given light but frequent grooming. This mainly involves deadheading—removing spent and browning blossoms—and tidying away any yellowed or disfigured foliage. If allowed to set seed, many species and old-fashioned annuals will stop flowering in order to ripen that seed crop. Deadheading prevents seed set and promotes rapid replacement of faded flowers, stimulating fresh crops of buds all summer long.

If pinched back every month or so, leggy annuals like petunias and African daisies will refurbish themselves and bloom anew for months. To keep plants looking attractive, don't decimate the whole thing at once, but shorten a third of the stems by two thirds of their length each week. By the time you have trimmed the last batch, the first ones will be refurbished. Daily or weekly grooming keeps plants looking in the pink and takes only a few minutes. It also keeps us closely in touch with our plants, making us aware of pest or disease problems almost as soon as they start.

SIX: NATURAL PLANT CARE

What do plants want and need? Most plants thrive when given good garden soil, ample mulch, and water as needed. The key to having sturdy, healthy plants lies in encouraging strong root growth. Conflicting advice comes at us from magazines, books, and garden centers. Listen, think, and do some homework before being talked into the idea that good gardens must be expensive. Gardening is a multibillion dollar industry, and all product marketers want your piece of the pie. Look for a nursery or garden center whose staff encourages you to make your own compost and offers inexpensive classes on natural care. Avoid buying garden products in big-box stores, where well-informed staff members are rare and product pushers pay fees to have their merchandise closer to the register.

Though many gardeners spend a lot of time worrying about how to feed plants, we are better off feeding the soil and letting the plants feed themselves. As a rule of thumb, when we build great garden soil, we will have happy, healthy plants (although we may need to work on making situationally appropriate plant choices). Whether we are focusing on edibles or ornamentals, our plants will be as healthy as the soil we build.

Healthy plants that are well rooted can take environmental stresses in stride, from pests and diseases to drought, wind, hail, and winter rains. The average overfed plant grown in poor soil has shallow roots that can't support its lush top growth. Such plants collapse in rain and wind storms, succumb to rots and mildews, and attract whiteflies and aphids. Weakly rooted plants are more attractive to pests and more vulnerable to diseases. Invariably, if one or two plants in a row are having problems while their neighbors look fine, the unhappy plants are extremely likely to have some kind of root damage.

The essence of natural care lies in supporting the underlying solution—plant and soil health—rather than attacking a given problem.

FEEDING PLANTS

To avoid problems and encourage vigorous growth, we need to feed our plants properly. Like human nutrition, plant nutrition is complex, but just as we can make simple rules about proper human nutrition, we can generalize some basic rules about feeding plants.

The primary building blocks of plant nutrition are called N-P-K, expressed in a ratio such as 5-5-5 or 1-50-3. N stands for nitrogen, P is for phosphorus, and K stands for potassium (I know, it seems as if it ought to be another P; sorry). This simple formula baffles a lot of us, but here's something that might help: A Master Gardener of my acquaintance made this nutrient trio unforgettable by associating it with John Travolta dancing on the *Saturday Night Fever* poster. Start humming "Stayin' Alive" and try this image:

The finger thrusting insistently skyward evokes nitrogen, which encourages plants to grow up. Nitrogen! N! Sky high! The finger jabbing earthward evokes potassium, which promotes healthy root growth. Potassium! K! Get down! Roots, baby! That loose-hipped, gyrating knee evokes phosphorus, the energy exchanger that circulates nutrients throughout the plant. Phosphorus! P! Round and round! True, this enchanting image doesn't help us to understand why phosphorus gets to be a P and potassium has to be a K, but even John Travolta can do only so much.

It may also help to consider these essential soil elements as the plant equivalent of the human need for proteins, fats, and carbohydrates, while the many trace elements are similar to vitamin and mineral supplements, helping to build healthy plant tissue. Nitrogen is the "green" element, promoting strong foliar growth and putting the green in leafy greens. In concert with trace elements, nitrogen also helps build the proteins in green plants. Like insulin in humans, phosphorus controls the transfer between cells of energy (plant sugars) and other nutrients. Teamed with trace elements, potassium builds strong root systems and promotes flower formation. Trace elements, including calcium, iron, magnesium, and other minerals, also help plants in many ways, notably in developing sturdy root systems. A balanced blend of all these elements will meet the nutritional needs of pretty much everything in the garden, from trees and shrubs to annuals and perennials, vines and bulbs, grasses and ground covers.

Lightly scratch organic fertilizers and amendments into the top few inches of soil. To retain moisture better, top the addition off with a 2- to 3-inch layer of compost mulch.

FEEDING PLANTS BY IMPROVING SOIL

Whenever we think about feeding plants, we need to think about feeding the soil first. Even when we start with poor-quality soil, we can improve soil tilth and texture dramatically simply by mulching regularly with compost and other humus producers. Farmers talk about the tilth of their soil when they want to discuss its texture and structure. Soil scientists call this a soil's "state of aggregation." Both are referring to the way soil looks and feels; healthy soils crumble rather than clump into balls, and they don't sift away like sand between your fingers. When we create healthier soils, we can see for ourselves that improving soil texture or tilth favors root growth and results in sturdier, healthier plants.

All this information helps us understand why organic ornamental gardens can largely be fed with soil amendments such as compost and manures instead of concentrated commercial fertilizers. However, when we come to growing vegetables, we need to provide more concentrated feeding mulches at planting time and throughout the growing season. Chapter 3 discusses soil amendments and feeding mulches in more detail.

SOIL SUPPLEMENTS

Once again, the better the soil quality, the better the health and vitality of the plants it supports. Although each kind of plant has specific needs, we rarely need to mix special soils for each crop we grow. Plants take what they need from soil and leave the rest behind. A soil test can tell you whether your soil is providing plants with everything they need. However, if certain elements are missing, many plants can't readily absorb others. For many crops, simply recycling green wastes into compost mulches can't provide enough of all the important nutrients plants need. A plant's needs can also vary depending on its time of life and the season. Thus, we try to offer our plants a smorgasbord of necessary food items and let them choose their own diet as they need it over time. Organic growers often use soil supplements to boost soil's nutritional quality and to correct mineral imbalances or deficiencies.

Most plants make do nicely on a diet that contains nitrogen, phosphorus, and potassium, the N-P-K of standard plant food labels. Nitrogen encourages overall plant growth, assists in photosynthesis, and promotes string leaf formation. Nitrogen is available to plants from a number of natural sources, including air, water, compost, the soil, and fertilizers. Nitrogen-fixing legumes such as peas, vetch, alders, and brooms all contribute nitrogen to soils as well.

In Northwestern soils, nitrogen is rarely in terrific supply, thanks in part to their low natural humus content and in part to our high winter rainfall and dry summer weather cycle. Thus, adding compost and other organic material helps our plants access available nitrogen better. We can also add nitrogen in the form of bat guano, blood meal, cottonseed meal, and other natural sources. Chemical sources for nitrogen include urea and ammonium nitrate. Well-balanced fertilizers may include a quick-releasing chemical nitrogen such as urea as well as slower-releasing organic sources to ensure a steady and long-lasting supply.

Phosphorus helps build healthy root systems as well as promoting strong cell formation and the production of flowers. Since our native soils are generally low in phosphorus, adding it in moderate amounts is wise. Some growers like to use superphosphates to give an immediate release of available phosphate in combination with slow-release sources such as bone meal and fish meals that include bones. Phosphorus must be blended into the root zone of a plant at planting time, and phosphate-based soil amendments should be dug in rather than layered on.

Potassium is used to promote overall nutrient circulation in plants and helps build strong, sturdy "immune systems." It is especially important for fast-growing plants such as annuals, vegetables, flowering perennials, and lawns. Small amounts of water-soluble potassium (often kelp meal or kelp extracts) are included in most blended fertilizers that will be watered in or washed into the plants' root zones by rain.

Three vital elements—oxygen, hydrogen, and carbon—are immediately available to plants from air and water as well as from the soil. Additional important micronutrients include boron, calcium, chlorine, copper, iron, magnesium, manganese, molybdenum, sulfur, and zinc. Some plants will absorb relatively large quantities of some micronutrients yet use only a tiny amount of others. By providing moderate amounts of each kind, we help our plants to help themselves to the nutrients they need. All of these micronutrients are commonly available from companies such as Whitney Farms or Grow More.

Even when using organic sources of micronutrients, it is possible to overdo things when it comes to soil amendments. Just as with vitamins for humans, the symptoms of a plant overdose of most micronutrients mimic the symptoms of their lack. Before you add significant amounts of any nutrients, check your soil test and read the application directions on any packaging carefully to be sure you are using an appropriate quantity.

ALFALFA MEAL

Alfalfa meal is a well-balanced source of nitrogen, phosphorus, and potassium and an excellent soil conditioner. Apply from midspring into high summer. Avoid medicated forms intended as animal feeds.

BLOOD MEAL

High in nitrogen, this water-soluble material should be applied in spring. Highly attractive to dogs, it is repellent to deer, squirrels, and many rodents.

BONE MEAL

Raw bone meal releases phosphorus slowly, while steamed bone meal is immediately available and continues to provide phosphorus and some nitrogen as it breaks down. Both forms are attractive to dogs unless covered with soil or compost. Be sure to use domestic bone meal to avoid any possibility of mad cow disease contamination. Fish bone meal is an excellent clean phosphorus source that is also repellent to deer. Dig it into the root zone of bulbs when planting, or scratch it lightly into soil around established plants in spring and cover with compost.

COTTONSEED MEAL

High in nitrogen, this slow-release amendment also contains moderate quantities of phosphorus and potassium. It is best used in spring or early summer. Scratch it lightly into the soil around established plants in spring, and cover with compost.

GREENSAND

Use this natural, slow-release source of potassium to blend into new beds. One application lasts for many years.

GYPSUM

Natural gypsum helps improve texture in sticky clay soils, especially where salt content is high (not uncommon conditions in western drylands).

KELP MEAL

An excellent source of potassium, kelp meal should be used sparingly (once a year is fine) to prevent accumulating excessive amounts of potassium. Kelp is the fastest-growing plant on the planet and contains a number of growth hormones as well as many micronutrients. Scratch it lightly into the soil around established plants in spring, and cover with compost.

LIME

Slaked lime is used in outhouses, not in gardens. Dolomite lime is a natural buffering agent that helps to neutralize acid soils. In the Northwest, lime is an important soil amendment for lawn areas, and moderate amounts can be added every other year. Otherwise, add it to new beds only. Do not use lime around acid-loving plants such as blueberries, heathers, rhododendrons, and azaleas.

ROCK PHOSPHATE

A natural, slow-release form of phosphate, rock phosphate lasts for many years in beds and borders. Moderate amounts can be added to compost piles to improve N-P-K balance.

SULFUR

Sulfur is most useful as an amendment in alkaline soils. It is rarely needed in Northwestern soils west of the mountains. Small amounts may be appreciated by acid lovers like blueberries if large quantities of compost have neutralized soils. Scratch it lightly into the soil around established plants in spring, and cover with compost.

PLANT DISEASES

Plants diseases of many kinds can ravage a garden where soil is poor and plants are already stressed. If one plant seems to be targeted over its companions, dig it up; more than likely, you will find some kind of root damage. Injured and stressed plants actually send out chemical distress signals that attract pets and predators.

FIGURING OUT WHAT'S WRONG

Quite often, gardeners find a plant problem and rush off to buy a quick-fix chemical killer without really knowing what the problem might be. For instance, one gal brought in a juniper branch, asking for something to kill the bugs that were harming the shrub. The problem turned out to be caused by an incurable viral disease, not an insect. Treating pests and problems with the wrong solution can lead to worse problems as well as environmental damage.

So how can we tell what is going on with a sad plant? Often it will be obvious that there is a problem, yet it can be tricky to figure out what is really wrong. Here are some simple guidelines for sorting out what the causal agent might be.

Most plant problems are caused by pests and diseases of various kinds. These are called biotic agents because, like the soil biota, they are alive. There are three main kinds of biotic damage. For instance, when mice or slugs eat our seedlings, that is considered to be biotic damage caused by macroorganisms. When aphids attack our nasturtiums, that is biotic damage caused by insects. When a virus or root rot weakens a tree, that is pathogenic damage.

Other problems are called abiotic because they are caused by various conditions or situations. Damage-producing physical conditions might include poor drainage and waterlogged soil, lack of water, or freezing weather. Leaving a load of new plants in the car all weekend in July would very likely cause serious damage. Cutting a bulb in half with your shovel is abiotic damage (even though a living person wielded the shovel). Chemical causes might include chemically damaged soil or overdoses of fertilizer, herbicide, or pesticide. Problems arising from nutritionally depleted or exhausted soil would also be considered to be chemical damage because vital chemical elements are missing from the soil.

Sometimes improper pruning leads to what we call mechanical damage. For example, a careless pruner might nick a tender hydrangea leaf bud. As it opened, the leaf would display a series of holes that were not caused by insects. When a tree blows down and snaps the limbs off a companion, that too is mechanical damage.

How can you tell the difference? As a rule of thumb, the more random the damage pattern, the more likely it is to be caused by a living agent. The more evenly distributed

HOMEMADE FUNGICIDE
To control powdery mildew and other fungal foliage diseases, mix up this classic spray:

1 tablespoon baking soda
1 tablespoon horticultural oil
1 gallon water

Blend all ingredients and spray on affected foliage. Morning or evening spraying is best.

the damage, the more likely it is to be caused by an abiotic agent. For example, if one plant or one kind of plant is having a problem and everything else around it looks fine, you are probably seeing pathogen or macroorganism damage. If all your rose bushes in a certain bed are half the size today that they were yesterday, look for little cloven hoofprints. If one rosebush wilts overnight and the others look fine, a mole may have burrowed underneath, disturbing its roots. Flooding the hole and packing it with compost should restore the fading plant quickly. If several rosebushes grouped in one part of the yard are turning pale and yellowing while others at some distance look fine, consider a virus or a pest such as rose mites.

Abiotic problems tend to affect everything in the area of damage. For instance, when that tree fell down, it probably caused a lot of damage to understory shrubs nearby as well as to the companion tree. If we forget to water a newly planted bed, all the plants in it will suffer from drought stress. If your neighbor sprays an herbicide on a windy day, you may see a swath of damage along an entire hedge or garden section.

Another deciding factor is the speed of a problem's progress. It would take a virus or a colony of insects a long time to cause as much damage as a single misguided sweep of the herbicide sprayer. If evenly distributed damage seems to occur overnight, look for an abiotic agent. A plant that dies fast without warning is usually affected by an abiotic agent: improper planting with major root damage, a broken neck, or accidental chemical poisoning are possibilities.

A third factor is whether many species and varieties of plants are affected or just one or a few. Abiotic damage is usually fairly uniformly distributed; that uncontrolled herbicide is likely to adversely affect pretty much everything it hits. On the other hand, living agents usually display preferences: clematis wilt will affect only clematis, and aphids are more often found on soft foliage than leathery leaves.

You can also examine the suffering plant for signs of insect presence, such as webs or eggs, or patterns of discoloration and swellings that might indicate fungal diseases. Look too for patterns of damage; a plant that dies from the top down and from the stem tips inward nearly always has root problems. However, many problems have similar symptoms, from yellowing or browning foliage to wilting stems. To become better acquainted with the symptom patterns presented by common pests and diseases, take samples of your afflicted plants to your local nursery or to a Master Gardener clinic for diagnosis.

NATURAL CARE FOR PLANT DISEASES
AEROBICALLY BREWED COMPOST TEAS

Machines for brewing aerobic compost teas are discussed in Chapter 3. These teas are of great value in improving the tilth of soil and in boosting soil biota, but they have other benefits as well.

If, for example, you have a Japanese maple suffering from verticillium wilt, you may be able to halt and even reverse the disease by treating the soil around the tree with aerobically brewed compost tea. To brew a tea that can be specifically helpful, collect some soil from underneath a thriving Japanese maple and add it to the feeder compost before brewing your tea. The finished product will have a high concentration of just the right kinds of beneficial soil biota. Initial studies also seem to show that soil taken from healthy forests can be brewed into teas that will help heal stressed woodland plants. These teas can also help stop root rots like phytopthora, a common scourge of farmers and gardeners alike.

Research now in progress also indicates that these teas, when used as a soil drench or sprayed directly on foliage, can help plants resist rust, black spot, mildews, and other foliage diseases. Unlike many other disease treatments, these living tea sprays do not rinse off. Rather, they are actually integrated into the living leaf. Thus, they are longer acting and provide more lasting protection to the foliage.

Dr. Elaine Ingham of Oregon State University wrote to me that, upon returning home from a summer trip, "my roses had a serious case of mildew, so I sprayed with a bacterial tea. The tea prevented any further spread of the mildew, but the one spray did not remove the fungus. I sprayed again two days later, and most of the infection was gone by the next day. I sprayed a third time two days later, and the mildew disappeared. I couldn't get the dead leaves to recover, of course, but those leaves that had just begun to succumb recovered to some extent."

This is, of course, great news for rosarians who are tired

of using toxic sprays on their roses. It's also a boon for those whose peonies get botrytis, whose peaches get peach leaf curl, and so on.

In my own garden, I begin a regular (usually weekly) spray programs for roses, peonies, and other susceptible plants as soon as the foliage emerges in spring. Once the foliage has fully developed, I switch over to a monthly spray schedule. For most gardeners, this is enough to maintain clean, healthy foliage even on trouble-prone plants like roses and phlox.

Cautions: Be sure to use a pathogen-free compost.

COPPER SULFATE

A nonsystemic contact and protectant fungicide, copper sulfate is an effective treatment for a wide range of bacterial blights and fungal diseases, notably powdery mildew, downy mildew, blossom brown rot, apple scab, peach leaf curl, anthracnose, European canker, Dutch elm disease, botrytis, and several kinds of blight. It is also used to control mites on black currants, beans, carrots, and tomatoes and to keep rose foliage clean. Copper sulfate is available as a dustable powder or in spray form, often mixed with carriers in dormant oil sprays for fruit trees. Bordeaux mixture is a classic though very toxic fungicidal treatment. It is highly toxic to mammals, bees, and aquatic life, but less so to birds.

Cautions: Copper sulfate may cause serious irritation to eyes and skin and can cause significant health problems if inhaled. It is extremely toxic if ingested. Wear protective clothing, eyewear, and gloves when applying. Do not use when children or pets are present. Do not use when beneficial insects are present, and do not spray open blossoms. Avoid spraying soil, as copper may harm or kill soil biota, including worms. Do not use near water or where runoff may reach water. It is safest when used in dormant oils during cold weather.

FUNGICIDAL SOAP

A blend of fatty acids and powdered copper, fungicidal soap suppresses a number of pathogens that cause powdery mildew and other disfiguring foliage disorders.

Cautions: Avoid contact with skin and eyes.

MEADOW FOAM

A native Northwestern wildflower, meadow foam *(Limnanthes alba)* has a number of interesting uses and properties. Though the plant is mostly grown for its oils, which are used in cosmetics and as a fungicide, the seed meal works like corn gluten, with a similar ability to act as a natural preemergent to suppress weed sprouting.

Cautions: None.

MYCORRHIZAE

Stressed plants are more susceptible to root rots and other common soil pathogens. Rather than attacking the pathogen, try supplementing the soil around a suffering plant with beneficial mycorrhizae. These fungal biota are discussed in Chapter 3.

Since nearly 90 percent of known plants enjoy mycorrhizal relationships, most plants will benefit from an inoculant containing beneficial mycorrhizae. These products come as wettable powders or tablets as well as in liquid and gel forms. To serve a wide range of plants, look for products that list both ectomycorrhizae (generally associated with woody plants) and endomycorrhizae (most commonly associated with grasses, perennials, and some woody plants); the plants will take on the ones they need and leave the rest.

To use the tablets, you push them into the root zone of transplants or existing trees and shrubs, making sure that they come into contact with feeder roots. You use the other forms by mixing them with water to activate the mycorrhizae and then watering them into plant root zones. Either form can be used at planting time or applied to plants in the ground and in containers. Both types can make a dramatic difference if used when planting or transplanting, and both help to reduce the results of other environmental stresses as well. In several nurseries and in my own garden, adding mycorrhizae to roses has significantly reduced the incidence of foliar diseases.

The use of mycorrhizae also seems to be a key to success when transplanting certain finicky native plants, such as madronas and Nuttall's dogwood. In early experiments, transplants given a mycorrhizal booster outperformed those planted without this benefit.

In addition, many arborists use a product called LASE to help nurture stressed or damaged trees and shrubs. LASE is a liquid concentrate that contains specific nutrients needed to support the active growth of the dominant types of beneficial mycorrhizae. A similar product, BLEND, creates optimal conditions for the colonization of beneficial bacterial biota. See the Resources section at the end of the book for information on obtaining these products.

Cautions: A few plant families, notably azaleas and rhododendrons, orchids, rushes, and proteas, do not benefit from mycorrhizal relationships. Mycorrhizal treatment won't harm these plants, but it will not be useful.

NEEM OIL

Extracted from the nuts of the neem tree, neem oil concentrates contain azadirachtin and related compounds (liminoids) that have many uses. In India, neem oil is added to toothpaste to reduce tooth decay. Though safe for mammals, neem oil is an effective suppressant for molds, mildews, and fungal diseases. It is also used on aphids, whiteflies, and many sucking insects. Neem oil smothers the eggs and larvae of many insects as well.

Cautions: An effective antibiotic, neem oil can harm soil biota if overused. Do not spray when beneficial insects are present. Do not spray open blossoms.

SULFUR DUST

Sulfur is a critical element used by plants in modest quantities. It is sometimes used to neutralize alkaline soils. Although relatively low in toxicity, sulfur is effective both as a fungicide and an insecticide. It acts primarily on fungal disorders, brown rot, powdery mildew and other mildews, rust, red spider, and gall mites. Nontoxic to birds, sulfur is considered to be only a minor toxin for bees. Sulfur dust or sprays are used to keep rose foliage clean of mildews and fungal diseases.

Cautions: Sulfur is irritating to eyes and skin and can cause lung problems if inhaled. Do not use when beneficial insects are present, and do not treat open blossoms. It can burn the foliage of sensitive plants, including cucurbits (members of the cucumber family), apricots, and raspberries. Do not use near water.

WEED CONTROL

Judging by my mail, many readers are plagued by weed problems. Indeed, weeds rank right up there with slugs and deer as ongoing annoyance factors. The problem is that this is one of the best places in the world to garden. Plants from all over the world love being part of the lush Northwestern scene.

Unfortunately, this means weeds as well as imported border beauties. Some of our worst weeds are deliberate imports that were brought here by misguided (if well-intentioned) gardeners. Scotch broom, for example, was planted by several homesick gardeners who longed for the golden hills of Scotland. Isn't that touching? Similarly, ox-eye daisies and English ivy were imported as elegant ornamentals.

Other common weeds are termed "seeds of disturbance," plants that mostly show up where the ground is broken. Fireweed *(Epilobium angustifolium)* is a classic example. This handsome, hot pink native is circumpolar, found in much of the temperate world. Most common along roadsides and farmed fields, fireweed also turns up in new developments. In the wild, fireweed is often the first plant on the scene after forest fires, but it is less successful at infiltrating healthy stands of native plants.

In gardens, fireweed is a wicked runner that can tear through beds and borders in a single season. The choice white-flowered form is far less invasive, but the common pink fireweed must be relentlessly pulled on sight.

Giant Himalayan blackberries were brought in by Luther Burbank, who ought to have known better. The rationale? He felt they would "add vigor to the native strain," whose lax strands seemed weenie to him. Given the choice, I'll stick with the natives, thank you.

Sadly, we are not given the choice. It's amazing how many of our annual weeds, from sow thistles (*Sonchus* species) to dock and spurge and chickweed, hail from other shores. Most came as passengers (often in seed form) on deliberately imported plants. Until fairly recently, nobody worried or cared that weed seeds might come along for the ride. Now we know better, but the Euro-trash weeds will always be with us.

Many common weeds can be kept at bay with mulch. Long a tradition in organic vegetable gardens, mulching is less common among ornamental gardeners. However, a

*Hand weeding is relaxing when
there isn't much of it, but when the
weeds are winning, it gets a whole
lot more like work.*

*Sheet mulching with straw or shredded
leaves is a far simpler way to keep
larger areas clean.*

good, thick mulch is effective anywhere and can be quite attractive. Besides suppressing weeds, mulches conserve moisture and add insulation to soil, keeping our plants cooler in summer and warmer in winter.

In established beds where weeds are winning, start with a coarse smother mulch of chopped bracken or meadow grass (hay or straw may contain clopyralid, and so they should be used with caution). Use 6 to 12 inches where weeds are already established.

WORKING WITH WEEDS

The key to having fun in the garden is being in control. This means different things to different people. Recently, the jolly fellow in line in front of me at the hardware store announced that he was getting ready to do some gardening. Heaped on the counter beside him were four kinds of chemical poisons, chain-saw oil, a gas can, and a new pair of loppers. Some kinds of control are a guy thing.

For many people, the natural world is an enemy. Weeds, bugs, bees, and bats are all on the hit list. Plants are too, especially hedge and foundation plants. If any sign of natural shape arises, don't worry, just whack 'em back.

There is, however, a large problem with the Wild West way of seeing the world as an enemy to be taken out: It is not sustainable. Sooner or later (probably sooner at this point), man wins. Nature loses. What's the problem? Well, when nature loses, we all lose. Big time.

Much as we hate to admit it, we depend on trees for the air we breathe. We depend on undeveloped farmland for the food we eat. We depend on national forest land to support our beef consumption. We depend on plants to filter water we pollute, making it clean enough to drink and to support the fish we eat.

This is pretty basic information, and most people acknowledge it in theory. In practice, however, it's a different story. Nature's all right in its place, but not in my backyard!

Some eco-activists feel that all gardens should be "natural," using only native plants and encouraging wildlife in many forms (but rarely deer). Other folks may just want a tidy-looking space where they can play games and hang out. They are not deliberately setting out to harm the environment, but when everything from TV and radio to publications push the usual practices, why question them? Yard work is Big Business. Financial interest pushes the

NORTHWESTERN WEEDS: TOP FOUR HIT LIST

If part of the satisfaction of toxic "yard work" is hand-to-hand combat, here are some safer ways to channel that energy.

Weed: Himalayan blackberry, European cutleaf blackberry

Control: Cut at least four times a year. Once plants are reduced to stubble, continue to mow or weed-whack at least quarterly (monthly is better). Chip or chop rooted stems and let dry completely before composting. Cut stems without roots can be added to static (slow) compost or brush piles while green.

Weed: Scotch broom

Control: Pull young plants. If plants are too big to pull (most are), cut stems at ground level. Repeat every two months until dead. Scotch broom that's *not* in seed can be added to static (slow) compost or brush piles while green. Those that are in seed should be bagged and burned.

Continued on page 184

In beds and borders, if you have a lot of weeds, you don't have enough plants. Interlayer shrubs and perennials as they are in nature, so plants barely overlap, with enough room to achieve their natural size and shape.

Weed: English ivy

Control: Smother ivy with deep (12- to 24-inch) mulches. After three months, about 80 percent will be dead. Hand-pull the remaining vines and let dry out completely on a tarp. Never put green ivy on the compost pile.

Weed: Bindweed or morning glory *(Convolvulus arvensis, Calystegia sepium)*

Control: Bindweeds are beautiful but amazingly destructive. If you just have spot problems with bindweeds, they can be controlled fairly quickly. Larger patches require serious work. This two-part program will keep small patches of bindweed at bay.

1. Harvest as many of the green tops as possible, frequently. The idea is to prevent the plant from blooming. Dry out the stems completely on the driveway or a tarp, then add to compost. Do not compost any root scraps—these must be bagged and burned. Do not include any stems with flowers, since there may also be seeds.

purchase of many unnecessary things that are more lucrative than beneficial.

Before investing a lot of time and energy on removing weeds, it's worth considering that the weeds—at least some of them—just might be doing something for us. Certain weeds, like chickweed, are terrific at smothering out the competition. Chickweed is also an indicator of good garden soil, so it's telling you that you're doing a good job of soil building. Except in the rock garden, those wide, lacy mats of chickweed don't bother the garden plants they surround, and they are acting as a living mulch, conserving moisture and shading out worse weeds with their frilly foliage. Chickweed's fine roots are easy to uproot, making it a good candidate for temporary ground cover, and chickens really do love it.

Northwestern natives like brooklime *(Veronica becca-bunga)* are charming ground-cover weeds, spreading in dainty, embroidered mats of rounded foliage and bright blue flowers. It makes quick cover in moist, partially shady beds without ever challenging its bedmates for nutrients. Besides being charming to look at, it is great fun to say ("beccabunga" rolls off the tongue so easily).

Our native self-heal *(Prunella lanceolata)* has English cousins whose folk name is "loveliness." This is a coarse-textured, wandering ground-cover plant in the mint family (though it's far less rowdy than mint) with a pinky-purple cluster of flowers on each rounded head. It scrambles around happily in part shade or sun and willingly fills in beds full of shrubs and larger perennials. So will creeping Charlie *(Glechoma hederacea)*, a pretty little nonnative European with heart-shaped leaves and tiny, tubular pinky-purple flowers. Its winning ways and ability to cover poor ground earns Charlie willing acceptance from gardeners with small budgets and even tempers.

Though native to Oregon and California, yerba buena *(Satureja douglasii)* has appeared in several of my gardens. Evidently it has been grown by native people for centuries, and these spontaneous populations may trace their ancestry back to a local potlatch. The trailing stems hold pleasant-smelling leaves and inconspicuous white flowers.

Three members of the great saxifrage clan are terrific ground covers, though all might be classed as weeds by the unknowing. I call this group the "three T's" and use them extensively as free ground covers in shady gardens. Fringe-cup *(Tellima grandiflora)* has curly, heart-shaped, scalloped foliage and fluffy stalks of pinky-white flowers. This willing spreader makes a splendid evergreen ground cover in poor soil, especially in shady gardens. Foam-flower *(Tiarella trifoliata)* has a basal rosette of foliage with triplet leaves scrambling up slim stems tipped with airy sprays of dainty white flowers. Piggy-back plant *(Tolmiea menziesii)* has similar but flatter and more elongated foliage with the charming ability to produce baby plantlets at the base of each large leaf. You may know this one from college days, when it probably graced your windowsill. A fast spreader, piggy-back plant comes in plain and variegated forms such as 'Taff's Gold' (which is really a soft, splotchy chartreuse). The pinkish flowers are often tinged with green and may turn a soft chocolate brown.

2. Add large quantities (12 to 24 inches) of coarse bark mulch to the area where the roots are coming in. This creates a smother mulch; as wood products break down, they deplete nitrogen from the soil and starve out weeds. The mulch also creates better drainage and an open, loose-textured soil. Keep pulling those stems, as often as possible (once a week is the minimum).

In time (after around three months), you can rake away the bark chips and haul out armloads of bindweed roots. Replace the mulch, using fresh sawdust and more coarse bark, and repeat as above. To keep roots out along a fence line, use the metal or plastic sheathing sold at nurseries to contain bamboo roots.

LESS LOVELY, BUT NOT ALL BAD

Certain common weeds are also helping by building soil nitrogen. When I'm working with little time and a small budget, I often call on local weeds to help me out until I'm ready to install "real" plants. Annual clovers can always be considered for use as temporary ground covers, particularly those that are easily uprooted (not the tight little creepers). Clovers are nitrogen fixers, absorbing atmospheric nitrogen and storing it in little white nodules on their roots, where it will eventually improve nitrogen levels in the soil. Some of the oxalis tribe (sorrels and false clovers) are also worthy temporary workers, including pretty little *Oxalis annua,* which comes in lovely shades of copper, bronze, red, and purple. This one in particular makes a dense and handsome ground cover and can be sheared back if it gets shaggy late in the season.

There are, however, weeds to avoid at all costs, notably wild and ferocious spreaders like bindweed (wild morning glory), tap-rooted terrors like Canadian thistle, and relentless roamers like creeping buttercup. Where aggressive weeds proliferate, it's a good idea to clear the ground well before trying to garden. We now know that fast-acting chemical killers like Roundup are not a benign solution (check out the website of the Northwest Coalition for Alternatives to Pesticides at www.pesticides.org to learn more about Roundup and its relatives). Methods that involve soil disturbance also generally only make matters worse. The seeds of many weeds are called "seeds of disturbance," because they can lie buried for decades, waiting patiently until some chance movement stirs the soil, bringing them up to the light and air. These opportunists love it when we till the soil for a fresh bed; that is their finest hour! Other weeds also enjoy the chance to proliferate that tilling offers. Each time we till, each scrap of weed root strives to become a whole new plant. Next time you decide to till, think twice. Instead, consider soil solarization with clear or black plastic or a deep smother mulch (discussed later in this chapter).

To tame rough grass and open meadows, mow them high, and they can be whipped into reasonable shape surprisingly fast. Even rough-cutting a meadow a few times a year will control all but the very wildest weeds. Frequent mowing of weeds and wild meadows keeps them from flowering, and without a steady seed crop, many weedy plants are easier to control. High-mow a rough meadow regularly for a few seasons and you will have a not-that-bad lawn. Because mowing selects for fine-textured grasses and perennials, it gets rid of coarse grasses, reeds, and taller weeds quite quickly. Tap-rooted weeds that make flat basal rosettes, such as dandelions, hawkweeds, and many thistles, can slip beneath the mower and persist for years, unless they are dug out by hand or controlled

The best defense is a good offense. In a well-filled border, there is no room for weeds to infiltrate. A combination of appropriately close planting and deep mulching keeps weeds at bay until beds and borders have time to fill in naturally. Once well knit, there is very little opportunity for weeds to enter.

with a broadleaf weed killer (several safe versions are now available from companies like Safer and Bioganic). To control tap-rooted weeds like dock and dandelions by hand, use a Japanese farmer's knife (a hori-hori), a long, thin-bladed weeder, or an old kitchen knife to remove at least 4 or 5 inches of the root, and any remaining root usually rots away.

WEEDING WITH FIRE

The most fun way to weed is definitely with flame. I use a 3-gallon, backpack model of the Red Dragon flame weeder to keep my garden's gravel paths clean. I also flame the sidewalks, driveways, and other paved areas several times a year, usually in winter. Because I don't water my borders much, if at all, in summer, most of the weeds germinate in winter, when the rains are in full spate. If I can get a jump on the weeds during the cool seasons, I rarely have trouble with them later. I'm not alone in this flaming business; organic growers have used flame to keep orchards, vineyards, and vegetable beds weed-free for many years.

The best place to find a really good selection of flame weeders, along with cart or backpack fittings to make them easier to use, is in an organic farm and garden supply catalog such as Peaceful Valley (see their website at www.peacefulvalley.com). You'll find several styles and sizes of flame weeders, including finesse nozzles that allow fine-tuning and directing of the open flame.

The point of flame weeding is not to charbroil your weeds, but to bring the water in the cells of the foliage to a boil. It takes about three to five seconds in most cases to bid each weed a respectful farewell. Young weeds are easiest to kill, but larger, tap-rooted weeds can take several flaming sessions to conquer. Prairie grasses bounce right back from burning, thanks to millennia of natural genetic programming, though young grass seedlings are far less resilient. Flaming grass seedlings in gravel will usually kill them fast.

It is extremely satisfying to clear large infestations of weeds with a flame weeder, but in closer quarters, it's hard to use this tool selectively. In the garden, the fierce heat will rebound, scorching shrubs and frying perennials that are too close to the target area. Flame weeders can be dangerous during droughts, when wildfires start easily and quickly escape control. Starting a fire is almost impossible in winter, when ground and plants alike are soaking wet. In summer, keep flaming sessions safe by having a reliable water source on hand. Anytime you flame weeds in a dry summer, ask someone to help you watch for sparks and smoke. To avoid harming garden plants, use flame weeders only on paths and patios with nonflammable surfaces.

Here's another hot tip: Tempting though it is, don't let your teenaged sons or pyromaniac partners loose with a flame weeder. Although both will take on this job with alacrity and zeal, an excess of zeal can burn down the house. Something happens when guys get behind the flamer; old movies resurface, the unconscious takes over, and if nobody is around to stop the action, the garden may never be the same. However, I do think that every gardening girl should have her own flame weeder. It's a great gardening skill to master, one that stretches our sense of self in a healthy way.

BOILING WATER

Any place that open flame won't work (such as near the deck or along dry bark paths, for instance), try plain old boiling water. Though most of us don't want to lug vast cauldrons of boiling water into the garden, a daily visit with a teapot can keep a small area weed-free all year-round. Here, too, persistence pays: Where persistent weeds such as thistles and morning glory are sprouting from narrow sidewalk cracks, spot-watering with boiling water will eventually overcome the weeds. Mortaring the crack shut is another good solution to this perpetual problem.

CORN GLUTEN

A by-product of the manufacture of cornmeal, corn gluten is nature's own preemergent herbicide. Since it also provides a good source of nitrogen (most forms are 10-1-0), you could call it the original natural weed-and-feed. When spread over bare soil and wetted down, corn gluten releases substances that cause weed seedlings to dry out before they can fully germinate. Tests conducted at Iowa State University showed that corn gluten performance improves over time; crabgrass was reduced by 86 percent the first year and by 98 percent the second. Dandelions were reduced by 100 percent over a period of four years of seasonal applications.

Corn gluten is sold in two forms. Pelletized, or prilled, corn gluten is easy to spread and makes an excellent source of nitrogen for lawns, where it will also act as a weed suppressant. (See Chapter 4 for a discussion of using corn gluten on lawns.) However, where weed suppression is desired on bare earth, the raw or powdered form is far more effective because it provides better coverage. Meadow foam seed meal, discussed earlier in this chapter, has a weed-suppression effect similar to that of corn gluten.

Because it does not discriminate, corn gluten will kill the seeds you sow as well as nature's choices. Thus, it should be spread on lawns after any grass seeds you sow have germinated and in vegetable beds after all vegetable and flower seeds have germinated. Those allergic to corn may experience a reaction to corn gluten if they inhale the dust while spreading it. Since most corn grown in the United States is genetically modified, those who don't want to use genetically modified corn will need to seek out organic corn gluten.

CITRUS- AND VINEGAR-BASED PRODUCTS

Both citrus oils and vinegar concentrates are effective herbicides and can be used to rid beds, borders, and lawns of persistent weeds. Some kill by drying out plant foliage. Others, such as Blackberry Block, work by lowering soil pH until plants can't survive. This acidifying effect lasts for varying periods of time, from several months to a year, depending on soil type and weather. All work best on warm, dry days, when signs of damage can be seen within minutes of use. However, these products may not work at all if applied shortly before a rain or watering. Overdilution of concentrates or application before rain or watering may cause these products to act like fertilizers instead of herbicides.

Products such as BurnOut that combine both citrus oils and vinegar concentrates kill broad-leaved weeds and certain grasses on contact. These products are usually top-killers that strip protective, waxy coatings off foliage, allowing the plants to desiccate. Tap-rooted weeds like dandelions will need several applications, but many young weeds will be killed with a single exposure. Do not use these products near edible crops. They are safe for mammals but may harm beneficial insects that are accidentally exposed to direct spray. Use with extreme care, as nontarget plants and wildlife may be killed by accidental exposure.

Cautions: May be extremely irritating to the eyes and to skin. Use eye protection and wear gloves when using, and wash well after use. Do not spray where beneficial insects are present. These products are most effective when temperatures are above 65 degrees F. They may be washed away if applied within an hour before watering or rainfall. Citrus- and vinegar-based products are not safe for use on food crops but can be used around the perimeter of vegetable gardens or orchards.

Blackberry Block and similar vinegar-based concentrates are best used in small amounts for spot-killing persistent weeds such as blackberries, horsetail, and morning glory (bindweed). Never use these on a septic field, or you will destroy it. Do not use near natural water, as these products can damage all forms of aquatic life. Do not use in the root zone of established trees, or you may accidentally kill or damage the tree.

BIOGANICS

This interesting line of products is made from food-grade essential plant oils such as sesame, lemon and orange, eucalyptus, and clove oils. Broadleaf Weed Killer can be used on lawns, while Grass and Weed Killer works well on paths, seating areas, and driveways. Most of these products work within twelve to twenty-four hours, though repeat applications may be needed for tap-rooted weeds.

Cautions: Avoid contact with skin and eyes.

SMOTHER MULCHES

Smother mulching is the answer to many serious weed infestations. It is also one of the best ways to work toward a large soil-clearing project. Anywhere you have an infestation of annual weeds, you simply heap a mixture of green grass clippings and shredded dry leaves or straw on top of the area. Be generous here; a 2-foot-thick layer is not too much. This makes a small, static compost pile that will work away quietly while you think about what you want to the bed to look like. Almost anything already growing there will be smothered by that heavy a blanket, and no new weeds will grow through it.

Worse weeds, such as English ivy, nettles, and blackberries, need coarser cover. For these, I use deep (2- or 3-foot) layers of very coarse bark chips. My supply comes from the road crews who trim trees around power lines. These chips are not suitable for garden use in the ordinary sense, but they do make a superior smother mulch. As it breaks down, the coarse bark draws a lot of nitrogen from the soil, leaving it depleted and very lean. Coupled with the weight of the bark and the lack of light and air, this is enough to discourage almost any weed from growing. Before dumping the bark, cut back any weedy top growth (be sure to wear heavy gloves and long-sleeved, protective clothing), and heap it over the vulnerable root zone of the problem spot.

If the weeds are especially thuggish and well established, consider removing as much root as possible before applying the smother mulch. The more you take away, the less you need to starve out. Short-handled mattocks are great tools for root removal, as are heavy picks. If the

COVER CROPS

Cover crops are seed-grown blankets of fast-growing annuals that carpet soil, acting as placeholders until your garden crop is ready to plant. Plants used as cover crops are often nitrogen fixers that help build up soil quality as well. Anytime you need to clear up a large quantity of weeds, consider enlisting a cover crop to keep the weed at bay. Many best bets are fast growers like vetch, Dutch clover, winter rye, and buckwheat, which will outperform the weeds. When your real crop is almost ready, the temporary cover crops are tilled under to replenish the soil with stored nitrogen and other nutrients.

To avoid tilling, simply mow your cover crops and let them compost right on site. When you are ready to sow your garden or field crop, loosen the soil with a heavy comb rake (a large gravel-leveling rake covers a lot of ground in a hurry), or simply broadcast your seed a bit more heavily than usual.

Though cover cropping helps build better soils, it does take time. Several cycles of cover cropping may be needed to

Continued on page 192

coax lean, exhausted, and weed-ridden soil into better shape. Even so, those with large properties to manage find this system to be an excellent way of getting and keeping wild areas under control while building tilth and boosting soil nutritional levels.

For hundreds of years, the standard English weed-cleansing cover crop for lawn making has been potatoes. Few weeds can successfully compete with the sprawling mats of potato foliage aboveground and their tangled roots below. The potatoes can be harvested before their greens are chopped and tilled into the soil or mown into compostable shreds. Over the winter, you can grow secondary cover crops like winter wheat or rye, which can be tilled or shredded before the next batch of potatoes goes in. A quick-growing crop of alfalfa or buckwheat can be inserted between the rye and the potatoes. These multiple crop cycles leave the soil in good heart, weed-free and ready to plant.

work is too difficult, just use more chips and keep a watchful eye on the area. You will need to be vigilant about removing any and all shoots and stems as they appear, but by cutting the tops and starving the soil, you will win out in time.

The most effective way to use a smother mulch is in combination. Begin by mowing or cutting back all weeds, and then layer on a 2- or 3-foot blanket of a hot-composting mulch such as grass clippings and dry shredded leaves in equal quantities. The heat helps to discourage the weeds from making a comeback, and when this layer has broken down, the soil beneath it will be loosened, making it much easier to dig out any persistent weed roots. Now you can add the smother mulch of coarse chips, making it at least 2 or 3 feet deep. Any weeds that do emerge will be easy to pull out, and the heap will rot peacefully for as long as you like. When you want to garden in that spot, pull the chips away (they make a fine path material), and replace them with compost and manure, with a booster of alfalfa. This will restore the nitrogen level of the underlying soil in a hurry.

Within three months, there is an average of eighty percent kill.

LET'S GET THE IVY OUT!

One of the legacies of the last century was an influx of persistent weeds from Europe and elsewhere. We can all help to clean up the bioregion of these Euro-trash invader weeds, starting in our own backyards. My favorite candidate for eradication is English ivy. One of the worst pests around, this pesky creeper displaces native plants and harms host trees and shrubs. It also harbors rats and other rodents, not to mention slugs. Out with the stuff! Whenever I write about removing ivy, I get questions about whether removal is really necessary. It is confusing to read that ivy is a dreadful invader and then find it for sale at your local nursery.

The confusion arises because ivy gets treated as both a wonder worker and an evil weed. Garden books written back East or in Europe sound ivy's praises as a ground cover and a climber. Garden designers routinely plant ivy in containers and as bed edging. Nearly every nursery carries ivy, often in several colorful forms. These days, however, many nurseries also post small warnings with the ivy plants, mentioning its wicked ways. In some parts of the country, gardeners struggle to grow English ivy and cherish the fancy forms for their horticultural cache. Shouldn't we delight in our abundance of ivy, when it grows so well here? Well, no.

The problem is that plants can display very different behavior patterns in different parts of the world. For instance, back home in Asia, kudzu is not a problem plant. In the American South, it is an ecological disaster. Kudzu has recently been found in Oregon, probably introduced by well-meaning gardeners who thought it was pretty (which it is). Early attempts to eradicate the runaway kudzu are not progressing very well. Let's pray that kudzu can be stopped, since it could make English ivy look like a lazy slacker.

Like kudzu, ivy is well behaved at home. I once visited a French arboretum where ivy delicately draped the trees in a decorative and decorous manner. When several of us commented that ivy is dangerously aggressive in our region, the arborist became angry. He insisted that there was nothing wrong with letting ivy run anywhere it liked and that it never harmed any plant.

Well, that seems to be so in Europe, where ivy has been growing for millennia. Here, however, this comparative newcomer has taken over large sections of the urban and suburban landscape, from Vancouver and Victoria, British Columbia, down through California, where it continues to be the most popular ground cover sold. Ivy is also infiltrating native woodlands.

How did ivy get out into the wilderness? In some cases, it escaped from gardens into nearby woods, sometimes as much as a century ago. In other cases, the vector has wings—birds help ivy fly to places it couldn't easily reach by the ground.

This is a big problem because ivy is an opportunist that takes over ecological niches. It smothers native climbers like honeysuckle and clematis. It destroys native ground covers such as creeping dogwood and trilliums. Ivy adapts very well to a wide range of conditions. That adaptability is what makes it and other weeds dangerous. It is finally on the noxious and toxic weed lists for both Oregon and Washington and is considered a serious problem in several other states.

Ivy's very popularity has long protected it from the

noxious weed listing or quarantine regulation that its rampant tendencies might otherwise trigger. It sells well. It is also so widespread that many people simply feel that control would be unenforceable. This is shortsighted, because without some regulation, the problem will continue to grow. Ivy has already created serious damage, not only in urban and suburban settings, but in the wild. In Washington's national forests and parks, ivy infiltration causes what foresters call "ivy desertification." In ivy deserts, ivy vines choke out native plants, displacing smaller understory as it spreads. The vines then scale trees, where the dense growth can catch the wind and bring trees to the ground before their time.

When ivy climbs, it changes character and leaf form. Virtually all of the many kinds of ivy—fancy leaf, laceleaf, variegated, and so on—develop the same adult form. A study done through Seattle's Center for Urban Horticulture revealed that most ivy damage comes from the larger-leaved forms of *Hedera helix* and that the tiny laceleaf forms are less destructive, even over time. However, all mature or arboreal ivy produces flowers and lots of fruit. Birds eat the fat, black ivy berries, processing them so effectively that little ivy sprouts can be found almost everywhere.

Europeans argue passionately that ivy can't hurt trees, and perhaps in Europe it doesn't. Here, however, when it gets a stranglehold on trees that are not adapted to its embrace, ivy can stunt growth. Arborists talk about hearing the "pop" as tree bark expands in relief when they remove girdling vines.

It may be true that ivy won't hurt healthy trees, but environmental challenges like excess summer water from lawn runoff, air pollution, and acid rain have stressed most trees. The considerable weight of mature ivy can destroy a stressed tree. Like a sail, high-climbing ivy catches wind, causing even healthy trees to snap.

HOW TO REMOVE IVY

Every time I write about ivy removal, I receive a generous flow of reader responses. I'd like to share the best tips, some of which are real time-savers. I'm also including a couple of horror stories in the hope that you can avoid similar problems.

A reader on Vashon Island reported good results from mowing her ivy. She explained, "We decided to try mowing it a few years after the ivy had been planted (yes, planted, by a professional landscaper yet!), and it works! Now every two years we mow the bank of ivy in the fall with a mulching mower, and that keeps the ivy down, under control, and tidy."

Where ivy covers a relatively flat area and you know what's underneath it, mowing can be a good temporary control. In unfamiliar territory, it's important to cut ivy (or any ground cover) with a machete or weed whacker before risking your mower. This initial clearing session will reveal any hidden hazards such as stumps, holes, or rocks that can seriously damage expensive machinery.

On steep slopes where mowing is dangerous, ivy can be trimmed with a weed whacker or brush cutter. Trimming once each year will keep ivy in its juvenile state, which means it can't produce seeds. However, it can still get away quickly, and a lapse of even a few seasons can create an ivy wilderness. You may well be responsible enough to keep the ivy under control. Even so, if you move or sell your home, the next person may not be so responsible, and the potential problem will simply be passed along.

Thus, you should supplement mowing or trimming with a staged removal program. Plan to replace the ivy slowly. Each time you hold a removal session, don't work for more than a few hours. During that period, stop each hour and do something that uses different muscles and motions. For instance, if you have been pulling ivy, stop pulling and chop the vines into pieces or stuff them into black plastic collection bags. Why? For many people, more than a few hours of vigorous, repetitive action like pulling ivy can lead to problems. One reader reported that a prolonged session of ivy removal ended up in a torn shoulder (rotator cuff), an exquisitely painful experience I'd like to spare the rest of you.

Here's a little reminder list for ivy removal:

1. Warm up first, stretching and loosening up all body joints.
2. Actively pull ivy for no more than an hour (or less).
3. Take a break and do something totally different for half an hour.
4. Shake out your hands and shoulders every fifteen minutes.
5. Remember that ivy removal can be done all year-round. An hour a week is plenty.

Another reader wrote that his acre site was infested with ivy (also installed by a landscaper). Mature trees on the site were burdened with it. A professional horticulturist/arborist had told him that English ivy changes its basic nature a few feet off the ground and becomes a tree parasite and that cutting it at the base would therefore not do any good. The only remedy, the reader was told, was to bring in a bucket truck and have the ivy pulled manually out of the trees.

The arborist had gotten it wrong, however. As ivy climbs, it becomes mature or arboreal. The leaf shape changes, and flowering and fruiting spurs appear. However, it is not parasitic (able to live off the host plant). If you remove the bottom 4 to 6 feet of ivy from a tree trunk, the ivy on the tree will die. It takes about a year for the leaves to turn brown and several more years for the vines to fall off. But it happens naturally, at no cost.

To prevent regrowth, pull as much ivy root from the ground as possible. After the trees are set free, spend an hour or two each week removing ivy from the ground. A small pick or mattock works beautifully for this chore. This is also an excellent family project, and most kids really enjoy ivy removal days.

As I learned at Plant Amnesty workshops, two people can remove sheets of ivy quickly if one end is loosened with a sharpened edging tool or sharp, flat shovel. Start anywhere and make a long cut with the tool. Next, one person rolls the ivy back like a rug, and the other chops the roots with the tool. Finally, pull all the big root pieces that protrude from the ground.

There will be some resprouting from this, but the reappearing ivy is quite manageable if you follow this simple program.

SMOTHER-MULCHING IVY

Experiments held in Kitsap County, Washington, have demonstrated that deep smother mulching (12 to 24 inches) with coarse bark chips can reduce ivy stands by 80 percent in about three months. The remaining ivy can be hand-pulled easily after the mulch has softened the ground. These studies show that where it is possible to get large quantities of mulch in place, you do not need to remove any ivy ahead of time. Patches that were cut back before mulching were not killed off any better than the control patches that were just mulched without any pre-cutting. The deep mulch is not harmful to the surrounding trees and can be removed for use in another area once the ivy has been cleaned up. After clearing and replanting, check up on the site two or three times a year, and remove any ivy that resprouts or reseeds.

SEVEN : DEALING WITH INSECT PESTS AND CRITTERS

Before "solving" a problem with a pesticide, improve cultural conditions such as poor drainage and nasty soil, and the problem will often resolve itself.

Over the years, I've experienced remarkably few serious garden problems. I've found that when we garden cooperatively rather than controllingly, pests are simply far less of a problem. In fact, most common garden problems are created by people. Many pests can be avoided or eliminated through good garden design. For instance, by not allowing plants to touch your house, you'll have healthier foundation plants and fewer pest problems such as ants and spiders in the house. Plant a lot of shrubs right up against the walls and windows and you'll have the opportunity to learn about molds, mildews, carpenter ants, heavy pruning, and vanishing views.

How can we learn the best times to deal with pests and problems? Grab a copy of *Pests of the West* by Whitney Cranshaw (Fulcrum Press). This handy book describes the life cycles of everything from molds and mildews to codling moths and whiteflies. The huge flaw in this book is that it suggests the use of toxic, long-lasting organophosphates, some of which are now banned in Washington. However, botanicals and organic controls are also recommended, so stick with those and your natural pest control program will be off to a great start.

COMMON PESTS
APHIDS AND WHITEFLIES

Aphids and whiteflies damage foliage and weaken plants. They are most commonly found on stressed plants, especially ones with weak or damaged root systems. Start by hosing off an infestation with the hose; plain water may be enough to dislodge the pests and water the stressed plant as well. Next, try ladybugs. These invaluable pest controllers feed voraciously on soft-bodied bugs like aphids and whiteflies.

Spotted Asian ladybugs were deliberately imported by

INTEGRATED PEST MANAGEMENT AND NATURAL CARE

I hear a lot of questions about integrated pest management (IPM) and natural care. As school districts, counties, and cities adopt IPM and natural care programs, homeowners are wondering if they should too. They wonder also if IPM is the same as organic gardening. The answer is, sort of.

Natural care is the term for the safe and least-toxic gardening techniques being actively promoted in Metro-King County by a number of public agencies. Natural care programs encourage gardeners to wean their landscapes off excess water and fertilizers. Natural care principles encourage minimal use even of less-toxic pesticides and herbicides.

The idea behind natural care is not to attack a given problem, but to support and encourage the solution: healthy environment and healthy plants. The main goal is to protect our local and regional soil, water, and air quality through reduced use of dangerous pollutants, including common herbicides and pesticides.

Natural care practices also benefit the practitioners by protecting their own health

the U.S. Department of Agriculture to help farmers prevent pest damage. Since many commercial crops, from vegetables and salad greens to annuals and perennials, are plagued by aphids, ladybugs are released in huge numbers into growers' greenhouses and fields. When growers can get rid of pests by harnessing nature's own controls, it saves time and money and reduces chemical pollution. Most nurseries sell packaged ladybugs in spring.

You may also be able to collect your own, since large populations of spotted Asian ladybugs overwinter in Northwestern homes. The ladybugs on your walls and windows are called *Harmonia axiritis*. Their species is young and variable, so in any given group, you can find lots of different colors and patterns. On my windows, some of the ladybugs are spotless. If they weren't mixed in with spotty buddies, I might not even know them for ladybugs. These can be solid red, tomato orange, or glossy black, but they are all the exact same thing, genetically speaking. A closer look may also show you ladybugs with just a few big spots and others with many smaller ones.

You might see a black one with orange spots, and an orange one with black spots as well as the "normal" red ones with black spots. You may not want them decorating your inner walls, but these charming bugs can be very helpful in their proper place—the garden. Unfortunately, they usually appear well before it's warm enough for them to go outside safely.

If your house fills up with Asian ladybugs as the days grow warmer, you can collect them for aphid-eating duty later on. When they first start covering the south-facing windows, the sleepy bugs move slowly enough that they are quite easy to catch. Use a soft whisk broom to scoop them into a dust pan, or put a clean bag in the vacuum and suck them up. From there, transfer them to a canning jar with a tight lid.

You can put a lot of ladybugs in the same jar, filling the jar half full without danger of crushing anybody. However, they need a bit of water to survive, so add a piece of slightly damp (not wringing wet) paper towel to each jar. Store them in the refrigerator until the weather warms up more consistently. I usually begin releasing ladybugs when I spot the first aphids in early May, and within a few days, the good bugs have eaten up the bad ones. To keep ladybugs from leaving your garden, sprinkle the foliage of the aphid-infested plants you want them to clean up. The first thing ladybugs need after emerging from dormancy is water, and they'll fly long distances to find it. Offer it first and they'll stick around to mate. Newly released adults eat a moderate amount of pests, but the babies that start hatching soon after release will eat enormous quantities. The larval ladybugs look like black, articulated crocodiles. Don't panic; they are on their way to ladybughood.

SLUGS

Slugs present a perpetual challenge to gardeners in the maritime Northwest. The region is well endowed with slugs in many sizes and colors; our native wood slug earned its nickname, the banana slug, for both its color and its size. However, these local slugs are allies, not competition. Natural composters that feed on dying foliage, banana slugs are important recyclers in woods and damp meadows and should be welcome in gardens as well. Most garden damage is done by several species of accidentally imported Euro-trash slugs. The European field slugs and snails feast on live foliage and can cause an amazing amount of damage in a bad year.

My kids earned a lot of money by using their super squirt guns to off slugs with ammonia water (1 part ammonia to 2 parts water). At a penny a pop, they could make several dollars a day before breakfast by cruising the garden and squirting slugs. Ammonia water causes slugs to fizzle up into little balls of nitrogen. It is not harmful to most plants but can burn foliage on delicate woodlanders like trilliums and Jack-in-the-pulpits.

There are many other relatively benign ways to control slugs, from beer traps (containers that hold enough beer to drown an unsuspecting mollusk) to diatomaceous earth, which consists of tiny, ground-up particles of ancient siliceous creatures that are sharp-edged enough to slice slugs to sushi. Slugs and snails have a terrific taste for beer and are also attracted to bran, the main (nonactive) ingredient in many kinds of slug bait, especially those based on metaldehydes. These are alcohol analogues that kill slugs as beer does. Unfortunately, most can also do significant harm to birds and larger animals like cats and dogs, so they are best avoided.

The most exciting development in recent years is the rise of environmentally safe slug deterrents based on iron phosphate. The best of them (such as Sluggo) are made

Slugs are a terrific pest in the Northwest, yet the problem is less with our native banana slugs than with European invaders. Native slugs mainly feed on decaying foliage, while European slugs are chiefly live foliage eaters. Vanquish them with iron-phosphate based baits that don't harm other wild life.

and well-being. For home food producers, natural care practices will boost soil health and thus food quality.

IPM is a carefully designed program that combines prevention and timed treatments to control pests and diseases. It is more often adopted by professional pest control companies than by gardeners, but the principles apply to home gardens equally well.

For instance, when tent caterpillars ravage trees and shrubs, the chemotherapy cure would be to spray the whole area with a toxic pesticide that would kill all caterpillars and quite a lot of other bugs as well. Indirect targets such as beneficial insects, fish and wildlife, pets, and people would also be adversely affected, either by direct contact, through wind drift, or through runoff into water systems.

Continued on page 202

Approaches shared by IPM and natural care would be to hand-pick caterpillars, burn nests, and/or spray favored foliage with Bt (*Bacillus thuringiensis*), neem oil, or pyrethrin. When eaten, these botanicals paralyze the digestive system of the caterpillars or disrupt the hormonal cycles that trigger life changes such as pupation.

The IPM approach looks at the specific life-span stages of each pest and then offers tactics for each stage. For instance, tent caterpillars eat leaves for only six to eight weeks after emergence. Thus, leaf treatment needs to happen within this window of opportunity. Once caterpillars have eaten their fill, spraying foliage is useless.

White dots on the caterpillars indicate that tiny parasitic wasps or tachinid flies have laid eggs in the soft-bodied hosts. Caterpillars with dots need no further intervention. Indeed, we should leave them to allow the parasitic wasps to proliferate.

When the caterpillars have eaten enough, they start spinning white cocoons. About two weeks later, the chunky brown moths appear. The moths lay eggs in blobby

like pasta with an extra dose of iron. The iron phosphate gives slugs an incurable case of anorexia. One bite and they crawl away to die. This has several advantages over other methods, notably the lack of disgusting masses of slime where poisoned slugs have been feasted on by friends, who then succumb in turn. Iron phosphate-based baits are listed as safe for use in vegetable gardens as well as in ornamental situations and will not harm birds or animals. They seem expensive but are very rainproof and so long lasting that a little goes a very long way. I find that one medium-sized box of iron phosphate bait lasts a whole season. If birds eat your bait, you are probably using too much. Tuck it more closely to your plants, or switch to a coconut soap gel called Slug Stop. It looks just like slug slime and fits well in naturalistic garden settings.

To be on the safe side, use these or any slug baits sparingly, placing a small amount (usually a quarter teaspoon) close to the point of emergence of susceptible plants such as hostas. It's also wise to place a few tiny pellets (again, about a quarter teaspoon) where bulbs will appear in spring and around each bulb cluster as soon as new growth appears. Many slugs will burrow underground to start chewing on fritillaries, ornamental onions, and narcissus. Later in spring, they may gnaw away at emerging lilies and dahlias as well. By safeguarding your bulbs before they come up, you ensure an undamaged display.

Copper tape is a classic slug stopper because there is enough salt in slugs' bodies to electrocute them when they touch copper (at night you may even see tiny sparks). Use copper tape on table legs to keep slugs earthbound. You can also wrap it around the base of large containers, or use it to line the sidewalls of raised beds and the entryways to your greenhouse.

WASPS

Bugged by pesky wasps and yellow jackets? Before you reach for the toxic spray, check your local listings for wasp removal services. Most charge a low fee for removing wasps, hornets, and yellow jackets from places where insects and people collide. Adult wasps are considered beneficial, preying on small insects and spiders (including many pests). When it becomes necessary to remove wasps from the house, begin by plugging entrance holes to their nests or by spraying diatomaceous earth in the nest at night.

Victor also makes a line of nontoxic pesticides, including a spray that destroys wasp nests. Any attempt to destroy a nest is best attempted at night, when wasps are inactive.

NATURAL CARE PRODUCTS FOR INSECT CONTROL
BENEFICIAL INSECTS

These days, gardeners can buy many kinds of beneficial insects, from tiny aphid-eating wasps to mason bees, lacewings, ladybugs, and praying mantises. All help to control a generous range of insect pests, and many also assist in the pollination of edible crops. Each package will include specific directions for timing and methods of release for most effective use.

Green lacewings (*Chrysopa rufilabris*) are delicate-looking insects, but their larval form look like ferocious if minuscule alligators that gobble down hordes of garden pests, including mealybugs, thrips, aphids, and whiteflies. Sprinkle the eggs and larvae in areas with pest problems, repeating with a new release every three to four weeks as needed.

Ladybugs are best known for their charming spots, but these little bugs do more than look cute; they can wipe out enormous quantities of aphids and other soft-bodied pests. Sprinkle the release area with water to keep them close to the pest problem. The soon-to-hatch larvae will eat even more aphids than the parents.

Pirate bugs (*Orius insidiosis*) are sold as mixtures of adults and nymphs. Both will eat lots of aphids, thrips, mites, spider mites, and whiteflies, among other pests. Release pirate bugs during the evening for best results. They are one of the best controls for persistent thrips infestations.

Praying mantis (*Tenodera sinensis*) eggs will hatch in warm weather (usually about a month after refrigeration stops), releasing up to two hundred little mantises. These voracious eaters will consume huge quantities of insect pests, from aphids to mites and whiteflies. Release by late July to ensure a full hatch.

Cautions: Praying mantises eat anything and everything, including other beneficial insects. Insecticides may harm your beneficial bugs as well as the target pests, so do not use insecticides before or during release of beneficial insects.

strips on tree and shrub branches, favoring (but not limited to) dogwoods, alders, cascara, and fruit trees of all kinds. At first the egg strips look shiny and almost crystalline. Soon they turn gray and look like dirty Styrofoam.

Interventions vary for each stage. As soon as you notice the caterpillars, they can easily be hand-picked and squashed or discarded. The clearly visible tents can be cut or knocked down and burned. Cocoons can be picked off and burned (as long as you are sure they are tent caterpillar cocoons, not precious butterflies). Egg strips can be smothered with horticultural dormant oil sprayed in winter. They can also be pulled off easily by hand, a leisurely, meditative winter chore.

The same concept works for aphids. When aphids appear in force, buy a packet of ladybugs, wet down the foliage, and let those girls loose. There's no point in releasing ladybugs before the food supply is in place. If you don't wet down the foliage, the ladybugs will take off in search of water. Provide both water and aphids and you have happy ladybugs.

BENEFICIAL NEMATODES

Most gardeners know that predator nematodes are bad news for plants, but not many realize that their good-guy cousins can come to the rescue. All nematodes are nonsegmented roundworms that occur naturally in native soils. Beneficial nematodes prey on many plant pathogens, from borers and beetles to grubs and weevils, including plant-eating nematodes. Some will even kill off the fleas that live on dogs and cats. These tiny critters come in a powdered form that is mixed with water and sprayed or sprinkled on lawns and planting beds. A packet of predator nematodes contains up to a million of the critters and can be sprayed over about 2,500 square feet.

Cautions: Nematodes must be used when soil temperatures reach the 50s or growth will be very slow and erratic. They can usually be used by May in the Northwest.

ESSENTIAL PLANT OILS

Lemongrass, eucalyptus, sesame, and other essential plant oils can act as very effective pesticides and herbicides. A company called Bioganic makes a wide range of such products that work quickly and smell great to boot. Bioganic Crawling Insect Killer, which targets ants, roaches, and more, is safe enough to use indoors on carpenter ants or termites. Used around the perimeter of a building, Bioganic Barrier Treatment is an excellent way to keep the house free from bugs, spiders, ants, and so on.

Cautions: Can irritate skin on sensitive people; wash well after use. Avoid prolonged use, which may lead to nausea, dizziness, or headaches. Do not use near natural water, as certain oils (especially eucalyptus) may harm aquatic life.

BACILLUS THURINGIENSIS (Bt)

Bt is a naturally occurring microbial insecticide found in soils all over the world. Substrains of various kinds have remarkable properties, including the ability to paralyze the digestive system of most caterpillars and some grubs or to kill larval stages of mosquitoes, leaf beetles, and blackflies. Caterpillar, fly, and beetle control is usually achieved with dustable powders or wettable sprays, while mosquito dunks come in hard "doughnuts" that float in water bowls, ponds, and water features.

Safe for use on edible and ornamental crops, Bt is not

CATERPILLAR SMOOTHIES

This time-tested method of ridding the garden of specific pests requires an old blender (one that is not used for food). Gather a quantity of pests (singly or combined), such as cabbage loopers, gypsy moth caterpillars, or even slugs. Combine them with a cup of water, and blend them to a fine slurry. Remove the strainer from a spray bottle and spray the mixture on the target crops and on nearby plants as well. Rumor has it that this works so well with slugs that you'll need to repeat it only once a year. (Strain slug and snail mixtures to remove shell bits, says my informant, a well-known California organic gardener.)

toxic to mammals and is thought to be safe for most insects. However, the surfactants (sticking agents) and other carriers used may not be as benign. As a precaution, do not apply when beneficial insects are present, and do not treat open blossoms.

Cautions: Read package instructions with care, since dilution rates may vary according to the target pests. Avoid direct contact with Bt spray or powder for humans, pets, and wildlife, since it may irritate eyes and skin and can be harmful if inhaled. Do not apply when beneficial insects are present, and do not treat open blossoms. Bt will kill or harm all caterpillars that eat treated leaves, so use with care and confine treatment to problem areas.

CITRUS- AND VINEGAR-BASED PRODUCTS

The rinds of lemons, oranges, tangerines, grapefruits, and other citrus fruits contain volatile oils and related compounds with potent properties. Many are natural insecticides, killing aphids, fleas, mites, and more on contact. Vinegar concentrates are also potent weed killers. (See Chapter 6 for more on vinegar-based herbicides.)

DIATOMACEOUS EARTH

This powdery substance contains tiny diatoms, ancient life forms with hard bodies that slice through many insects and other pests. Sprinkle it around plants for slug and snail control, or rub it on household pets to kill fleas.

Cautions: Garden forms of diatomaceous earth are not heat treated. Heat-treated forms used to filter swimming pools are not suitable for garden use and can cause health problems if inhaled.

HOT PEPPER WAX

Not everybody loves hot stuff, and a wide range of insect pests can't bear it. Thus, extracts of hot peppers such as capsaicin and related compounds make effective repellents for aphids, lacebugs, leafhoppers, mites, spider mites, and many other pests. These products are usually bound with food-grade waxes that help the hot stuff stick to the plants. They are safe for use on most ornamental and edible crops, even up to the day of harvest, but you'll need to wash all edibles well before eating.

Cautions: Hot pepper extracts are extremely irritating

to eyes and skin, so use protective gloves and eyewear and wash hands and arms well after applying these products. Avoid spraying on open blossoms, and don't spray when beneficial insects such as bees are active.

INSECTICIDAL SOAP SPRAYS

Among the first organic products to appear on the market, insecticidal soaps come in many strengths and kinds. Most are made from potassium salts of botanically derived fatty acids, which kill a long list of plant pests. The main targets are aphids, caterpillars (many), cinch bugs, earwigs, grasshoppers, leafhoppers, mealybugs, mites, mole crickets, scale, spider mites, tent caterpillars, and thrips. They generally work on contact; you must see and target the pest to kill it.

Insecticidal soaps that also include neem oil can smother eggs and larvae of many pests, from aphids to whiteflies. Neem soaps can be used on lawns for fungal problems, red thread, cinch bugs, and mole crickets.

Insecticidal soaps can be used up to the day of harvest on many garden crops, though all treated edibles must be well washed. They are also safe on most trees, shrubs, perennials, annuals, and houseplants.

Cautions: Some plants, especially euphorbias, show sensitivity to insecticidal soaps. Direct contact may harm beneficial insects, especially bees; avoid treating open blossoms. Do not use near natural water (such as streams and ponds) to avoid injuring aquatic vertebrates such as frogs and salamanders.

PYRETHRINS

Many botanically based insecticides contain pyrethrins, toxic compounds extracted from several species of chrysanthemum flowers. Available as dusts or powders or as sprays, pyrethrins work on contact, paralyzing the nervous system of many insects, though sometimes only for a brief period. Because certain insect pests produce enzymes that can break down pyrethrins and other botanical toxins quickly, most insecticides combine pyrethrins with synergists that markedly increase their effectiveness.

Pyrethrins are used to control many pests, from ants and aphids to beetles, bugs, caterpillars, earwigs, leafhoppers, thrips, gypsy moths, stinkbugs, and whiteflies, among others. Other forms are used to control body lice, mosquitoes, cockroaches, and flies. Because they are rapidly broken down by exposure to light, pyrethrin products are best used early in the morning or in the evening. Pyrethrin dusts are used on tubers, corms, and storage roots to prevent damage from borers and grubs. Powders and sprays are used on many vegetable crops to control damage from sucking and chewing insects. They can be used on edible crops, but all treated edibles must be rinsed and washed thoroughly.

Pyrethroids such as allethrin are semisynthetic derivatives of chrysanthemumic acids that tend to be less toxic to mammals, though they are even more effective as insecticides. In combination, pyrethrins and pyrethroids are highly effective insecticides. Insecticides based on certain pyrethrins (pyrethrin-I) are classified as Restricted Use pesticides and available only to certified applicators.

Cautions: Pyrethrins are irritating to the eyes and skin, and inhalation can trigger asthma, nausea, and headaches as well as itching and burning sensations in adults. Although pyrethrins are rapidly broken down in the adult human body, skin rashes may persist for two days. If cuts, sores, or open skin lesions are exposed to pyrethrins, irritation may result, especially if the wounds are exposed to sunlight. Infants cannot break down pyrethrins efficiently, so children must be protected from direct contact with any and all forms of pyrethrin. Large doses of pyrethrins may be fatal to mammals, including humans, pets, and wildlife. They are highly toxic to aquatic life and moderately toxic to some birds. They are also harmful to bees. Do not use when beneficial insects are present, and do not use on open blossoms.

STICKY TRAPS

These plastic or foil-backed traps are coated with sticky substances that attract flies, whiteflies, and many other small flying pests. Yellow traps are especially attractive to whiteflies.

Cautions: Do not place sticky traps where they might accidentally catch small birds.

If your rhododendrons are attacked by root weevils, wrap the trunk with foil spread with Tanglefoot. Trim away all branches that touch the ground, and the now-sticky trunk will become the access point for the yummy foliage.

TANGLEFOOT

A mixture of castor oil, natural gum resins, and vegetable wax, this sticky substance is used on traps to collect ants, apple maggots, caterpillars, cutworms, gypsy moths, rootworm weevils, and other climbing or flying insects. Where strawberry rootworm weevils have disfigured rhododendrons badly, prevent further damage by removing all lower branches that touch the ground (or other plants), reducing access to the main trunk. Wrap waxed paper or tinfoil around the trunks, then coat it with sticky Tanglefoot to trap the soil-dwelling pests as they climb. Paint round balls red and coat with Tanglefoot to catch apple maggots and other pests. In greenhouses or homes, yellow plastic strips painted with Tanglefoot capture aphids, whiteflies, flies, and other pests.

Cautions: This stuff is really sticky. Insect traps coated with Tanglefoot have been known to accidentally trap small birds, so use large-area traps with discretion, placing them where birds can't come into accidental contact with the sticky surface.

PROBLEM ANIMALS AND NATURAL CARE DETERRENTS

CATS AND DOGS

In urban settings, cats and dogs can wreak as much havoc as a herd of deer on a country estate. The best way I've found to keep cats from using a freshly prepped bed as a litter box is to drape the bed (or the cats) softly with large pieces of plastic netting. The kind used for keeping birds out of fruit trees is perfect. Stake the sides and edges down with long metal staples, but be sure to bunch up the main mass of the stuff loosely in the middle. Cats dislike the uncertain feeling of this netting underfoot. To lure cats out of the garden, plant catnip along the back alley or near the trash cans.

Where dogs disrespect the garden, fencing is the best remedy. If that is not possible, consider making or purchasing an automatic scarecrow device (discussed in the section on deer). These noisy ratcheting water sprayers can be adjusted for height from very low (cat height) to average dog height. True, you can replicate this with a hose, but these gadgets have the advantage of working even when you are not around.

DEER

Throughout the Northwest, gardeners are constantly searching for effective ways to deal with deer. As new housing appears in formerly wooded areas, their habitat shrinks daily. However, these adaptable creatures make do by replacing their traditional diet of native plants with the sumptuous salad bar of garden tidbits we prepare for their delectation.

Despite the popularity of lists of plants deer don't eat, in heavily populated areas there are very few plants that won't be browsed. For years, I have planted the outer areas of my gardens with strongly scented foliage plants, finding that deer rarely eat them. These days I'm finding that while adult deer seldom graze on intensely flavorful herbs, like scented geraniums, rosemary, and lavender, young deer will eat at least some of pretty much anything.

So well are the deer adapting to their new circumstances that it is becoming common to see twins and even triplets wandering through suburban and formerly rural gardens. In spring, as the deer population increases rapidly, gardeners often find their precious plants ravaged overnight.

My present home backs onto a large wooded area, and we see deer every day. My ornamental beds even hold a few mashed spots where fawns like to nestle down at night. Over the years, I've tried many remedies to keep deer at bay. Many work quite well, for a while. Most, however have a downside, whether it is eventual loss of effectiveness or sheer ugliness. I really can't admire the garden when it is full of hair and soap and similar substances bobbing from every tree branch. Besides, for every report I get about how well something works, another gardener will rebut. For instance, an Alaskan gardener told me that he faithfully hung big bars of Irish Spring soap from his fruit trees, on the advice of many friends and neighbors. He was fascinated to see how eagerly the elk ate the soap but, sadly, they showed an equal appetite for the trees.

I have found that the best way to protect my plants is with a frequently changing program of deer repellents. I've also learned that the garden is most vulnerable in its early years, as are the plants. Now that many of my plants have been in the ground for three or four seasons, they are less fatally attractive to our frequent furry visitors.

The following are some of the most successful techniques and products I've found so far.

MALE PREDATOR URINE

Coyote urine is sold in nurseries and is a highly effective deer repellent. It is placed in rubber-sealed plant picks (the kind that hold cut flowers) and wicked out with thick cotton string or sponge wicks. Stick these near attractive plants (peas, roses, lilies), and deer won't come near.

Pro: It really works.

Con: The coyotes are penned in inhumane conditions in order to collect their urine.

Solution: Many of us keep a male predator around the house. Humans are even higher on the food chain than coyotes. If you have access to a free supply of male predator urine, by all means, give this organic technique a try.

ROTTING SALMON PRODUCTS

A number of gardeners recommend products containing decayed fish from Maine to keep deer away from their wild roses.

Pro: These products do seem quite effective, at least initially.

Con: Rotting fish smells like rotting fish. I prefer to wake up and smell roses. Also, I see no point in buying rotting fish from Maine when we have perfectly good rotting fish right here in the Northwest.

Solution: I prefer to use a somewhat similar product from Oregon called Fishtown Fish Bone Meal. This gritty, partially deodorized substance recycles fish wastes and by-products that formerly polluted our coastal waters. Scratch fish bone meal lightly into the soil around susceptible plants; the plants will appreciate it and the deer won't. Rabbits also seem to dislike the smell of fish bone meal.

BITREX

Said to be the most bitter compound known to humans, bitrex is safe for mammals and beneficial insects, and it is biodegradable. When this bittering agent is applied to foliage, the leaves smell and taste bad to deer. Most of these products are mixed with a clear latex carrier that coats stems and foliage. A new form called Repellex Systemic Tablets promises to repel not only deer but rodents, gophers, rabbits, and other herbivores, providing up to two years of protection for roses, lilies, and so forth.

Pro: I added Repellex Systemic Tablets when planting bulbs in the fall. Come spring, the deer did not touch the crocuses or the tulips (that was a first). Used on evergreens, this stuff really does seem effective, though some damage was done (mainly by fawns, as far as I could tell). The systemic tablets also provide a 14-2-2 fertilizer. The Repellex company offers numerous field studies, performed by Rutgers and other institutions, to back up their claims.

Con: It takes about a month or two for the bittering agents to enter the plant's system fully. Thus bulbs, roots, shoots, and foliage may need physical protection during that window of vulnerability. Also, if not used according to package directions (tablets inserted about 3 inches into the soil), the product may not be as effective. Never touch this material with your bare hands, and never apply it to edible crops. If you do accidentally get it on your hands and mouth, the most effective antidote is chocolate taken orally.

AUTOMATIC SCARECROWS

Battery-powered devices sold as scarecrows are triggered by a motion detector. A ratcheting device and a hose end combine to create a surprise attack: When deer, raccoons, dogs, and cats pass by, they are hit by a strong spray of water. The scarecrow combines sound and motion to intimidate.

Pro: These devices are extremely effective if they are moved often. Otherwise, critters simply avoid the spray area and make a new path. Scarecrows can be adjusted in height for various animals, so you can set one by your pool at a low height to chase away raccoons and otters and set another higher to catch wandering dogs or deer. They also help keep cats out of newly prepped vegetable beds.

Con: Despite the name, the one critter they do not work on is crows, which delight in setting these things off on a hot summer day and then preening themselves in the cool shower. Also, the cost is high for some folks, about $65 for each unit. However, those who are handy can make their own, or so I am told.

PROTECTING BULBS
FROM DEER

To discourage deer from eating spring flowers, set loose nets of black plastic fruit tree or pea vine netting over bulb beds. Deer also prefer tulips to daffodils, so those with frequent deer visitors may decide to eschew tulips in favor of daffodils. Planting bulbs with Repellex Systemic Tablets may prevent spring browsing.

METAL TREE STAKES

Where trees and shrubs are disfigured, damaged, or killed by deer rubbing their antlers, try setting a heavy-duty metal tree stake close to each trunk. You don't need to fasten the tree to the stake. The deer are trying to cure a ferocious itch, and since the metal works better than mere wood, they quickly learn to rub their heads and horns on the metal tree stakes instead of your tender trees.

Pro: This is an inexpensive and fast fix that really works.

Con: It looks a little funky but is not half as ugly as mangled trees.

HOG WIRE HOOPS

Heavy-duty hog wire can keep deer from grazing on young trees and shrubs. Buy a roll of 4-foot-wide hog wire and make hoops large enough to encircle the plant. For taller plants, stack two hoops and fasten them together with plastic twist-ties or wire. Use long metal staples to fasten the hoops to the ground.

Pro: This is a very effective, inexpensive, and flexible protection system that can be used over and over for many years. Lightweight hoops store easily and can be resized easily as needed.

Con: Some folks find the looks of the hoops objectionable. Again, wire hoops are more attractive than broken trees.

GEESE

In some areas, large flocks of geese may become a nuisance, covering lawns and garden beds with their droppings and damaging plants in beds and borders. To avoid attracting geese, never feed water birds. Geese can be repelled with streamers of foil or bright plastic or by automatic scarecrow devices, discussed in the section on deer. Bobbex-G, a new form of a common deer repellent, is said to keep geese off lawns as well.

MOLES

Moles make a lot of gardeners crazy. Each spring, dormant moles wake up hungry. They cruise from garden to garden, seeking their favorite foods, which are worms and grubs. During the summer, mole visits are usually sporadic, but in fall, as they prepare to enter dormancy once again, the determined search for food is repeated. Lawns are decorated with heaps of burrow soil, and plants may

Rabbits and moles won't get your tender lettuces if they aren't in the ground. Container plantings are often unbothered by soil-dwelling pests.

wither overnight, distressed by root disturbance and air pockets left in the wake of a hungry mole.

Why do moles pick on certain gardens more than others? When we make rich, healthy soil, we encourage our worm population as well as our plants. Because moles eat worms, the better a job we do of soil building, the more hungry moles will like our gardens. The solution to this is emphatically not to kill off the worms (as some pesticide manufacturers suggest), nor is it to stop improving the soil. Impoverished soil and plants invite a wide variety of problems, from failure to thrive to pests and diseases. In addition, lousy soil won't stop moles from visiting, though they won't stay as long in poor environments.

Readers with low pest tolerance are reminded that it is illegal (in Washington, at any rate) to trap moles with spring traps that maim or kill them. Live trapping is legal, but it leads to complications: What do I do with this innocent mole? Patience may be the best tactic. In truth, moles are a good sign, not a bad one. They are carnivores that dine on crane fly larvae, grubs, and worms, not plants or roots. (When plant root damage is present in a mole run, it is nearly always caused by opportunistic voles and mice.)

Moles help aerate compacted soils, acting like living rototillers that turn the soil. They are most active and tend to linger longest where soils are damp, so overwatered lawns are a primary target. On average, the mole population is only one or two critters per acre. If we don't attract them by overwatering our lawns, they are rarely a nuisance. Where moles are a bother, reduce watering to no more than an inch once a week or less. Gradually replace water-guzzling landscape plants with handsome

CONCENTRATE TO REPEL MOLES

Here is a simple and effective version of the liquid commercial mole repellents. This recipe was sent in by a reader some years ago and has been tested by many home gardeners, who report satisfying results. The key ingredient is the dish soap; as we all know, there is no substitute for Joy. One part may equal 1 cup or 1 tablespoon.

Mix together until foamy:

2 parts castor oil
1 part Joy dish soap

To use, add 2 tablespoons of the mixture to 1 gallon of water, and spray in and around mole holes daily. This usually works within a day.

native shrubs and drought-tolerant ground covers. It also makes sense to give preference to attractive plants from other regions with wet winters and dry summers. For instance, a handsome landscape can be woven with evergreen grasses, seasonal bulbs, sedums and succulents, and evergreen hardy Mediterranean herbs such as rosemary, sage, lavender, and thyme. In the meantime, reduce incidental damage to plants by gently tamping down any visible mole runs with your feet.

MOLE FENCE

To keep moles out of new beds, install 10-inch-high mole fences of ¼-inch-mesh hardware cloth. To make these, fold a 20-inch-wide length of hardware cloth in half, forming an L shape. Install the fences below soil level, pointing the lower stroke of the L in toward the garden. Set just below the soil surface, these invisible fences won't catch the lawnmower or be visually obtrusive, but they will block moles, voles, and mice from your new beds. That's a lot of work when large areas are involved, and though they work well, these little fences are pretty hard to retrofit into a mature garden.

WORM BARS

In my garden, my favorite way to deal with moles is to create small mock compost piles near the points of attack. I hide a wheelbarrow load of almost-finished compost and blended kitchen scraps behind a handy plant, then add in some red wigglers from the worm bin or the manure heap. Cow manure is another irresistible lure for worms (and thus moles). Simply dump a wheelbarrow load of dairy manure here and there near the perimeter of your property. In both cases, the resulting rich concentration of worms convinces the moles to dine in your worm bars instead of digging through the garden. This is a bit like putting a pot of jam out for wasps when they appear at a picnic.

MOLE CHASERS

Another option is to use one of the ultrasonic or sonic mole chasers, which transmit sounds that annoy moles and certain other rodents, notably gophers. These work best in lighter soils; heavy clays may limit the passage of sound. They seem to work best when moved periodically. Both battery- and solar-powered models are available.

MOLE REPELLENTS

Yet another highly effective way to deal with moles is to use a repellent made from castor oil. Nearly all commercial mole repellents include castor oil, which does not kill moles but does encourage them not to linger. If as a child you were ever dosed with castor oil, you will understand why this is so.

Most commercial mole repellents are sprays that can be applied with a hose attachment. They typically last for only a week or so, especially during the rainy months, when the castor oil is quickly washed away. A new version called Mole No More is prilled (pelletized) and can be spread on lawns and flower beds with a whirlybird (hand seeder) or a drop spreader. This solid stuff is quite persistent, lasting through six or eight weeks' worth of rain or garden watering.

MOUNTAIN BEAVERS

A very unhappy gardener once told me about wrestling with a mountain beaver that had dragged a good-sized azalea halfway down its hole. The critter was pulling it one way and she was furiously tugging on the other end. She eventually won that round but lost the war. I've not dealt with these tough critters myself, but I'm guessing I'd probably move.

RABBITS

The only rabbits native to the maritime Northwest are pygmy rabbits, mostly found up on the Gulf Islands. All the others are escapees from suburbia (except those that are deliberately let loose by "owners" without a conscience). Rabbits are hard to discourage, but a combination of the following tricks usually works:

- Line the bottom of all garden fences with 3-foot-tall hog wire or chicken wire, sinking the wire an inch or more below ground.

- Use hot pepper sprays or bitrex (see the deer section) on nonedible foliage.

- Sprinkle coarse fish bone meal and/or blood meal around the perimeter of each bed.

- Set a scarecrow water spray device (discussed in the deer section) at the lowest possible setting near natural approach areas or known critter pathways.

- Make cages of chicken wire reinforced with metal screen material at the sides to fit over rows of susceptible edibles.
- Grow little "hedges" of rosemary, lavender, garlic, and other strongly scented foliage plants around each garden area.

RACCOONS

To avoid attracting raccoons, be careful not to create problems by leaving food where they can get it. Put all garbage in tightly closed tins. Dig food scraps well into the compost heap, or buzz them in the blender before adding them to your worm bin. Never leave pet food where raccoons can find it, and never, never feed them. Raccoons that excavate lawns or raid worm bins, compost heaps, and ponds can be dissuaded with one or more automatic scarecrow devices (discussed in the deer section). To be a successful deterrent, each scarecrow needs to be moved at least a few feet every few days, or the raccoons learn to ignore it.

RODENTS

Rats, mice, voles, and other rodents can cause a lot of damage in a garden. In greenhouses, you can plug in electric "silent scream" devices that are said to repel rodents with a high-pitched sound humans can't hear. Outside, you can try battery-powered or solar sonic and ultrasonic rodent chasers, devices that are shoved into the soil, where they transmit sounds at levels humans can't hear. Boxes or cages of chicken wire can be reinforced with metal screen material at the sides to cover greenhouse flats, single plants, or whole rows. If the garden is heavily damaged or you are losing chickens to rats, consider using one of the new bio-safe (for nonrodents) rodent killers (several types are now available). Protect bulbs with rodent-proof wire cages. Several sizes are commercially available, or you can make your own with heavy-gauge wire screening, such as hog wire. See also the earlier section on making mole fences. The squirrel-proof bird feeders are usually rat-proof as well, and there are also several effective rodent repellents based on plant essential oils.

SQUIRRELS

Squirrels are apt to dig up fall-planted bulbs, sometimes trading them for nuts of their own. To protect bulbs, plant them in wire cages (described in the section on rodents). Planting bulbs with lots of black pepper may help as well. There are several squirrel repellents based on plant essential oils that can be used indoors (in attic crawl spaces and so on) as well as outside. There are also good, if expensive, bird feeders that are designed to be squirrel-proof.

EIGHT: GARDEN BONES

To ensure your trees have a long and healthy life, choose appropriate trees, place them where they can succeed, and plant them with care.

In the Northwest, trees are sometimes horribly abused in the name of preserving views. Before topping or mutilating a tree, remember that trees are themselves a view, just as water and mountains are.

A friend once made a provocative comment. "Here in the Northwest," he observed, "relationships between neighbors are based on trees." He explained that people are drawn here by the expansiveness of forest and mountains and sky. When they build a new house, the first thing they do is clear-cut the property to let in the sunlight. The next thing they do is start reforesting, nearly always right along their property line.

Since trees grow at a great rate in these parts, before you know it the neighbors' yard is half full of half-trees that don't belong to them. Their lawns are invaded by roots, their houses are shaded, and their views may be lost, but they can rarely do anything about it without starting a pitched battle that may quickly involve the entire neighborhood. Even worse, the original lot still enjoys a terrific view and plenty of sun. Such inequity makes for hard feelings, and rightly so.

The solution, happily, is simple. Before planting trees, think long and hard about their future. Unless you live in a rural area, think small. Think apple, think bay laurel, think Irish juniper. Think ahead, and think of your neighbors.

For one thing, thoughtless tree placement can trigger guerrilla tactics when neighbors (or new owners, or the power crew) are moved to action. Overnight, beautiful trees are butchered into grotesque obscenities. Half a tree is not better than none. Few sights are more depressing than mutilated grandeur. It's one thing when trees are battered and broken by natural storms. It's quite another when they are brutally hacked out of shape simply to serve human convenience. Mangled trees make enduring monuments to selfish insensitivity.

MAKING SMART TREE CHOICES

Fortunately, tree trauma can be avoided by intelligent, thoughtful action. Where mature trees spark neighborly difficulties, selective limbing can restore lost views and bring light to dark places. Where too many trees are tightly clustered, selective thinning will create a healthier environment for the survivors. Tree topping is never an acceptable option, for not only is it unspeakably ugly, but the brutal practice is very hard on the tree. It is far better to remove a troubled or troublesome tree entirely and replace it with a healthy, more appropriately sized substitute.

Here in the Northwest, we are deeply attached to our rights. Indeed, sometimes I think the more we want to insist on our rights, the further west we move. However, in this land of trees, as far west as one can get, arboreal rights should also be respected. We can move a lot faster than the trees, so we seem to have the upper hand. The trees, however, can long outlast us, and let us hope they do. If we succeed in killing most of our trees, we will discover that we literally cannot live without them. Without trees to clean it, our world's polluted air would be unbreathable.

Although we come to the Northwest because we admire the lushness, many of us react to the overwhelming green by attempting to control it, to assert our human power over the forces of nature. Any gardener can tell you that this is a mistake. Just watch the way a lone daffodil or horsetail can push its blind way through layers of asphalt, splitting sidewalk or roadway asunder with soft green leaves.

Rather than pitting our strength against nature, we can benignly harness that green energy by making smart choices about what we plant. When we plant trees, native or not, we can select choice forms that won't outgrow their position. Instead of setting ourselves up for years of heavy pruning and damage control, we can enjoy watching our young trees develop, secure in the knowledge that what they do naturally is exactly what we want of them. That cooperative spirit makes for good neighbors, human and arboreal.

SMALL GARDEN TREES WITH CHARACTER

Since most gardens have room for only a very few trees, it is vital to choose them with care. Poor choices can cause significant inconveniences, from diseases, pruning problems, root infiltration, and excess shade to roof or car damage from falling limbs. At worst, choosing the wrong tree can trigger an ongoing battle for control that ends only with death (generally that of the tree).

In contrast, well-chosen trees play a key role in garden design, providing numerous practical advantages as well as intangibles such as strong character, majesty, and a sense of maturity. At best, garden trees also offer serial pleasures season after season, year after year.

With so many tantalizing trees to choose from, it can be difficult to narrow our choices down to just the right few. The most satisfactory way to do this is to begin intellectually, setting stringent standards and requirements such as the following:

Spectacular fall color in Japanese maples can be enhanced with deep compost mulches. Compost provides the sugars that create vivid, sunset tints when chlorophyll drains away from dying foliage.

- The trees in question must size up fairly quickly or be available in adequately large size to make an immediate impact, yet never outgrow their position.

- The trees must be mannerly, sharing ground without spreading an excess of hungry, thirsty roots.

- The trees must not be messy, shedding quantities of berries (think of mulberries or madronas) or large, smothering leaves (like many oaks or bigleaf maples) or prickly ones (like hollies and mahonias).

- The limbs must not be so brittle that any wind strews beds and borders with their branches (like locust trees) or that large limbs drop without notice (as with many willows).

- The trees must be adapted to the soil and site we can offer them, accepting whatever is involved in the way of wind or shelter, sun or shade, acid or alkaline soil, and sand or clay.

- To be truly choice, garden trees must also possess outstanding attractions in every season.

The amazing thing is the number of trees that meet all these criteria. Applying this list of qualifications refines the possibilities down from thousands to mere hundreds that remain appropriate choices.

The second part of the equation involves an emotional response to the real thing. We need to look at the candidates, and not just in nursery cans but in garden contexts. When we visit established gardens and arboreta, our attention will likely be caught by trees with character. By this I mean plants that have developed something close to personality, qualities of shape and form and color that give them genuine presence.

Such trees shape the space around them, leading the eye as well as the foot, demanding acknowledgment from nearby plantings and reigning as undisputed queens of their territory. Ancient apples, hoary with lichen, limbs sagging in elegant swags; twisted pines, wind-blasted and seemingly bent with the snows of centuries; elderly birches whose chalky, black-eyed trunks are peeling and tattered—all build a powerful impression of distinguished maturity in a garden.

Sadly, unconventionally shaped mature trees are not readily available to the average garden maker. For one thing, older trees don't always move well. Fruit trees in particular can be highly resentful of disturbance. Try as we may to entice them into our garden, that enchanting old pear that's far too close to the house or the pick of the crop from the abandoned apple orchard down the road would rather die.

Certain small trees, among them many graceful maples and arboreal rhododendrons, are less fussy and will accept a move with ease. However, mature specimens rarely come cheap. A few years ago, the talk of Seattle's Flower and Garden Show was a gigantic old sumac, shaggy with moss, its arching branches leafless but decorated with faded seedheads. Priced at over $16,000, such a tree is not within every gardener's budget but would unarguably become the centerpiece of any garden it graced.

All across the country there are garden designers who specialize in locating and installing mature plants. Gardeners who can afford these services may take advantage of the instant stability and cachet that older trees will bring to the rawest new garden.

On the other hand, we may overlook treasure that's hidden in our own backyards. Overgrown, neglected gardens new to us only as new owners frequently contain aging trees that simply await artful pruning to unveil long-concealed beauties.

Some trees are beyond repair, but others need only be freed of deadwood and distorted branches to be revealed in glory. Indeed, if there is any doubt at all about a tree's possible worth, a judicious, inquisitive pruning session is always more appropriate than immediate removal. If what is revealed is more gory than glorious, rip it out and replace it with something better. Before removing older trees (or large shrubs, which can fulfill the same function in small yards), consult with an arborist or garden designer who specializes in restorative work.

If you haven't got an elderly tree in place or a sizable chunk of cash to pay for somebody else's, the best option is to grow your own. True, it will be a long time before a young plant will fulfill its potential. However, by selecting trees that are lovely in youth and that will age with grace, you can enjoy them at every stage of life, watching their character develop along with your own. Below is a sampler of fine garden trees, any of which will be an asset to your garden from the day you plant it.

Any or all of these choice little trees will serve as the centerpiece for border or bed, create a focal point for a much-used house window, or act as sentinel at the entryway to the garden. Through the seasons and over the years, they will steadily increase in beauty and strength of character, aging with a grace and dignity we can only admire and try to emulate.

FRINGE TREE

The southeastern native fringe tree, *Chionanthus virginicus* (12 to 20 feet), is a splendid creature in any season. Like the catalpas, the fringe tree leafs out late, and the long, tapered foliage is still expanding as the flowers appear in early summer. Even young trees bear good crops of faintly fragrant flowers, which hang, clustered and creamy, in long, silky panicles that give the tree its common name, old man's beard.

The simple foliage remains handsome well into autumn, slowing turning clear gold as cold weather arrives. The dangling berries, dark blue with a bloom like Concord grapes, are eagerly sought out by thrushes and robins, which weigh down the branches when the fat little fruits are ripe. In winter, the sleek gray trunks and netted branches make a shapely silhouette against hedge or sky or rise like rugged stone columns amid a flurry of golden-stemmed dogwoods.

Young plants may be single or multitrunked, open and airy or densely branching. Whichever form you prefer can be selectively pruned to clarify the overall growth pattern but should otherwise be allowed to achieve its natural shape. Don't stake sinuous young trunks, but let them wind their way upward. As the plant matures, those little kinks and wiggles become graceful swoops and turns that give the adult tree its distinct character.

Fringe trees are occasionally bothered by the diseases their cousins, the lilacs, are prone to, notably mildews and scale. However, such problems occur mostly on stressed plants. Given good garden soil, adequate supplemental water in hot or dry summers, and a site offering plenty of light and free passage of air, fringe trees adapt even to difficult urban conditions with aplomb.

PARROT TREE

Gaudy as a parrot (though named for a naturalist), Persian parrot tree, *Parrotia persica* (20 to 50 feet), ranks among the world's best plants for fall color. Like its hamamelid kin, which include witch hazels, fothergillas, and *Disanthus cercidifolius,* its boldly rounded leaves color vividly, their long-lasting display building slowly to spectacular effects. Generally broad headed with curving, multiple trunks, the adult parrot tree has limbs marbled with pewter and cream (though young bark is a solid gray-brown).

The strongly horizontal branches are eccentrically tiered, creating wavelike layers rather than neat stacks. This structural pattern creates a striking outline that remains potent in every season. In winter, its strong skeletal form has the power of sculpture. In spring, the glossy new growth is suffused with bronze and burgundy. Quietly handsome in summer, Persian parrot tree comes into its own in fall, when it colors with all the familial intensity, in captivating combinations of yellow and gold, tawny orange and copper, flaming scarlet and glowing ember crimson.

Young or old, parrot tree resents transplanting, so it's wise to choose its place with care to avoid repeated displacement. It adapts to average garden soils but prefers well-drained, mildly acid clays enriched with copious quantities of humus. Parrot tree regards wet feet with dismay, but willingly tolerates dry soil once established. It looks perfectly at home at the edge of a meadow or woodland. The tree grows well in light shade but colors most spectacularly in full sun.

Generously sized (6- to 10-foot) specimens of this moderate grower provide the greatest initial impact, but younglings can be treated as charming shrubs if planted with an eye to their future development. Healthy and sturdy, the Persian parrot tree has no common pests or diseases, though Japanese beetles may riddle the leaves in bad years. Allowed ample room for its multiple trunks to develop their characteristic curves, it shares space happily with the smaller shrubs and perennials of the mixed border, which can flow smoothly beneath its spreading arms.

CRABAPPLE

Crabapples of many kinds offer lovely, fragrant flowers, bright fruit, terrific fall color, and a charming winter silhouette.

Even the most ordinary apple tree has significant charms, but a few members of the apple clan are outstanding in every season. Among the ornamental crabapples, pride of place goes to the Sargent crab, *Malus sargentii* (12 to 15 feet). This shrublike little tree takes its time about gaining height but enchants the eye at every stage of its long life.

A heavy bloomer in late spring, its masses of scented white flowers (appropriately apple blossom pink in the form 'Rosea') are followed by remarkable quantities of persistent cherry red fruits. Its fall color is remarkable for dazzle and duration even where summers are cool. In the garden, Sargent crabs make splendid company for incendiary dogwoods and azaleas, or mingle excitingly with sumacs and large grasses in meadows and at the skirt of dark woods. Winter bares the branches to reveal interesting herringbone branch patterns that look especially pretty when encased in ice or outlined with snow.

Another excellent little crabapple, weeping *Malus* x 'Red Jade' (to 15 feet) is perfect for smaller gardens where space is at a premium. Narrowly mounded and almost fountainlike in shape, its slim branches look too frail to bear their loads of foamy flowers, let alone the bountiful crops of fat little fruits that follow. These linger well into winter, bobbing daintily from the long, hanging stems, which make strong verticals in the winter landscape. Like most apples, this one is exceptionally appetizing to deer, over which it seems to exercise a fatal attraction. String soaked in coyote urine (contained in capped florists' vials) is an effective repellent but, unfortunately, it repels me as well.

CAMPERDOWN ELM

Camperdown elm, *Ulmus glabra* 'Camperdownii' (10 to 20 feet), is a tidy little weeper with a rounded head and long, pendulous arms that brush the ground. Very much at home in formal settings, its soft outline also blends readily into the complex interior topography of the mixed border or cottage garden. In the East, elm leaf beetle may decimate the foliage, but they are not a problem in Western gardens.

Where winters are mild, these little trees can be grown in large pots and set on decks or in courtyards or used in pairs flanking the front door of the house, for they offer pleasures in every season. The intricate tracery of the bare branches is delightfully apparent in winter. The coppery new leaves are prettily pleated in spring. The summer shape is strong and graceful, and even a light breeze is enough to ruffle the dark leaves, showing their downy, silvered undersides. In autumn, summer's green brightens to old gold and then darkens to rich mahogany brown, the perfect foil for warm lilacs and lavenders, so set colchicums and fall crocus thickly at its feet, to point this up at leaf fall.

PHOTINIA

Perhaps because it lacks a common name, *Photinia beauverdiana* (to 20 feet) remains rare in gardens. Collected from western China by Ernest Wilson in 1900, this delightful deciduous tree deserves wider distribution.

When young, its habit is so lax that the large leaves appear to pour down in rippling cascades from the humped crown. As it matures, it straightens into a narrow, upright little tree with flexuous branches. Where summers are warm, these are studded in late spring with crowded corymbs of creamy little florets, followed by loose clusters of ruby fruits. In cooler climates, both flowers and fruits are scanty, but in every setting, the autumn foliage display is noteworthy. Long and tapering, the marvelously tinted foliage turns scalding yellow, burnt orange, burnished copper, and smoldering red before falling.

Though easygoing, healthy, and less intolerant of limy soils than most deciduous photinias, this one is hard to find in nurseries. That's too bad, because this tree has ample character from the gallon.

KATSURA TREE

Among the most beautiful small garden trees are Asian katsuras, *Cercidiphyllum japonicum* (20 to 60 feet), whose heart-shaped leaves recall the redbud family. The whole tree is astonishingly graceful, rising like a slim flame when young, wiry arms curved to embrace the sky, and then spreading with maturity into billowy domes. In the wild, katsuras can achieve great heights, and in open landscapes, they may reach 40 to 60 feet, but in gardens, they rarely exceed 30 feet.

However handsome the sinuous skeleton and the glazed brownish-gray bark, which grows attractively ragged in older specimens, foliage is these trees' dominant beauty. Flushed with plum purple, the infant leaves are as decorative as blossoms. Rich bottle green in summer, they begin to take on autumnal tints in early fall. Their coloration can be exceptionally varied; my own garden holds several katsuras, as does my neighbor's, and no two of them share the same tints or the same time line. Some produce and drop their leaves early, while others trail weeks behind.

In the most open part of the garden, the katsura leaves turn shades of singing yellow and muted gold. On trees in slightly more shade, they are buff overlaid with salmon, coral flushed with rose, peach veined in old gold on red stems, or pale tangerine suffused with apricot and veined in lemon. One tree in dampish soil and little direct sun colors incandescently, the lower branches golden and the upper ones searing reds and oranges, veined in purple and stemmed in fuchsia.

To enjoy them fully, we float the leaves in bowls of water, for though their lovely confetti decorates the garden floor for weeks, the leaves dry out and darken quickly indoors. The ripening foliage has a delicious scent like milky caramel, faintly spicy and intensely sweet, which can permeate the whole garden. This, too, is a variable feature, for in my garden, only the eldest tree (which is over fifteen years old) produces strongly scented leaves.

FRAGRANT SNOWBELL

Japanese fragrant snowbell, *Styrax obassia* (18 to 30 feet), outshines our native snowbell *(S. americanum)* in every respect. From youth, its twisting arms cradle the curving trunk protectively, forming a netted web of stems that make lovely lacework in winter. Its big, rounded leaves appear early—indeed, fragrant snowbell needs a protected spot in cold gardens to keep leaves and flower buds from frost damage.

Whether single or multiple, its sleekly turning trunks are a luminous dove gray, while the horizontally stacked branches are clothed in coppery orange-brown bark that gleams like Thai sari silk when soaked by winter rains. In spring, big buds unfurl into coppery leaves that green up quickly, making a dramatic backdrop for its long, clustered bunches of white blossoms. These dangle under the branches as well as on top, and when this little tree is placed above a path or stairway, the passerby looks up into an open umbrella filled with fragrant white flowers. In fall, its coloration is more subtle than sumptuous, yet its warm gold and mellow browns make an effective foil for more brilliant companions.

SOUTHERN MAGNOLIA

Because fall color is among my major interests, my lone evergreen example is a petite form of the southern native, *Magnolia grandiflora* 'Little Gem' (15 to 20 feet). Unlike the parent species, 'Little Gem' blooms as a young plant, and its lustrous, hand-sized evergreen leaves are half the typical size, though similarly lined with cinnamon fuzz on their back sides. Densely furnished to the ground, 'Little Gem' makes an impressive front entry plant, especially when planted in matching pairs along the path or set out in ornamental containers beside the garden gate. The waxy white flowers, cupped and filled with gold stamens, are intoxicatingly fragrant, and their heady scent carries clear across the garden on warm spring nights. The first flowers open in late spring and continue in bursts through November, at times opening beside plump pods bursting with glossy red seeds.

TREES IN MIXED BORDERS

Certain specimen trees and shrubs can also be placed within planting beds, where they become the focal point of a mixed border. Mixed borders hold combinations of plants of all kinds, usually integrated into layered communities. The canopy layer might be small trees or large shrubs, with understory shrubs carrying the eye back down to border shrubs, perennials, and ground covers.

In this setting, a choice small tree will become the focal point for the entire border. Placed as the centerpiece, all its subsidiary companions will help lead the eye back to the main attraction. In a sunny spot, a weeping 'Red Jade' crabapple might be flanked by masses of peachy 'Daydawn' potentillas, pink floribunda 'The Fairy' roses, and white coneflowers (*Echinacea purpurea* 'White Swan').

In a shadier place, a weeping goat willow (*Salix caprea* 'Weeping Sally') could be surrounded by sweet box (*Sarcococca* species), fluffy astilbes, evergreen ferns, and lenten roses (hellebores). In both cases, the small, shrublike tree has enough sculptural quality that it will carry quite a large planting with panache.

If an evergreen tree is wanted, a multitrunked strawberry tree (*Arbutus unedo* 'Compacta') has enough character for the role yet won't overplay the part. This madrona relative has white, bell-shaped flowers followed by fat little fruits that have a sour tang (but they are great in salads).

Emphasizing the sculptural quality of the specimen tree is the key to successful placement. If the tree is too crowded, it can't develop its characteristic shape properly. If the understory plantings are too tall, we won't be able to see the lead character very well.

Planting a specimen tree close to a house wall (or any wall) is not a good idea. In such a position, a plant can achieve only half its true shape. What's worse, the back sides of plants placed too close to walls are nearly always centers for disease, mildews, molds, and other problems. The main culprits are poor air circulation and dry soil (rain can't reach under roof soffits, and walls create a rain shadow).

Huge specimen trees can be a gift to the whole neighborhood, but they must be placed with thoughtful care. Never put a tree where it will grow into overhead wires of any kind. Likewise, keep those deep roots well away from underground water mains, cables, and sewage lines.

It makes sense to place specimen trees where they will frame a desirable view or screen a regrettable one. Do, however, consider your neighbors as well; if your favorite tree will get 40, 60, or 100 feet tall, what will happen to the view from nearby homes? Might roots and leaves and litter from your tree eventually fill other folks' yards?

If not, you are lucky indeed. Those with large properties can indulge in almost any kind of tree and revel in the results for years to come. Evergreen magnolias, bigleaf

A well-spaced grove of birch trees
underplanted with perennials, ground
covers, and daffodils provides year-
round beauty.

The same scene in autumn's mellow
gold: This is the garden of Margaret
de Haas van Dorssen in Oregon.

maples, beeches, and chestnuts are all splendid large trees that increase in magnificence decade after decade.

However, in a typical small yard large trees will quickly outgrow the available space. To avoid a host of expensive problems, those with modest lots will be best off planting smaller, more compact trees. Fortunately, there are many exceptional small trees that offer beauty in every season. Here are some favorites in the 20- to 30-foot category.

STEWARTIAS

First come the stewartias, graceful small trees with lovely bark, a handsome branching habit, exceptional fall color, and white flowers in summer. Graceful as a dancer in winter, any stewartia leafs out in midspring and blooms in June. In fall, these small trees burn like a living flame in hot reds, coppers, oranges, and yellows.

Stewartia monadelpha can exceed 30 feet in time, but may take over forty years to do so. Smaller Japanese stewartia (*S. pseudocamellia*) has larger flowers and lovely leaves and looks especially splendid rising behind large rhododendrons. Korean stewartia (*S. koreana*) has a delicate branching pattern and a pronounced upright habit as well as fragrant white flowers.

CRABAPPLES

Smaller still are the crabapples, a large and mixed group. Look for crabs that resist scab and other apple diseases, since both can afflict crabapples throughout the Northwest. (Compost tea helps control these and other foliar and fruit disease problems; see Chapter 6 for more information.) The narrowly upright 'Centurion' combines rosy flowers, round red fruit, and ruddy tinted foliage in spring and fall. Grandiflora crabs combine plump buds with rosy flowers, attractive long-lasting fruit, good fall color, and lovely form.

MAPLES

Maples come in all sizes, from modest to massive. Native vine maples (*Acer circinatum*) are choice small trees, while Japanese maples (*A. japonica*) range from 8 to 10 feet up to 20, 30, and even 40 feet, depending on which one you select. It is imperative to place larger maples (and all larger trees) where they can form their natural shape without being hacked back.

THE 20-FOOT RULE FOR TREES

If you are planting trees and large shrubs, you need to know about the new 20-foot rule. As of 1998, throughout much of the Northwest any tree or large shrub growing within 20 feet of a power line may be pruned or topped.

This new 20-foot zone has been adopted by many electrical companies. The rule is enforced by the pruning crews that work for public and private utilities. These are the folks that keep the roadways clear and trim around phone and electrical lines.

The crew will contact homeowners and get permission to cut privately owned plants. However, in cases where trees and shrubs are growing near or into power lines, it is extremely probable that the trees will be topped, which leaves them permanently disfigured.

Planting 20 feet back from power lines may not protect your plants, since many large trees and shrubs have considerable lateral spread. To avoid this unhappy event, take heed and don't plant anything with a mature height of more than about 12 feet under power lines.

Our magnificent native Pacific dog-wood, Cornus nuttalli, *does beautifully in gardens as long as it isn't watered or fertilized. Most natives prefer a lean diet and no summer water and can be killed with kindness.*

Even a common red alder makes a splendid shade tree when mature. Our native red alder has won awards of merit from England's Royal Horticulture Society and is well worth cherishing in the right spot.

PLANTING TREES

Autumn is prime time for tree planting. It is also the ideal time to plant or transplant trees and shrubs. In spring, most plants are trying to produce foliage, flowers, and even fruit. In fall, they are more single-minded, settling for strong root growth.

Since trees can outlast their planters by many years, it makes sense to give them a good start. Dig each planting hole as deep as your tree's container and at least twice as wide. Firm up the bottom of the planting hole well (you can even stomp on it) to make sure there are no air pockets, which can make roots dry out very fast. Add an inch of compost, pack it firmly, and then place your tree, making sure that the "collar" of the tree is exactly at grade. The collar is a slight swelling at the base of the trunk; below it, you'll notice that the tree's roots are spreading out rather than down. Help them spread out a bit, then fill in around them with a mixture of half the removed bed soil and half compost. Firm this down well, and water your new tree in generously.

Give each tree at least 5 gallons of water at planting and each time you water it for the first year. Water the roots, not the foliage. Use a mild transplanting fertilizer (an N-P-K ratio of 2-4-2 is fine) that incorporates beneficial biota and mycorrhizae (Whitney Farms Lifelink is a good one).

Now give your tree a fresh blanket of compost to keep weeds away. Be sure the trunk is not smothered; there should be no more than ½ inch of compost from the trunk to about a hand span away. Increase the depth of the compost mulch until it is about 3 to 4 inches deep at the tree's dripline. The compost mulch should always extend at least 2 feet beyond a tree's dripline.

CHOICE SPECIMEN TREES FOR SMALL YARDS

COMMON NAME	BOTANICAL NAME	HEIGHT
Chinese stewartia	*Stewartia sinensis*	To 30'
DESCRIPTION: *Fragrant white flowers; flaming fall foliage; flaking bark; tiered form*		
Columnar crabapple	*Malus x 'Centurion'*	15 to 20'
DESCRIPTION: *Narrow, ruddy foliage; fragrant flowers; small fruit*		
Fragrant snowbell	*Styrax obassia*	To 30' (slow growing)
DESCRIPTION: *Showy white flowers in summer; splendid fall color; likes moist soil*		
Japanese maple	*Acer japonica*	8 to 30'
DESCRIPTION: *Lovely flowers; fabulous foliage and seasonal color; good structure*		
Japanese stewartia	*Stewartia pseudocamellia*	20 to 30' (slow growing)
DESCRIPTION: *Large, fragrant white flowers; fabulous fall color; flaking bark; fine form*		
Korean stewartia	*Stewartia koreana*	30 to 40' (slow growing)
DESCRIPTION: *Large, fragrant white flowers; fabulous fall color; flaking bark; fine form*		
Persian parrot tree	*Parrotia persica*	20 to 50'
DESCRIPTION: *Tiny flowers and fruit; broad form; fabulous bark; splendid fall color*		
Pink snowbell	*Styrax japonicus 'Pink Chimes'*	To 30'
DESCRIPTION: *Fragrant, baby pink bells; golden fall color; graceful, upright form*		
Sargent crabapple	*Malus sargentii*	12 to 15'
DESCRIPTION: *Fragrant flowers; berrylike fruit; terrific fall color*		
Strawberry tree	*Arbutus unedo 'Compacta'*	12 to 15'
DESCRIPTION: *White bell flowers; red fruit in fall; evergreen; multitrunked, good form*		
Vine maple	*Acer circinatum*	12 to 20'
DESCRIPTION: *Handsome, slim form; great fall color; pretty silhouette*		
Weeping crabapple	*Malus x 'Red Jade'*	12 to 15'
DESCRIPTION: *Fragrant flowers; graceful weeping form; holds fruit well into winter*		
Weeping goat willow	*Salix caprea 'Weeping Sally'*	12 to 15'
DESCRIPTION: *Long catkins in late winter; soft golden fall color; graceful weeping form*		

Shrubs offer multiple advantages to the gardener seeking sustainability. Once established, shrubs are nearly independent. Most need only a few minutes of care each year (the time it takes to scatter compost mulch and alfalfa or remove winter damage). Shrubs make excellent screening and backbone plants, offering structure and privacy all year-round in exchange for very little time and attention. Well-chosen shrubs can also offer a steady supply of seasonal interest, from spring flowers and summer foliage to fall fruit and winter bark and berries.

The downside of shrubs is that most don't really change much through the seasons or over the years, particularly evergreens. To create that desirable ongoing seasonal interest, we need to provide a blend of the reliable but relatively static evergreens and the constantly changing deciduous shrubs. The staunch evergreens can be placed to block unwanted views and to create enclosure and a sense of privacy. Deciduous shrubs can be placed where their seasonal flow will be appreciated most and where their lack of leaves won't present privacy problems during the cooler months.

Here's how to select and place shrubs in the garden successfully.

THE RULE OF THIRDS FOR LOW-CARE GARDENS

- One third evergreen shrubs
- One third deciduous shrubs
- One third plants with seasonal color

Well-chosen shrubs are garden glue, holding your bed and border vignettes together all through the year.

Evergreen native leatherleaf, Garrya elliptica, *is handsome year-round, but especially so in winter, when male plants produce their elegant catkins. Best in a sheltered site with morning light and afternoon shade, garrya is drought tolerant and prefers compost over fertilizer.*

EVERGREEN SHRUBS

Using lots of shrubs can greatly reduce garden chores. However, a preponderance of woody plants can also make the garden feel totally boring or lacking in life and flow. To avoid a static quality and rigid appearance, no more than a third of any garden planting should consist of structural evergreen shrubs. Most of these will be the larger transitional layering shrubs that enclose the garden and form a backdrop for the beds and borders. The remainder of them may be fine-textured border shrubs such as hebes, rosemary, sages, and lavenders or small woodlanders like sweet box (*Sarcococca* species), huckleberries, camellias, and small rhododendrons. The smallest evergreen subshrubs, such as miniature boxwoods and shrubby thymes, can be used as edging plants.

DECIDUOUS SHRUBS

Another third of the garden's plants may be devoted to deciduous shrubs, including spring and summer bloomers as well as those with persistent berries and handsome winter bark. Members of this group may range from large shrubs like beautyberry (*Callicarpa* species) and 'Midwinter Fire' twiggy dogwoods *(Cornus alba)* to smaller border foliage shrubs like 'Goldflame' spiraea, black-leaved 'Diablo' ninebark, and many barberries. These may provide blossoms and fruit as well as colorful leaves. The smallest deciduous shrubs, such as dwarf barberry and miniature roses, can edge beds and pathways.

PLANTS WITH SEASONAL COLOR

The final third of our plants will be made up of perennials, annuals, grasses, and bulbs. The compact border shrubs can be clustered with evergreen grasses to create island plantings that present pockets of winter interest within beds and borders. The ephemerals (bulbs, annuals, and perennials) can then be placed in and around these island groupings, where they will be supported during their show times and masked during decay and dormancy. If we take care to include early and late bloomers as well as summer performers, such a blend offers a pleasing balance of privacy, winter presence, and seasonal color.

Because a high percentage of these plants are woody, such a garden is far less needy than the usual flower borders. If closely planted and deeply mulched, the beds will need very little feeding or weeding and will require only occasional watering, except during prolonged hot or dry spells. Fall cleanup will consist of chop-and-drop tidying, cutting up spent leaves and stems and letting them compost in place between the shrubs. Evergreen grasses and shrubs carry the borders in winter, and in spring, bulbs and early bloomers tucked between the structural shrubs will begin the ongoing annual cycle of color once more.

Glossy native huckleberry takes shade or part sun in stride and can grow in full sun if given soil improved with compost. Fragrant flowers become delicious berries that attract both birds and hungry gardeners.

GARDEN SHRUBS

While most of the tallest shrubs will be planted about the perimeter of the site and others may be used as trees within the garden itself, the majority of intermediate shrubs can be used to form backdrops for borders as well as to create interior garden "walls." Most of these transitional layering shrubs should be selected from those that mature at between 8 and 12 feet in height. The smallest shrubs, mainly dwarf and compact border shrubs that mature at between 1 and 5 feet, can be integrated into mixed borders and texture gardens, where they lend strength and substance to perennials, annuals, grasses, and bulbs.

SHRUBS FOR FALL COLOR

COMMON NAME	BOTANICAL NAME
Azalea (many)	*Rhododendron* species
Barberry (many)	*Berberis* species
Beautyberry	*Callicarpa* species
Fothergilla	*Fothergilla* species
Cotoneaster	*Cotoneaster* species and hybrids
Disanthus	*Disanthus cercidifolius*
Enkianthus	*Enkianthus* species
Hydrangea (many)	*Hydrangea quercifolia* and others
Smoke bush	*Cotinus* species and hybrids
Spiraea (most)	*Spiraea* species
Sumac (all)	*Rhus* species
Witch hazel (all)	*Hamamelis* species

SHRUBS FOR SUNNY SPOTS

COMMON NAME	BOTANICAL NAME
Abelia	*Abelia* species and hybrids
Barberry	*Berberis* species and hybrids
Beautyberry	*Callicarpa* species
Bog rosemary	*Andromeda polifolia*
Boxwood	*Buxus* species and hybrids
California lilac	*Ceanothus* species and hybrids
Cotoneaster	*Cotoneaster* species and hybrids
Dwarf conifers	Many
Escallonia	*Escallonia* species and hybrids
Euonymus	*Euonymus alatus*
Flowering currant	*Ribes* species and hybrids
Forsythia	*Forsythia* species and hybrids
Lavender	*Lavandula* species and hybrids
Lilac	*Syringa* species and hybrids
Madrona	*Arbutus menziesii*
Manzanita	*Arctostaphylos* species and hybrids
Mexican orange	*Choisya ternata* and hybrids

Mock orange	*Philadelphus* species and hybrids
Oregon grape	*Mahonia* species and hybrids
Pacific wax myrtle	*Myrica californica*
Potentilla	*Potentilla* species and hybrids
Pyracantha	*Pyracantha* species and hybrids
Quince	*Chaenomeles* species and hybrids
Rockrose	*Cistus* species and hybrids
Rose	*Rosa* species and hybrids
Rosemary	*Rosmarinus* species and hybrids
Sage	*Salvia officinalis* and other species and hybrids
Salal	*Gaultheria shallon*
Silk tassel	*Garrya* species and hybrids
Spiraea	*Spiraea* species and hybrids
Sumac	*Rhus* species and hybrids
Viburnum	*Viburnum* species and hybrids

SHRUBS FOR SHADE

COMMON NAME	BOTANICAL NAME
Azalea (some)	*Rhododendron* species and hybrids
Camellia	*Camellia* species and hybrids
Enkianthus	*Enkianthus* species and hybrids
Flowering currant	*Ribes sanguineum* and others
Fothergilla	*Fothergilla* species
Fuchsia	*Fuchsia* species and hybrids
Hazelnut	*Corylus cornuta*
Huckleberry	*Vaccinium* species and hybrids
Hydrangea	*Hydrangea* species and hybrids
Indian plum	*Oemleria cerasiformis*
Leucothoe	*Leucothoe* species and hybrids
Mountain ash	*Sorbus* (some)
Oregon grape	*Mahonia* species and hybrids
Rhododendron	*Rhododendron* species and hybrids
Snowberry	*Symphoricarpos* species and hybrids
Sweetbox	*Sarcococca* species and hybrids
Thimbleberry	*Rubus parviflorus*
Twiggy dogwoods	*Cornus* species and hybrids
Viburnum	*Viburnum* species and hybrids
Witch hazel	*Hamamelis* species and hybrids

LAYERING FOR LIGHT

Chapter 1 introduced the concept of layering as a way of placing plants so that they step down from trees to shrubs to garden plants, giving the garden a natural look. Layering is also used to create open space around the house. This is especially important in the Northwest, where natural light is at a premium for much of the year. Instead of cluttering up the house with excessively large foundation plantings that shade the windows and block views, we can place our shrubs about the perimeter of the site, creating a soft green wall that is viewed from house windows. Rather than feeling gloomy and overgrown, the house thus sits in a golden bowl of light with ruffled green sides sloping up to the sky.

These tiered plantings look best and are most easily cared for when they consist of unsheared shrubs with handsome natural shapes. Unsheared shrubs are highly attractive to birds, which flock to gardens that offer such natural shelter and feeding opportunities. Naturally shaped shrubs are gentle on the eye and never demand the constant maintenance that tightly sheared shapes require.

In urban and suburban settings, the majority of layering shrubs should mature at heights between 8 and 20 feet to avoid problems arising from overscreening. Since few small modern lots have space for more than one large tree (if any), larger shrubs can be treated like small trees. Given pride of place and limbed up to look treelike, shrubs such as dwarf magnolias, weeping crabapple or goat willow, golden privet, California lilac, and large rhododendrons will approximate the presence and majesty of trees with far less height and bulk. (For more on arborizing shrubs, see Chapter 5.)

EVERGREEN LAYERING SHRUBS

COMMON NAME	BOTANICAL NAME	HEIGHT	FOLIAGE	HABIT
	Abelia (several)	6–8'	Fine textured	Upright or broad
Andromeda	*Pieris* (several)	8–20'	Tapering	Upright or broad
California lilac	*Ceanothus* (many)	8–12'	Fine textured	Upright or broad
	Camellia (many)	12–20'	Glossy	Upright
	Cryptomeria (several)	8–12'	Winter color	Upright
	Escallonia (several)	8–15'	Fine textured	Upright or broad
	Eucryphia (several)	10–20'	Glossy	Upright
False cypress	*Chamaecyparis* (several)	8–12'	Many colors	Upright or broad
	Ilex (many)	8–20'	Hollylike	Upright or broad
Madrona	*Arbutus menziesii*	8–15'	Glossy	Upright or broad
Mountain laurel	*Kalmia* (many)	8–15'	Tapering	Upright or broad
Oregon grape	*Mahonia* (several)	8–12'	Hollylike	Upright
Pacific wax myrtle	*Myrica* (several)	12–20'	Glossy	Upright
	Phillyrea (several)	8–15'	Tapered	Upright or broad
	Rhododendron (many)	5–20'	Glossy	Upright or broad
Strawberry tree	*Arbutus unedo*	12–20'	Fine textured	Upright
Various berries	*Vaccinium* (several)	5–20'	Fine textured	Upright or broad
	Viburnum (several)	5–20'	Various	Upright or broad

DECIDUOUS LAYERING SHRUBS

COMMON NAME	BOTANICAL NAME	HEIGHT	FOLIAGE	HABIT
Azalea (many)	*Rhododendron* species and hybrids	8–20'	Fall color	Upright or broad
Beauty bush	*Kolkwitzia amabilis*	8–20'	Fine textured	Upright or broad
Bottlebrush buckeye	*Aesculus parviflora*	8–15'	Bold	Upright or broad
Butterfly bush (many)	*Buddleia* species and hybrids	8–20'	Tapering	Upright
Forsythia (many)	*Forsythia* species and hybrids	8–12'	Fall color	Upright or broad
Honeysuckle (many)	*Lonicera* species and hybrids	6–12'	Fine textured	Upright or broad
Hydrangea (many)	*Hydrangea* species and hybrids	8–12'	Bold	Upright or broad
Lilac (many)	*Syringa* species and hybrids	12–20'	Oval	Upright
Mock orange (many)	*Philadelphus* species and hybrids	6–8'	Fine textured	Upright or broad
Quince (many)	*Chaenomeles* species and hybrids	6–15'	Fine textured	Upright or broad
Rose (many)	*Rosa* species and hybrids	6–20'	Fall color	Upright or broad
Smoke bush	*Cotinus* species and hybrids	12–20'	Fall color	Upright
Sumac (many)	*Rhus* species and hybrids	8–15'	Fall color	Upright or broad
Twiggy dogwoods (many)	*Cornus* species and hybrids	6–12'	Fine textured	Upright or broad
Viburnum (several)	*Viburnum* species and hybrids	8–20'	Various	Upright or broad
Witch hazel (many)	*Hamamelis* species and hybrids	12–20'	Bold	Upright or broad

Glorious fall color makes sumacs sing when temperatures tumble. Tall and leggy, sumacs are terrific layering plants, bridging huge trees and garden-scale understory.

COMPACT BORDER SHRUBS

In sustainably designed gardens, the beds and borders are likely to be gracefully layered with woody plants. Whether placed as specimens, backbone plants, or screening plants, larger trees and shrubs can be treated very simply. The same is true for most compact border shrubs, the smaller shrubs woven into the furnishing layer of garden plants. Like their larger counterparts, border shrubs will thrive on benign neglect, needing only a few minutes of attention each year to keep them tidy and healthy. Border shrubs in this category include broad-leaved evergreens such as andromeda (*Pieris japonica* and hybrids), sheep laurel (*Kalmia angustifolia* and hybrids), and border rhododendrons. Deciduous shrubs like fothergilla, star magnolia, and the smaller Japanese maples are also included in this category.

All of these are what I call character shrubs, plants with a definite shape of their own. All have a strong internal branching pattern, with one or more main trunks. These plants should never be sheared or shaped except with thoughtful attention to the plant's true nature.

In terms of nutrition, most shrubs grow best in decent, well-drained soil, without commercial fertilizers. An annual feeding mulch in spring and a comforting layer of compost in fall will amply provide for their nutritional needs.

Shrubs vary in their needs for water. When we are designing for sustainability, we need to consider what plants prefer, whether damp shade or full sun and dry soil, before placing them in the garden. Even when we can offer our shrubs conditions they like, they will need to be watered well for their first full year and situationally watered for another year or so before becoming independent. Some shrubs, such as hydrangeas, will flag sadly in dry years, even in good soil and well-mulched beds. It's worth clustering thirsty shrubs in the garden and winding a soaker hose around their feet. When dry summers make your shrubs look sad, run the soaker once a week until the rains return.

A second group of border shrubs includes root-hardy plants that may die back to the ground in cold winters but will reappear in spring. The fluffy pink California lilac, *Ceanothus* x pallidus 'Marie Simon', is typical of this group. Shrubs like potentillas and spiraeas that have a natural bun or blob shape fall into this category as well, since they can be restoratively whacked or sheared as needed and will recover quickly and nicely. For instance, when you want to tidy up the masses of old blossom on small spiraeas, you can simply grab handfuls of twigs and clip the ends, or you can shear the shrub back by a third all over. Either way, it will rebound in a hurry without looking artificial or stiff.

It's best to do this remedial trimming in late winter or early spring, rather than in fall. The extra top growth provides protection from frost damage, and the seedheads will attract goldfinches, chickadees, and other small seed feeders. A few broad-leaved evergreens fall loosely into this category. Certain daphnes, various leucothoes, and salal *(Gaultheria shallon)* are all amenable to regular clipping, though they may become unnaturally congested if overly controlled.

Larger cane-growing shrubs include arctic willow, forsythia, quince, and lilac. All of these can be whacked to the ground if need be, to restore their natural shape. When the roots resprout, selectively choose as many as you think right (you may want three or five trunks on a lilac, and as many as twenty or so on a large, old forsythia). Thin all other shoots rigorously, allowing only the chosen ones to mature. In a few seasons, you'll have a well-shaped plant that does not need coercive shearing to stay in bounds.

This common practice can be stressful for the plant, however. Even easygoing shrubs like willows and twiggy dogwoods (such as *Cornus alba*) will weaken over time when they are cut back too hard too often. To keep your twiggy dogwoods colorful, remove about a third of the oldest, most dully colored canes each year, cutting them clear to the ground. This way, each plant will be fully renovated every three years, and you'll keep a steady supply of handsome winter twigs coming without overly stressing your plants.

FOUNDATION PLANTINGS

Foundation plantings are the plants that surround the house. Nearly always evergreen, foundation plantings are intended to visually link the house to the landscape or garden. Typically, small trees or large shrubs flank the front doorway to mark its importance and create a sense of entry. Low-growing shrubs are grown beneath windows,

When choosing compact border shrubs, blend deciduous shrubs with a mix of broadleaved evergreens and conifers for year-round good looks. For ease of care, give preference to drought-tolerant shrubs with a naturally tidy habit, like heathers and dwarf conifers.

COMPACT EVERGREEN BORDER SHRUBS

COMMON NAME	BOTANICAL NAME	HEIGHT	FOLIAGE	HABIT
Barberry	Berberis	2–5'	Winter color	Upright or broad
Bog rosemary	Andromeda polifolia	1'	Blue-gray	Low, mounded
Boxwood	Buxus	1–2'	Variegated	Upright
Cedar, arborvitae	Thuja (several)	1–6'	Fine textured	Upright
	Cryptomeria (several)	2–8'	Winter color	Upright
	Escallonia (several)	4–8'	Fine textured	Upright or broad
False cypress	Chamaecyparis (many)	2–8'	Many colors	Upright or broad
	Gaultheria (several)	2–5'	Winter color	Upright or broad
Heather and heath	Calluna + Erica	1–3'	Many colors	Spreading
	Hebes (many)	2–6'	Blue-gray, green	Upright or broad
Honeysuckle	Lonicera (several)	3–4'	Glossy	Spreading
	Ilex crenata (many)	1–5'	Winter color	Upright or broad
Lavender	Lavendula (many)	2–4'	Silver, green	Upright or broad
	Leucothoe (several)	4–6'	Fall color	Arching
Mexican orange	Choisya ternata	4–6'	Glossy	Upright or broad
Mountain laurel	Kalmia (some)	2–5'	Winter color	Upright or broad
Oregon grape	Mahonia (several)	1–4'	Winter color	Upright or broad
	Rhododendron (many)	1–6'	Glossy	Upright or broad
Rockrose	Cistus	2–6'	Several colors	Upright or broad
Rosemary	Rosmarinus (many)	3–5'	Several colors	Upright or broad
Sage	Salvia (many)	2–3'	Several colors	Spreading
Sweet box	Sarcococca	2–4'	Green	Spreading
Various berries	Vaccinium (many)	2–8'	Fall color	Upright or broad

COMPACT DECIDUOUS BORDER SHRUBS

COMMON NAME	BOTANICAL NAME	HEIGHT	FOLIAGE	HABIT
Arctic willow	Salix glauca	5–8'	Fine textured	Mounding
Azalea (many)	Rhododendron	2–8'	Fall color	Upright or broad
Barberry	Berberis	1–5'	Many colors	Upright or broad
Bluebeard	Caryopteris (many)	3–5'	Several colors	Upright or broad
Butterfly bush	Buddleia (many)	4–8'	Many colors	Upright or broad
Fothergilla (several)	Fothergilla	2–6'	Fall color	Upright
Fuchsia (many)	Fuchsia	2–8'	Many colors	Upright
Hydrangea (many)	Hydrangea	1–5'	Several colors	Upright or broad
Lilac	Syringa (several)	4–6'	Green	Upright
Ninebark	Physocarpus (several)	6–8'	Green, black, gold	Upright, informal
Potentilla	Cinquefoil (many)	1–4'	Fall color	Upright or broad
Quince	Chaenomeles (many)	2–5'	Green	Upright or broad
Rockrose	Cistus (many)	2–5'	Several colors	Upright or broad
Spiraea (many)	Spiraea	1–6'	Many colors	Upright or broad
Sumac	Rhus (many)	2–8'	Fall color	Upright or broad

while larger ones may decorate large sections of bare house wall.

Often, foundation plantings are remedial in nature, designed to disguise architectural flaws. When well chosen and well placed, structural evergreens can improve the looks of an awkwardly shaped or poorly sited house. Conversely, the wrong foundation plantings can create remedial situations. It is easy to assume that certain plants must be "the right ones" because we see them everywhere. However, thousands of homeowners can indeed be misguided, if not flat-out wrong. When we think in terms of sustainable design, it seems silly to set ourselves up for years of repetitive chores, and it makes perfect sense to select foundation plants that will remain the right size for many years.

The most common error is to select foundation plants that will quickly outgrow their desired size. To avoid this, figure out the dimensions of the various foundation spaces you want to fill, and then choose plants that will mature to fill somewhat less than those spaces. Remember that plants are three-dimensional; they gain in bulk as well as height. Thus, if your windows are 4 feet above the ground, you'll choose shrubs that mature at or below 4 feet in height. If those shrubs will be around 6 feet wide at maturity, you'll plant them about 6 feet apart. If the spaces look empty to you, fill in with short-lived shrubs like rockroses or easily moved ones like hydrangeas. As your plants mature, the fillers can be edited out.

Typically, however, we pick plants that will be far too big, place them too close together, and then complain that they are growing too fast. The usual solution to overgrowth is to shear foundation plantings. This plan has two major flaws. First, it creates a self-perpetuating chore that can't be skipped. Even worse, it stresses the plant. Nothing enjoys being continually frustrated. In time, sheared plants look as tired as the people who constantly struggle with them. This is called a lose-lose proposition.

The sustainable solution is to seek out plants that will do exactly what you want them to by nature. If you love the formal look, select formally shaped plants. Many compact and dwarf conifers will fill the bill, and lots of broad-leaved evergreens look groomed and dapper in every season. True, none are actually rectangular, but here in the Northwest, casual beauty looks more at home than the chilly perfectionism of pure formality anyway.

In general, it's best to avoid chain-saw relationships with our plants. Until recently, few people questioned the wisdom of standard texts that blithely presented some pretty odd ideas as gospel. Even the *Sunset Western Garden Book* advises that the giant sequoia makes a fine hedge plant and can be kept indefinitely at 8 to 12 feet. Anybody who has seen a mature sequoia can sense that there is something intrinsically wrong with the concept of a sequoia hedge.

Doesn't it seem more sensible to find plants that will be 8 to 12 feet for life by nature? Why not use Hicks' yew (*Taxus media* 'Hicksii') instead? This is a handsome, columnar shrub with a natural buzz cut that matures at 10 feet or so. There are dozens of compact conifers with naturally formal shapes that can serve as excellent hedging plants without necessitating constant shearing and annual hard pruning.

Rhododendrons provide excellent examples of both successful and disastrous foundation plantings. Many a Northwest home is darkened by looming arboreal rhododendrons that soar skyward instead of remaining low and compact. That sweet young thing in a nursery pot looked so demure and tidy. Who would guess that it longed to be a tree?

Rhodies can be terrific foundation plants, but only if we pick the right ones. If you want a rhododendron that remains 2 to 4 feet tall, start by looking at yaks, hybrids of *Rhododendron yakushimanum*. All have dense, felted foliage and lastingly trim figures as well as lovely flowers. If you don't like fuzzy leaves, look for dapper little 'Moonstone', a 2-footer with creamy moonlight flowers, or 'Bow Bells', a tidy 4-foot shrub whose glowing pink bells ring in midspring.

Once you've chosen the right plant, make sure you put it in the right place. No matter what your situation, the right place is never smack against the house. The right place is more likely to be 4 to 6 feet out from the house. That may look silly at first, especially if you are starting with small plants. However, in just a few seasons, the plants will fill in and the look will be right. In the meantime, fill those empty spaces with bold annuals. Just don't let them crowd your young shrubs, for evergreens can be permanently damaged by leafy overgrowth.

Because it doesn't "look" right when it's done right, almost all foundation planting is done wrong. Most foundation shrubs are inappropriately large and are placed too close to the house for health or beauty. As a result, most foundation plantings have disease or growth problems on the side facing the house. Pollen buildup and fungus, molds, and mildews are common on plants that lack good air circulation.

What's more, when snow slides from the roof, it generally lands right in the middle of poorly placed foundation plants. To avoid broken or misshapen shrubs, set them well out from under the roof or gutter line.

All such problems will be prevented if we surround the house with a band of gravel at least 18 inches wide and 6 inches deep. Consider this a plant-free zone, a place to stand while changing screens, putting up shutters, washing windows, and so forth.

Next, create your planting beds outside this gravel strip. The foundation beds should be a minimum of 3 feet wide, to accommodate the girth of your structural shrubs as they mature. If your soil is heavy clay, creating mounded beds with a base layer (8-inch minimum) of sandy loam topped with a layer of good soil (8-inch minimum) will greatly improve the health of your plants. (See Chapter 3 for more on building beds.)

These beds need not be edged; simply smooth them down to the gravel on the back side and to the lawn, walkway, or whatever is at the front. The soil will settle within a season, so they won't look out of proportion. Top the beds off with a 2- to 4-inch layer of mulch. Aged dairy manure or compost works well to conserve moisture and suppress weeds. Wood chips and peat moss are not appropriate mulching materials; wood products leach nitrogen from the soil as they decompose, while peat moss sheds water when dry and is difficult to rewet.

When you plant, center those young shrubs in the bed, placing their stems or trunks at least 4 to 6 feet from the house wall. If the scale of your home demands that you use large shrubs, place them proportionately further out from the house walls. Do all this and you will have handsome, healthy, easily maintained foundation plantings that grow old gracefully.

Remember too that you don't have to use the same plant on each face of the house. If the front of the house is sunny, the sides are shaded, and the back offers dappled light, you'll be most successful if you choose sun lovers for the front yard and shade lovers for the remaining sides.

EVERGREEN FOUNDATION PLANTS

NAME	HEIGHT	CULTURE
Ceanothus thyrsiflorus	3 to 6'	Sun
DESCRIPTION: *California lilac, fine-textured foliage, takes pruning in stride, drought tolerant*		
Dwarf conifers (many)	3 to 6'	Sun
DESCRIPTION: *Dwarf Hinoki, gold thread, or blue Chamaecyparis; many more excellent choices for the careful label reader*		
Hebe species (many)	3 to 6'	Sun, light shade
DESCRIPTION: *Dapper, fine-textured foliage, many foliage colors, drought tolerant*		
Leucothoë axillaris 'Nana'	To 3'	Shade, some sun
DESCRIPTION: *Several other dwarf forms, good winter color, drought tolerant*		
Lonicera nitida	3 to 4'	Shade, sun
DESCRIPTION: *Box honeysuckle is neatly tiered, takes pruning well, drought tolerant*		
Nandina domestica 'Gulfstream'	To 6'	Shade, sun
DESCRIPTION: *Many fine choices among the nandinas, most very drought tolerant*		
Osmanthus heterophyllus 'Purpureus'	3 to 4'	Sun, light shade
DESCRIPTION: *Purple, hollylike foliage, drought tolerant*		
Pernettya mucronata	2 to 3'	Sun, light shade
DESCRIPTION: *Showy winter berries in white or pink, fine-textured foliage, drought tolerant*		
Rhododendron 'Moonstone'	To 3'	Shade, some sun
Rhododendron yakushimanum (many)	2 to 4'	Shade, some sun
DESCRIPTION: *Many excellent choices, will never need pruning; best with regular moisture*		
Rosmarinus officinalis 'Arp'	3 to 5'	Sun
DESCRIPTION: *Many good choices, including some columnar forms, drought tolerant*		
Sarcococca species	2 to 5'	Shade, some sun
DESCRIPTION: *Dapper sweet box has fragrant winter flowers, best with regular moisture*		
Senecio greyi 'Sunshine'	3 to 5'	Sun
DESCRIPTION: *Silver foliage, can be pruned, drought tolerant*		

SUSTAINABLE ENTRYWAY PLANTINGS

The point of entryway plantings is to frame the doorway, arch, arbor, or gate that leads us from a public space into a more private one. As with foundation and screening plants, the most common error is to overplant and to use plants that will become excessively large for the available space. Sustainable design encourages us to pick appropriately sized plants and to place them where they can develop their full size and shape without blocking traffic flow or obstructing views into or through the garden. Where space is limited, choose columnar plants, or consider making entryway plantings in large containers filled with seasonal color plants (conifers in winter, annuals in summer, and so on).

Use the following guidelines when choosing plants for an entryway:

- Entryway plantings should not have prickles or thorns that could scratch a child in a stroller (or anybody else).

- Entryway plantings should not crowd the doorway, creating an unsafe situation for an older person whose footing is insecure.

*Dapper, drought-tolerant strawberry trees (*Arbutus unedo) *make a charming entryway tree and blend well into an informal tapestry hedge.*

- Entryway plantings should not shed slippery leaves in autumn or drop unsightly litter in any season.
- Entryway trees and shrubs should not be brittle or susceptible to wind damage.

Compact or dwarf conifers and leafy shrubs of any kind can be used next to an entryway, but the majority should be evergreen to provide year-round interest. Adding a lively assortment of evergreen or multiseasonal foliage perennials such as ferns and spurges (Euphorbia species) will also help keep entryways attractive. See the list of foundation plants given earlier for some ideas. Where taller accents are wanted, consider using narrow, columnar shrubs or small trees, such as ones in the following list.

COLUMNAR PLANTS FOR ENTRYWAYS

NAME	TYPE	SIZE
Juniperus chinensis 'Hetz's Columnaris'	Evergreen	3' wide, 10 to 15' tall
Juniperus communis 'Stricta' (Irish juniper)	Evergreen	2' wide, 10 to 15' tall
Juniperus scopulorum 'Skyrocket'	Evergreen	3' wide, 10 to 15' tall
Malus 'Pink Spires' (crabapple)	Deciduous	8' wide, 15' tall
Malus sargentii (Sargent crabapple)	Deciduous	8' wide, 12' tall
Rosmarinus officinalis ('Miss Jessup's Upright')	Evergreen	3' wide, 6 to 10' tall
Rosmarinus officinalis 'Tuscan Blue'	Evergreen	3' wide, 8 to 12' tall

SCREENING PLANTS

If specimen trees are showpieces, the plants that frame and define the garden space are more structural, acting like living green walls. Shrubby screening plants are usually evergreens, which can perform their multiple functions all year-round. Thoughtfully chosen and well placed, they become a firm basis for the garden's design, their strong forms clearly dictating the position of subsidiary plants.

Though they are seldom showboats, backdrop evergreens can screen unwanted views and frame attractive ones. Again, in the interests of maintaining our sustainable garden, we do not want to pick plants that will outgrow their position, forcing us into a chain-saw relationship. Instead, we want a selection of adaptive, easygoing plants that will size up quickly and mature to an appropriate size.

For most yards, the largest screening shrubs may top out at 10 to 15 feet. The bulk of them can be smaller, in the 8- to 12-foot range, and where we want to frame and preserve views, they probably won't need to exceed 6 to 8 feet. We also want plants that will maintain a pleasing natural shape for many years, requiring little or no regular pruning.

Happily, plenty of evergreen shrubs will give us everything we need from them. To find good candidates for your own yard, start by consulting your favorite local nursery folk. Visit lots of different nurseries, both big chain garden centers and small specialty places, seeing what's available. Check out some library books, including a few good regional references that offer listings of appropriate evergreen plants. A good one to start with is *Trees and Shrubs for Pacific Northwest Gardens* by John and Carol Grant (Timber Press, 1994).

Once you have some attractive choices in mind, tour public gardens, parks, and arboretums to see what that growing list of possible screening plants will look like in maturity. Don't skip this eye-opening experience, because no matter what the label says, it's hard to imagine just how big those cute little baby trees and shrubs will really be at maturity.

SMALL-SCALE EVERGREENS FOR SCREENING

COMMON NAME	BOTANICAL NAME	HEIGHT	FOLIAGE	HABIT
Barberry	*Berberis* (several)	2–5'	Winter color	Upright or broad
Bog rosemary	*Andromeda polifolia*	1'	Blue-gray	Low, mounded
	Cryp—meria (several)	2–8'	Winter color	Upright
False cypress	*Chamaecyparis* (many)	2–8'	Many colors	Upright or broad
	Gaultheria (several)	2–5'	Winter color	Upright or broad
	Ilex crenata (many)	1–5'	Winter color	Upright or broad
	Leucothoe (several)	4–6'	Fall color	Arching
Mountain laurel	*Kalmia* (some)	2–5'	Winter color	Upright or broad
Oregon grape	*Mahonia* (several)	4–6'	Winter color	Upright or broad
	Thuja (several)	1–6'	Fine textured	Upright
	Vaccinium (several)	2–8'	Fall color	Upright or broad

MIDSIZED EVERGREENS FOR SCREENING

COMMON NAME	BOTANICAL NAME	HEIGHT	FOLIAGE	HABIT
	Abelia (several)	4–5'	Fine textured	Upright, wide
Andromeda	*Pieris* (several)	8–20'	Tapering	Upright or broad
Blue juniper	*Juniperus virginiana* 'Manhattan Blue'	10–15'		
Columnar juniper	*Juniperus scopulorum* 'Wichita Blue'	15–20'		
	Euonymus (several)	5–20'	Glossy	Upright or broad
	Ilex (many)	6–20'	Hollylike	Upright or broad
	Lonicera (several)	5–10'	Tapering	Upright or broad
Mountain laurel	*Kalmia latifolia*	15–30'	Tapering	Upright or broad
Oregon grape	*Mahonia* (several)	5–10'	Hollylike	Upright
Pacific wax myrtle	*Myrica californica*	10–15'		
	Rhododendron (many)	5–20'	Broad	Upright or broad
Strawberry tree	*Arbutus unedo*	10–20'	Fine textured	Upright
	Vaccinium (several)	5–20'	Fine textured	Upright or broad
	Viburnum (several)	5–20'	Various	Upright or broad

SUSTAINABLE HEDGES

Hedges are a long-term investment and should be planned carefully. Usually we create hedges to provide privacy, to screen views, or to protect the garden from wind. How we enclose each section of the garden will depend in part on how we plan to use it. Once we decide which activities best suit each available area, we can think about ways to put appropriate and practical visual boundaries between them. For the outer "walls" of the garden perimeter, traditional choices include evergreen or deciduous hedges as well as fences or walls. Where any or all of these are already in place, the garden is half made from the start.

In new gardens, however, there is often no enclosure at all. If there is a hedge, it is probably too young to create effective enclosure. Because large hedges require several years to size up, they should be planted early on and backed up by a secondary screen or visual baffle.

Common, quick-growing hedge plants will be relatively inexpensive and are frequent sale items at large nursery chains. However, it's important to think about how you want that hedge to work and how much time you want to spend on it. Sustainable choices include shrubs that don't outgrow their allotted space and don't require endless pruning and shaping. Most common hedge choices are huge plants that will need constant shearing for the rest of their life (or yours).

Before you buy a hundred baby photinias or Leyland cypresses, ask yourself a few questions. Do you really need an evergreen hedge, or could a dense row of twiggy deciduous shrubs work just as well? Evergreen hedge plants are usually quite a bit more expensive than deciduous ones, but if you aren't out in the yard much during the winter, the extra protection may not be worth the extra expense.

Consider as well whether you want to trim your hedge or not. In the city, formal homes and garden designs seem to demand clipped hedges. However, tightly spaced evergreens with a naturally upright habit, such as Italian or Irish junipers (*Juniperus communis* 'Stricta' or 'Hibernica'), can look quite dapper even when unclipped. In some situations, notably in suburban or country gardens, an excess of clipped hedges may look pretentious, while a shaggy row of unsheared arborvitae (*Thuja* species) will make a convincing visual link with native trees and shrubs nearby.

Untrimmed hedges are not necessarily casual or sloppy looking; much depends on the plants you choose. Evergreen lily-of-the-valley shrub (*Pieris* species, slow growing to 10 feet) has a naturally tidy habit and needs only occasional minor pruning to maintain a formal appearance. Arching bridal wreath spiraea (*Spirea prunifolia,* to 6 feet) is a densely twiggy deciduous shrub with enough natural architecture that a wide row of it appears equally charming when flanking a driveway circle before a country house or lining a broad walkway in front of a formal townhouse.

To further refine your possible choices, consider whether the available hedge space offers adequate width for large shrubs. If you don't have at least a 15-foot-wide strip available for your hedgerow, plan to use narrow, tightly columnar plants like Irish junipers. In general, you can assume that a mature hedge will be about as wide as it is tall. This means that plants like photinia and Leyland cypress that get 15 to 20 feet high will also get that wide. They'll keep on getting that wide for their whole life, even if you keep cutting them in half. Thus, the chain-saw relationship is born.

The same principle holds true on a smaller scale as well.

When you are creating lower green walls for interior garden spaces, keep in mind that if you want the little hedge between the vegetable patch and the swing set to be 4 feet high, you'll need to allocate a 4-foot-wide strip for it. If that big front hedge is to be 12 feet tall, you'll need to leave 6 feet of clear space on both sides of the baby hedge to allow for future growth.

This brings us to a major point: It is not polite, considerate, or in some cases, legal to plant a hedgerow smack on your property line. Half the width of that hedge will be growing in somebody else's yard for years to come. Similarly, half the hedgerow may be growing into the neighbor's driveway or a public sidewalk. Before you decide where a hedge will go, walk the site, tape measure in hand, and see exactly what kind of space you have to work with. Narrow spaces don't mean that you can't have a hedge: There are plants, like 'Skyrocket' junipers (*J. scopulorum* 'Skyrocket') and weeping sequoias *(Sequoia dendron giganteum* 'Pendulum') that rarely grow more than 3 to 4 feet wide, no matter how tall they become. However, it is very important to be realistic about what will happen to that hedge over time.

If in laying out the planting strip you realize that your hedge will encroach on the sidewalk and fill the entire front yard, you may prefer to enclose that particular area with a fence instead. Fences are often the enclosure form of choice for small, urban lots. If you decide to use plants, keep in mind that as a good rule of thumb, anything you plant should remain on your property, even in maturity. A hedge placed where it will intrude on public or private property stands a good chance of getting more of a trimming than you want it to, either from irate neighbors or a zealous city pruning crew.

Once you have decided what the physical limitations of the site are, make a few notes about the soil and light or shade along the potential hedgerow. Sites with dark and light sections are good candidates for mixed hedges, using different kinds of plants instead of all one kind. That way, you can mix shade and sun lovers as needed without stressing plants or getting the irregular look of happy and unhappy plants.

When you know the ultimate size your hedge plants can be and the site conditions you can offer them, it becomes relatively simple to select appropriate candidates. Now you can go shopping with something very specific in mind. Even if you aren't sure just what the plant may be, you know you are looking for an 8-foot-tall shrub that doesn't get more than 6 feet wide, seldom needs pruning, and adapts well to both full and partial sun and clay soil. Chances are good you'll come home with something like redtwig dogwoods or arctic willows *(Salix glauca),* both of which would work just fine. If you want an evergreen, you might use Hick's yews *(Taxus media* 'Hicksii') or *Magnolia grandiflora* 'Little Gem' instead.

FORMAL OR INFORMAL HEDGES

Sustainable hedges can be made in several ways. Most commonly, hedges are made of a single row of a single kind of plant, planted very close together for quick fill-in, and then sheared or not. When unsheared, they are called informal hedges. When windbreaks are needed, hedges can be planted in double, staggered rows or a soft W formation, using tall, slim trees or shrubs such as poplars or columnar cypress at the back and bulkier, lower growers like Pacific wax myrtle, barberry, or spiraea along the front or garden side. Most often, double-row hedges are not sheared.

Tapestry hedges are made of several kinds of plants mixed together. These can be sheared (which to my eye looks like a real mess) or left natural. For instance, a famous tapestry hedge at Hidcote in England contains plain and copper beech. It is also possible to create mixed hedges using many kinds of plants. Indeed, putting all the loose, sloppy-shaped but beloved shrubs of spring like forsythia at the border back helps to free up precious garden space.

Good candidates for mixed hedging include forsythia, lilacs, quince, shrub rose, wild rose, rosemary, viburnum, snowberry, and twiggy dogwoods. Even if you are making tapestry or mixed hedges involving several kinds of plants, the result will be more pleasing when all the shrubs are similar in size and shape. When a hedge mixture offers too much variety, it creates visual chaos. Instead of blending into a solid backdrop, the mixed plants remain stubbornly separate, offering the eye a distracting jumble of forms.

Tapestry hedges often appeal to plant lovers who prefer variety over repetition. One good way to indulge plant lust without spoiling the design of the garden is to keep the main green walls simple but to combine the most interesting plants you can find for smaller, interior hedges. Inside the garden, you can combine striking backdrop shrubs in satisfyingly creative compositions. Because the overall area involved is not great, there won't be room to create chaos, since only a few compact or dwarf plants will fit. In a tiny garden room, a plain hedge can look pretty boring, but a vividly mixed tapestry of shrubs makes a fascinating wall that never looks dull.

Even ardent plant collectors may decide to opt for plain hedges when they realize what splendidly understated backdrops they make. Where complex plantings are to be framed, the simplicity of plain yew or privet is highly complementary, whereas a long run of brightly colored leaves or wildly textured greenery can become overwhelming, distracting the eye from the beds and borders that are intended to be the visual heart of the garden.

On the other hand, there are places where such a hedge becomes a work of art. When paired with potent modern architecture, a visually aggressive hedge becomes as compellingly eye-catching as the building it encloses. In such a situation, a garden design combining extreme simplicity and boldness will be most successful anyway, and an extravagantly woven tapestry hedge will look terrific.

LITTLE HEDGES

Low hedges are often used to divide spaces within the garden into rooms, to frame vegetable or rose gardens, and to edge beds, paths, and walkways. These inner hedges can be as simple as a shaggy row of unpruned lavender or as contrived as an arrow-straight line of sheared boxwoods, depending on the style and feeling you want to evoke.

Where a low interior garden hedge is meant to guide the feet but allow the eye to see beyond the barrier into adjacent garden areas, compact shrubs such as box honeysuckle (*Lonicera nitida,* to 6 feet) or one of the shorter privets (*Ligustrum* species, 6 to 10 feet) can be kept to height of 3 or 4 feet by annual clipping. Those who want a looser, unclipped low hedge can consider dwarf barberries (*Berberis* species) or glossy Japanese hollies (*Ilex crenata* forms).

As always, the main points to consider are the ultimate height and width of the unpruned plant and how frequently it requires clipping to remain tidy. If your chosen shrub produces pretty flowers and fruits, find out whether it will still do so when constantly pruned. (Some shrubs flower only on new wood, so each time you cut away the young growth, you are also removing potential flowers.)

Compact edging shrubs like dwarf boxwood or lavender can be clipped or left natural in shape. Even if you plan to shear your hedges, you can minimize the work by selecting dwarf plants. Their slow growth will reduce the amount of control you will need to exert to keep your edging hedges looking trim. Where space is tight, there may not be room for unclipped shrubs unless they have a naturally upright, narrow form. In such a spot, you will probably need to do a light annual pruning no matter what kind of plant you pick for the job.

Again, one good solution is to choose slimmer plants. For taller hedges, Irish junipers (*Juniperus communis* 'Stricta' or 'Hibernica', 12 to 20 feet) are good choices where soils are poor, for they tolerate both heavy clay and sand, as well as persistent dampness or drought. They take up relatively little ground space, maturing at between 12 and 20 feet in height but rarely exceeding 5 feet in width. The even skinnier ones called 'Skyrocket' (*J. scopulorum,* 10 to 15 feet) are almost as adaptable and seldom get wider than 2 feet across, even when reaching their ultimate height.

HOW MANY PLANTS?

I wish I could offer you a specific formula for calculating how many hedge plants you will need, but there is none. The right number will be determined by considering the following points:

• Which plants you will use

• How long the hedge needs to be

• How closely the plants should be spaced

This last consideration also depends on several variables:

• The kind of plants you have chosen

• How big they are

• What size you want the hedge to be

• What kind of soil and conditions you can offer them

For instance, a shady site is less than ideal for most hedge plants, so your plants will need closer spacing and harder pruning to shape well. In a sunny site with good soil, you'll get quick coverage even if your plants are spaced farther apart. Set 5-gallon shrubs farther apart than gallon-sized plants or whips (unbranched cuttings).

Any hedge handbook will give you guidance on the calculating process, as will the nursery that sells you the plants. Common sense helps, too; if you have decided on 'Skyrocket' junipers and you know they will be about 2 feet wide at maturity, you can safely set them on 18-inch centers. If you buy young 'Skyrocket' trees between 6 and 8 feet high, this spacing will give you a dense, interwoven barrier quite quickly.

If you have room, you can arrange a double hedge in staggered rows for almost instant coverage. This way, the plants in the second row mask the gaps left between those in the first. With slender, columnar trees, even a double row takes up less space than an ordinary hedge. A 15-foot hedge of beech or laurel would be at least 15 feet wide, but a double hedge of 15-foot columnar trees (the slimmest sorts) might fit into a mere 6-foot-wide strip.

How closely you can space your hedge plants also depends somewhat on the kind of soil you have. Some plants will thrive in rich soil, but others will get overly lush and be more prone to diseases than when grown in leaner soil. Before you fertilize the hedgerow, find out what kind of soil and feeding your chosen plant needs. Most common hedge plants do best in ordinary garden soil that has been improved with soil-building amendments rather than fertilizers. Compost, aged manure, and rotted sawdust are all good for promoting root growth without encouraging excessively fast top growth.

Fast growth seems desirable in a hedge, yet it can lead to problems. In the garden, as elsewhere, steady, unchecked growth gives better long-term results than quick spurts boosted by artificial stimulants. What's more, plants that grow extremely fast often don't live very long. If you aren't planning to stick around for a while, you may not mind that drawback, but it's amazing how quickly the years fly by. Plants that have a 15- or 20-year healthy life span, like certain poplars and some false cypress (*Chamaecyparis lawsoniana*), may size up quickly, but when they start dying off, they leave unsightly gaps in your hedge that are impossible to fill properly.

CHOOSING SUSTAINABLE HEDGE PLANTS

Hedges are traditionally made with adaptable, vigorous plants like privet and honey locust. These plants are tough troupers that are not easily discouraged. This is important, because traditional hedge plants are subjected to repeated stresses to make them conform to our desires. First they are planted very close together, causing root competition almost immediately. Next, they are cut back hard to encourage bushy growth at the base and keep the leader (main trunk) from getting too tall. Throughout their life, their new growth is removed almost constantly.

Unless the hedge is carefully sheared so that it is considerably wider at the base than at the top (this is called giving a hedge "batter"), the lower limbs are shaded by the upper ones, making them weak and scrawny. Only the strongest plants can take this kind of abuse for long. It is not too surprising that such plants may also need frequent restraining. Count on shearing a happy privet hedge two or three or even more times each year.

Unless you have reliable garden help or really enjoy clipping hedges, you will probably prefer more sustainable hedge plants that do much of the work for you. These include any plant, deciduous or evergreen, that has a handsome natural shape and neat habit (manner of growth) and that achieves an appropriate height at maturity. When made into hedges, these cooperative plants will probably require a modicum of shaping at first (see "Unshearing Shrubs" in Chapter 5), but when properly spaced and appropriately fed, your natural beauties will fill in quickly and do their job for many years without much help from you.

What they won't do is provide instant screening. When spaced to allow for full, natural shapes, hedge plants may take several years to fill in enough to become an effective visual screen. Where time is not of the essence and you are planting for the future, this is not a problem. Where you want both future beauty and present coverage, coupling the young hedge with a fence of some kind will meet both needs.

Another excellent way to provide quick coverage is by pairing young hedge shrubs with large grasses. Spaced on 3- or 4-foot centers, 5-gallon plants of tall eulalia grass

(*Miscanthus sinensis*, 6 to 10 feet) will create a visually effective boundary in a single season. Indeed, many of the big grasses are potent enough in form to be used this way. They don't hold their shape in winter and take a while to leaf out in spring, but anywhere that a summery screen is wanted, big grasses will fill in fast.

Needled evergreens with a trim natural shape are splendid candidates for unclipped hedges. The slimmest fit snugly anywhere, so they are best bets in smaller gardens (see "Columnar Plants for Entryways," earlier in this chapter). Pyramidal shrubs are skinny in youth but bulk out a bit at maturity. These provide dense coverage for the lower 10 feet or so of hedge, while their airier tops let plenty of light and air into the garden. Pyramidal hedge plants work best where there's plenty of room.

Where no space constraint exists, nearly any sort of evergreen shrub or tree can be used. In such cases, space your hedge plants generously, allowing room for them to develop their full natural shapes, which will take several years. If quicker screening is wanted, set the trees in staggered, double rows. In a couple of seasons, you will have a magnificent hedge, bushy and beautiful, which provides a lifetime of enclosure with very little care.

In mild climates, any of a number of mannerly, shapely broad-leaved evergreens can be used for hedging. Camellias, rhododendrons, viburnums, and many kinds of laurel come in lastingly handsome forms, some of them columnar. Any of these can do hedge duty well and without causing a lot of extra work for the gardener.

No matter what you decide, be sure to double-check your choice with a reliable regional resource or two before investing in a whole hedge's worth of expensive plants. To find these reliable resources, start at the library, where you ought to find lots of regionally appropriate books. (There will also be plenty of less appropriate books, so pay attention to where they are written and published.) As I've mentioned before, *Trees and Shrubs for Pacific Northwest Gardens* by John and Carol Grant (Timber Press, 1994) is a good place to start.

Master Gardener clinics and workshops are great places to get solid information, as are classes at good nurseries. Your county extension agent can usually provide both tips and plant lists. The entire maritime Northwest is rich in native and hardy plant societies as well as garden clubs of various sorts. Reputable nurseries abound, all terrific places to find regionally specific information. If your site has suitable soil and climate and offers no pests and diseases to plague your chosen plants, you can be pretty sure that your hedge will repay your installation efforts it many times over.

PLANTS FOR UNSHEARED HEDGES

In the Northwest, rhododendrons grow extremely well and are widely available. The larger forms make excellent screening plants and look very attractive as an informal hedge. One of my favorites is 'Lodestar' (to 10 feet), a chunky, well-furnished shrub with glossy leaves and enormous trusses of white flowers with pale golden hearts. These blend beautifully into gentle springtime color schemes, as will those of 'Hong Kong' (to 10 feet), which are imperial yellow touched with lacquer red. For perimeter plantings, consider taller arboreal forms like 'Sir Charles Lemon' (to 20 feet). This big guy has large, dark green leaves lined with cinnamon-orange fur (indumentum) and generous clusters of buttery yellow flowers that smell delicately (and appropriately) of lemons.

Many conifers are beautiful, mannerly, and easy to please. Where winter winds are severe, broad-leaved evergreens may look burned and stressed during the colder months. In such places, needled evergreens are always the bone plants of choice, but their many graces make these sturdy plants welcome in warmer gardens as well.

For instance, narrow, columnar *Juniperus scopulorum* 'Wichita Blue' (15 to 20 feet) is a knockout, both in youth and in maturity. Steely blue-gray and fluffy as a cloud, its color and texture complement an enormous range of plants, making it a natural for back-of-the-border duty. Though it thickens a bit at midlife, it remains upright and shapely for many years.

Bluer still is *Juniperus virginiana* 'Manhattan Blue' (10 to 15 feet), another fine columnar form that makes a lovely background plant in mixed borders. Paired with lustrous green cherry laurel (*Prunus laurocerasus,* a 10- to 12-foot shrub or 18-foot tree), it makes a sumptuously textured tapestry hedge.

Among my favorites for screening and informal hedging is the admirable Pacific wax myrtle (*Myrica californica*,

10 to 15 feet). Upright and densely clad, its slim, leathery leaves have a bronzed, healthy sheen all year round. It tolerates windy sites and adapts well to dry or acid soils. Wax myrtle loves full sun but performs well in light or partial shade.

Another good performer is laurustinus (*Viburnum tinus*, to 12 feet). This chunky evergreen is covered in small, glossy, fine-textured leaves all year. In spring, it produces copious sprays of softly pink and white flowers, followed by metallic blue berries in fall.

If you investigate good nurseries and visit public parks and open gardens, you will discover hundreds of likely candidates to choose from. Be guided by manners and looks in maturity as well as in the nursery pot, and you will soon develop a worthy palette of plants to give your garden good bones.

HEALTHY, HARDY, HANDSOME NATIVE SHRUBS

Our lovely native red flowering currant, Ribes sanguineum, *is a hummingbird magnet and a beautiful low hedging shrub for an informal setting.*

Tough, hardy, and independent, native plants thrive on benign neglect if given a good start. As well, a surprising number of Northwest natives, from red alder to flowering currant, have been given the Award of Merit by England's Royal Horticulture Society. Perhaps as a result of seeing our natives in English gardens, Northwest gardeners are experiencing increasing interest in our own flora.

A few years ago, it was hard to find any but showboat natives, like trilliums and red currants. Today, most nurseries have at least a few gardenworthy natives, such as the Lewis mock orange *(Philadelphus lewisii)*, which commemorates the Lewis and Clark expedition. This highly adaptable plant grows in many kinds of situations, from moist woodland edges to rocky island bluffs. This makes it a good bet for gardens, where it takes anything but excess summer water or fertilizer.

The same is true of most natives, which prefer average soil, amended with compost, to lush border conditions. Give them summer water while they are getting their roots established, but after the first year or two (if the winters are dry, as they have been), let them fend for themselves. Once they are growing strongly, an annual mulch of compost is enough to keep them in good health.

Lewis mock orange is a heavy bloomer whose swooningly fragrant white flowers can really pull in the bees.

These shrubs can get as much as 8 to 10 feet tall, with beautifully peeling, rusty bark that gleams in winter. To hide their knobbly knees, give them a skirt of snowberry.

Snowberry is one of my favorite thicketing shrubs, perfect for lining a driveway or filling a rough spot in sun or part shade. In winter, the bare stems are spangled with white berries that shine like captive stars amid twiggy nets. The Northwest boasts numerous snowberry species, of which the upright *Symphoricarpos albus* is the most common in nurseries. If plain versions don't tempt you, try the lovely gold and silver variegated forms ('Aureus' and 'Albovariegatus').

If you want to keep deer or dogs at bay, highly effective hedgerows can be woven of snowberry, redtwig dogwood *(Cornus stolonifera)*, and wild roses. Though twiggy dogwoods are often grazed by deer, this only makes them denser. As they fill in, these plants create a dense and handsome barrier that can stop all critters bigger than a bird.

Wild roses often intertwine with redtwig dogwood in nature. This combination is breathtaking in winter, when the glowing burgundy stems and bright red rose hips catch the pale winter light. Though they flower only in pink, wild roses have many virtues. They are resistant to the woes of hybrid tea roses. They have great hips that attract lots of birds. They are totally drought tolerant. They don't need pruning, and they smell like heaven.

Baldhip rose *(Rosa gymnocarpa)* is often found in the islands and takes drought and poor soil in stride. So does *Rosa acicularis,* whose plump red hips taste terrific in tea. Even so, you may prefer to let the birds have them, since their chirping grocery shopping expeditions make chilly winter days seem brighter.

The tall nootka rose *(R. nutkana)* has the largest flowers of the family, followed by juicy red hips. The foliage turns soft gold in fall, leaving vivid red, head-high stems in winter. Western Cascade rose *(R. pisocarpa)* tolerates more summer moisture than most wild roses and is an excellent hedging candidate. Woods rose *(R. woodsii)* is found in all sorts of places and adapts well to anything except an excess of kindness.

If you want to attract hummingbirds to your yard, consider planting a wild honeysuckle or two. The scrambling western trumpet honeysuckle *(Lonicera ciliosa)* opens its orange trumpets along the roadsides, weaving itself up

WHERE TO FIND NATIVES IN QUANTITY

Each spring, conservation district offices sell native plants very inexpensively. Generally the availability lists go out in February, and plants are picked up in March. Many are rooted whips, cuttings that have not yet branched much. If planted out directly into unimproved soil and watered sporadically (or not at all), the survival rate runs 40 to 60 percent.

To boost it closer to 100 percent, pot up your youngsters in 2- and 5-gallon containers. Treat them like a nursery crop for a season, watering them weekly. Planted in the fall, these well-rooted plants will establish quickly and grow strongly. To learn how to receive these lists of native plants, contact your local Master Gardener program. (In Seattle, call 206-296-3900.)

wild cherry trees and into stands of native rhododendrons *(Rhododendron macrophyllum)*. Still common in woodland gardens, this pretty climber can be found by following the hummingbirds, which flock to its succulent flowers. Native people wove baskets of the twining honeysuckle stems but left the inedible berries for the birds.

Shrubby honeysuckle, *Lonicera involucrata* (also called twinberry)*,* is a very attractive shrub with dainty yellow flowers in dangling pairs, followed by plump purple or black fruit that bring in the birds come fall. The showy bracts start out coppery pink and deepen to a soft burgundy by autumn, when the leaves turn gentle gold.

Hardy fuchsias are drought tolerant and tough once established. They, too, are favorites for hummingbirds and bloom over a very long period.

Given our generally wet autumns, it works best to plant native trees and shrubs in midfall or early winter (October and November), thus reducing the need to supplement their water supply.

To learn which natives will grow best in the conditions you have to offer, consult good regional guides such as *Gardening with Native Plants of the Pacific Northwest* by Arthur Kruckeberg (University of Washington Press, 1997), *Plants of the Pacific Northwest Coast* by Jim Pojar and Andy MacKinnon (Lone Pine Publishing, 1994), and *Landscaping for Wildlife in the Pacific Northwest* by Russell Link (University of Washington Press, 1999).

BIO-SPONGE PLANTINGS

Native shrubs can help increase the sustainability of the garden in general terms, but they are especially valuable when we are dealing with drainage and runoff issues. Many natives, from twiggy dogwoods and sword ferns to wild roses and snowberry, can also help protect banks and slopes from erosion. There are several common situations in which bio-sponge plantings of natives will help resolve both kinds of issues.

First, wherever homeowners have to cope with excessive seasonal water, plantings that take up ample water in winter yet don't need much in summer are clearly of tremendous service.

Next come waterfront gardens, whether high-bank, low-bank, or no-bank. The Departments of Ecology for both Washington and Oregon variously demand (when possible) or suggest that landowners create no-water zones of native plants. Typically, these are 20-foot buffers of native plants that won't need watering, fertilizing, or pesticide treatments. The goals here are to reduce or eliminate water pollution from lawn chemicals and to help stabilize banks prone to slippage. Reducing watering needs by making bio-sponge plantings that take up excess water readily in winter but need little or no supplemental water in summer will help reduce the danger of slope slippage (often triggered by garden watering).

The maritime Northwest is considered to have a modified Mediterranean climate. The modifications mainly involve accumulated heat, but the crucial similarity is the typical pattern of wet winters and dry summers. Often we receive little or no measurable rainfall between May and October. On the other hand, we may get as much as 20 inches of rain in January alone. Clearly, native plants are better primed to deal with such a moisture range than those from regions with more even moisture distributions.

So, too, are plants from other Mediterranean-type climate zones. Parts of South Africa offer us winter lilies (*Schizostylis* species), honey bush (*Melianthus* species), and many bulbs, from agapanthus to watsonia. Parts of New Zealand, Australia, and Tasmania offer coppery carexes, silvery *Senecio greyi* 'Sunshine', shrubby hebes, and smoky New Zealand flax (*Phormium* species).

Parts of Asia offer us countless plants, from trees to ground covers, that thrive in our climate. Central and South America contribute hardy tropicals like red bananas and fan palms, as well as many fuchsias, mallows, and lantanas.

The Mediterranean itself gives us hardy evergreen herbs like rosemary, sage, and lavender as well as perennials like hellebores and wood arums. In all, thousands of plants from these regions and our own will grow well here, needing little or no supplemental water once established.

Such plants are appropriate choices for the no-water zones that protect slopes and banks, for greenbelts, and for perimeter plantings. Excellent native choices include vine maples and serviceberry, redtwig dogwoods and salal, wild roses and huckleberries. Elderberries, flowering currant, Indian plum, ocean spray, wild mock orange, wild apples, hawthorns, mountain ash, and sumacs are also great candidates. All are inviting to birds and butterflies.

EVERGREEN NATIVE SHRUBS

COMMON NAME	BOTANICAL NAME	HEIGHT	HABIT
Bog rosemary	*Andromeda polifolia*	1'	Low, mounded
California lilac	*Ceanothus* species and hybrids	1–20'	Upright or prostrate
Flowering currant	*Ribes* species (some)	3–6'	Upright or broad
Huckleberry	*Vaccinium* species and hybrids	4–10'	Upright
Manzanita	*Arctostaphylos* species and hybrids	1–8'	Upright or prostrate
Oregon grape	*Mahonia* species and hybrids	1–8'	Upright, spreading
Pacific rhododendron	*Rhododendron macrophyllum*	6–12'	Mounded
Pacific wax myrtle	*Myrica californica*	20–30'	Upright
Salal	*Gaultheria shallon*	2–6'	Spreading
Silk tassel	*Garrya* species and hybrids	8–12'	Upright

DECIDUOUS NATIVE SHRUBS

COMMON NAME	BOTANICAL NAME	HEIGHT	HABIT
Bitter cherry	*Prunus emarginata*	8–12'	Upright
Bog birch	*Betula glandulosa*	6–10'	Upright
Chokecherry	*Prunus virginiana*	8–20'	Upright
Elderberry	*Sambucus* species and hybrids	8–20'	Upright
Flowering currant	*Ribes sanguineum*	6–10'	Upright
Golden currant	*Ribes aureum*	3–6'	Upright
Hard hack	*Spiraea douglasii*	5–8'	Spreading
Hazelnut	*Corylus cornuta*	10–20'	Upright
Highbush cranberry	*Viburnum trilobum*	6–10'	Upright
Huckleberry	*Vaccinium* species and hybrids	4–10'	Upright
Indian plum	*Oemleria cerasiformis*	8–12'	Upright or broad
Lewis mock orange	*Philadelphus lewisii*	6–10'	Upright
Mountain ash	*Sorbus* species and hybrids	6–10'	Upright
Ninebark	*Physocarpus capitatus*	8–15'	Upright
Ocean spray	*Holodiscus discolor*	8–15'	Upright
Salmonberry	*Rubus spectabilis*	5–8'	Spreading
Serviceberry	*Amelanchier alnifolia*	8–20'	Upright
Snowberry	*Symphoricarpos* species and hybrids	3–5'	Spreading
Sumac (many)	*Rhus* species and hybrids	8–15'	Upright or broad
Thimbleberry	*Rubus parviflorus*	3–6'	Spreading
Twiggy dogwoods (many)	*Cornus* species and hybrids	6–12'	Upright or broad
Twinberry	*Lonicera involucrata*	6–8'	Upright
Wild azalea	*Rhododendron occidentale*	3–8'	Upright or broad
Wild rose (several)	*Rosa* species	3–8'	Upright or broad

PLANTING SHRUBS

Because shrubs are long lived, they grow best in soils improved with long-lasting organic nutrients. Like trees, shrubs prefer a soil that is rich in humus, and they have relatively low nitrogen requirements. When planted with compost and fed with organic feeding mulches, shrubs perform better and live longer than when planted in poor soil and fed with chemical fertilizers.

To give garden shrubs a good start, dig each planting hole as deep as your plant's container and at least twice as wide. Firm up the bottom of the planting hole well (you can even stomp on it) to make sure there are no air pockets, which can make roots dry out very fast.

Add an inch of compost, pack it firmly, place your shrub so its neck is at soil grade, and then fill in around it with a mixture of half the removed bed soil and half compost. Firm this down well, and water your new plant in generously. Give each shrub at least 5 gallons of water at planting. Use a mild transplanting fertilizer (an N-P-K ratio of 2-4-2 is fine) that incorporates beneficial biota and mycorrhizae (Whitney Farms Lifelink is a good one).

PLANTING TIPS FOR SHRUBS

- Where the native soil is heavy clay, subsoil, or hardpan, plant shrubs in mounded beds (see Chapter 3) that drain well and are generously amended with organic material.

- Plant shrubs so that their trunks remain at the same level as when in the nursery pot. The rim of the root system should not stick up above grade. The main trunk or branching structure should not be buried.

- Mulch can be added generously as long as both soil and mulch are graded down as they approach the trunk. Compost or aged dairy manure are good mulch choices; bark or wood by-products are not suitable mulches for shrubs.

- Annual mulches of aged manure and compost will keep your shrubs healthy for many years.

- Give each shrub at least 5 gallons of water at planting time and each time you water it for the first year. Water the roots, not the foliage.

Now give your shrub a fresh blanket of compost to keep weeds away. Be sure the trunk of your shrub is not smothered; there should be no more than ½ inch of compost from the trunk to about a hand span away. Increase the depth of the compost mulch until it is about 3 to 4 inches at the shrub's dripline. The compost mulch should always extend at least 1 to 2 feet beyond a shrub's dripline.

Perennials are the lifeblood of the garden, bringing an ongoing flow of color and textural interest to beds and borders season after season.

What are perennials? The basic definition is a nonwoody plant with a life span of at least three years. (Some perennials can last for decades, while others are short lived.) Being nonwoody, even the longest-lived perennials lack permanent trunks or branching structure. Most are deciduous, dying to the ground each fall or winter and reappearing in spring from a dormant crown. In the mild-winter regions of the Pacific Northwest, quite a few perennials are evergreen, often producing a fresh resting rosette in the fall, a low tuft of new foliage that persists through winter before the plants refurbish fully in spring. (Columbines are a good example of semievergreen perennials of this type.) A handful, like the winter roses (hellebores), are fully evergreen, refreshing their foliage even as the old leaves fade.

Perennials are the lifeblood of the garden, providing the pulsing flow of color and change that enlivens the relatively static framework of woody plants. For nearly a century, woody plants dominated Northwest gardens. Flowering shrubs (especially rhododendrons) were the queens of nearly every landscape. In more recent years, perennials have become horticulturally hot. A well-chosen succession of herbaceous perennials can provide dramatic seasonal change even in the smallest gardens. When selected to flower in sequence, perennials create overlapping waves of color from earliest spring through darkest winter.

Enticing as they are, perennials must be brought into the garden thoughtfully. The sustainable designer will recall that woody plants require very little care. Perennial plants are high-maintenance, second only to lawns in terms of frequent need. In truth, the highest-maintenance garden model you can find is the perennial border encircled by grass. That said, perennials can bring unmatched excitement to the garden, which would look sadly static if it were furnished only with evergreens and shrubs. The secret to success with perennials is to be very picky and to edit them ruthlessly, so they never get out of control.

Though far longer lived, few perennials can match annuals for sheer flower power. Typically, perennials bloom more briefly, flowering from a mere week or two to several months. However, the best perennials are cooperative, adaptive plants with merits that gain them a respected place in even a sustainably designed garden. Good perennials prosper without much help from the gardener and without crowding out their neighbors. Some can rebloom steadily, providing a flush of flowers every month or so from late spring into fall. Many boast handsome foliage that makes a strong and lasting contribution to the garden picture.

Foliage perennials can be massed in colorful drifts that don't rely on flower power for punch. Instead, foliage combinations play up contrasts of leaf size, texture, and tint. Perennials play an important part in mixed borders, which may also contain trees and shrubs, bulbs, vines, and grasses. Here, perennials soften the stiffness of evergreens, mask dying bulb foliage, and fill the bays between shrubs with flowers. Perennials can burst out of the borders as well, tumbling from tubs and containers at entryway or patio, pouring in richly textured carpets that can replace unused lawn, and weave ground cover tapestries beneath shrubs and trees.

HOW TO GARDEN EFFECTIVELY WITH PERENNIALS

When most gardeners think of perennials, they see in their mind's eye a bountiful, luxuriant English border. Unfortunately, as they quickly discover, those traditional English perennial borders are extremely labor-intensive. Without a well-trained staff to do your bidding, perennial borders mean a lot of work for the hapless gardener.

What's more, borders based on perennials are practically empty for fully half the year. That model was fine for folks with significant acreage, with room for many seasonal borders. (It was also developed at a time when most landed families spent the cooler months in London, so empty borders were not a big deal.) Here in the maritime Northwest, we often use our yards all year-round and want them to look furnished and attractive in every season.

Few of us have room for big summer borders that look blank and empty from fall until spring.

Happily, England's cheerful cottage gardens make a fine model for gardeners who lack vast acres and a trained staff. Simple in design, traditional cottage gardens combine a profusion of easily grown perennials with annuals and bulbs, fruits and vegetables.

One important English design principle is that flowers are best displayed in a framework or structural context. Both the English border and cottage garden design styles stress the need for enclosure and structure, whether from clipped hedges or stone walls.

Few of us have Elizabethan stone walls to garden against, yet many of our own native plants are potently structural, from evergreen huckleberries and Oregon grape to towering firs and cedars. In our modest backyards, we can arrange perennials successfully in either formal or naturalistic settings as long as we provide a solid framework for our flowers. Often called "garden bones," this backdrop can come from hardscape (manmade structures) such as walls, arches, and arbors; from evergreen trees and shrubs; or from a mixture of both.

PERENNIAL PARTNERSHIPS

To be lastingly effective, perennial partnerships must involve more than mere color. As in any relationship, the best companions have compatible cultural needs and habits (manner of growth). Perennial partners should also complement each other in form, size, texture, and period of bloom. Well-chosen, well-paired, and well-placed perennials will be happy, healthy plants. To this end, we must seek perennial cooperators, adaptive plants that share space and resources well. Beware of bargain-priced perennials, which are often thugs that can take over a garden, crowding out companions and stripping soil of nutrients.

Beware as well of the novelty factor. Newly introduced plants often get rave catalog reviews for a few years, then sink quietly out of sight as gardeners and nurseryfolk begin to realize that these new plants may have quite a few flaws after all. Brand-new perennials are often in short supply and thus very expensive. However, these same perennials often need coddling and may be so new to horticulture that not much is known about their garden needs and behavior. Since it's difficult to succeed

GUIDELINES FOR CHOOSING PERENNIALS

- To get the best performance from your perennials, be selective.

- Look for cooperators: easygoing plants that adapt well to many cultural conditions but don't turn into thugs.

- Don't buy every pretty flower that catches your eye; make sure you can please each plant you bring home.

- Avoid prima donnas. Some plants are difficult unless you give them exactly what they want. Start with easygoing perennials.

- Give preference to perennials that prefer the conditions you can offer them (such as dry, rooty shade or full sun and sandy soil).

- Base perennial combinations on plants with similar cultural needs (plants that like damp shade or dry, sunny spots).

- Choose long-blooming perennials and reliable rebloomers.

- Pick plants with fascinating foliage and terrific textures.

Continued on page 277

with so many unknowns, hold off for a few years until more information about habits and needs is available. If the plants are really so terrific, rest assured that they will be widely available in just a few seasons. The price will usually come down dramatically, too, so patience pays off.

Perennials provide the flow of color and contrast in mixed borders at Gossler Farm Nursery in Oregon. Placing perennials in the bays between shrubs provides much-needed backdrop and support for floral displays.

FINDING PERENNIALS FOR CHALLENGING PLACES

Many sites have difficulties that make life hard for most plants. If your garden poses special problems, consider them when selecting your perennials. For instance, if you garden on a bluff, near a windy open space, or in an urban setting where both wind and light are reflected off nearby buildings, choose perennials that are drought and wind tolerant. Seaside gardens' plants must adapt to wind and salty sea spray. Woodland gardens may have permanently soggy spots or become utterly dry in summer.

To find appropriate plants for each place, seek out specialty nurseries that grow plants for those specific situations. Here in the Northwest, we are rich in excellent regional nurseries, many of which carry site-adapted natives and other perennials for every imaginable need, from dry coastal bluff gardens to shady bogs. Such nurseries and their catalogs are often invaluable sources of information, ideas, and assistance.

Regional handbooks on native plants will also be helpful. One of the best books is *Gardening with Native Plants of the Pacific Northwest* by Arthur Kruckeberg (University of Washington Press, 1997). Another terrific native plant handbook is *Plants of the Pacific Northwest Coast* by Jim Pojar and Andy MacKinnon (Lone Pine Publishing, 1994). Both of these books offer great information about where natives are commonly found in the wild and what conditions they appreciate.

Here are some more pointers for growing perennials successfully in less-than-ideal spots:

- Choose site-adapted natives that grow happily in garden settings.
- Coddle perennials planted in tough places for two full seasons before expecting them to hold their own.
- Small, young plants usually transplant better into challenging places than big, mature ones.
- Amend soil in tough spots with plenty of compost.
- Mulch site-challenged perennials two or three times each year with compost.

- Choose perennials with an attractive natural form.
- Give preference to perennials that don't require staking.
- Select perennials that look great fresh or dry; these last the longest.
- For greater winter interest, plant perennials that die with grace.

COMPOSING WITH PERENNIALS

Much has been written about artful or colorist gardening, mingling and matching colors, shapes, and textures and creating color-themed gardens. Both color work and garden composition are matters of personal taste. If you love a certain grouping, it's right for you. The Taste Police are not coming to your garden, so do whatever delights your eye.

If you find the process of combining plants to be frustrating rather than rewarding, a few organizational rules can help you turn a jumble of unrelated plants into a balanced composition:

- Play with your plants. Arrange them while still in their pots into pleasing partnerships. When you love them, plant them.
- Focus on creating contrasts of foliage and form. Flowers are fun, but when the whole plant contributes to the picture, the result will be visually stronger and the pleasing effects will last far longer.

- Ultimate size counts. Big perennials don't always need to be banished to the border back, but unless they are airy scrim plants, they'll soon swamp shorter companions placed behind them.

- If you find yourself rearranging more than you think you should, relax. The average perennial will move at least three times before finding its proper home. Call the process "editing," and accept that you'll be doing a lot of it.

- Edit often. Good gardeners are good editors, and the best gardens are frequently revised.

PLANTING IN LAYERS

Because they often lack winter interest, perennials are best grown in combination with plants of many kinds, in a layered style. These layers can be formally arranged or naturalistic, giving the garden the relaxed, abundant look of native woodlands. In each case, the first layer is the canopy, the treeline or skyline created by the tallest plants. Next come intermediate plants (usually tall shrubs), which make a visual ladder between the front of the border and the larger elements. The middle layer is like forest understory, knit from compact shrubs and perennials. Ground covers carpet the floor, while vines lace the layers together. In a large garden, each layer can be full sized. In a smaller garden, the layers are scaled down, with shrubs playing the role of trees and narrow, space-saving plants chosen over wide ones.

The largest layering plants generally define the shape of the garden. Most of these will be evergreen trees and shrubs, which enclose the garden like a green wall. However, bold backdrop perennials can be woven into the woody plants with a wonderfully softening effect. Whatever the components, the first layer establishes the line of the garden plantings, often creating a powerful silhouette against the sky. Their arrangement will also set the tone for the garden, making it formal or casual.

The style or feel of each garden is strongly influenced by how the layers are put together. For instance, a straight line of a single kind of plant, especially one with an architectural shape, will look best in a crisp, clean-edged design. Formal gardens are often based on geometrical framing, with formal first-tier plants whose lines are echoed within the plantings. These layers are usually

simplified and very clearly defined (this kind of layering is sometimes called "stair-stepping"). Formal beds are generally edged with neatly shaped or sheared plants and filled with massed plants of regular habit, perhaps arranged in colorful or interestingly textured patterns.

Ruffled, irregular layers appear more natural and lend themselves to soft-edged, naturalistic plantings. In these designs, the back line or perimeter plantings are usually mixed rather than monotonous. Backbone plants may be grouped in soft W shapes to avoid straight lines, and second- and third-layer plantings may blend into the backdrop plants, creating a wavy, multitiered look. Within the beds, carpet-level plantings of irregular sizes may create an inner topography that plays up the variety of shapes and textures. These relaxed, informal interior arrangements can create a fascinating flow of form as well as color.

Second-tier plantings create an intermediate layer between the skyline and the border front. In larger gardens, there may be two or three intermediate levels, while in smaller gardens, one intermediate layer will suffice. Intermediate shrubby layers help to link trees to tulips, creating both a visual and physical transition between the largest backdrop plants and tiny ones tucked at the border's edge.

In formal plantings, the goal of the intermediate layer is uniformity. Plants are chosen for regularity of size and appearance and arranged in patterns that emphasize specific qualities. Naturalistic garden design encourages a multiplicity of intermediate layers, with less strict ranking by size. Midborder plants often display a charming informality, with taller plants occasionally placed in front of shorter ones. This technique gives the beds an inner topography, offering a surprisingly different appearance when approached from fresh angles. It also creates a visual scrim or veil that creates an intriguing sense of mystery.

To emphasize form and texture, midborder plants are not crowded, but are given enough room to develop their distinctive shapes. Partnerships offer contrasts of color, texture, and form and a pleasing balance of size and mass. To avoid a skimpy appearance, they are placed close enough so that when fully expanded, their slightly overlapping foliage completely hides the soil.

Border front perennials are generally the lowest growers, many of which may also qualify as ground cover plants. Silvery artemisias, creeping and woolly thymes, black ajugas, and silver-striped lily turf are double-duty perennials that can serve as reliable ground covers as well as attractive border plants.

PLANTING BY SHAPE

The most lastingly attractive and visually interesting combinations are those that emphasize not just color but contrasts of form. When creating combinations, many garden designers concentrate more on plant shape than on any other aspect, including color. This simple trick works best with each plant's true shape; controlling plant shapes by heading back or shearing makes for lots of repetitive work and physically stresses the plants. However, since many plants offer strong innate architecture, we have a wide range of natural shapes to play against each other. Fans and fountains, mounds and sprawlers, sturdy towers and slim turrets, all can be endlessly recombined into exciting and attractive partnerships.

To experiment with partnering perennials by shape, select a good supply of perennials with distinctive forms. Start by playing with those shapes, looking for pleasing contrasts. Initially, you might pair a fan-shaped variegated water iris with foamy blue flax or a chocolaty mound of sweet spurge, *Euphorbia dulcis* 'Chameleon'. Add a silky, small grass like *Stipa (Nassella) tenuissima* to soften the look and line of this initial partnering, and pick a structural tall sedum, 'Autumn Joy', for its upright solidity. Now let a spill of lacy beach wormwood (artemisia) or creeping thyme carpet the ground beneath them all. The result? A combination that reads well as a whole vignette, with impact through much of the year.

Part of the challenge is to combine plants with equal "weight" or visual strength. A fluffy, formless baby's breath can't balance a potently structural *Rodgersia pinnata* 'Superba'. Architectural plants need equally powerful partners to create balanced compositions. Instead of matching the rodgersia with an airy baby's breath, we need boldly scaled plants that bring different forms, new textures, and complementary colors to the match. Long-stemmed, vase-shaped royal ferns are rich green, with coppery sori that echo the rodgersia's leaf edges and new growth. A burgundy-leaved ligularia like 'Desdemona' would also match up well. We could also balance the mass of a large, architectural plant with clustered groups of mounding plants such as hardy woodland geraniums (*Geranium macrorrhizum*) or lacy-leaved astilbes.

When placed with care, unusual plant shapes provide pleasing contrasts to the more common mounds and billows of the typical perennial. Eccentric spires of silvery verbascums can disappear in a chaos of color but become magnificent when placed against large, simply shaped plants such as a maiden grass (*Miscanthus sinensis*) or rosemary. A smooth mound of creeping Canterbury bells makes a shapeless mass on its own, but when contrasted with stiff, finely textured yarrows and a multiarmed sea holly, it brings the simplicity of smooth stone to a complex combination.

PERENNIALS BY SHAPE

FANS AND FOUNTAINS
Daylily (*Hemerocallis* 'Happy Returns')
Evergreen pampas grass (*Cortaderia richardii*)
Needle grass (*Stipa gigantea*)
New Zealand flax (*Phormium tenax*)
Siberian iris (*Iris sibirica*)
Sword plant (*Yucca filamentosa*)
Water iris, also Yellow flag (*Iris pseudacorus* 'Variegata')

SPIKES AND TURRETS
Delphinium belladonna 'Peace'
Foxglove (*Digitalis purpurea* 'Apricot')
Gayfeather (*Liatris pycnostachya* 'Alba')
Pencil plant (*Verbena patagonica*)
Poker plant (*Kniphofia uvaria* 'Primrose Beauty')
Verbascum 'Helen Johnson'

MOUNDERS AND SPRAWLERS
Beach wormwood (*Artemisia stellerana* 'Silver Brocade')
Baby's breath (*Gypsophila paniculata*)
Blue spurge (*Euphorbia myrsinites*)
Catmint (*Nepeta* 'Six Hills Giant')
Chameleon spurge (*Euphorbia dulcis* 'Chameleon')
Creeping Canterbury bells (*Campanula poscharskyana* 'Stella')

ECCENTRIC AND ARCHITECTURAL SHAPES
Chilean gunnera (*Gunnera manicata*)
Himalayan rhubarb (*Rheum australe*)
Purple coneflower (*Echinacea purpurea*)
Rattlesnake-master (*Eryngium yuccifolium*)
Sea holly (*Eryngium* 'Blaukappe')
Verbascum bombyciferum 'Arctic Summer'

ARCHITECTURAL PLANTS FOR THE BORDER BACK

Canopy or backdrop plants marry garden plantings to surrounding trees or buildings. They provide enclosure and help to bring the garden into balance with the scale of its surroundings.

Traditional garden design nearly always uses shrubs and small trees for such a role, but a host of perennials will fill the bill as well. In large gardens, a hedge of tall maiden grass will provide screening, privacy, and a textured backdrop for flower beds. American pokeweed *(Phytolacca americana)*, joe pye weed *(Eupatorium* species), and prairie sunflowers *(Rudbeckia maxima)* weave into a majestic backdrop, rising shrublike to enclose the garden. In smaller spaces, a 4-foot wall of bell-flowered knotweed *(Polygonum campanulatum)* will provide both enclosure and lacy pink or white flowers from May until hard frost. Where less solid walls are wanted, airy masses of pencil plant, *Verbena patagonica* (also sold as *V. bonariensis*), weave into a fine scrim, veiling all that lies behind it in a haze of purple blue.

Many backdrop perennials spend spring and summer climbing skyward, reserving their bloom for late summer or autumn. If these are chosen for flowers or fall foliage color as well as size, the garden framework changes from quiet backdrop into a climax planting. Grasses are natural candidates for this role, brightening their autumn bronze with bursts of flame. Dapper, compact evergreen pampas grasses such as *Cortaderia fulvida* and *C. richardii* spread their great silken plumes above the borders. Late-blooming goldenrods like 'Fireworks' rise head high, while towering *Aster tataricus* looms taller still, its great, arching arms studded with blue.

In many cases, the backdrop is where these buxom beauties belong. Within beds and borders, such outsized plants can throw off the balance of scale, making everything else look dwarfed in comparison. It is certainly possible to place larger plants close to the front of a border, where they create intriguing topography, making us peer past them for a glimpse of the border's unseen depths beyond. However, it's vital to choose airy plants for such a role rather than those with bulky foliage that will swamp their neighbors by summer's end. Border back

Well-orchestrated mixed borders at Joy Creek Nursery in Oregon were designed by Lucy Hardiman to provide color and textural interest over an extended season.

placement turns these potential thugs into bold, dramatic plants that create a skyline celebration of exciting form and ebullient color.

Where space permits, indulging in garden gigantism can be tremendously appealing, giving the gardener the opportunity to be utterly embraced by plants. Modern life is so full of straight lines and rigid routines that a garden where plants dominate and Nature rules with her own wild ways is a constant refreshment to the spirit. This concept influences a number of developing design schools that stress plant-driven rather than florally driven gardenscapes. In these new gardens, boldly shaped plants often play the space-defining role traditionally assigned to hardscape, from walls and trellises to arches and arbors.

In warmer parts of our region, where many true tropical plants can flourish, it's easy to give any garden a lush, junglelike appearance. No substitutes are needed, because warm climates support the real thing. Birds-of-paradise; pink, orange, or luscious purple giant succulents; and New Zealand flax (*Phormium* species) grow to amazing proportions where heat and moisture are in ample supply. Dryer hot climates nourish a wide range of astonishing desert plants, including dozens of kinds of day- and night-blooming cactus and spurges (*Euphorbia* species), as well as broad-bladed grasses and swirling, sword-leaved yuccas.

In mild-winter areas, we can use hardy tropicals, large-leaved foliage plants that create the impression of jungle abundance yet take moderate frosts in stride. In recent years, plant explorers have increased our palette with dozens of relatively cold-hardy perennial forms of former houseplants, such as Rex begonias and black taro *(Colocasia esculenta)*. Many of these new introductions are finding their way into tropicalismo gardens, a design school that celebrates joyful gigantism.

Characterized by exuberance, this ebullient design style feature mixtures of sculptural character plants with spunky style. Tropicalismo designers mingle large-scaled native plants from their own regions with allies and exotics from all over the world, creating a world-mix of fascinating plants that cohabitate with ease. Often hardy perennials are blended with tender ones that are stored in protected areas for the winter. These gardens are often entirely given over to plants, so that any space that isn't a path or a seating area is planted.

Even where winters are consistently cold, gardeners can create a surprisingly convincing jungle garden by selecting the largest possible members of common perennial families. Giant lobelia, for instance, rises 8 or 10 feet high in a damp spot, sending up lovely spears of white or red flowers. Several ornamental giant joe pye weeds that are considered horticultural hot news in England hail from chilly New England. Garden rhubarb comes in enormous and decidedly decorative versions from China and the cold Himalayan peaks (don't try to eat them, however; most are toxic). Several forms boast splendidly carved foliage in shades of red and purple, while others bear great plumes of bracted blossoms. Hardy grasses of many kinds and colors can tower overhead, from zebra-striped maiden grass to gold- or silver-striped pampas grasses.

Shady gardens can also support certain oversized perennials in style. Hardy bamboos bring majestic height (and wandering roots) to shady or partially sunny sites. A number of hostas (notably *Hosta sieboldiana* 'Elegans') reach remarkable proportions, with mature plants achieving 5 feet or more in all directions. The fern family presents numerous large candidates, from the fluffy ostrich fern to our lacy native lady fern. Even lowly bracken ferns can bring a pleasingly feral quality to garden plantings, and the soft gold of their autumnal coloration provides a happy contrast with the deep greens of autumn fern and silvery swirls of Japanese painted fern. The pale pink spires of Chinese *Astilbe grandis* can top 6 feet in a damp spot, as will several of the hollow-stemmed rush grasses (*Juncus* species).

BOLDLY SCALED PERENNIALS

Asian rhubarb (*Rheum palmatum*)
Giant tatar aster (*Aster tataricus*)
Hosta 'Blue Umbrellas'
Hosta 'Sum and Substance'
Joe pye weed (*Eupatorium* 'Gateway')
Lobelia 'Red Giant'
Magellan gunnera (*Gunnera magellanica*)
Pinnate rodgersia (*Rodgersia pinnata* 'Superba')
Plume poppy (*Macleaya cordata*)
Pokeweed (*Phytolacca americana*)
Variegated pampas grass (*Cortaderia selloana* 'Sunningdale Silver')

SANDWICH GARDENING: SEQUENCING SEASONAL COLOR

Most of us begin by filling the garden with spring and summer perennials. Over time, we may come to want more for and from the garden. We may begin adding earlier bloomers as well as late ones. Eventually we seek to stretch the garden year into an endless loop of seasonal color. Here in the maritime Pacific Northwest, we are truly fortunate, because we can grow a terrific range of perennials from all over the world. To create serial color effects, we simply group perennials throughout the garden in combinations that will shine in studied sequences.

While most winter-blooming perennials do best in mild climates, anywhere in the region the flow of perennial color can begin in late winter and end only when the snows return. To learn how to arrange such sequential bloom, we can look to the beautiful, long-flowering natural models offered by riparian, mountain, or woodland meadows. All of these remarkably sustainable models display the tightly interwoven tapestry of perennials, annuals, grasses, and bulbs that I call sandwich planting.

These natural sandwiches or layered plantings encourage us to be more creative when planting in our own backyards. We usually think of garden soil in terms of square feet, but by thinking cubically, we increase our planting options dramatically. In meadows and woodlands, the same cubic foot of earth may house five or six (or even more) kinds of compatible plants—most often perennials and bulbs—that perform in turn. As the low-growing early bloomers go dormant, taller summer stars arise to take their place. These give way to the towering flowers of fall, many of which persist as strikingly beautiful skeletons well into the winter.

Again, if we are shooting for a sustainable garden, it's important to select cooperators, plants that tolerate benign neglect and close company. If we cut out a slice of prairie sod, we would see roots layered and intertwined, filling the soil in a tight-knit tapestry. These companions are all site-adapted plants that have learned to live together and under certain conditions over thousands of years. Clearly, we can't toss together any six perennials at random and expect them to get along this way. However, if we start by selecting plants that are adapted to communal living, they probably will cooperate similarly in our gardens.

Portland garden designer John Caine takes perennials out to the street in a garden advance that welcomes and envelops passersby. In sunny, dry, exposed sites, many high country desert plants like penstemons thrive and rowdy perennials can't get away to take over the garden.

Although much of the maritime Northwest was climax forest before it was settled, pockets of prairie have existed for millennia. In recent times, humans have created many more of these pockets by clear-cutting trees and creating open space where dryland grasses and flowering plants can flourish (or at least grow). Thus, the tallgrass prairie can also make a good resource for us when we seek out natural models for gardens. The tallgrass prairie is home to a host of hardy perennials that double as border beauties. So are open meadows and shady woodlands, here and all across the country.

For example, the prairie's purple coneflower *(Echinacea purpurea)* is represented in borders by award winners like rosy 'Magnus', enormous 'Bravado', and gleaming 'White Swan'. A common eastern meadow aster, *Aster novae-angliae,* has dozens of garden forms, including the recent 'Purple Dome', a fine plant that appears on many "top ten" lists. Native goldenrods (which are not allergenic) come in compact hybrid forms like 'Peter Pan' and 'Golden Baby' as well as exuberant tall forms like *Solidago rugosa* 'Fireworks'.

As garden plants, these selected forms will perform as well in your border as their parents do on their native ground. What's more, none are demanding or persnickety and all get along well with others. Even in the smallest yards, we can assemble an array of similarly cooperative perennials that repay moderate attention with major rewards.

To weave a year's worth of color into your beds and borders, start with adapted natives like these, then add in others that seem likely to be compatible in needs, looks, and habits. The sections that follow describe what a typical annual cycle of bloom might look like.

FINDING EARLY BIRD BLOOMERS

In early spring, glossy new leaves gleam on the crowns of sleepy perennials, which begin to stretch skyward as temperatures rise. Spring bulbs and flowering shrubs make excellent company for early perennials, the hardiest of which begin to bloom, though leafless, as the snow melts. Other perennials leaf out first, their fresh foliage followed quickly by plump buds and cheerful flowers.

To find early bloomers that will enjoy your yard, cruise local nurseries and garden centers frequently. Mail-order catalogs will increase your choices, as will joining local plant societies (plant swaps are an important social function for these groups). Read garden books written for mild-winter regions, from England to the American South, seeking plants that might brighten late winter here as well as there. The hunt for first flowers presents a delightful challenge that can excitingly extend the garden year.

COMBINING FIRST FLOWERS

To develop more vivid color early in the year, we can arrange our first flowers in companionable clusters. Instead of dotting them in small patches around the garden, group plants with similar needs and compatible colors in sufficient quantities to make a pleasing visual impact. Just as they are found growing in meadows and prairies, these early perennials can be sandwiched with later bloomers—literally planted together into the same piece of ground, so that first flowers are followed by second and third waves. For instance, snowdrops and bluebells (*Mertensia virginica*) can be interplanted with columbines (*Aquilegia* species) and hostas to create a carpet of color from late winter well into fall.

In most gardens, spring's flowers are provided by trees, shrubs, and bulbs. However, if we consult our natural

models, we'll find plenty of early-rising perennials to bolster our spring borders. For instance, as winter fades, our
woodlands are full of violets, trilliums, and spring beauty
(*Claytonia* species). Meadows and prairies are bright with
bird's foot violets *(Viola pedata),* various anemones, and
shooting stars *(Dodecatheon meadia).*

In gardens, too, violets and violas may appear with the
tulips and daffodils. Many native violet species flower in
spring, as do large-flowered hybrid violas and pansies.
Tuck any of these tufting clumpers between larger, later-
rising plants where they can bloom early and then perform as an airy ground cover. As long as they are not
smothered, violets thrive as an understory carpeter.

The anemone family is another terrific source for early
color, offering fuzzy-budded pasque flowers *(Anemone
vulgaris)* for sunny sites and lacy-leaved wood anemones
(A. nemorosa) for shade. Both species pass gently into early
dormancy, leaving room for summer-blooming companions to take center stage. In sunny settings, penstemons,
goldenrods, and salvias will take over handily. In shady
gardens, columbines, rodgersias, and astilbes can be
densely interplanted with wood anemones.

SEQUENCING SPRING COLOR

In prairies and meadows around the world, the tufted
grasses are still sound asleep, but the crowns of summery
perennials are showing signs of life. The same is true in
our gardens, where perennials often mingle with ornamental grasses. Dormant grasses can be heavily underplanted with early perennials like spotted lungworts
(*Pulmonaria* species), which need some shade in summer.
With their showy striped and speckled foliage, the lungworts are at their best in spring, when their pink and blue
(or white) flowers arrive. Snugged beside midborder
grasses, these sprawling perennials can be admired during
their spring peak and then hidden by taller neighboring
foliage as they decline.

In most of the Northwest, evergreen grasses can provide
visual continuity between the seasons. Steel blue oat grass
(Helictotrichon sempervirens) can anchor cluster plantings
of minor bulbs such as crocus and snowdrops along with
early perennials. Pair oat grass with glossy leatherleaf
(*Bergenia cordifolia* 'Morning Red') for long-season punch.
This sturdy evergreen perennial produces red-veined,

plum purple flowers in spring, above rounded, leathery leaves that are still stained with ruddy winter color.

Late-rising perennials like peonies and Russian sage (*Perovskia*) can be similarly partnered with early flowers. Creeping *Phlox subulata* spreads in fragrant pools in spring, encircling silvery sage stems with puddles of blue (or pink, or white) blossoms. Primroses in deep-toned colors emphasize the wine-dark stems and coppery new leaves of emerging peonies.

Early perennials like leopard's bane (*Doronicum* species) partner well with tulips and narcissus, joining them in flower, and then hiding browning bulb foliage with their own expanding skirts. Lenten roses (*Helleborus* x *orientalis*) are woodland and meadow dwellers that flower in splendor when their companions are dormant, then are swallowed up (and shaded by) maturing foliage. In gardens, hellebores do best in partnerships that provide spring sun and summer shade, and their lustrous foliage remains attractive all year-round. Give them wide skirts of snow crocus, followed by reticulated iris or sheets of dainty scilla in white, pink, or blue.

Full or partial sun suits many of the most common spring bloomers to the ground. Quite a few will perform nicely if they receive plenty of reflected or filtered light, even if they can't get much direct sun. The true sun lovers, like rock cress and basket of gold, generally demand excellent drainage. All of these first flowers look best when grown in ordinary garden soil with a compost mulch.

Shady gardens are ideal spots for woodland flowers, many of which bloom early and then go dormant as summer heat builds. To hide the gaps they leave, mingle them with ferns and hostas, whose unfurling fronds and foliage come into their own later in the year. Combinations based on such sequencing succeed because they take advantage of each plant's natural cycle. To make the relationships last, select adaptive partners that don't mind sharing the same ground space with others.

SEQUENCING EARLY SUMMER BLOOMERS

By early summer, many gardens are sweet with roses and honeysuckle, but apart from peonies, foxgloves, and coral bells, early perennials may be in short supply. A look at the tallgrass prairie may inspire us to add blue or white wild indigo (*Baptisia* species) and lacy-leaved meadow rues (*Thalictrum* species), early bloomers that double as splendid foliage plants.

Our wild indigo *(Baptisia australis)* is much admired in England, where it is prized as much for its lustrous, blue-gray foliage as for its blue, sweet-pea flowers. Wild indigo partners pleasingly with long-fingered peonies and slender wands of peach-leaved bellflowers *(Campanula persicifolia),* which repeat their bloom if deadheaded. Because wild indigo remains sturdy well into winter, later bloomers like daylilies, autumnal asters, and goldenrods must be clustered nearby rather than interplanted, but early bloomers like violets and anemones can share its space.

Meadow rues are ideal sequencing plants, rising early, needing little room at ground level, and tolerating close companions. Taller types, such as columbine-leaved meadow rue *(Thalictrum aquilegifolium),* will screen sweeps of browning bulbs nicely. The airy scrim of their feathery foliage adds a lovely sense of mystery to small gardens, making a little space seem larger. Meadow rue's lacy, open structure contrasts strikingly with big grasses, mounded *Spiraea* 'Goldflame', and slim stems of brilliant purple pencil plant *(Verbena patagonica).*

In early summer, meadow plants reach knee height and lush grasses hide the drying leaves of the earliest flowers. In our gardens, the same sort of sequencing can occur. Fading first flowers are masked by summer bloomers already fluffing out wide skirts spangled with buds. When we create layered or sandwich plantings of perennials, a look at our natural models demonstrates that combinations of clump formers and moderate runners work well.

For instance, coral bells *(Heuchera)* like wine-leaved 'Plum Pudding' shrink to small crowns in autumn and then expand rapidly in early summer. These pair effectively with early-flowering carpeters such as *Veronica peduncularis* 'Georgia Blue', a fine-textured sprawler that reblooms in fall, taking on hot foliage tints as well.

By May or June, foliage perennials such as bold rodgersias, rounded hostas, and unpleating lady's mantle *(Alchemilla mollis)* come into their own, ably assisted by ligularias and ornamental rhubarb, whose leaves are as impressive as their flowers. All have relatively small resting crowns that enlarge dramatically by midsummer. Thus, their early-performing partners must prefer summer shade and drought or retreat into dormancy early.

Shady woodlands provide plenty of possibilities, from bluebells and anemones to violets.

Larger plants can also overlap if their cycles are compatible. Summer-blooming baby's breath sets off jagged-leaved Oriental poppies to perfection when the huge blooms open in late spring. By midsummer, foamy clouds of baby's breath will disguise the poppy wreckage once

Seek out choice native shade perennials like trillium (Trillium ovatum), now available as tissue cultured rather than wild collected plants.

SPRING BLOOMERS FOR SUN

Aubretia	*Aubretia* species and hybrids
Basket-of-gold	*Aurinia saxatilis*
Compact leopard's bane	*Doronicum hirsutum* 'Miss Mason'
Cushion spurge	*Euphorbia polychroma*
Double yellow marsh marigold	*Caltha palustris* 'Multiplex'
Golden globe flower	*Trollius* x *cultorum* 'Orange Queen'
Horned viola	*Viola cornuta*
Leatherleaf	*Bergenia cordifolia* 'Morning Red'
Leopard's bane	*Doronicum caucasium* 'Magnificum'
Pasque flower	*Anemone pulsatilla* (also sold as *Pulsatilla vulgaris*)
Sweet violet	*Viola odorata*
Variegated rock cress	*Aurinia saxatilis* 'Dudley Neville Variegated'
White globe flower	*Trollius* x *cultorum* 'Alabaster'
White marsh marigold	*Caltha palustris* 'Alba'

Native foam flower (Tellima grandi-flora), Solomon's seal (Polygonatum biflorum), and forget-me-nots (Myoso-tis) carpet a shady pocket in photographer Janet Loughrey's home garden.

SPRING BLOOMERS FOR SHADE

Black Labrador violet	*Viola labradorica*
Bleeding heart	*Dicentra eximia* 'Zestful'
Blue corydalis	*Corydalis flexuosa* 'China Blue'
Blue-leaf bleeding heart	*Dicentra oregana* 'Boothman's'
Lenten rose	*Helleborus x orientalis* hybrids
Purple bishop's hat	*Epimedium grandiflorum* 'Violet Queen'
Red-stemmed hellebore	*Helleborus foetidus* 'Wester Flisk'
Red wood spurge	*Euphorbia amygdaloides* 'Rubra'
Snowy bishop's hat	*Epimedium x youngianum* 'Niveum'
Spotted lungwort	*Pulmonaria x* 'Berries and Cream'
Variegated lungwort	*Pulmonaria rubra* 'David Ward'
Wood anemone	*Anemone nemorosa* 'Vestal Virgin'
Wood bleeding heart	*Dicentra formosa*
Wood violet	*Viola glabra*
Yellow corydalis	*Corydalis lutea*

those fabulous flowers are gone. (Trim back the poppy foliage, give it some compost tea, and the crowns will refurbish with far better-looking new leaves.)

Certain second-flush perennials can fill several roles at once. Fuzzy lamb's ears *(Stachys byzantina),* a common edger, creeps companionably among all sorts of summery perennials, covering bare earth with silver. The form 'Big Ears', which rarely flowers, makes an ideal mid- to front-border filler. Low, densely furnished companions will cause it to drop its leaves by midsummer, but taller, airy ones allow 'Big Ears' to remain clothed well into fall. Flowering forms like *S. b.* 'Cotton Ball' produce spikes studded with pale purple spheres, which persist decoratively into winter.

In shady sites, carpeting bellflower *(Campanula takesimana)* plays a similar part, lapping over the border edge and winding between clumps of foxgloves, long-blooming hardy geraniums *(Geranium maculatum* 'Album'), and evergreen fans of ivory-banded *Iris foetidissima* 'Variegata', an early bloomer that produces fat red fruits in fall. If the spent stems are trimmed back, the bellflower (like many of its kin) sends up several flushes of flowers from early summer into fall.

SUMMER SEQUENCING

In high summer, both native prairie grasses and perennials are head-high and bloom approaches its peak. Hot pinky-purple wands of brilliant gayfeather or prairie blazing star *(Liatris pycnostachya)* sizzle in the sun. Rattlesnake-master *(Eryngium* species) tips sheaves of stiff, yuccalike leaves with dramatic candelabra stems that end in explosions of spiky silver-green globes. Stately culver's root *(Veronicastrum virginicum)* sends its slim white spires skyward with architectural dignity.

High summer is also showtime in the garden, where a dazzling array of perennials create nonstop visual fireworks for several months. We can re-create the rich floral tapestry of the tallgrass prairie by learning the average bloom periods of our favorite perennials. Once we know how they behave in our own backyards, we can concoct potent and pleasing combinations, interweaving flowers and foliage so that when one plant takes a breather, another can step in and take its place.

Sun-soaked and abuzz with bees, open gardens can host a tremendous number of summer bloomers. Many native prairie flowers adapt well to garden conditions, growing larger and blooming longer than they do in the wild. Coneflowers *(Echinacea* species) and blanket flower *(Gaillardia* species), black- and brown-eyed Susans *(Rudbeckia* species), and penstemons all provide multiple possibilities.

Shaded woodland gardens are often quite dry by midsummer, when the early wildflowers have disappeared. Damp or dry, shade makes it easier to arrange eye-catching displays of foliage plants, some of which offer striking blooms as well as gorgeous leaves. Hostas, which burn to a crisp in hot sun, can develop their full magnificence in light or dappled shade. Glowing gold, gleaming green, or steely blue, striped with cream or stippled with silver, their puckered and quilted leaves offer enough variety of form, color, and texture to fill a whole border. For heightened contrast, mix in rounded and ruffled coral bells (*Heuchera* species), lace-webbed ferns, and fine-textured astilbes.

The best way to enjoy an unbroken summer of bloom is to develop a full and varied palette of perennials. That way, despite quirky weather, disease, or straying animals, something will succeed. The key is to select a core palette of garden workhorses, plants with staying power in almost any situation.

First on many must-have perennials lists are yarrows (*Achillea* species), whose elegant, ferny foliage remains lush despite heat and drought. The remarkably persistent flowers rebloom for months, and modern hybrids come in all sizes and almost every color but blue. Yarrows combine effectively with early-blooming peonies and poppies as well as fall-flowering sedums like 'Autumn Joy' and ornamental grasses.

Daylilies are another "top ten" plant that offer a delicious array of colors. Choose with care and you can enjoy daylilies from late spring until fall. Many have handsome foliage, and a few boast striking seedheads as well. Their ribbony foliage is a good foil for fine-textured grasses and blue globe thistles.

Plenty of prairie plants make the list as well. Our native joe pye weed (*Eupatorium* species) is another trouper that is horticulturally hot these days. Vanilla-scented *Eupatorium fistulosum* 'Gateway' holds its inflated purple balloons for months, and the stems stay strong into winter. Rugged joe pye weed (*E. rugosum*) 'Chocolate' has melting brown leaves that set off icing-white flowers to perfection. Both blend well with large grasses, salvias, and bold-leaved perennials such as purple pokeweed *(Phytolacca americana)*.

Mallows (*Malva* species) and lavateras are abundant bloomers that produce clouds of hollyhock flowers nonstop until frost. If pink-and-white *Lavatera thuringiaca* 'Barnsley' is too confectionery for your color scheme, its cousins, 'Burgundy' and 'Alba', could fill the bill handily. These bushy plants act like shrubs in the border and can be interplanted with long-flowering bellflowers and spiky blue sea hollies or prairie rattlesnake-master *(Eryngium yuccifolium)* for utterly reliable bloom.

EARLY SUMMER BLOOMERS FOR SUN

Double peach-leaf bellflower	*Campanula persicifolia* 'Victoria'
Fern-leaf peony	*Paeonia tenuifolia* 'Flore-pleno'
Golden daylily	*Hemerocallis* 'Goldrush'
Golden hardy geranium	*Geranium* 'Ann Folkard'
Gold-leaf creeping bellflower	*Campanula garganica* 'Dickson's Gold'
Hybrid peony	*Paeonia* 'Coral Charm'
Pale bellflower	*Campanula lactiflora*
Peach-leaf bellflower	*Campanula persicifolia* 'Percy Piper'
Siberian iris	*Iris sibirica* 'Snow Queen'
Threadleaf coreopsis	*Coreopsis* 'Moonbeam'
Variegated iris	*Iris pallida* 'Variegata'

EARLY SUMMER BLOOMERS FOR SHADE

Apricot foxglove	*Digitalis purpurea* 'Apricot'
Blue-crested wood iris	*Iris cristata*
Crimson coral bells	*Heuchera* 'Crimson Clouds'
Double-flowered bellflower	*Campanula trachelium* 'Bernice'
Japanese wood bellflower	*Campanula takesimana*
Mourning widow geranium	*Geranium phaeum* 'Variegatum'
Red-stemmed wood spurge	*Euphorbia* x *martinii*
Silver coral bells	*Heuchera* 'Silver Shadows'
Variegated Gladwin iris	*Iris foetidissima* 'Variegata'
Velvet geranium	*Geranium renardii*
White crested wood iris	*Iris cristata* 'Alba'
Wood anemone	*Anemone sylvestris*
Wood phlox	*Phlox divaricata* 'Clouds of Perfume'

Daylilies come in almost every color now, from the midnight red of 'Black Cat' to the snowy 'Sunday Gloves'. Plant these tough long bloomers near a path to facilitate removal of spent flowers.

SUMMER PERENNIALS FOR SUN

Alpine sea holly	*Eryngium alpinum* 'Blue Star'
Balloon flower	*Platycodon grandiflorus*
Burgundy tree mallow	*Lavatera thuringiaca* 'Burgundy'
Dusky joe pye weed	*Eupatorium rugosum* 'Chocolate'
Dwarf daylily	*Hemerocallis* 'Stella d'Oro'
Himalayan spurge	*Euphorbia griffithii* 'Dixter'
Joe pye weed	*Eupatorium fistulosum* 'Gateway'
Moonlight yarrow	*Achillea taygetea*
Pastel summer phlox	*Phlox* x 'Phlox of Sheep'
Pink tree mallow	*Lavatera thuringiaca* 'Barnsley'
Purple-blue daylily	*Hemerocallis* 'Prairie Blue Eyes'
Rosy geum	*Geum* x 'Paprika'
Striped meadow mallow	*Malva sylvestris* 'Zebrina'
Summer Pastels yarrow	*Achillea* 'Summer Pastels'
Threadleaf tickseed	*Coreopsis* 'Zagreb'
White satin mallow	*Malva moschata* 'Alba'
Yellow reblooming daylily	*Hemerocallis* 'Happy Returns'

SUMMER PERENNIALS FOR SHADE

Bamboo-leaved rodgersia	*Rodgersia podophylla*
Blue hosta	*Hosta* 'Blue Heron'
Chevron plant	*Tovara virginiana*
Columbine	*Aquilegia* species and hybrids
Coral bells	*Heuchera* 'Snow Storm'
Golden hosta	*Hosta* 'August Moon'
Golden meadowsweet	*Filipendula ulmaria* 'Aurea'
Japanese painted fern	*Athyrium goeringianum* 'Ursula's Red'
Lady fern	*Athyrium filix-femina*
Maidenhair fern	*Adiantum pedatum*
Obedient plant	*Physostegia virginiana* 'Variegata'
Plateleaf	*Astilboides tabularis* (formerly *Rodgersia*)
Purple astilbe	*Astilbe taquetii* 'Purple Lance'
Sweet spurge	*Euphorbia dulcis* 'Chameleon'
White toad lily	*Tricyrtis latifolia* 'White Towers'

SEQUENCING LATE BLOOMERS

Flowers may be scarce in fall, but as late summer slides into autumn, warm days and cool nights waken hidden flames in foliage. Certain perennials join the blaze, such as blue star *(Amsonia tabernaemontana)* and balloon flowers *(Platycodon* species), both of which turn to masses of fiery gold. Meadows and prairies gleam with the burnish of brass and bronze as ripe grasses are streaked with hot sunset colors and heavy with seedheads.

Our native showy goldenrod *(Solidago speciosa)* burns sun yellow against the blue autumn sky. The silphiums—compass plant, prairie dock, and cup plant—soar 8 and 10 feet high, their spangled seedheads thronged with goldfinches. Native asters haze the prairie with smoky blue and slumberous purple. Though rough and weedy in the wild, many make magnificent garden plants. Indeed, in England, these prairie belles are considered indispensable border beauties.

In home gardens, similarly stunning effects can be achieved by incorporating plenty of ornamental grasses into borders bright with fall flowers. Native bluestems ripen to a smoldering copper red, while selections of switch grass *(Panicum virgatum)* such as 'Heavy Metal' and 'Cloud Nine' shimmer like spun gold. Combine them with broader-bladed Chinese maiden grasses *(Miscanthus sinensis)* such as 'Morning Light' or zebra-striped 'Strictus', as well as daintier dwarf clumpers like silken palomino Mexican feather grass *(Stipa* or *Nassella tenuissima)*, and ruddy blood grass *(Imperata cylindrica* 'Red Baron').

Shady gardens can be as full of flowers in fall as in spring. Bugbanes *(Cimicifuga* species) spill honeyed scent from slim white bottlebrush flowers. Cheerful pink bells of *Polygonum campanulatum* still ring out gaily, even in deep shade. Rosy or creamy, Japanese anemones *(Anemone japonica)* bloom long and hard in dappled light. Arching wands of Asian toad lilies *(Tricyrtis* species) gleam with tiny flowers that stud the stems like so many orchids. Stippled and speckled, freckled and spotted, the little flowers reward the gardener who takes time for closer inspection. Obedient plant, *Physostegia virginiana* 'Variegata', thrives in light shade, where ivory-striped leaves turn the same raspberry as the flower spikes in fall.

In order to have a good show in autumn, we need to

dedicate a fair percentage of garden space to late bloomers. It needn't mean a summer sacrifice: If 10 to 20 percent of your plants offer strong flower or foliage fall color in fall, they can carry the day. For one thing, many late performers are large plants with plenty of character. For another, they can be placed behind reliable rebloomers, perhaps yarrows, blanket flowers, and daylilies, whose now-minor contribution will be amplified by good company.

To make the most of the autumn display, it helps to group our late bloomers and to provide some reinforcement. As with the spring flowers, fall performers can look forlorn and unconnected if dotted about the garden. Set in clusters and sweeps, and given supportive companions (like those reliable rebloomers), they gain significant visual impact.

Fortunately, many fall flowers have striking foliage, which contributes to the texture and fullness of the beds while these slow developers are on the way up. The trick is to select fall flowers that pull their weight over several seasons. Asters, for example, can be splendid in fall but dogs in summer, when their lanky stems flop and their foliage mildews.

The solution is to seek out superior forms, such as bushy *Aster* x *frikartii* 'Monch', which makes a fine backdrop for summery penstemons before creating its own long-lasting cascade of periwinkle stars. Calico aster, *A. lateriflorus* 'Horizontalis', has a marvelously tiered structure that makes it outstanding on its own or mixed in a border, where its lavender flowers glow against its dusky, purple-black leaves.

Sedum 'Autumn Joy' is a border classic precisely because it offers so many periods of interest. In spring its fat, scale-encrusted stems pierce the ground early. In summer the plump stems are packed with green buds with the texture of broccoli. In fall they burst into clouds of rusty rose, followed by tarnished seedheads that attract small birds through winter, when its battered skeleton remains upright beneath the snow. Good old 'Autumn Joy' has dozens of equally gardenworthy relatives, such as sizzling pink 'Brilliant', dusky 'Indian Chief', and frosty 'Stardust', which are similarly fascinating to watch over the seasons.

LATE PERFORMERS FOR SUN

Blue star	*Amsonia tabernaemontana*
Boltonia	*Boltonia asteroides* 'Pink Beauty'
Burgundy blanket flower	*Gaillardia grandiflora* 'Burgundy'
Calico aster	*Aster lateriflorus* 'Horizontalis'
Copper Helen's flower	*Helenium autumnale* 'Moerheim Beauty'
Dwarf tickseed	*Coreopsis grandiflora* 'Flying Saucers'
Japanese anemone	*Anemone japonica*
Frikart's aster	*Aster* x *frikartii* 'Monch'
Himalayan knotweed	*Polygonum* 'Dimity'
Leadwort	*Ceratostigma plumbaginoides*
New England aster	*Aster novae-angliae* 'Alma Potschke'
Purple Dome aster	*Aster novae-angliae* 'Purple Dome'
Tumbling sedum	*Sedum* x 'Vera Jameson'
Variegated goldenrod	*Solidago* 'Gold Spangles'
White tall sedum	*Sedum telephium* 'Stardust'

LATE PERFORMERS FOR SHADE

Blue monkshood	*Aconitum carmichaelli* 'Barker's Variety'
Cardinal flower	*Lobelia cardinalis*
Gladwin iris	*Iris foetidissima*
Ostrich fern	*Osmunda cinnamonea*
Purple toad lily	*Tricyrtis formosana* 'Amethystina'
Rosy Japanese anemone	*Anemone tomentosa* 'Robustissima'
White Japanese anemone	*Anemone japonica* 'Whirlwind'
White snakeroot	*Cimicifuga simplex* 'White Pearl'
White toad lily	*Tricyrtis latifolia* 'White Towers'
White wood aster	*Aster divaricatus*

SEQUENCING WINTER EFFECTS

Winter in the garden is often downtime, a season without much flow of color and change. With a little planning, any Northwest garden can provide an attractive assortment of colors, shapes, and textures well into winter. For starters, many summer beauties can hold their own through autumn and into winter. When sturdy, structural summery perennials like sea hollies, coneflowers, and Russian sage are left to stand through wind and snow, the resulting shapes can work the same magic that transforms the native prairie from stubble to sculpture. The educated eye quickly discovers winter's subtle beauties of line and form and appreciates the quiet season's gentle gradations of delicate color. Brown is revealed as beautiful indeed, from tender tints of toast and biscuit to dark chocolate and rich molasses.

In our meadows, winter is a time of deep peace and quiet. Susurrating grasses whisper in every wind, the hollow stems of big bluestem grasses clacking softly above softer seedheads of little bluestem. Blanketing snow emphasizes the graceful silhouettes of pale purple coneflowers, false indigo, and bush clover, whose stems are now the warm, rich color of burnt sienna.

Skeletons of joe pye weed cast long shadows on the snow, joined by angular rattlesnake-master, seed-studded cup plant, and densely plumed goldenrods. Brown and burnished, the remaining seedheads of native grasses and perennials nourish hungry birds in deep winter when other food is scarce.

Clearly, not all perennials are good candidates for winter beauty. To learn which perennials will look dramatic in your winter garden (instead of merely overlooked), try leaving likely perennials untrimmed, and then evaluate their looks through fall and winter. Leggy asters, bushy Russian sages, and late-blooming salvias are all good plants to experiment with when seeking interesting off-season performance. So, too, are the many border versions of those native coneflowers and rudbeckias, joe pye weeds and goldenrods. Through selection and editing, you can develop your own winter palette to enliven this underappreciated season.

SEQUENCING MILD-REGION WINTER COLOR

In many parts of the Pacific Northwest, mild winters are the rule. Here, the garden possibilities become far more plentiful. Evergreen perennials act as foliage plants all year long, then come into their own when brasher competition retreats. Grouped companionably and given the support of compact border shrubs (evergreen herbs, rhododendrons, and dwarf conifers), even the least showy winter flowers can make a cheerful splash.

When perennial borders are traditionally bare, a well-chosen array of winter performers will keep the coveted color coming. Glossy, rounded foliage of leatherleaf (*Bergenia* 'Red Star') turns sumptuous shades of ruby and garnet in winter, setting off stubby spikes of snapping pink or red flowers. Blue spurge (*Euphorbia myrsinites*)

tips its lax, blue-scaled arms with lime-colored flower-heads in sunny spots, while taller spurges like *E. wulfenii* 'Golden Balloons' open round-headed flowers in lemon and chartreuse. Set amid a flurry of evergreen candytuft (*Iberis* species) and rock cress, the effect is charmingly gay all winter long.

Tall sedums like 'Brilliant' (cousin to the better known 'Autumn Joy') look terrific from early spring well into winter. These easy-growing season-extenders are drought tolerant and prefer compost to fertilizers. Divide every few years for best behavior (they get floppy in time).

In shady places, red wood spurge offers stiff stems ruffled with whorling leaves in holiday reds and greens. Stinking hellebores (*Helleborus foetidus),* which don't stink at all, produce clusters of icy green bell-shaped flowers above dramatic leaves that are like spoked wheels without rims. At their feet, spotted lungworts (*Pulmonaria* species) are lush with new foliage that may be not just spotted but marbled, striped, or spattered with silver. Red-flowered 'Christmas Cheer' may be joined by pink and blue cousins anytime after the New Year.

Some of winter's flowers are even fragrant. Those so-called stinking hellebores, for example, may have perfumed flowers (as in 'Miss Jekyll's Scented Form'). Sweet violets (*Viola odorata)* may start to open in midwinter, including those like 'Blue Remington', a rebloomer that flowers both early and late in the year. Primroses, which often begin to bloom around the winter solstice, have their own distinctive fragrance, which smells like the breath of spring.

Copper carexes are splendid winter evergreen perennials in the maritime Northwest. Give Carex comans *'Bronze' a knee-high trim in fall, rather than a flat-top buzz cut that can lead to winter rots in evergreen grasses.*

SEQUENCING WINTER COLOR

Evergreen perennials, including grasses, usually need a light autumn grooming to remain lovely all winter. With a bit of help, shimmering half-globes of steel blue oat grass *(Helictotrichon sempervirens)*, carexes in coppery fountains or cream-edged whirls, and tufted blue fescues can stay on duty indefinitely. Interplant these stalwarts loosely with silvery creeping artemisias, woolly thymes *(Pseudo lanuginosus)*, and carpeting knotweeds *(Polygonum* species), leaving space for early bulbs and summer perennials that can be tidied away as they go dormant.

Strong winter shapes are contributed by strapping, swordlike New Zealand flax *(Phormium* species), which has both upright and weeping or cascading forms with variously tinted foliage. In general, the more colorful, attractive, and expensive the New Zealand flax, the less hardy it is. Protection with a few evergreen boughs keeps these semihardy plants healthy and whole during cold snaps. In winter windstorms, the protection of light row-cover cloth (such as Reemay) can save tender leaves from unsightly windburn.

Similarly spiky and completely hardy, the yuccas can rise dramatically above carpets of evergreen herbs and

SKELETAL WINTER PERENNIALS

Alpine sea holly	*Eryngium alpinum* 'Superbum'
Autumn Sun rudbeckia	*Rudbeckia nitida* 'Herbsonne'
Big bluestem	*Andropogon gerardii*
Bigleaf pokeweed	*Phytolacca americana* 'Bigleaf'
Globe thistle	*Echinops banaticus* 'Blue Glow'
Golden needle grass	*Stipa gigantea*
Joe pye weed	*Eupatorium purpureum* 'Selection'
Little bluestem	*Schizachyrium scoparium*
Russian sage	*Perovskia* species and hybrids
Tall sedum	*Sedum maximum* 'Atropurpureum'
White false indigo	*Baptisia leucantha*

winter flowers. For visual continuity, encircle these winter performers with easygoing evergreen carpeters such as speedwells (*Veronica* species) that can gently fill in gaps where summer plants are slumbering but won't mind being overshadowed later. Masses of minor bulbs like squills, snowdrops, and snow crocus can also be laced through perennial borders without harm.

MILD-WINTER PERENNIALS

Algerian iris	*Iris unguicularis* 'Walter Butt'
Apricot New Zealand flax	*Phormium* x 'Apricot Queen'
Christmas rose	*Helleborus* niger
Copper carex	*Carex buchananii* 'Red Racer'
Cream variegated carex	*Carex morrowii* 'Fisher's Form'
'Dragon Skin' kale	
Golden yucca	*Yucca filamentosa* 'Gold Sword'
Leatherleaf	*Bergenia* 'Winter Glow'
Pink New Zealand flax	*Phormium* x 'Maori Maiden'
Rainbow kale 'Bright Lights' kale	
'Russian Red' kale	
Variegated stinking iris	*Iris foetidissima* 'Variegata'
Winter hellebore	*Helleborus atrorubens* 'Early Purple'
Winter iris	*Iris cretica*

BUYING PERENNIALS

Finding perennials can be as simple as taking a trip to the nearest garden center. If you find a good selection of healthy, attractive plants that are well rooted and growing strongly, you're in luck. Use these guidelines when making your choices:

- Choose the best specimens to take home, giving preference to those with vigorous good looks and plenty of lush new growth.

- Avoid plants with limp, brittle, puckered, or discolored foliage, all of which may be symptoms of stress or disease.

- Discoloration can be harder to detect in variegated plants, so check the overall appearance; if the plant basically appears to be flourishing, it's probably a good bet.

- Happy plants have sturdy stems and are firmly seated in their pots.

- Poorly rooted plants teeter or flop, and their anchor roots may be partially exposed above the soil level.

- A small but sturdy plant is preferable to a larger one that's lank and flopsy.

How do you know a plant has been at the nursery too long? A few roots poking from the bottom of a pot can simply mean that the plant is raring to go, but if you suspect a plant is rootbound, turn it carefully out of its pot

Hellebores thrive in the maritime Northwest, and many new forms are being bred for larger blossoms, new colors, and intriguing flower shapes.

and take a look. Ideally, the roots will make a solid web through which you can still detect some soil. A solid mass of tightly wound roots means the plant has been waiting too long. To set it free, you'll need to rough up those tight roots a bit before setting the plant into fresh soil. Unless you do this, the plant won't even know it has a new life waiting and may stay balled up for several seasons.

Though perennials are more popular than ever, not all parts of the Northwest are equally well served with specialty nurseries, so the local selection may not include the enticing plants shown in books and magazines and at plant lectures. Plant sales sponsored by garden clubs and plant societies are excellent places to seek the uncommon. Field trips are also in order, since our region is, on the whole, so very well endowed.

Buying through mail order has never been easier, but even by mail, it's best to buy locally. Plants raised in your region will adapt better to your garden than those grown across the country.

How many plants to buy depends on several factors. If you aren't in a hurry, you can buy a single plant of each favorite perennial, grow it for a year, and then divide it into several or many offspring. Given good conditions, less-expensive, smaller plants will fatten up quickly, providing as good a show as large plants in a season or two. Many common, easily grown perennials can be divided soon and often, providing the patient gardener with a large supply of freebies in just a few seasons.

If you need a lot of plants and want them soon, growing from seed offers an attractive alternative to blowing the budget. Many perennials are as easy to grow from seed as annuals and vegetables. The high cost of new or rare perennials often reflects their scarcity, so the cost comes down as the supply increases. Those that remain expensive for many years are generally more difficult to propagate, even for professionals.

FINDING THE RIGHT PLANT FOR THE RIGHT PLACE

Which perennials will grow best for you depends in good part on where you live, because our varied region includes many distinct climatic areas, and both soil and water types can vary greatly even within short distances (like across the yard). As a rule, most perennials will grow well anywhere in the Northwest.

Nominally, the entire maritime region is considered to be USDA zone 7 or 8, meaning that plants rated for anything lower than or up to that (zones 2 through 7 or 8) will be hardy here. However, while the hardiness zones assigned to perennials reflect their ability to withstand cold, these zones don't tell us whether perennials adapt well to hot nights, acid clay, constant spring or winter rain, or other such conditions. Regional resources such as local garden clubs, plant societies, and your county extension service can be extremely helpful guides. Libraries and good nurseries can also provide excellent information.

Regional factors must guide your choices when you choose perennials, but it is also important to thoroughly explore your own garden, learning its specifics as well. Every garden has its own microclimates, pockets of warmth or cold, sites that are usually wet or very dry, windy or protected. Discovering these will help you place your perennials well, since each plant family has its own requirements.

ALTERING THE SOIL

In general, it's wise to grow plants that enjoy the conditions your garden offers. Most perennials tolerate a wide range of soil types but do best in soils that are close to neutral in pH. Adding plenty of humus (compost and aged manures) will neutralize pH somewhat and boost root growth as well. Though it's impossible to change the nature of the whole garden, you can alter pH in a small area for special plants. Here is a quick look at some ways to improve or amend soil. For detailed information, see Chapter 3.

- To sweeten acid soils, add agricultural or dolomite lime (*not* the slaked lime used in outhouses) as directed on the package.

- Alkaline soils can be brought closer to neutral by adding sulfur and mulching with pine needles (which are very acid).

PLANTING PERENNIALS

Thoughtful placement and proper planting are the keys to a healthy, handsome garden. When arranging perennials, consider their relative vigor and ultimate size. In well-filled borders, neighboring plants are not crowded, yet they lightly overlap, presenting an unbroken tapestry to the eye but allowing free circulation of air. For a generous look, you may opt to space young plants closely, then move them farther apart as they mature. When planting, follow the old adage and dig a gallon hole for a 4-inch pot.

In new beds, blend the sandy loam and compost with a potful of potting soil (a gallon-sized plant receives a gallon of soil, and so on). In an established bed, blend the removed soil with an equal amount of compost or aged manure. Fill the hole halfway, making a conical mound in the center. Loosen the roots of the plant with your fingers or a garden knife, and then center the plant's crown on the mound, fanning the roots out on all sides. Sprinkle soil over them, firming it in with your fingers. Make sure the crown remains at soil level (just as it was in its pot). Water well and renew the mulch or top-dressing around it.

Bare-root plants are easy to plant this way, but if potted plants are a bit rootbound, you will need to tease out their tangles before planting. Although a few perennials such as bleeding heart have brittle roots, most are very sturdy, so don't worry about hurting them.

- Lean soils can be enriched with soy and cottonseed meals for a slowly released source of nitrogen.

- For a quicker boost, add composted manure and alfalfa meal or pellets, which synergistically produce extra nitrogen when used together.

- Digging in horticultural grit or coarse builder's sand may improve drainage slightly, but can create sinkholes.

ELEVEN: GROUND COVERS

Ground covers don't have to be diminutive. In a shady setting, dense, evergreen epimediums and hellebores make a delicate looking but tough ground-covering carpet beneath shrubs and trees.

For most gardeners, the subject of ground covers rivals only dirt as the ultimate dull topic. If the term conjures up a stultifying sweep of vinca or a blank expanse of pachysandra, try thinking instead about garden carpets. Why not break up those blah green rugs with clusters of seasonal bulbs and clumps of contrasting foliage plants? Make stylish, magical carpets, decorated with imaginative detail. What's more, ground covers need not be uniformly green. Roll out a rich red carpet of *Ajuga reptans* 'Burgundy Glow' to add pop to a pastel planting. Pour sparkling 'White Nancy' lamium (*Lamium maculatum* 'White Nancy'), with whitewashed foliage and clean white flowers, beneath a dusky purple smoke bush (*Cotinus coggygria* 'Royal Purple').

We often assume that ground cover plants are intrinsically boring, fit only for a life of servitude. Happily, only mental habit, not horticultural law, demands that they be homely or inconspicuous. Escape the constrictions of conventional wisdom by ignoring routine choices like ivy (a noxious weed) or St. John's wort (hard to remove even with a bulldozer) in favor of equally hard workers that are delightful plants in their own right.

Similarly, we may profitably reexamine ground covers' expected garden roles. They do indeed suppress weeds, yet they also perform other vital tasks willingly and well. In spring, they protect bulb blossoms from being mudsplashed by the rain. Throughout the growing season, they conserve moisture, reducing evaporation and shading shallow-rooted perennials. Repeated groups of ground covers can unify complex border plantings, leading the eye gracefully while subtly linking disparate areas.

Evergreen ground covers can make permanent placeholders for ephemeral plants or can act as the stage for a succession of "sandwich" plantings, interlayered bulbs and perennials that chase each other through the year. Evergreen ground covers also provide winter interest while insulating borderline tender plants from deep ground frosts. As for the prime directive, the best ground covers suppress weeds artfully, creating a neutral zone between warring colors, softening primary colors or emphasizing secondary tints.

GROUND COVERS IN COMBINATIONS

While every garden holds numerous niches that are best filled by cooperative ground covers, we need not use the same plants over and over again. Rather than perpetuating those drab, impersonal stretches of creeping cotoneaster or vinca that give ground covers a bad name, we can try a new approach. We can plant each niche individually, employing a full range of plants with foliage and flowers in uncommon colors or subtle shades.

Not convinced? Tuck some lacy, prostrate beach wormwood, *Artemisia stellerana* 'Silver Brocade', under 'Black Joker' pansies and vivid red roses. Surround ashy blue *Iris sibirica* 'Summer Skies' and deep purple trumpet lilies with the crinkly rosettes of black bugleweed, *Ajuga reptans* 'Metallica Crispa'. Loop swirls of sheep bur, *Acaena* 'Blue Haze', around salmon and apricot daylilies. Circle a creamy pink miniature rose with tidy tweed sheets of pinky-purple *Sedum spathulifolium* 'Roseum'. Let a treasury of golden piggy-back plant, *Tolmiea menziesii* 'Taff's Gold' (a Northwest native), glow like lost sunshine beneath leathery rhododendrons.

By now, you may be wondering whether we are talking about plant combinations or ground covers. The point is to think about both. One clump of golden piggy-back under a canary yellow *Rhododendron* 'Hotei' is a combination (or at least the start of one). An encircling crowd of golden piggy-backs becomes a ground cover. Their circle need not remain unbroken, of course; it might be punctuated by clumps of ostrich ferns, daffodils, and blue summer onions *(Allium azureum)*.

Similarly, that creeping wormwood, 'Silver Brocade', that spills over the path edge can also crawl back into the border, accentuating gray 'Krossa Regal' hostas and hazy catmint. Blue sheep bur can both surround and echo glittering clumps of steel blue oat grass and quivering, blue-leaved meadow rues like *Thalictrum glaucum*. The ruddy sedum might play host to purple crocus in spring, set off the pleated, silver-green leaves and rosy flowers of clover-like *Oxalis adenophylla* in summer, and then play backdrop to the tiny, fragrant annual violet cress, *Ionopsidium acaule,* from autumn well into winter.

GREAT SERVANTS, TERRIBLE MASTERS

When they perform as intended, ground covers can be the busy gardener's best friend, but if they exceed their commission they may rank among our worst enemies. Essentially, we are asking plants to grow where we want them to and not where we don't, which is rather like explaining to the cats that they are welcome on the couch but not on the computer keyboard. To reduce conflict, be chary in your choices. This necessitates self-education, for the more you know your conditions—dry, sandy soil in full sun; heavy acid clay in half shade—the better able you will be to create a list of plants that will grow in those situations.

Next, find out how each of your candidates behaves in your part of the region. Even in the maritime Northwest, differences in climate and soil type can make plants behave quite differently in different gardens. A plant that acts demure in Seattle may turn rowdy in Eugene or vice versa. This underlines another important point: If your experience differs markedly from that of gardeners in other counties (or countries) or from information offered in gardening books (even this one), don't assume that either you or they must be wrong. Many environmental factors can significantly influence plant growth and behavior. Overall, the experience of maritime Northwest gardeners and nursery folk will prove more practically helpful than English garden books or even North American ones intended for a general readership.

Since ground covers are by definition plants that readily carpet the ground, unfamiliar candidates for garden placement should be handled with caution. Play it safe and give experimental selections—especially natives—a trial season or two in a nursery (separate) bed to prove themselves before unleashing them in your favorite border. This practice is especially recommended when dealing with plants from families with bolting tendencies, like mints and campanulas. Rampant spreaders often act deceptively meek for their first season, and only the following year do you discover what their roots have been up

Pick ground covers with care, avoiding troublemakers like St. John's wort (Hypericum calycinum), *which is a rampant spreader and extremely difficult to remove.*

Another challenging choice is archangel (Lamiastrum galeobdolon), *a beautiful but treacherous scrambler that can strangle smaller plants and cover amazing amounts of territory.*

to underground. This doesn't mean that there is no place in the garden for strong, aggressive carpeters; some situations are best served by garden thugs. However, knowing in advance what to expect from your ground covers can save a lot of hard work and heartache.

CHOOSING GROUND COVERS

When choosing candidates, remember that ground covers don't have to be flat or tiny; any plant that suits the style and scale of the planting and fulfills your requirements for a designated area can do the job. If you aren't sure where to start looking for replacements for insufferably dull old standards, check their family connections, for many of them have cuter cousins. Periwinkle, or creeping myrtle (*Vinca minor,* to 5 inches), is much prettier when painted with gold or silver variegations such as 'Variegata' and 'Argentea', and delicate, airy 'Miss Jekyll's White' is a collector's plant. Ordinary bugleweed is a weed indeed, but buxom, blue-spiked *Ajuga reptans* 'Catlin's Giant' and the richly textured 'Purple Brocade' are knockouts. The eastern native Allegheny spurge, *Pachysandra procumbens,* is attractive enough to plant as a specimen, with its bronzed and marbled foliage and fluffy ivory flowers.

Certain creeping herbs make gorgeous garden rugs, especially the prolific mother-of-thyme (*Thymus serpyllum,* 1 inch). The species is variable, producing sheets of tight-textured green foliage smothered from late spring well into autumn with tiny flowers of purple or lavender. It boasts numerous named forms, such as white 'Albus', clear red 'Coccineus, 'Pink Chintz', and 'Reiter's Red'. The most enticing form, woolly thyme *(T. lanuginosus),* spreads in soft gray rugs over any light or open soil, wanting only full sun and quick drainage in order to thrive.

Golden marjoram (*Origanum vulgare* 'Aureum') forms low, cascading tussocks of rounded, banana yellow foliage before sending up thickets of taller stems tipped with frizzy purple flowerheads. This strapping form (often sold at specialty herb nurseries) is a willing worker that goes very well in larger-scale settings, but where space is limited, you might prefer the choicer 'Norton's Gold', a dwarf mounder some 5 or 6 inches high, its mild pink flowers held on 12-inch stems. A good many other marjorams and ornamental oreganos are worthy of consideration where you want ground covers to be both lovely and luxuriant yet tough and drought tolerant. All grow well in hot, dry situations, doing nicely beside heat-reflective staircases, sidewalks, and driveways as well as swimming pools.

There are many diminutive forms of favorite border plants as well, such as prostrate baby's breath, *Gypsophila repens,* a ground-hugging mat that foams with white froth (or pink, in the case of 'Rosea') from late spring through midsummer. Like its larger cousins, creeping baby's breath prefers sun and open, limy soils, sulking or dying away in heavy, acid clays.

Several mat-forming veronicas are enchanting carpeters, including the very dwarf *Veronica pectinata,* with toothed, silvery leaves crowded in summer with short spikes of sky blue flowers. An even grayer version, 'Rosea', has warm, blushing pink flowers that accord nicely with peonies and old roses. The slightly larger *Veronica prostrata* (also sold as *V. rupestris* or *V. teucrium*) has leathery little green leaves and vivid, purple-blue flowers, softer in the form 'Heavenly Blue' and rosy in 'Mrs. Holt'. A daintier, golden-leaved version, 'Trehane', has sea blue flowers. All the veronicas like full sun but prefer moister soils than the hardy thymes.

Whether you choose traditional or uncommon ground covers for a given setting, it is vital to balance plant and situation for vigor and scale. Where a good deal of ground needs to be covered, perhaps beneath mature trees and shrubs, our carpeters must be determined but not outright thugs. Running comfrey, *Symphytum grandiflorum,* weaves an evergreen tapestry of coarse, hairy leaves trimmed from spring into summer in dangling clusters of ivory bells tipped with china blue in 'Hidcote Blue' or pastel pink in 'Hidcote Pink'. A chalky blue-flowered form with leaves handsomely streaked in buttery yellow and cream is called 'Variegatum'. It makes a wonderful, stippled flooring for a sun-dappled woodland, consorting well with shrubby dogwoods (*Cornus* species) and flowering currant (*Ribes* species).

Among big, bold plants like hostas, rodgersias, and tall ostrich ferns, we need understory plants that can hold their own without overpowering the main events. A vigorous, white-flowered carpeter, *Houttuynia cordata,* is an aggressive traveler in damp soils but more restrained in drier, wooded gardens. Its pretty variegated form,

Native bunchberry (Cornus canadensis) *looks beautiful under rhododendrons and witch hazels. Give it plenty of compost but no fertilizer and avoid summer water after plants are well established.*

'Chameleon', is more moderate in growth, and its heart-shaped leaves (which smell like marmalade) are cheerfully splashed with copper pinks and bronzed reds. It will fill in between the crowns of larger perennials or shrubs while adding depth and finish to the planting. In a modest border, ground covers like the above-mentioned veronicas and bugleweeds will be hearty enough to compete successfully among taller plants, yet never overweening. In a tiny urban courtyard, restraint and long-term company manners are musts, and diminutive alpines will be the ground covers of choice. An orchestrated group of evergreen border shrubs could be fronted down with prostrate rock plants, sheets of choice thymes, and ornamental oreganos in sun or a glossy evergreen East Coast native, *Galax urceolata,* and thick club mosses in a shady situation.

Clearly, our choices are many, which makes plant selection more fun than ever. Chosen well, these garden workhorses are not only helpful but harmonious, enhancing, even exciting. If we carpet the garden as thoughtfully as we do our living quarters, choosing ground covers with an eye both to practical functions and to intrinsic beauties, the results will be anything but dull.

Oregon wood sorrel, Oxalis oregana, *comes in several evergreen forms as well as the usual deciduous type. Durable, drought tolerant, and hardy, this is an invaluable native carpeter for woodland gardens.*

NATIVE EVERGREEN GROUND COVERS FOR SUN

Barrett's penstemon	*Penstemon barrettiae*
Beach sedum	*Sedum spathulifolium*
Beach strawberry	*Fragaria chiloensis*
Bog rosemary	*Andromeda polifolia*
Dwarf Oregon grape	*Mahonia pumila*
Hummingbird trumpet	*Epilobium canum (Zauschneria latifolia)*
Kinnikinnick	*Arctostaphylos uva-ursi*
Point Reyes creeper	*Ceanothus gloriosus*
Salal	*Gaultheria shallon*
Shrubby penstemon	*Penstemon fruticosus*

NATIVE GROUND COVERS FOR SHADE (EVERGREEN AND DECIDUOUS)

Bunchberry	*Cornus canadensis*	Evergreen
Cascade Oregon grape	*Mahonia nervosa*	Evergreen
Creeping Oregon grape	*Mahonia repens*	Evergreen
False lily-of-the-valley	*Maianthemum dilatatum*	Deciduous
Foamflower	*Tiarella trifoliata*	Evergreen
Fringe cup	*Tellima grandiflora*	Evergreen
Inside-out flower	*Vancouveria* species	Evergreen and deciduous
Marbled wild ginger	*Asarum marmoratum (hartwegii)*	Evergreen
Miterwort	*Mitella breweri*	Evergreen
Piggy-back plant	*Tolmiea menziesii*	Evergreen
Speedwell	*Veronica beccabunga*	Evergreen
Starflower	*Trientalis* species	Deciduous
Twinflower	*Linnaea borealis*	Evergreen
Vanilla leaf	*Aclys triphylla*	Deciduous
Violets	*Viola glabella, V. glabra, V. nuttalli*	Semievergreen
Western leucothoe	*Leucothoe davisiae*	Evergreen
Wild ginger	*Asarum caudatum*	Evergreen

OTHER RELIABLE EVERGREEN GROUND COVERS

Beach wormwood	*Artemisia stellerana*
Brass buttons	*Cotula squalida* (several color forms)
Creeping lamium	*Lamium maculatum* (many color forms)
Creeping myrtle	*Vinca minor* (many color forms)
Hardy geranium	*Geranium macrorrhizum* (many color forms)
Heath	*Erica carnea* (many color forms)
Heather	*Calluna vulgaris* (many color forms)
Leatherleaf	*Bergenia* species (several flower colors)
Sheep bur	*Acaena* species (several color forms)
Sweet woodruff	*Galium odoratum*

WALKABLE EVERGREEN GROUND COVERS

Beach strawberry	*Fragaria chiloensis*
Brass buttons	*Cotula squalida* (several color forms)
Sandwort	*Arenaria montana*
Scotch moss	*Sagina subulata*
Sheep bur	*Acaena* species (several color forms)
Woolly antennaria	*Antennaria dioica tomentosa*
Woolly thyme	*Thymus lanuginosus*

Creeping thyme is a reliable ground cover where drainage is very fast in winter. On heavy soils, use a moisture-tolerant substitute.

Beach strawberry, Fragaria chiloensis, *is both drought tolerant in summer and able to take wet clay soils in winter. It makes a terrific, walkable carpet in lean soil in full sun. Mulch with compost but don't fertilize to avoid lank, overly lush growth.*

GROUND COVERS WITH COLORFUL FOLIAGE

YELLOW

Golden creeping Jenny	*Lysimachia nummularia* 'Aurea'
Golden lily turf	*Liriope muscari* 'Gold-banded'
Golden marjoram	*Origanum vulgare* 'Aureum'
Golden piggy-back plant	*Tolmiea menziesii* 'Taff's Gold'
Golden veronica	*Veronica prostrata* 'Trehane'
Golden vinca	*Vinca minor* 'Variegata'
'Moonshadow' euonymus	*Euonymus* 'Moonshadow'

BLUE

Asian bluebell	*Mertensia simplicifolia*
Blue beach sedum	*Sedum spathulifolium* 'Blue Chalk'
Blue clover	*Oxalis adenophylla*
Blue sheep bur	*Acaena* 'Blue Haze'

CHARTREUSE

'Emerald Gaity' euonymus	*Euonymus* 'Emerald Gaity'
Lady's mantle	*Alchemilla ellenbeckii*

COPPER OR BRONZE

Brass buttons	*Cotula squalida*
Bronze sheep bur	*Acaena microphylla* var. *inermis*

PURPLE

Burgundy bugleweed	*Ajuga reptans* 'Burgundy Glow'
Purple bugleweed	*Ajuga reptans* 'Purple Brocade'
Purple clover	*Trifolium repens* 'Purpurascens'
Purple grape	*Vitis vinifera* 'Purpurea'

PINK AND MAUVE

Mauve beach sedum	*Sedum spathulifolium* 'Mauve Chalk'
Pink beach sedum	*Sedum spathulifolium* 'Roseum'
Variegated houttuynia	*Houttuynia cordata* 'Chameleon'

BLACK

Black bugleweed	*Ajuga reptans* 'Metallica Crispa'
Black buttons	*Cotula squalida* 'Pratt's Black'
Black labs	*Viola labradorica* 'Purpurea'
Black mondo grass	*Ophiopogon planiscapus* 'Nigrescens'

SILVER-GRAY

Beach wormwood	*Artemisia stellerana* 'Silver Brocade'
Silver artemisia	*Artemisia canescens*
Silver buttons	*Cotula* 'Silver Buttons'
Silver veronica	*Veronica pectinata* 'Rosea'
Silver vinca	*Vinca minor* 'Argentea'
Stone plant	*Raoulia australis*
Woolly antennaria	*Antennaria dioica tomentosa*
Woolly thyme	*Thymus lanuginosus*

WHITE

'Harlequin' euonymus	*Euonymus* 'Harlequin'
Silver lily turf	*Liriope muscari* 'Silvery Sunproof'
White beach sedum	*Sedum spathulifolium* 'Cape Blanco'
White lily turf	*Liriope muscari* 'Variegata'
'White Nancy' lamium	*Lamium maculatum* 'White Nancy'
White variegated speedwell	*Veronica prostrata* 'Miffy Brute'

GROUND COVERS TO REGARD WITH CAUTION

ARCHANGEL *Lamuim galeobdolon*, **also sold as** *Lamiastrum galeobdolon*
This beautiful terror is so pretty, with its shimmering, metallic silver leaves and yellow flowers, that it is very tempting to use it in rough areas. However, this extremely aggressive plant is capable of climbing 6 to 8 feet into trees and will choke out choicer plants in short order. As a rule, it does *not* belong in intimate parts of any garden. It is also not suitable for woodland gardens (where it can become a menace). Archangel can be used in parking strips and parking areas where it is bound by cement and can't escape. It is best controlled by twice-annual cutting back (shear plants to the ground in spring and again in fall). Running roots can be pulled twice a year to keep it in bounds. Vigilance is a must.

BISHOP'S WEED

Aegopodium podagraria
Plain or variegated, this unassuming looking plant can eat its way through sidewalks and house foundations in time. Like many aggressors, it is a slow starter, but once this pretty weed gets its roots into a garden, eradicating it is a lifelong struggle. Bishop's weed is best controlled by twice-annual cutting back (shear plants to the ground in spring and again in fall). Running roots can be pulled twice a year to keep it in bounds. Vigilance is a must.

STARTING GROUND COVERS ECONOMICALLY

It is quite easy to grow a large amount of most ground covers by starting them in trays or flats. This can be done in spring (March and April) or in fall (September and October). Take some of the nursery flats that 4-inch pots come in and line the bottoms with newspaper. You can also use seed-starting trays with drainage holes. Fill the trays or flats with good potting soil or compost, and tamp it down lightly.

Next, take a clump of ground cover and tease it into as many pieces as possible. With vinca or ajuga, cut away the long stems between rosettes. If you are starting with a well-grown 4-inch pot of a close grower like Scotch moss or thyme, cut off the bottom half, then slice the remainder into as many postage-stamp-sized chunks as you can. Some bits will have more roots than others, but it doesn't matter.

Arrange your starter pieces a few inches apart in the flats, and tuck them in. Water well and set them out of direct light for a week or so (under a potting bench is the classic recovery spot). Once the new plants are growing well, bring the trays out into more light. Keep them well watered and you will have solid flats of ground covers to transplant in a few months.

PLANTING GROUND COVERS

If you are planting ground covers into established shrub beds or giving your mixed beds edging plants, simply prep the areas you plan to plant. Cover the area to be planted with 3 to 4 inches of compost, and rake it out. Set your ground cover starter plants in place, and water them in well. Using a drop seeder or whirlybird seeder, scatter raw corn gluten meal over any exposed soil and water it to retard weed seed sprouting. Keep newly planted ground covers watered during any dry periods for a full year.

If you are preparing a whole bed that will mainly be filled with ground covers, more work is required. Start by removing all tap-rooted weeds with a hori-hori or hoe. If the area is very weedy, use a black plastic mulch to clean the soil (see Chapter 6). Once the soil is clean, cover the new bed with 3 to 4 inches of compost and rake it out, then proceed as just described.

TRANSPLANTING GROUND COVERS FROM FLATS

Planting from flats involves the same general process as the one just described, except that you need to gently tease or slice (depending on texture) the plants that fill the flat into well-rooted chunks. Tuck these into raked compost, setting the pieces a few inches apart. You will get the quickest coverage of solid carpeters such as thyme and veronica by using 1- to 2-inch pieces set 2 to 3 inches apart. The least expensive method is to use 1-inch chunks set a hand span apart (6 to 8 inches), which works just as well but more slowly. For runners like strawberries and vinca, set rooted pieces 3 to 5 inches apart. Scatter raw corn gluten meal over any exposed soil and water it to retard weed seed sprouting. Keep newly planted ground covers watered during any dry periods for a full year.

TRANSPLANTING RUNNING GROUND COVERS

Here's an extremely quick way to cover ground with running plants like beach strawberry, ajuga, vinca, and piggyback plant. Cover the new bed with 3 to 4 inches of compost and rake it out. Pull up some extra plants from an established bed, keeping them attached on their long stem strings. Now arrange the running plants loosely over the new bed with the root sides down. Scatter more compost over the whole business and water in well. Scatter corn gluten meal over any exposed soil and water it to retard weed seed sprouting. Keep newly planted ground covers watered during any dry periods for a full year.

WEEDING AND WATERING NEW GROUND COVERS

Newly planted ground covers are vulnerable to drought the first year, even if they are drought tolerant once established. Coddle your plantings through the first full year, making sure the young plants do not dry out during hot spells. Fall planting usually gives better results than spring planting, since plants set out in September or October put on six or eight months' worth of root growth before hot weather arrives in May or June. To avoid getting weeds established in new ground cover areas, keep patches of bare earth covered with corn gluten meal, respreading it every six weeks in summer and every four to five weeks in winter.

SNOW-IN-SUMMER
Cerastium tomentosum
Its silvery, woolly foliage is beautiful, but snow-in-summer is an implacable foe in mild climates. Even when carefully segregated by cement, this relentless creeper sneaks under sidewalks and driveways, appearing in the middle of your favorite plant. Where summers are hot, it remains dense and silvery, but in cooler climes, it loses its luster, growing rank and sprawling. Just say no. It is best controlled by shovel pruning (remove plants whenever they appear). Vigilance is a must.

ENGLISH IVY
Hedera helix
English ivy is a serious pest in the Northwest, where it has infiltrated the forests, causing "ivy deserts" by choking out native plants. Now listed on the Noxious and Toxic Weed Lists in both Oregon and Washington, ivy must be removed wherever it appears. See Chapter 6 for more information.

TWELVE: BULBS

Sturdy, drought-tolerant daffodils are easy to naturalize in a shady woodland or along a sunny roadside. Blend them with ground covers for summer good looks, and give them a compost mulch each year when you see the shoots come up.

Bulbs come in many shapes and sizes and kinds, but in general they can be thought of as storage packets filled with future flowers. Bulbs, corms, rhizomes, and tubers are usually lumped together in garden books and in nurseries, since all are a form of storage root with relatively similar cultural requirements.

Most true bulbs belong to one of three large clans. The lily family (Liliaceae) encompasses lilies, tulips, agapanthus, ornamental onions, and a host of minor bulbs. The amaryllis family (Amaryllidaceae) holds daffodils and snowdrops as well as many half-hardy bulbs like Guernsey lilies and spider lilies. The iris family (Iridaceae) includes bulbous iris as well as crocosmia, crocus, blue-eyed grass, freesias, and gladiolus, along with less-familiar bulbs such as South African winter lily and angel's fishing rods.

Many iris relatives (such as gladiolus and crocosmia) produce corms rather than true bulbs. Other common corms include hardy cyclamen (members of the primrose family, Primulaceae) and some anemones (notably *Anemone blanda,* the windflower), which are buttercup kin (Ranunculaceae). A handful of other families include a few bulbous or tuberous members, including the geraniums (Geraniaceae) and the begonias (Begoniaceae).

WHAT BULBS LIKE AND DON'T LIKE

Above all, bulbs need good drainage. Most grow best in well-drained, gritty soils rather than heavy clay, and they persist longest in mounded beds or on berms. In addition, because so many bulbs have evolved in Mediterranean-type climates where winters are wet and summers are dry, most demand a dry period during their dormancy, which is usually summer. In the Northwest, we lose more bulbs to root rots than to cold (or even to mice). When placed where they receive water in summer, during their dormant stage, they often rot. To keep them blooming for years to come, plant bulbs where their planting soil won't get wet in summer.

In sunny gardens, good spots to plant bulbs include sidewalk parking strips, narrow beds between the house and the garage, along hedges, and between established shrubs. Shady gardens tend to be dry in summer, which suits woodland bulbs perfectly.

Where summer water is part of the program, you can reduce bulb losses by improving drainage. To make better conditions for bulbs, mix fine gravel or coarse builder's sand into their planting holes to promote quick drainage. Most bulbs also tend to rot if planted with an immature, manure-based compost placed too close to the bulb body (though the roots will feast on the stuff). See "Planting Bulbs," later in this chapter, for more on getting bulbs into the ground.

Bulbs need reliable partners to keep them in good health. Avoid planting summer-dormant spring-blooming bulbs between perennials with floppy, smothering foliage (like daylilies). In general, lower-growing companions like hardy herbs (thyme, oregano, and so on) are more lastingly supportive than big boomers. Our evergreen native *Penstemon barrettiae* makes an excellent ground cover for bulbs, and its purple flowers are a lovely bonus.

Most bulbs enjoy wet winters because during the winter months, spring bulbs (and many summer bloomers) are producing significant root growth. You may not see any action aboveground, but great expansion is happening beneath the soil blanket. At this stage, bulbs can take a lot of water in stride.

Bulbs continue to need water as they open their flowers, so spring rains are also not a problem. Once the flowers fade and the foliage begins to ripen off, however, water becomes a liability. During summer dormancy, excess water can be fatal.

CHOOSING BULBS BY SEASON

SPRING BLOOMERS

Most common spring bulbs require full sun, quick drainage, summer drought, and appropriate companions. Full sun is a tall order in the maritime Northwest, but most bulbs need at least six hours of sun to thrive. If your yard is shady, you may find yourself with lots of foliage and few flowers. See "Bulbs for Shady Gardens" later in this chapter.

SPRING-BLOOMING BULBS

COMMON NAME	BOTANICAL NAME	CULTURE	COLOR	BLOOMS
Checkered lily	*Fritillaria meleagris*	Sun, light shade	Rose, white, purple	Mar.–May
DESCRIPTION: *Will not survive being smothered by floppy companions. Summer dormant.*				
Crown Imperial fritillary	*Fritillaria imperialis*	Sun, light shade	Red, orange, yellow	Mar.–May
DESCRIPTION: *Will not survive being smothered by floppy companions. Summer dormant.*				
Dogtooth violet	*Erythronium dens-canis, E. revolutum, E. tuolumnense*	Sun, light shade	White, yellow, pink	Mar.–May
DESCRIPTION: *Rapid multiplier. Summer dormant.*				
Dutch crocus	Many hybrids	Sun, light shade	White, blue, yellow	Feb.–Apr.
DESCRIPTION: *Must ripen foliage to multiply. Very persistent.*				
Hardy cyclamen	*Cyclamen repandum*	Sun, light shade	Rose	Mar.–May
DESCRIPTION: *Excellent under trees or in dry, rooty shade as well as in intimate beds. Will not survive being smothered by floppy companions.*				
Hyacinth	Many hybrids	Sun	Rose, yellow, blue, white	Mar.–May
DESCRIPTION: *Very long lived in the garden in well-drained soil. Deadhead after blooming.*				
Persian fritillary	*Fritillaria persica*	Sun, light shade	Purple-gray	Mar.–May
DESCRIPTION: *Will not survive being smothered by floppy companions. Summer dormant.*				
Spring onion	*Allium karataviense, A. neopolitanum, A. oreophilum*	Sun	White, pink	Mar.–May
DESCRIPTION: *All need full sun and well-drained soil. Lastingly attractive seedheads.*				
Windflower	*Anemone blanda*	Sun, light shade	White, blue, pink	Feb.–Apr.
DESCRIPTION: *Self-sows abundantly; great spreader in difficult places.*				

Persian fritillary, Fritillaria persica, *is a dramatic bulb for container plantings or a sunny hillside with good drainage. Plant the big bulbs with a little tilt to keep rain from rotting their collars.*

Native camass are edible, but look much too pretty to pick. These true Northwesterners need wet soil in winter and dry soil in summer, so keep them well away from irrigation.

SUMMER BLOOMERS

Summer-flowering bulbs, like gladiolus, dahlias, and crocosmias, can be treated pretty much like perennials. These bulbs are more tolerant of summer irrigation, though none like standing water or constantly soaked soil. Any can be incorporated into beds and borders where they will receive regular mulching and occasional summer water. All grow best in well-drained garden soil. Where winters are harsh, semitropical bulbs such as dahlias and gladiolus may prove tender. Deep planting (6 to 8 inches below the soil level) and a deep (4- to 6-inch) winter mulch can often bring them through the winter unscathed.

There are dozens of summer bloomers to try, so experiment freely with any you find available in nurseries. To learn their ways, try unfamiliar bulbs in pots or window boxes, giving them bright annuals for companions.

SUMMER-BLOOMING BULBS

COMMON NAME	BOTANICAL NAME	CULTURE	COLOR	BLOOMS
Acidanthera	*Acidanthera bicolor*	Sun	White	July–Sept.
DESCRIPTION: *Tender. Rapid multiplier, especially in containers. Fragrant.*				
Angel's fishing rod	*Dierama pulcherrimum*	Sun	Pink, rose	June–Aug.
DESCRIPTION: *Tender in coldest gardens. Will not survive being smothered by floppy companions. Semievergreen.*				
Blue dicks	*Brodiaea lactea, B. laxa*	Sun	Blue, lavender	May–July
DESCRIPTION: *Will not survive being smothered by floppy companions. Winter dormant.*				
Camass	*Camassia leichtlinii, C. quamash*	Sun	Blue, lavender, white	May–July
DESCRIPTION: *Will not survive being smothered by floppy companions. Winter dormant.*				
Crocosmia	*Crocosmia* x *crocosmiiflora*	Sun	Yellow, orange, red	June–Sept.
DESCRIPTION: *Tender in coldest gardens. Rapid spreader. Blooms best if thinned frequently.*				
Freesia	Many hybrids	Sun	Yellow, white, rose	July–Aug.
DESCRIPTION: *Tender in coldest gardens. Will not survive being smothered by floppy companions. Winter dormant.*				
Gladiolus	Many hybrids	Sun	Yellow, white, rose, blue	July–Aug.
DESCRIPTION: *Tender in coldest gardens. Rapid multiplier. Dig and store to overwinter.*				
Lily	Many species and hybrids	Sun, light shade	White, rose, orange, yellow	July–Aug.
DESCRIPTION: *Need deep, enriched soils, good drainage, and good air circulation.*				
Ornamental onion	*Allium christophii, A. giganteum, A. schubertii,* and many more	Sun	White, rose, purple	May–Aug.
DESCRIPTION: *Attractive, long-lasting seedheads.*				
Pineapple lily	*Eucomis autumnalis, E. bicolor, E. undulata*	Sun	White, greenish	June–Aug.
DESCRIPTION: *Tender in coldest gardens. Will not survive being smothered by floppy companions. Winter dormant.*				

FALL BLOOMERS

Fall crocus (such as *Crocus zonatus*) and false autumn crocus (such as *Colchicum autumnale*) are easily grown in well-drained soils. Since they require only three or four hours of daily sun, they grow well in shady gardens that offer plenty of reflected light or dappled shade. False fall crocus make heavy rosettes of foliage in spring that ripen in June and July. It is important to place these late bloomers where their flowers are an asset to the fall garden yet their yellowing, cabbagelike leaves do not mar the summer display. In general, they look best in a spot at the border back that is visible in autumn, after summers bloomers have retreated, yet is screened in summer by early-rising perennials or annuals. True fall crocus produce slim, fine-textured foliage in winter and spring. This is not especially showy in life or death and requires no special placement measures.

WINTER BLOOMERS

A few stalwart bulbs flower well into winter in the Northwest. In a mild year, some (like the hardy cyclamen and Guernsey lilies) will continue to bloom clear into spring. To help them give their best, provide a snug, sheltered spot where they can bask in whatever sun may be available. Of the plants listed here, only the daffodils have lingering foliage that needs tidying. To minimize the effect of browning leaves in spring, give small, early daffodils a low ground cover such as leadwort *(Ceratostigma plumbaginoides)*.

FALL-BLOOMING BULBS

COMMON NAME	BOTANICAL NAME	CULTURE	COLOR	BLOOMS
Autumn crocus	*Colchicum autumnale*, *C. speciosum*	Sun, light shade	White, rose	Sept.–Nov.
DESCRIPTION: *Spring foliage may smother fragile companions. Summer dormant.*				
Autumn snowflake	*Leucojum autumnale*	Sun, light shade	White	Sept.–Nov.
DESCRIPTION: *Will not survive being smothered by floppy companions. Summer dormant.*				
Fall crocus	*Crocus goulimyi*, *C. speciosus*, *C. zonatus*	Sun, light shade	Blue, lavender	Sept.–Nov.
DESCRIPTION: *Will not survive being smothered by floppy companions. Summer dormant.*				
Guernsey lily	*Nerine bowdenii*	Sun, light shade	Rose	Sept.–Dec.
DESCRIPTION: *Will not survive being smothered by floppy companions. Summer dormant.*				
Hardy cyclamen	*Cyclamen hederifolium*, *C. purpurascens*	Sun, light shade	White, rose	Sept.–Dec.
DESCRIPTION: *Excellent under trees or in dry, rooty shade as well as in intimate beds. Will not survive being smothered by floppy companions. Semievergreen.*				
Naked ladies	*Amaryllis belladonna*	Sun, light shade	Rosy	Aug.–Oct.
DESCRIPTION: *Will not survive being smothered by floppy companions. Summer dormant.*				
Oriental lily	*Lilium auratum*, *L. speciosum*, *L. s.* var. *rubrum*, many hybrids	Sun, light shade	White, rose	Aug.–Oct.
DESCRIPTION: *Will not survive being smothered by floppy companions. Winter dormant.*				
Rain lily	*Zephyranthes candida*	Sun, light shade	White, rose	Sept.–Dec.
DESCRIPTION: *Will not survive being smothered by floppy companions. Summer dormant.*				
South African winter lily	*Schizostylis coccinea*, *S. c.* 'Major'	Sun, light shade	White, pink, rose	Sept.–Mar.
DESCRIPTION: *Rapid spreader. Floppy foliage in summer. Divide frequently for best bloom. Semievergreen.*				

WINTER-BLOOMING BULBS

COMMON NAME	BOTANICAL NAME	CULTURE	COLOR	BLOOMS
Daffodil	Narcissus 'February Gold', N. 'Dove Wings', N. 'March Sunshine', N. 'Tête-à-tête', N. bulbocodium conspicuus (hoop petticoat), N. cantabricus, N. cyclamineus	Sun, light shade	Yellow	Feb.–Apr.

DESCRIPTION: *Must ripen foliage. Will not survive being smothered by floppy companions. Summer dormant.*

Hardy cyclamen	Cyclamen coum	Sun, light shade	White, rose	Jan.–Mar.

DESCRIPTION: *Excellent under trees or in dry, rooty shade, as well as in intimate beds. Will not survive being smothered by floppy companions. Summer dormant.*

Iris	Iris danfordiae, I. reticulata	Sun, light shade	White, blue, yellow	Feb.–Apr.

DESCRIPTION: *Must ripen foliage. Will not survive being smothered by floppy companions. Summer dormant.*

Snow crocus	Crocus ancyrensis, C. chrysanthus, C. fleischeri, C. tommasinianus	Sun, light shade	White, blue, yellow	Jan.–Apr.

DESCRIPTION: *Rapid spreader if allowed to set seed. Summer dormant.*

Snowdrop	Galanthus nivalis, G. iberiae	Sun, light shade	White	Jan.–Mar.

DESCRIPTION: *Rapid spreader if allowed to set seed. Summer dormant.*

South African winter lily	Schizostylis coccinea S.c. 'Major'	Sun, light shade	White, pink, rose	Sept.–Mar.

DESCRIPTION: *Rapid spreader. Floppy foliage in summer. Divide frequently for best bloom.*

Squill	Scilla bifolia, S. siberica	Sun, light shade	White, blue, pink	Feb.–Apr.

DESCRIPTION: *Moderate spreader. Fine-textured foliage. Summer dormant.*

Windflower	Anemone blanda	Sun, light shade	White, blue, pink	Feb.–Apr.

DESCRIPTION: *Rapid spreader if allowed to set seed. Summer dormant.*

Winter aconite	Eranthis cilicica, E. hyemalis	Sun, light shade	Yellow	Feb.–Mar.

DESCRIPTION: *Rapid spreader if allowed to set seed. Summer dormant.*

BULBS IN SHADY GARDENS

We can't usually change our sun allotment, but we can adjust our bulb buying. In shady gardens, few tulips or daffodils will be lastingly great performers. However, woodland bulbs like starry wood anemone and Italian arum will multiply happily.

Most bulbs that prefer shady, woodland gardens prefer fairly deep planting (3 to 6 inches) and enjoy an annual feeding mulch of compost and aged manure. Hardy cyclamen and many scillas are particularly good choices for the dry, rooty shade found under trees and mature shrubs. Woodland lilies require improved soil and may need supplemental water in dry summers.

Certain crocuses are very easy to naturalize in light shade as long as their foliage is not mowed before it ripens. Once the leaves turn brown, they can be mowed without harm. This is Crocus tommasinianus, *a very fast, easy multiplier.*

WOODLAND BULBS FOR THE SHADY GARDEN

COMMON NAME	BOTANICAL NAME	CULTURE	COLOR	BLOOMS
Dogtooth violet	*Erythronium dens-canis,* *E. revolutum,* *E. tuolumnensis*	Sun, light shade	White, yellow, pink	Mar.–May
DESCRIPTION: *Rapid spreader if allowed to set seed. Summer dormant.*				
Italian arum	*Arum italicum* 'Pictum'	Light shade	Orange berries	Oct.–Jan.
DESCRIPTION: *Fresh fall foliage, handsome in winter. Summer dormant.*				
Hardy cyclamen	*Cyclamen coum*	Sun, light shade	White, rose	Jan.–Mar.
DESCRIPTION: *Excellent under trees or in dry, rooty shade as well as in intimate beds. Will not survive being smothered by floppy companions. Semievergreen.*				
Hardy cyclamen	*Cyclamen repandum*	Sun, light shade	Rose	Mar.–May
DESCRIPTION: *Excellent under trees or in dry, rooty shade as well as in intimate beds. Will not survive being smothered by floppy companions. Summer foliage.*				
Jack-in-the-pulpit	*Arisaema candidissimum,* many other species	Light shade	White, pink	June–Aug.
DESCRIPTION: *Late riser, often with long-lasting berries. Winter dormant.*				
Lily	Many species and hybrids	Sun, light shade	White, rose, yellow, orange	July–Aug.
DESCRIPTION: *Need deep, enriched soils, good drainage, and good air circulation.*				
Snowdrop	*Galanthus iberiae,* *G. nivalis*	Sun, light shade	White	Jan.–Mar.
DESCRIPTION: *Rapid spreader if allowed to set seed. Summer dormant.*				
Windflower	*Anemone blanda*	Sun, light shade	White, blue, pink	Feb.–Apr.
DESCRIPTION: *Rapid spreader if allowed to set seed. Summer dormant.*				
Winter aconite	*Eranthis cilicica,* *E. hyemalis*	Sun, light shade	Yellow	Feb.–Mar.
DESCRIPTION: *Rapid spreader if allowed to set seed. Summer dormant.*				
Wood anemone	*Anemone nemorosa*	Light shade	White, pink, blue	May–July
DESCRIPTION: *Rapid spreader if allowed to set seed. Summer dormant.*				

PLANTING BULBS

When the first autumn rains begin to soften the earth, spring bulbs begin to wake up. This is also when we can begin planting new spring- and fall-blooming bulbs. Planting bulbs is not difficult as long as you practice this basic rule of thumb: pointy side up. Once you have that down, you can move on to finesse techniques.

Most bulbs will bloom at least once, no matter what we do to them. Next spring's flowers are already folded into those snug brown packets. Unless we plant our bulbs in puddles, in deep shade, or where constant foot traffic will crush them, the flowers will arise on schedule.

However, in successive years many bulbs dwindle instead of holding their own. To encourage ongoing bulb displays that reward us for years to come, we must provide for their long-term needs.

Most nurseries offer planting charts along with bulbs. Since many of our native soils are lean and don't drain well, it's best to dig wide as well as deep. Add generous amounts of grit, river sand (not sandbox sand), or finely crushed gravel to each hole to promote drainage.

Like tulips, most lilies prefer to be planted 6 or more inches deep. Plant daffodils, hyacinths, and fritillaries a bit more shallowly (about 4 inches deep). The smallest bulbs, like crocus and scillas, can be tucked under a mere inch or two of soil.

Few bulbs enjoy very shallow planting. One exception is the Madonna lily, which likes its top to be sticking up a bit above soil level. Madonna lilies should be planted immediately, because they need to make what's called a "resting rosette," or a tuft of foliage, before winter arrives.

Another bulb that prefers shallow planting is the nerine. This South African amaryllis relative lights up the autumn garden with satin pink, fine-petaled flowers like tiny floral explosions. Even if you plant them deeply, the bulbs will hike themselves up to soil level.

Nerines need excellent drainage and a sunny spot, and they seem to last longest when given the shelter of an accompanying shrub. I have had the best success with these somewhat tender bulbs when I set them among small, evergreen shrubs. Until the Big Freeze of 1990, nerines grew beautifully for me, nested amid a bed of Mediterranean herbs, including many kinds of rosemary, lavender, sage, and thyme, as well as New Zealand hebes.

STORING TENDER BULBS
FOR WINTER
To be safe, dig tender bulbs for winter storage in a cool, dry, dark place. Store bulbs in mesh bags for best ventilation, labeling each kind as you dig them. Let freshly dug bulbs cure until dry (usually about ten days), again keeping them in a cool, dry, dark place, before bagging. A handful of mothballs in the storage bag will keep hungry mice at bay.

None of these plants need regular watering once they are established, so the bulbs could ripen and rest well in this company.

Most bulbs appreciate compost mixed in with their soil, and bulb roots love manure. However, many bulbs rot quickly if planted with manure. To satisfy the roots, blend aged manure and compost into the root zone, topping it off with a few inches of grit or sandy soil. Set your bulbs on that gritty pad, then mix sandy soil and compost to fill in your planting hole.

A top mulch of dairy manure also works fine, helping to retain moisture, reduce mud splash, and keep weeds down. Just don't mix manure into the planting hole, where it could come into direct contact with your bulbs.

Mark the outline of each bulb planting with golf tees or small, unobtrusive rocks to jog your memory. The best planting care is wasted if you dig up slumbering bulbs to plant something else in what seems to be an empty spot.

We can also lose bulbs to mice, gophers, or voles during the winter. To discourage these pests, line bulb-planting areas with wire mesh. You can also mix a handful of smelly moth flakes into the soil.

Mice love crocus, but *Crocus tommasinianus* and its various named forms seem less tasty. They are also such strong multipliers that any winter losses are made up by spring.

Where chipmunks and squirrels insist on swapping stale peanuts for precious bulbs, mix ground pepper and moth flakes into their mulch. (This also keeps cats from disgracing themselves in the borders.)

Last, let the bulb foliage ripen fully in the spring. Don't cut, braid, wrap with rubber bands, spindle, or mutilate that foliage. Instead, tuck browning leaves gently beneath the surrounding greenery. Light, airy ground covers such as *Vinca minor*, leadwort, sweet woodruff, and bugleweed make it easy to disguise fading bulbs foliage.

BULBS IN CONTAINERS

Most bulbs can be grown very well in containers. Indeed, if you garden on heavy clay, you may find that your bulbs will persist longer when grown in pots than in the soil. We lose a lot more plants to winter rots than to cold, and most bulbs are very susceptible to both crown and basal rots. To please bulbs in pots, make sure that your potting soil drains well. Add several inches of crushed gravel to the base of your pot, and mix some charcoal (the aquarium filter kind) into the bottom third of the pot to keep the soil sweet.

Growing bulbs in pots can also be a temporary solution to problems arising from overordering. Sometimes, for instance, you may find yourself with a lot of unplanted

Big, bold ornamental onions like
Allium schubertii *look fabulous even after they bloom. Terrific container plants, they appreciate a boost of 20-20-20 fertilizer as they come into bloom when grown in pots.*

Our native Pacific Coast iris are exceptional plants for the sustainable garden. They prefer dry summers and don't like high-number fertilizers. They grow well in containers and prefer full sun with plenty of compost.

bulbs when winter comes. Unless they have been stored perfectly, in a cool, dry place, bulbs are apt to be in less than optimal condition by the solstice. It's still okay to plant them, but any that are soft, mushy, or crusted with mold should be burned instead. (Don't add them to the compost unless you are an accomplished compost maker. In piles that don't heat up well, rotting bulbs can introduce molds and mildews you really don't want.)

All kinds of bulbs can be packed into pots, layered like a wedding cake. Big bulbs like tulips and daffodils go deepest, with 8 to 10 inches—even a foot—of soil on top. Next come species tulips and daffodils, which are far smaller. These can be planted so they'll have 6 to 8 inches of soil over them. Fritillaries and other minor bulbs can be added in the 4- to 6-inch layer, while little crocus and windflowers *(Anemone blanda)* come last, needing only an inch or two of blanketing soil.

FORCING BULBS

I love to fill the house with flowering bulbs in winter. From Thanksgiving to Valentine's Day, my rooms are fragrant with the heady scents of narcissus. I grow mostly

WHICH WAY IS UP?

As a rule, bulbs are planted pointy side up. If you can't tell which side is the pointy side, plant sideways. Certain corms, notably those of many anemones, are just weird looking. If you have no idea which end of these knobbly objects is the "pointy" or stem end, plant them on their sides and let the roots figure out the proper orientation.

The flat, knobbly corms of hardy cyclamen can be tricky to plant, since the dormant roots look almost exactly like the dormant stems. Usually the smooth, rounded side goes down and the concave side goes up. If you aren't sure, set them in pots or flats with sandy, gritty soil and a light (1-inch) covering of compost. Keep your eye on them, and if you see roots emerging instead of tiny heart-shaped leaves, flip them over and cover again with compost.

'Ziga', an Israeli hybrid with huge white flowers that smell intensely sweet. I also love the spicy scent and sunny, cheerful look of lemon yellow 'Soleil d'Or'. My kitchen is full of queenly amaryllis, trumpeting boldly in royal crimson, icy white, salmon, and peach. In winter, I make a garden of potted plants in my bedroom, just below the windowsill, where they get plenty of east light. That way, the first thing I see when I wake up is a host of flowers, many of them sweet smelling. By early December, my bedroom garden boasts early snowdrops in pots, along with hardy cyclamen and Parma violets. As winter rolls on, they'll be joined (or replaced) by plump purple squills and wide-eyed anemones. These are all potted up in autumn and chilled outdoors in a cold frame, then brought in to blossom early indoors, where they brighten table and windowsill alike.

If the autumn stays warm, my refrigerator fills up with chilling bulbs by November. Why? In order to persuade bulbs to blossom early indoors, we need to give them an extended period of cold treatment. Here in the Pacific Northwest, autumn and early winter may be as mild as late summer, so simply potting things up and leaving them outside won't get the job done, as it does in colder climates. Instead, we must resort to refrigeration.

There are two ways to go about chilling bulbs, both of them good. Traditionalists insist that bulbs should not go naked into that chilly night. These people always pot up their bulbs first and then subject them to cold treatment, pot and all. To do this, arrange your bulbs in their pots, cover with soil, and water well, allowing excess water to drain away. Before chilling, cover the top of each pot with a plastic bag to conserve moisture, closing it loosely with a twist tie to allow for some air exchange.

Some families have been known to object when the refrigerator is suddenly fuller of pots than of food. Bulb pots do take up quite a bit of space, and some of us have found it politic to invest in an inexpensive secondhand fridge for just such activities. This may seem indulgent, yet the spare refrigerator can come in handy all year long, when the summer garden harvest arrives in a rush or during holidays when lots of entertaining is going on. Indeed, at times it can be hard to make room for both bulb pots and party food.

If you can't spare the space for an extra fridge, just slip your bulbs (still in their mesh or paper bags) into tightly closable plastic bags, including plenty of air. These can be tucked discreetly into the vegetable bin or behind the mustard, often without arousing comment. Since they don't have the protection of soil during their long weeks of chilling, check them periodically to be sure they are neither too damp (which may cause molds to grow) nor too dry (this makes them shrivel up like old onions or potatoes).

If the bulbs do look damp, take them out, wipe them dry, and repack them with a few teaspoons of dry milk powder in their package. This will absorb any excess moisture from the bag without desiccating the bulbs themselves. Should the bulbs look too dry, sprinkle them lightly with water and then repack them in a sealed bag. Check up on them in a few days, repacking in a dry bag if they now seem to be too moist.

These precautions may seem bothersome but, in fact, they are rarely necessary. Still, it's worth taking the time to check up on your investment rather than lose the lot to the creeping blue crud that lurks in many an outwardly respectable refrigerator. When the bulbs' time is up, pot them up in the usual way and set them aside to sprout.

Where you sprout your bulbs depends on how you keep your house in winter. Most people's comfort zone is too warm for plants, even bulbs that think spring is just around the corner. An unheated sunporch is an ideal place to sprout forced bulbs. Often the basement or garage will be cooler than the house, yet warmer than the out-of-doors. In an elderly, drafty house like mine, no place is really too warm for bulbs. I often set mine under the kitchen table, below the sunny windowsill where they will eventually bloom.

Wherever they end up, the forcing pots should be kept moist but not soggy. As soon as the first shoots appear, move the pots into a warmer, sunnier spot. Turn the pots each day so the shoots grow evenly, rather than stretching toward the light. Forced bulbs usually have lankier foliage than those outside, so some support is welcome. Short (18-inch) plant stakes with bendable metal arms are perfect for this task, since you can shape the arms into hoops the exact size of your foliage bundle. Skinny bamboo skewers (the long kind sold for kebabs) are often strong enough for this job as well. Use at least three sticks

BULB-CHILLING TABLE

Bulbs should be chilled at temperatures above freezing (32 degrees F) but below 40 degrees F. Normal refrigerator temperatures are about right. Use the following table to determine how many weeks of cold treatment your bulbs need. The longer times indicated are for bulbs chilled at relatively higher temperatures.

BULB	WEEKS OF COLD TREATMENT
Checkered lily	
Fritillaria meleagris	10–12
Crocus	
Crocus species	8–10
Daffodil	
Narcissus species and hybrids	12–15
Grape hyacinth	
Muscari species	10–14
Hyacinth	
Hyacinthus species	12–15
Reticulated iris	
Iris danfordiae, I. reticulata	10–14
Snowdrop	
Galanthus species	9–12
Squill	
Scilla species (most)	10–12
Tulip	
Tulipa species and hybrids	12–10
Windflower	
Anemone blanda	8–10

for each pot, and wind a discreet web of black thread or clear fishing line between them. Held by these threads, the foliage will remain straight and tidy. Add a disguising ribbon if the threads distract your eye.

AFTER-CARE FOR FORCED BULBS

Narcissus is not really hardy in the Northwest, except in very protected gardens. Daffodils, tulips, hyacinths, scillas, anemones, crocus, and other typical garden bulbs can all be returned to the garden after they have bloomed. Plant them right away where you want them to bloom, or let them ripen their foliage in the pot. If you do this, use ribbon or yarn to indicate the color of each pot of bulbs— this is impossible to tell once the flowerheads have faded.

Amaryllis performs best when grown like an evergreen houseplant. Feed it regularly with half-strength fertilizer (or use solid sticks of plant fertilizer). Repot amaryllis each year in fresh soil, using a wide but shallow bulb bowl that allows the top third of the bulb to remain above the soil level. It blooms best when its roots are slightly crowded, and a large mother bulb can be grown for many years in a generous container. In time, you may notice offsets called "pups," which will reach blooming size in two or three years. These can be detached or grown along with the original bulbs, making a slowly increasing colony that blooms abundantly.

FORCING NARCISSUS

Narcissus blooms longest and remains most upright if planted into soil instead of plain gravel. Set the bulbs in 3 to 5 inches of soil, then top them with gravel for a tidy presentation. To prevent flopping foliage entirely, plant your bulbs in large, straight-sided glass vases that are 12 to 18 inches deep. Use colorful gravel (red, green, or purple looks very festive) for more holiday cheer. Sprout as described in "Forcing Bulbs." Most narcissus sold in nurseries have already been prechilled and won't need any cold treatment. If this is so, you can stage them to bloom over several months by planting new batches every two or three weeks, starting in early November. In a house that averages 65 degrees, prechilled narcissus bulbs will be ready to bloom about three weeks after planting.

THIRTEEN : VINES AND CLIMBERS

Clearly, it's very important to know a lot about the climber you are buying. This matters greatly, both in terms of where to put it and what to put it on. For the most part, vines do best when given a clear job to do. Cover this trellis. Drape this wall. Hide the garage, or clamber into that Doug fir. Choose a vine of the right size for the job, give it a good root run and the basic conditions (such as sun or shade) it prefers, and let it rip. Choose the wrong vine, however, or put it in the wrong place, and you will have made a lot of ongoing work for yourself.

Choosing the right vine is largely a matter of educating yourself. This process involves reading plant labels, asking nursery folks for advice, and double-checking all the information you receive. The *Sunset Western Garden Book* tends to have a California bias, so sometimes sizes and bloom time are a bit skewed.

Here in the maritime Northwest, the best all-purpose guide is a book called *Gardening with Climbers* by Christopher Grey-Wilson and Victoria Matthews (Timber Press, 1997). It covers everything from wisteria (a real disaster in the wrong spot) to annual morning glories. The text is clear, the pictures are pretty and, best of all, the information is accurate.

Where to put vines is the next vital piece to consider. In one of my early gardens, I went through a serious clematis craze, buying every kind I could find. At first, it seemed charming to have a clematis threading through every shrub and climbing up every tree. I soon decided to combine several in each spot, so there would be flowers from early spring into fall. As the clematis grew, it became obvious that few gardens could support such an excess of vinery.

On a recent trip to Vancouver, I visited the University of British Columbia's botanic garden and saw huge clematis, ornamental grapes, honeysuckles, and species roses lacing through huge, mature Douglas firs. Each tree had just one vine on it, and in some cases, that one vine

Vines of all kinds, whether annual or perennial, belong well away from house walls. Always allow at least 18 inches of air space between a trellis-planted vine and a house or outbuilding wall. This encourages good air flow and cuts down on diseases. It also reduces insect access to house walls.

was almost too much for the tree. The lesson here is to keep your head at the nursery: Do not come home with any vine you don't really have room for.

That said, it's also delightful to find room for a big vine or two. Where would they be most at home? Most lusty vines will be best off scrambling into the arms of a really big tree. For best results, plant the vine well away from the trunk of the tree you want it to live upon. The same is true of a vine intended to cover a wall of any kind. Most vines hate root competition and grow poorly when they aren't given an adequate root run.

Smaller vines can be safely placed in beds and borders or grown in containers for years. Try putting smaller summery vines into large rhododendrons or purple-leaved plum trees for extra zip after the host plant's bloom has faded. Many small vines will make excellent ground covers, lacing through masses of junipers or low shrubs and grasses.

PLANTING RULES FOR VINES AND CLIMBERS

Rule 1: Vines need good air circulation.

To avoid fungal disorders, molds, and mildews, never place a vine support smack against a wall of any kind. Wall-mounted trellis panels or fans should be placed on blocks of wood that hold them well away from the wall (a foot is not too much space). As an alternative, you can mount them on heavy posts that are set outside of the dripline of the wall or associated roof. Trellises mounted on the soffits of the roofline and extending outward will place your vines exactly where they ought to be.

Rule 2: Vines are heavy.

If the trellis is to hold a large vine (such as a rampant species clematis or a wisteria), the minimum support post size is 8 x 8 inches. These posts should have at least 3 feet of their length in the ground and must be set in concrete. Otherwise, you risk losing the vine, trellis and all, to wind or snow. A healthy vine can weigh hundreds of pounds all by itself. The added weight of rain or snow can damage an insufficient structure.

Rule 3: Vines need a good root run.

Most vines do best without much direct competition in the root zone. Since they will spend the first year making roots, give them a terrific send-off by digging a

HONEYSUCKLES

Most honeysuckles are very vigorous vines that quickly outgrow their position without careful placement. All can be pruned hard (cut back to the ground in spring) if overgrown but otherwise need only occasional thinning of the oldest stems (which make great decorative wreaths). Favorites with birds and bees, honeysuckles appreciate annual feeding mulches (see Chapter 3) in spring and fall. To revel in their scent, place them near seating areas. Most bloom from May into July, offering red or black berries in late summer and fall.

generous hole and amending it well with compost and good garden soil. Never plant a vine smack against a mature tree, where greedy feeder roots will compete for nutrients. Set your vine at least a yard or two away from the intended host, where there is plenty of room for root growth. In time, the thriving vine will find its own way into the tree. If you can't wait, provide guidance with trellising.

Rule 4: Match the vigor of the vine with the size and strength of the host.

When you interplant vines with trees and shrubs, don't put big, fast-growing vines like hops on a small, choice, or slow-growing host like a Japanese maple. Use only one vine per host, and try not to put clematis on everything that is not moving. It is not lastingly rewarding.

Rule 5: Match the size of the vine with the size of your space.

If your space is small, stick to small vines. Unless you want to create an evergreen wall, give preference to vines that can be cut back clear to the ground each season. Most summer-blooming clematis, climbing hybrid roses, and many honeysuckles are ideal for smaller gardens.

Rule 6: Vines need care and feeding.

Most vines thrive on a feeding mulch of compost, aged manure, and alfalfa (see Chapter 3) in spring and fall. None need commercial fertilizer. Most are drought tolerant once established but need regular water through dry seasons for the first two or three seasons. Once the roots are well grown, most vines will need supplemental water only during prolonged dry spells.

GREAT GARDEN VINES

COMMON NAME	BOTANICAL NAME	HEIGHT

Blueberry creeper — *Ampelopsis brevipedunculata* — 12 to 20'
DESCRIPTION: *Inconspicuous flowers, vivid fruit. Several ornamental forms with variegated or lacy leaves. Several other decorative species.*

Blueberry vine — *Billardiera longiflora* — 6 to 8'
DESCRIPTION: *Tiny flowers, fat purple-blue fruit. Twine it through a callicarpa for a joyful autumn display. A favorite with ants and robins.*

Cat vine — *Actinidia kolomikta* — 12 to 30'
DESCRIPTION: *Fragrant white flowers, edible fruit. Bold foliage with pink edges, hairy stems. Cage young plants to keep cats from damaging shoots and foliage.*

Chilean potato vine — *Solanum crispum* — 15 to 30'
DESCRIPTION: *Semievergreen in mild years, fine-textured foliage, clusters of fragrant, white to purple flowers bloom well into autumn. Best in a sheltered spot.*

Chinese gooseberry — *Actinidia arguta* — To 60'
DESCRIPTION: *Fragrant white flowers, edible fruit. Bold foliage, hairy stems.*

Chinese hydrangea vine — *Schizophragma hydrangeoides* — 15 to 40'
DESCRIPTION: *Deciduous, long-leaved vine with white flowers in flat clusters. Vigorous climber, flowers well in low light (good for north-facing fences).*

Chinese rose vine — *Schisandra chinensis* — 15 to 30'
DESCRIPTION: *Deciduous, attractive foliage, fragrant, roselike flowers (white or pink) in clusters, followed by red fruits appreciated by birds. Several other decorative species are hardy in the Northwest.*

Chinese wisteria — *Wisteria sinensis* — 40 to 60'
DESCRIPTION: *Vigorous, heavy, and rampant, wisteria does not belong on or near a house or functional building. Heavy and sturdy support is required for this gigantic, implacable vine. Buy vines in bloom to be sure you don't get a nonflowering form. Difficult to eradicate, so plant with care. One wisteria is enough (or possibly too much) for any yard.*

Clematis: see "Growing Clematis," page 348

Climbing hydrangea — *Hydrangea anomala* — 15 to 60'
DESCRIPTION: *Slow to start, this is a vigorous climber with showy creamy flowers and splendid fall color. Put it up a Doug fir, and don't prune off the flowering shoots in the name of tidiness (a common cause of floral failure).*

Climbing monkshood — *Aconitum volubile* — 4 to 8'
DESCRIPTION: *Blue flowers, late bloomer. Likes compost, semishade, scrambling into light. Shrubs make good hosts. Grows like a perennial (dies back in winter).*

Climbing nasturtium, flame creeper *Tropaeolum tuberosum* — 6 to 12'
DESCRIPTION: *Semideciduous, this late bloomer may produce red, orange, or golden flowers. Edible tubers. Flowers well in low light (good for north-facing fences). Best in a sheltered spot.*

Wisteria can weigh hundreds of pounds when wet, so give it a sturdy support and keep it off your house. If you don't have much room, choose a tree form that will never outgrow its position.

Grape vines are also potentially extremely large and need more than a wobbly bit of trellis to keep them aloft. Purple leaf grape (Vitis vinifera 'Rubra') is a stunning vine for screening summery seating areas and looks terrific scaling a magnificent Douglas fir.

Chilean potato vine (Solanum crispum), above left, is a beautiful scrambler that will thread through a rhododendron or share a trellis happily with another vine. Here, it twines together with goldfish vine, Eccremocarpus scaber.

Great Garden Vines, continued

COMMON NAME	BOTANICAL NAME	HEIGHT
Dutchman's pipe	Aristolochia macrophylla	15–25'

DESCRIPTION: *Deciduous vine, decorative flowers, bold foliage. Very fast grower. Good bird cover.*

English ivy	Hedera helix	

DESCRIPTION: *This serious pest should be banned from nursery sales. To get rid of ivy (and learn why you should), see Chapter 6.*

Evergreen climbing hydrangea	Hydrangea integrifolia,	15–30'
	H. seemanii	10–15'

DESCRIPTION: *These handsome evergreen climbers have toothed, glossy foliage and lacy white flowers. Slow to establish, then vigorous, they need a sheltered spot.*

Five-leaf	Akebia quinata	20–30'

DESCRIPTION: *Fragrant white to cream flowers, edible fruit. Semievergreen. Ornamental fruit (like purple pickles). Several other decorative species and forms.*

Garden jasmine	Jasminum officinale	12–30'

DESCRIPTION: *In a protected spot, jasmine will be semievergreen and may flower into fall. Feeding mulches (see Chapter 3) in spring and fall boost bloom production.*

Holboellia coriacea (no common name)		15–25'

DESCRIPTION: *Semievergreen, this handsome scrambler looks great in a sheltered spot, protected from wind and hard frost. White to purple flowers, purple fruit.*

Hops	Humulus lupulus	10–18'

DESCRIPTION: *Deciduous, fast-growing, bold foliage; decorative bracts. The form 'Aureus' has golden to chartreuse foliage. Very vigorous. Spring shoots edible.*

Kiwi	Actinidia chinensis	To 30'

DESCRIPTION: *Fragrant white flowers, edible fruit. Bold foliage, hairy stems.*

Passion flower	Passiflora caerulea	15–30'

DESCRIPTION: *Deciduous vine, showy white or pink flowers with blue corona, attractive foliage, needs a warm, sheltered spot. Can be cut to the ground in winter but is usually root hardy. Orange fruit is enjoyed by thrushes.*

Trumpet creeper	Campsis species	30–40'

DESCRIPTION: *Big orange or yellow flowers. A vigorous, heavy, fast-growing vine. Needs very large and very strong support. Do not put this on your house.*

Virginia creeper	Parthenocissus henryana	15–24'

DESCRIPTION: *Handsome, lobed leaves and terrific fall color make this deciduous vine a popular choice for covering fences and walls. Several other decorative species and forms make fine choices where there is plenty of room.*

Wine grape	Vitis vinifera	20–60'

DESCRIPTION: *Grapes do best in open, sunny places with good air circulation. European varieties tend to develop mildews easily, though living compost teas (see Chapter 6) help control this and other leaf disorders. European grapes ripen best in Oregon and California. In cooler, maritime Northwest gardens, our best choices are the North American native grapes like 'Concord', grown from the eastern native Vitis labrusca.*

Winter jasmine	Jasminum nudiflorum	6–12'

DESCRIPTION: *Train this shapeless shrub against a wall, where its golden trumpets will shine in winter. Thin crowded older shoots to the ground annually (in spring).*

FRAGRANT VINES

Refer to the "Great Garden Vines" list for information about these vines.

Actinidia species (cat vine, Chinese gooseberry, kiwi)
Clematis species (some are fragrant)
Holboellia coriacea
Jasminum species (garden jasmine, winter jasmine)
Lonicera species (honeysuckle; most are fragrant)
Rosa species (rose; many are fragrant)
Wisteria species (Chinese wisteria)

SMALL TO MODERATE VINES AND VINES THAT CAN BE KEPT SMALL BY HARD PRUNING

Refer to the "Great Garden Vines" list for information about these vines.

Aconitum species (climbing monkshood)
Clematis species (some)
Humulus species (hops)
Jasminum species (many)
Lonicera species (many)
Rosa species (some)
Solanum species (Chilean potato vine)
Tropaeolum species (climbing nasturtium, flame creeper)

Put vigorous hops vines where you intend them to grow, because once in the ground, they are off and growing as fast as possible. Happily, young hops shoots are edible and make a lovely asparagus substitute.

GROWING CLEMATIS

Some 250 species of clematis grow worldwide, mostly in temperate parts of the world. Most are climbers, while others are semishrubby or perennial-like. Species clematis do not need routine pruning, except when older plants become congested or wildly outgrow their position. Judicious thinning of a few older stems by cutting them back to the main "trunk" in late winter takes care of congestion. Excess top growth can be removed anytime it annoys you.

Garden or hybrid clematis (the ones with names) are divided into two groups. The nursery label will tell you how to prune each particular type, so tape the label into your garden journal as a reminder. However, it's really pretty simple: The *Clematis viticella* and *C. x jackmanii* hybrids can be cut back hard each year, generally in late winter. This means cutting down all of last year's stems to their lowest set of buds—not a tricky operation, but one best done while the buds are still dormant. February is usually a good time for hard pruning.

The remainder can be pruned lightly or not at all, depending on how much of a tangle it is in. If it looks fine and blooms well, leave it alone. If it is foaming over everything in sight, it's wiser to move that happy clematis to a roomier location than to battle with it each season.

Clematis are gross feeders that appreciate lots of compost and aged manure and lashings of alfalfa pellets each spring. March and April are good times to give clematis feeding mulches (see Chapter 3). Clematis also appreciate regular water in summer, especially while they are young. Older vines are more drought tolerant, but all bloom best when kept adequately moist during dry or hot spells.

For more information on growing great clematis, join the Pacific Northwest Clematis Society (see the Resources section at the end of this book).

Summer blooming clematis will interlace with aplomb through conifers or broadleaved evergreen shrubs like rhododendrons. They can also be grown as ground covers, lacing through low-growing junipers for a dash of summer.

CHOICE CLIMBING ROSES FOR THE PACIFIC NORTHWEST

NAME	COLOR/TYPE	HEIGHT	BLOOM HABIT

None of these red climbers are fragrant, but all boast healthy, glossy foliage and are long flowering.

NAME	COLOR/TYPE	HEIGHT	BLOOM HABIT
'Altissimo'	Hot red tea type	10 to 12'	Long, repeat bloomer
'Dortmund'	Bright red, white eye	6 to 8'	Repeat bloom, takes shade
'Dublin Bay'	Velvet red	6 to 8'	Long blooming

Pink roses are the most popular. All of the following are long flowering, fragrant, and have handsome foliage.

NAME	COLOR/TYPE	HEIGHT	BLOOM HABIT
'Climbing Cécile Brunner'	Clustered, pink	8 to 12'	Repeats, fragrant, adorable
'Climbing Dainty Bess'	Single, pink	8 to 10'	Repeats, nice hips
'Climbing Shot Silk'	Single, rosy	10 to 15'	Repeats, very fragrant
'New Dawn'	Single, baby pink	10 to 15'	Repeats, just the best

White climbers and ramblers are not always fragrant. 'Lady Banks' is an exception, smelling like Parma violets. Rosa soulieana is a big girl, but what a beauty!

NAME	COLOR/TYPE	HEIGHT	BLOOM HABIT
'Bobbie James'	Single, clusters	15 to 20'	Blooms once, good hips
'Climbing Iceberg'	Double, tea buds	10 to 12'	Repeats, no scent
'Lady Banks' (*Rosa banksiae*)	Double	15 to 30'	Long, early bloom
Rosa mulliganii	White, golden eye	20 to 40'	Blooms once, good hips
Rosa soulieana	Single, clusters	15 to 30'	Gray leaves, good hips

Yellow roses are my own favorites (usually). I especially love 'Golden Showers', which can be trained as a long-blooming climber.

NAME	COLOR/TYPE	HEIGHT	BLOOM HABIT
'Golden Showers'	Big singles	10 to 12'	Repeats, tall shrub
'Royal Gold'	Double, tea buds	8 to 12'	Repeats, needs sun
Rosa banksiae 'Lutea'	Small doubles	15 to 30'	Long, early bloom

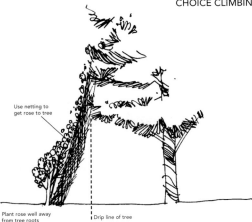

Use netting to
get rose to tree

Plant rose well away
from tree roots

Drip line of tree

Place the root ball of a climbing vine
outside the drip line of the host plant.
Use trellis, netting, or other support to
assist the vine to climb.

TIPS FOR GROWING CLIMBING ROSES

• Climbing roses are greedy feeders. Give them heaping mulches of aged manure, compost, and alfalfa pellets in spring (March and April), and follow up with a feeding mulch (see Chapter 3) in May.

• To avoid foliage diseases, spray the leaves of climbing roses as soon as they emerge with aerobically brewed compost tea (see Chapter 6). For total control, spray weekly for the first month and then monthly throughout the growing season.

• Prune species climbing roses only when they are damaged. Otherwise, leave them alone. If they are in the way of passersby, they are in the wrong place and should be moved.

• Hybrid climbers can be cut back to a strong framework of 4- to 6-foot stems each year in early winter (mid-February is usually a good time).

• Climbers and ramblers trained on fences and trellises should be tied in and pruned to encourage lots of lateral shoots (see illustration, above). The more side shoots, the more flowers you'll have.

• To get a big species rose into a tall tree with few lower limbs, toss a rope over the lowest branch. Attach the rope to a long section of black string netting (such as pea netting), and hoist the netting over the branch. Secure the near end of the netting to the ground (tent stakes work well) near where you planted your climbing rose. Tie a heavy stone to the end of the rope to keep it from slipping back over the branch. Once the rose reaches that branch, it will be able to get itself higher without help.

FOURTEEN: ANNUALS

Annuals in a naturalistic garden don't have to be a lot of work: Use them to add color and texture, and to fill in the gaps in your garden.

Annuals come in all shapes and sizes, from prostrate ground covers dense enough to prevent weeds to shrubby-looking creatures that can pass as small trees. They can climb or trail, creep or billow. Some bloom in late winter, while others persist into fall. By choosing with care and placing plants where their attributes are an asset, we can let annuals fill many of our garden's gaps, temporarily or for many years.

Modern annuals have been bred to offer an extended range of blossom colors as well as unusual foliage form, color, and texture. From pansies and forget-me-nots to fried egg flower and baby blue eyes, we can grow wild or refined versions of hundreds of annual species.

Annuals are often associated with lots of work, but this need not be so. If we want a carefree summer garden, selected forms of native wildflowers will work hard in return for a minimum of effort. For instance, in California, grassy hills are stained hot copper orange with wild poppies in late spring. Gardeners have their choice of longer-blooming strains in a shimmering run of related colors. If you have a white garden, a stand of 'Milky White' California poppies will carry on your theme for most of the summer. In a soft-toned sunrise-colored garden, the silk-petaled rose, pink, and bronze mixture called 'Thai Silk' may work best.

Most California poppies are best used in casual settings, given their informal habit. However, a few of the newest selections are choice enough for a special spot where each flower will be savored. There, you can set the double forms such as 'Apricot Flambeau', whose swirling, pleated skirts combine peach and coral, or the two-toned 'Rose Chiffon', with pale yellow hearts and ruffled rosy skirts.

California poppy selections can also be found to bloom in every color between these extremes, from butter and chalky yellow through apricot, salmon, and peach to copper red and pumpkin orange. All will flower abundantly in repeated flushes from spring into fall. These adaptable natives grow best in well-drained, lean soils with a minimum of supplemental water and no fertilizer. Thus, putting cooperative native plants to work around the garden can reduce chores like weeding, feeding, and watering.

Sweet alyssum is a fragrant, long-blooming self-sowing annual that makes an excellent living mulch in the vegetable garden. These almost ever blooming plants bring in the pollinators from spring into fall, increasing fruit and vegetable cropping dramatically.

BRINGING ANNUALS INTO THE BORDER

Annuals make valuable placeholders in young gardens, filling in the temporary gaps between slowly maturing shrubs and perennials. Where height is needed, look to the spider plants *(Cleome spinosa),* statuesque annuals whose airy spears are tipped with whorling heads of elongated flowers with prominent, thready stamens that give them a spidery look. In rich border soil, spider plants become bushy and need plenty of room to give their best performance. When planted late (after a wet, cool spring), they tend to be narrower plants that snug in comfortably between immature perennials.

Though large enough for the border back, it's pleasant to place a few spider plants where their delicate fragrance can be appreciated (butterflies like it, too). The color range is fairly limited; 'Helen Campbell' is spanking white, 'Violet Queen' a vibrant purple, 'Cherry Queen' a vivid rose, and 'Pink Queen' is a softer, clean pink that accords nicely with clary sages, *Salvia horminum.* These last are also hardworking annuals that will bloom for months, their tiny flowers surrounded by showy ornamental bracts in lively pinks and blues with deeper-toned veins.

Red- or green-leaved castor beans (*Ricinus* species) are also big and bold enough to serve as backdrop plants. Their huge, palmate leaves are deeply veined and glossy, and their luxuriance of foliage sets off the small flowers and curious, highly toxic fruit (which resemble a cross between a ping-pong ball and a porcupine). In warm summers, these tropical medicinals can exceed 8 or 10 feet in height. In a cold, wet year, they may only reach 2 or 3 feet, especially if planted late.

For the midborder, consider long bloomers like marguerites (*Argyranthemum* species). Common in containers, they are rare in gardens, though their daisylike flowers fit in anywhere. White forms may be single or double, and selections bloom in soft yellow or baby ribbon pink. The kind with gray, very lacy leaves looks terrific with hardy herbs like rosemary and sage.

Long-blooming cosmos comes in variously colored mixtures, from gentle pastels to hot, brilliant colors. The dainty Seashells series is especially pretty, with each petal curled into a little cornucopia horn. Where vivid colors are wanted, try the Bright Lights or Sensation series. Such warm colors can be cooled down with an infusion of cooling blues, perhaps from *Salvia farinacea* 'Victoria', a royal blue that also combines elegantly with the pewters and silvers of various artemisias and the stalwart dusty miller clan. More blues can be found among annual lobelias, like 'Crystal Palace' and the paler 'Blue Moon', as well as shaggy bachelors buttons and our native prairie-dwelling *Lisianthus,* now found everywhere in gorgeous if temperamental Japanese hybrids like 'Blue Lion' and 'Blue Prince'.

ANNUALS BY SHAPE

CREEPERS AND CRAWLERS

Bedding *Ageratum* 'Hawaii Blue'
Bedding *Alyssum* 'Carpet of Snow'
Bedding *Lobelia* 'Regatta Midnight'
Portulaca 'Sundial Cream'
Verbena x *hybrida* 'Raspberry Crush'

REGULAR MOUNDS

Basil 'African Blue'
Bedding *Salvia* 'Salsa Light Purple'
Flowering tobacco 'Domino Green' *(Nicotiana* hybrids)
Petunia 'Carpet Buttercream'
Species marigold 'Tangerine Gem' *(Tagetes)*

SPIKES AND SPIRES

Larkspur 'Exquisite Rose' *(Consolida ambigua)*
Green tobacco 'Lemon Tree' *(Nicotiana langsdorfii)*
Mexican sunflower 'Aztec Sun' *(Tithonia rotundifolia)*
Money plant *(Lunaria annua* 'Variegata')
Stock 'Ten Weeks Mixed' *(Matthiola* hybrids)

FANS AND FOUNTAINS

Celosia 'Pampas Plume'
Love-lies-bleeding *(Amaranthus caudatus)*
Ponytail grass *(Stipa* or *Nassella tenuissima)*
Red orache *(Atriplex hortensis)*
Squirreltail grass *(Hordeum jubatum)*

ECCENTRICS

Castor bean *(Ricinus communis)*
Cleome spinosa 'Helen Campbell'
Joseph's coat *(Amaranthus tricolor)*
Sunflower *(Helianthus annuus)*
Tree dahlia *(Dahlia merckii, D. sheriffii,* etc.)

LOW-GROWING ANNUALS

Creeping or prostrate annuals are often used as infill in pattern beds, where a tight edging of clipped boxwood or herbs frames a solid flow of colorful flowering plants. Within the linear edging, annuals can be used in sheets and masses or arranged in bright mosaic patterns. Since Elizabethan times, annuals have been included in the elaborate infill patterns that turn subtle, gray-green herbal knot gardens into the glowing, stained glass window plantings known as parterre.

Traditional parterre and knot gardens are largely woven with a combination of meticulously maintained herbs, subshrubs, and perennials. However, it's terrific fun to make an instant, all-annual knot garden that will look marvelous right away. True, it will last only a single season, but this way, we have the luxury of changing our minds completely each year, altering the plan or substituting something utterly new every spring.

Choose compact, fine-textured and naturally shapely plants for the outer edging of your bed, such as 'Globe' basil or rounded little cigar plant (*Cuphea ignea*) in lilac or rose. Next, set distinctive foliage plants like dusty miller 'Silver Leaf' or Irish lace marigolds (*Tagetes filifolia*) in crisscrossing rows to create diamond-shaped spaces within your beds. To get an amazingly multidimensional look, you can "break" the lines into basket-weave by alternating which plant "cuts through" the opposing line each time. When your framework is established to your satisfaction, fill the resulting diamonds with masses or patterns of annuals.

The Victorians often tucked statuary or bird baths into such schemes, and we can too—imagine a gaudy pattern bed full of hot purples, oranges, and reds, where each diamond is centered with a great gazing ball in similarly fiery tones. Instead of elevating the globes on pedestals, set them right on the ground, so their companion flowers are mirrored in their glittering surfaces. For a more traditional approach, center pattern beds with red bananas, clumps of striped cannas, or an arching tree fern. Less flamboyant centerpieces might include a simple sculpture or a basket stuffed full of flowers. In a country garden, use an old wooden chair whose seat has been filled with flowers. In the city, make a sensational centerpiece by painting a clunky old bicycle red or blue and packing its panniers with tumbles of trailing petunias.

Such found art is especially eye-catching when it fills the center of a solid mass of flowers: imagine a sea of golden marigolds centered with an ancient purple push mower. To make a visual pun, create a mower-sized swath of Irish lace marigolds behind the machine to look as if the flower tops have been tidily trimmed. Note that all of these schemes use ordinary plants, but none would appear ordinary to passersby!

In less formal settings, the same group of low-growing annuals can themselves act as edgers, delineating beds, softening the hard line of paving material, or trimming a curving path with a flowery fringe. In a wonderful garden in New Zealand, rainbows of shimmering portulaca fill the entire driveway, leaving only two bare strips the exact width of a car tire. Less cautious drivers might prefer to use this ebullient edger near a pool, where reflected heat and light distress less resilient plants.

The low growers can also serve to emphasize the sculptural qualities of taller companions. Plumes of pink feather grass (*Celosia* species) make a pretty haze in a tangled border, but when several clumps are set into a foamy

LOW-GROWING ANNUALS

Alyssum 'Apricot'
Basil 'Genovese'
Begonia 'Non-stop'
Calendula 'Bon Bon Mix'
Cigar plant (*Cuphea ignea*)
Creamcups (*Platystemon californicus*)
Dusty miller 'Cirrus'
Dusty miller 'Silver Lace'
Fried egg flower (*Limnanthes douglasii*)
Gazania 'Daybreak'
Lantana 'Camara'
Lemon thyme
Lobelia 'Regatta'
'Globe' basil
Irish lace marigold (*Tagetes filifolia*)
'Lulu' marigold (*Tagetes* 'Lulu')
Portulaca 'Sundial Mango'
'Ruby Field' twinspur (*Diascia* species)
'Silverleaf' snapdragon
Verbena 'Peaches & Cream'

pool of 'Ruby Field' twinspur (*Diascia* species), both plants gain tremendous distinction. Tender, upright fuchsias like soft coral 'Corale' are set off to perfection by trails of 'Silverleaf' snapdragon *(Antirrhinum majus),* whose white flowers are delicately veined in pale salmon pink. Such artful planting makes artwork of our plants.

Fluffy cockscomb, Celosia plumosa, *are too artificial looking for garden beds, but make intriguing accents in containers, blended with foliage plants like coleus and everlasting (*Helichrysum petiolare).

MIDBORDER ANNUALS

Middle-sized annuals can be difficult to use in traditional bedding schemes, where they tower over their low-growing companions. Bigger annuals like shrubby cat's whiskers *(Orthosiphon stamineus)* and husky Brazilian snapdragons *(Otocanthus* species) work just fine in larger-scaled beds where waist-high hedging creates garden "boxes" or "bins" to fill with plants. In such situations, carpeters and creepers are not impressive enough to take the eye, even when massed, but the intermediates will shine. Complex infill patterns can look fussy or confusing on a large scale, but simple combinations—whether delicately tinted runs of white larkspur and pale yellow marguerites *(Argyranthemum* species) or a more potent mixture of fancy-leaf geraniums and bloodleaf *(Iresine herbstii)*—provide powerful impact all summer long.

The new coleus are terrific foliage plants for sun or shade, making a distinctive contribution to container combinations.

In mixed borders and perennial gardens, medium-sized

plants are used as the middle tier in the beds, an intermediate layer that lifts the eye from the ground up to the
taller shrubs and trees that make the garden backdrop.
Though purists may scorn the use of annuals in perennial
borders, adventurous gardeners will offer purple-blue
Angelonia 'Hilo Princess', pink or white flowering 'Domino'
tobacco (*Nicotiana* species), and 'Raspberry Ruffle' sunproof coleus a midborder spot anytime. Few perennials
can rival the months of unbroken color these workhorse
plants provide.

Continual bloomers like royal blue honeywort
(*Melianthus major* 'Purpurascens'), 'Red Plume' blanket
flower (*Gaillardia*), and 'Aurora Yellow Fire' marigolds
(*Tagetes* species) keep the border bright with color while
repeat-flowering perennials rest between flushes of blossoms. Golden feverfew and creamy-variegated 'Powys
Pride' snapdragons *(Antirrhinum majus)* are strong
bloomers whose colorful foliage also holds interest even
when no flowers are in sight. Sunproof 'Rustic Orange'
and 'Burgundy Sun' border coleus bring out the shimmer
in coppery carexes and tawny daylilies, as will an under-
skirt of coppery 'Outback Sunset' creeping Jenny *(Lysimachia procumbens)*.

'Wild Lime' and gold-edged 'Flair' coleus make an
exciting second tier behind mats of creeping Mexican
petunias or lemon-lime 'Margarita' variegated sweet
potato vine *(Ipomoea)*. Where heavy-looking plants need
airy companions for contrast, baby's breath (*Gypsophila*
species) will make a foamy mound spangled with thousands of tiny florets of rose, pink, or white. Annual grasses
add similar lightness as well as movement, for all will
dance with every breeze. Feathery spumes of squirreltail
grass *(Hordeum jubatum)* make rosy golden fountains
amid mounds of pink mask flower (*Alonsoa* 'Bat-faced
Pink'). Love grass *(Eragrostis tenella)* boasts enchantingly
fluffy seedheads that look like miniature pillow fights
bursting out between clumps of starry, silver-leaved gaza-
nias and tall African marigolds. The braided seedheads of
quaking grass *(Briza maxima)* dangle like swaying birds
on thread-thin foliage, while ponytail grass *(Stipa* or *Nassella tenuissima)* blooms in a mass of pale golden floss that
looks like cornsilk.

Intermediate annual combinations can make showboat
contributions in beds and borders or in pots and containers.

Either way, to play up form and texture, mingle plumes of wiry dill with 'New Black' coleus and coral cockscombs (*Celosia* species), with hot purple trailing snapdragons spilling down in front. For a softer look, mix pale 'Frosted Pink' marguerites with white baby's breath and 'French Vanilla' marigolds, fronted with a sweep of *Bacopa* 'Snowflake'.

To create a handsome grouping with an enticing, ever-altering perfume that lingers into the night, mix 'Fragrant Cloud' flowering tobacco with night-scented stock *(Matthiola bicornis)*, mignonette *(Reseda odorata),* and sweet alyssum. For an extra treat, tuck in a few plants of night-scented phlox *(Zaluzianskya capensis)*, but arrange these last at the back of the border, where their untidiness won't detract from the composition. Their looks aren't much, but their fragrance is unforgettable.

MIDBORDER ANNUALS

Alonsoa 'Fireball'
African marigold (*Tagetes* x *hybrida*)
Angelonia 'Hilo Princess'
Bloodleaf *(Iresine herbstii)*
Brazilian snapdragon (*Otocanthus* species)
Browallia 'Amethyst'
Cat's whiskers 'Lavender' (*Orthosiphon stamineus* 'Lavender')
Coleus Sun Lover series
Cosmos 'Picotee'
Cosmos 'Sonata Mix'
Cuphea illavera 'Batface'
Cuphea micropetala 'Candy Corn'
Honeywort (*Melianthus major* 'Purpurascens')
Lantana 'Biarritz Red'
Love grass *(Eragrostis tenella)*
Marguerite (*Argyranthemum* species)
Mask flower (*Alonsoa* 'Bat-faced Pink')
Night-scented phlox (*Zaluzianskya capensis*)
'Outback Sunset' creeping Jenny (*Lysimachia procumbens* 'Outback Sunset')
Pink baby's breath (*Gypsophila elegans* 'Carmen & Rose')
Poor man's orchid (*Schizanthus* 'Angel's Wings')
Quaking grass *(Briza maxima)*
Upright *Lobelia* 'Blue Moon', *L.* 'Riviera Blue Splash'
White baby's breath (*Gypsophila elegans* 'Covent Garden')
Zinnia 'Pumila Cut & Come Mix'

BACKDROP ANNUALS

Magnificent backdrop annuals like castor beans (*Ricinus* species), sunflowers (*Helianthus* species), and angel's trumpets (*Brugmansia* species) can be used to create a quick privacy screen around a seating area, to make a fast filler for the back of a brand-new border, or just to blow your neighbor's socks off with their joyful exuberance. If you enjoy having a garden that stops traffic, just plant a few oversized annuals in the front yard. Start by painting the house walls with living color: set some huge and gloriously smudgy blue 'Tie-Dye' morning glories up a trellis, adding a few strands of scarlet runners or pink and purple lablab beans for even more visual splendor.

Next, bring in the astonishing angel's trumpets, with salmon or golden flowers the size of a bread loaf. Arrange several generous clumps of lanky, languid copper orache (*Atriplex hortensis* 'Cupreata') behind them, with a sweep of dusky golden broom grass *(Sorghum nigrum)* for pleasing textural contrast. Giant golden amaranths (*Amaranthus cruentus* 'Golden Giant') offer deliciously fluffy flowerheads on a bold scale, making a blazingly sunny backdrop for citrus-colored marigolds or a fiesta of tall zinnias. Other robust amaranths come in red or orange or mahogany, or in mixtures of several vivid colors. A few chunky castor bean plants whose tremendous leaves are tinted red or burgundy will add an intriguing touch of the tropics, as will a lusty banana tree *(Musa basjoo)* and enormous, striped and stippled elephant's-ear (*Caladium* species). If you still have room, try growing some variegated corn *(Zea mays)* and walking stick cabbages, whose knobbly stems are head-high by midsummer.

An extravagant jungle garden full of flagrant, flaunting flowers is surprisingly easy to accomplish, even in Northern gardens. Because they provide so much pleasure and excitement in a single season, tender tropicals of all kinds are now being marketed as annuals. Some exotics can be coddled indoors over the winter, but many gardeners are happy to enjoy their generosity of leaf and flower without the extra trouble.

Indeed, those with small homes should think twice before bringing their summer glory indoors. Even a single banana tree or angel's trumpet takes up considerable house room by summer's end. What's more, these lusty plants often sulk after being brought inside, even when kept in the same container without root disturbance. Once indoors, tropicals are prone to whitefly and aphid attacks that wouldn't trouble them a bit outdoors. Since small plant starts reach blooming size in short order with proper care, it's far simpler to start afresh each summer. That way, we can try new color forms or varieties each season, expanding our enjoyment without guilt.

If this scenario sounds unlikely (many gardeners can't imagine growing tropical plants in the garden), begin your exploration of the toss-away tropicals with a baby banana. Many species (including most of the *Musa* species, which are the easiest to find) will reach as much as 6 or 8 feet in four months from seed. Give them plenty of food and water and stand back, because these luxuriant plants grow very fast. Glory bower (*Tibouchina* species)—a shrub in its own land—and angel's trumpet reach similar heights, especially where summers are warm.

LARGE-SCALE BACKDROP ANNUALS

COMMON NAME	BOTANICAL NAME	HEIGHT
Amaranth 'Aurora Yellow'	*Amaranthus tricolor* 'Aurora Yellow'	To 3'
Amaranth 'Golden Giant'	*Amaranthus cruentus* 'Golden Giant'	To 4'
Angel's trumpet 'Alba,' 'Aurea'	*Datura metel* 'Alba, *D. m.* 'Aurea'	To 10'
Angel's trumpet 'Charles Grimaldi'	*Brugmansia* 'Charles Grimaldi'	To 10'
Banana tree	*Musa basjoo*	To 8'
Broom grass	*Sorghum nigrum*	8'
Burning bush	*Kochia trichophylla*	To 3'
Canna 'Bengal Tiger'	*Canna x generalis* 'Bengal Tiger'	To 8'
Castor bean 'Carmencita'	*Ricinus communis* 'Carmencita'	To 6'
Copper orache	*Atriplex hortensis* 'Cupreata'	To 6'
Elephant's-ears	*Caladium* species	To 3'
Glory bower	*Tibouchina* 'Athens Blue'	As annual to 5'
Lablab bean	*Dolichos lablab*	8'
Mallow 'Loveliness'	*Lavatera trimestris* 'Loveliness'	To 4'
Mexican sunflower 'Aztec Sun'	*Tithonia rotundifolia* 'Aztec Sun'	To 3'
Plume grass	*Celosia argentea* 'Pampas Plume'	2 to 3'
Red orache	*Atriplex hortensis*	To 6'
Rustic tobacco 'Sherazi'	*Nicotiana rustica* 'Sherazi'	3'
Spider flower 'Violet Queen'	*Cleome spinosa* 'Violet Queen'	4'
Striped corn	*Zea mays* var. *japonica*	6'
Sunflower 'Chianti'	*Helianthus annuus* 'Chianti'	4'
Sunflower 'Pastiche'	*Helianthus hybridus* 'Pastiche'	5'
Sunflower 'Velvet Queen'	*Helianthus debilis* 'Velvet Queen'	4'
Tower of jewels	*Echium pininana*	6'
Woodland tobacco	*Nicotiana sylvestris*	4'

ANNUALS FOR SCREENING

Annual climbers can be used to create fast screens where summer privacy is desired. Use them to baffle views from the backyard or the deck, porch, or patio. Where chain-link fences form part of the property line, use foamy, fast fillers like canary vine *(Tropaeolum peregrinum)* to disguise the unattractive fence. This rapid grower makes a multi-stemmed vine that can reach 8 to 10 feet by early summer. Each rambling arm is decked with rounded, five-lobed leaves and frilly yellow flowers that look like a flock of tiny canaries. In mild winters, it often self-sows moderately, producing cheerful volunteers that will scramble through almost anything, from tall ground covers to shrubs as well as fences or trellises.

If you want showier flowers, consider *Asarina* 'Victoria Blue', which pours like the waterfall it was named for, making a blue wall of flowers 4 to 6 feet high by midsummer. Sweet peas *(Lathyrus odoratus)* will also climb a fence or trellis, producing clouds of fragrant flowers through the summer. They bloom most heavily in early summer to midsummer, and the vines can get pretty ratty looking by August, when spring-sown crops will be blooming sparsely. If you have a cool place to start a second crop in summer, fall-planted sweet peas may bloom on (however sporadically) until the winter holidays.

For denser screening power, consider a luxuriant foliage plant. A handsomely variegated form of Japanese hops *(Humulus japonicus* 'Variegatus') is an annual in all but the warmest climates. This one makes quick work of covering almost anything, weaving its maplelike jade green and ivory leaves into a stippled tapestry some 10 to 15 feet high.

Annual climbers are multitalented performers that can play many roles. Use them for quick ground cover, letting them spill and sprawl over bare ground or between maturing perennials. Or use them to paint a big, bare wall in living color, making tapestries with as many shapes and textures as you like. They can also fill the air with fragrant flowers, drawing birds and butterflies into the garden. Drape them over a sloping hillside, or use them as blooming curtains for private parts of the yard. A narrow passageway between the house and garage can be enriched with spills of fragrant sweet peas or sheets of pink and purple snapdragon vine *(Asarina scandens)* growing from flat-sided wall baskets on masonry hooks.

Annual climbers like Thunbergia look great in containers and can be moved through the garden to highlight or screen areas as needed (use a hand truck for big pots).

A Mexican scrambler, Rhodochiton is a splendid mixer in windowboxes and containers, softening the edge of a pot or pouring down the side of a wall like a purple river.

To enchant a child, cover a stick tepee with purple and yellow wax beans, or weave a tunnel with ornamental gourds that dangle enticingly overhead. While waiting for foundation shrubs to grow in, disguise the foundation of a new house with annual vines by stretching netting across the area to be covered and planting some red-leaved Malabar spinach. A single vine of cathedral bells *(Cobaea scandens)* will cover half the house by high summer. Goldfish vine *(Eccremocarpus scaber)* is a determined traveler that can cover a garage or foam through a mature fruit tree in a single season. (It may also prove hardy in sheltered locations.)

Give spring-flowering shrubs a second season of bloom by setting lightweight scramblers like firecracker vine *(Mina lobata)* or sweet peas about their skirts. Heavier vines like the fernleaf cypress vine *(Ipomoea quamoclit)* need a sturdy host to handle the heft of their considerable bulk. Put that lusty cypress vine up a large tree, rather than a shrub. Its closely related cousins, the morning glories, are less massive but they, too, need stout support for their dense growth.

Rivers of blue morning glories will flow over a homely retaining wall or thread through strong netting to scale the house. To extend the show, combine morning glory and moon vine *(Calonyction aculeatum)*, whose fragrant white flowers light up the night. Send either of these impressive vines up an old ladder leaning into a tree, or give them runner guides of rubber-coated wire or heavy waxed twine rather than string, which soon sags under their weight.

Most annual climbers are small enough to work well in any setting. Lacy hyacinth bean *(Dolichos lablab)* will twine through a wall-mounted trellis or embroider evergreen vines with clusters of pink pea flowers and hot purple pods. Honeysuckle, clematis, and similar permanent plantings can carry a lightweight summer passenger like runner beans or firecracker vine without damage. Demure black-eyed Susan vine *(Thunbergia alata)* will wind itself through pea netting to make living curtains for house windows or screen your favorite sunbathing spot from the neighbors. Double nasturtiums *(Tropaeolum majus)* can cascade from an old wicker bicycle basket, spill from an old wheelbarrow, or dangle down in wide fans to hide the base of the deck.

ANNUALS IN CONTAINERS

Container planting allows even those with tiny gardens (or no gardens at all) to enjoy all the benefits of a garden in an area the size of a hug. Where ground space is limited, or when you want to make an empty entryway more welcoming, emphasize a handsome staircase, or enliven a paved poolside, any and all annuals can be generously packed into pots and containers. There are literally hundreds of ways to use annuals in containers, from window boxes and hanging baskets stuffed with trailing vines and cascading petunias to olive cans crammed with red geraniums.

To make a child's day, drape a tepee trellis with wandering vines of canary creeper, Tropaeolum peregrinum. *This easygoing vine is fast-growing, sturdy, and often self-sows to provide plenty of seedlings for next year's garden.*

CLIMBING ANNUALS (6 FEET AND GREATER)

Black-eyed Susan vine	*Thunbergia alata*
Canary vine	*Tropaeolum peregrinum*
Cathedral bells	*Cobaea scandens*
Cypress vine	*Ipomoea quamoclit*
Firecracker vine	*Mina lobata* 'Citronella', *M. l.* 'Revelation'
Goldfish vine	*Eccremocarpus scaber* 'Gold Select'
Hyacinth bean	*Dolichos lablab* 'Ruby Moon'
Mexican bell vine	*Rhodochiton atrosanguineum* 'Purple Bells'
Moon vine	*Calonyction aculeatum*
Morning glory	*Convolvulus* or *Ipomoea* 'Tie Dye', 'Heavenly Blue', 'Pearly Gates'
Nasturtium	*Tropaeolum majus* 'Jewel of Africa', *T. m.* 'Moonlight'
Ornamental gourds	Mixed cucurbits 'Large Bottle Mixed'
Scarlet runner bean	*Phaseolus coccineus*
Snapdragon vine	*Asarina scandens* 'Sky Blue'
Sweet pea	*Lathyrus odoratus* 'Antique Fantasy'

WEEDING WITH ANNUALS

Easygoing annuals can be used in many places where you don't want weeds to grow. Under established shade trees, shade-tolerant annuals like fried egg flower (*Limnanthes douglasii*) will act as a living mulch, conserving moisture and suppressing weeds. Because they have very low nutritional needs, these native annuals won't compete with your trees for food. What's more, by replacing grass next to the trunks, their presence helps protect trunks from weed-whacking damage.

Sun-loving natives like California poppy, ice plant, and clarkia (as well as nonnatives like sweet alyssum, gazania, and calendula) can be planted in rough places where weeds are likely to intrude. Put these heat lovers along sunny rockeries, driveways, parking strips, and hot sidewalks, where reflected heat and strong light would daunt fussy border beauties. They will resow abundantly, filling in the ecological niches that opportunistic weeds usually find with flowers.

As a rule, bigger is better; it's far easier to keep large containers well watered than smaller ones, which dry out quickly in summer heat. Anything that holds dirt can be used for planting, with a few modifications. Plant roots need air as much as they do water, so drainage holes are vital. Large volumes of soil can clog drainage holes easily, so line each container with a few inches of coarse gravel, broken pots, or beach stones to ensure free drainage. If you want to set a smaller planting pot within a larger ornamental one, build up this drainage layer to the height needed. (For best plant growth, the minimum size for interior pots is 5 gallons.)

The added weight of the drainage layer is helpful with lightweight terra-cotta look-alikes of cast resin, which can blow over in windy sites. Where excess weight is an issue (balconies and rooftop gardens), use plastic packing peanuts or crushed aluminum cans for your drainage layer. Before adding soil, insert a piece of weed barrier cloth over the drainage material. This allows water and air to pass through but keeps soil out. Large volumes of soil compact readily, turning "sour" after many waterings. To avoid this, add a few cups of activated charcoal (the kind used for fish filters) to your planting mix. To keep shallow containers such as window boxes from drying out too quickly, add half a cupful of hydrated hydrophyllic polymer (water-holding gel) to each 5 gallons of potting soil.

PLANTING IN CONTAINERS

Annuals grown in containers are highly vulnerable to heat stress and drought as well as nutritional deficits. Plants in the ground have expanded resources; they can stretch out their roots to reach distant water and nutrients, and the whole earth is their blanket. Even the largest container holds a limited volume of soil, which heats up faster and dries out sooner than the surrounding earth. This can work to our plants' advantage, offering a microclimate that will be appreciated by tropical and desert annuals. However, it also makes container-grown plants highly dependent on timely human intervention.

Regular watering is essential, and where there are many pots to tend, it may be worth investing in a drip system.

To disguise their presence, drip lines can be discreetly threaded through the slats of a deck or run along the edge of a balcony. Run them up the back of a large container or slip them through a drainage hole of a pot, taping the line in place before adding soil. The feeder tube can them be placed at the base of the main plant or split into several emitters so that each plant in a large container gets its own water source. Drip lines can be put on automatic timers to deliver water daily even when you are on vacation or too busy to water. Remember, too, that the frequent watering required by containers also washes out nutrients at a rapid rate, so it is vital to replace them with a regular feeding program.

SEASONAL CHANGE WITHOUT ROOT DAMAGE

With a bit of planning, large containers that hold permanent evergreen plantings can be dressed up with seasonal annuals. To avoid root disturbance, sink permanent place-holding gallon-sized pots around the inner edge of each large container. Transplant plants from 4-inch pots into gallons and slip them into the place-holding pots. You can slide an endless array of annuals in and out of these planting pockets without damaging the roots of your permanent plantings. In winter, use decorative foliage kales, followed by spring primroses and then cascading double nasturtiums and silvery helichrysums for summer show.

INSTANT GLAMOUR POTS

Annuals can be used freely in narrow-necked pots that would fatally trap perennials once their roots developed. For instant elegance, drop lushly filled hanging baskets of fuchsias or geraniums into tall, narrow-necked jars and let the plants tumble down the sides. Remove the hanging wires and you have a splendidly mature-looking planting in a flash.

Trailing annuals are delightful when grown in hanging baskets, along with or in combination with more upright bloomers. Trailers are also excellent for softening the sides of large containers, cascading down staircases, and pouring over sloping beds. Many will scramble upward if given support.

TRAILING ANNUALS

Asarina procumbens 'Yellow'
Asarina scandens 'Midnight Blue'
Baby blue eyes (*Nemophila menziesii* 'Five Spot', *N. m.* 'Pennie Black')
Baby's tears (*Helxine soleirolii* 'Golden Queen')
Bacopa 'Mauve Mist', *B.* 'Snowflake'
Basket begonias (tuberous) Cascade series
Bidens Compact series
Brachycome 'Amethyst', *B.* 'Purple'
Bush morning glory (*Convolvulus tricolor* 'Blue Ensign')
Candytuft *(Iberis crenata)*
Clematis 'Radar Love'
Coleus 'Trailing Red'
Floss flower *(Ageratum houstonianum)*
Forget-me-not *(Myosotis sylvatica)*
Fuchsia 'Gartenmeister Bonstedt', *F.* 'Korale', *F.* 'Swingtime', *F.* 'Tangerine'
Helichrysum 'Lemon Bush', *H.* 'Lemon Licorice', *H.* 'Licorice Splash'
Helichrysum microphyllum
Heliotrope 'Iowa Blue'
Hermannia verticillata
Ice plant (*Mesembryanthemum* species)
Ivy geranium (*Pelargonium* x *hortorum* 'Roller's Pilgrim')
Lobelia 'Double Kathleen'
Lotus vine *(Lotus berthelotti)*
Mexican creeping zinnia *(Sanvitalia procumbens)*
Moss rose (*Portulaca grandiflora* 'Sundial Mango')
Nasturtium 'Alaska', 'Empress of India'
Nolana paradoxa 'Blue Bird'
Periwinkle (*Catharanthus* 'Pretty in . . .' hybrids)
Petunia 'Supertunia', 'Surfinia', million bells
Scaevola 'Blue Fancy'
Sunrose (*Helianthemum* hybrids)
Sweet alyssum *(Lobularia maritima)*
Sweetpea (*Lathyrus odoratus* 'Cupid', *L. o.* 'Snoopea')
Twinspur *(Diascia barbarae)*
Verbena 'Tapien Blue'
Viola cornuta 'Bluebird'
Wahlenbergia 'Overshelf Gold'

FOLIAGE ANNUALS

Foliage annuals are traditional in flowerbeds, but they also contribute power to hanging baskets, window boxes, and other containers. Many foliage annuals do bloom, but their leaves earn their kudos. Silvery dusty millers *(Senecio cineraria)* and fine-textured lotus vine *(Lotus berthelotti)*, purple perilla *(Perilla frutescens)*, cream-streaked snow-on-the-mountain *(Euphorbia marginata)*, kales and cabbages, feathery dill, and spangled squirreltail grass *(Hordeum jubatum)* all bring unusual form, color, and texture to garden compositions.

In recent years, a new class of annuals has been introduced. Sometimes called "vegetative annuals," they are really vegetatively propagated tender perennials. Brilliant foliage plants like coleus and long bloomers like tropical begonias are hardy in warm climates but die with the arrival of frost. Grown from cuttings, these tender creatures act like annuals, flowering long and hard. If you like, you can lift them in early autumn to winter over indoors. However, most are so widely available and so inexpensive that it's more convenient to treat them as toss-aways.

Among the most exciting new annuals to hit the market are sunfast coleus. Older strains scorch or lose their brilliant patterns in the sun, even in the cool Northwest. These new coleus can take full sun in Georgia, where they were hybridized by Allan Armitage. What's more, they are day-neutral bloomers that don't flower in summertime. When coleus bloom, the plants disintegrate badly, growing leggy and skimpy of leaf in days. The new sunfast coleus bloom in winter, or would if they were still alive.

To keep them alive over the winter, root a few cuttings in a glass of water at summer's end. The cuttings can be grown indoors all winter, where they will be too young to bloom. Next summer, bring them out and enjoy a second season of color from these tropical beauties, which are perennials and shrubs in their native lands.

BEAUTIFUL LEAVES

Angel's trumpet (*Datura* and *Brugmansia* species)
Banana (*Musa* species)
Basil 'Purple Ruffles' (*Ocimum basilicum* 'Purple Ruffles')
Begonia x *semperflorens*
Bunny grass *(Lagurus ovatus)*
Burning bush *(Kochia scoparia)*
Canna hybrids
Castor beans (*Ricinus* 'Carmencita')
Cloud grass *(Agrostis nebulosa)*
Coleus Day-neutral series, Solar series, Sunlovers series
Dahlia 'Redskin'
Dusty miller (*Senecio cineraria* 'Silverdust', *S. c.* 'Cirrus')
Elephant's-ear (*Caladium* species)
Flowering cabbages and kales (*Brassica* species)
Fountain grass *(Pennisetum setaceum)*
Fuchsia 'Autumnale', *F.* 'Island Sunset'
Ginger (*Hedychium* species)
Helichrysum 'Lemon Licorice', *H.* 'Lime Splash', *H.* 'White Licorice'
Ivy geranium (*Pelargonium hortorum* 'Crocodile', *P. h.* 'Sunset', *P. h.* 'Variegata')
Love grass *(Eragrostis tef)*
New Guinea impatiens (*Impatiens* New Guinea hybrids)
Painted corn (*Zea mays* 'Variegata')
Perilla *(Perilla frutescens)*
Plectranthus (many, including *P. argentatus* and *P. australis*)
Ponytail grass *(Stipa tenuissima)*
Quaking grass *(Briza maxima)*
Red mustard 'McDonald's Red', 'Red Giant'
Rex begonia *(Begonia rex)*
Snow-on-the-mountain *(Euphorbia marginata)*
Squirreltail grass *(Hordeum jubatum)*
Sweet potato *(Ipomoea batatas* 'Blackie', *I. b.* 'Margarita')
Swiss chard 'Bright Lights', 'Rhubarb Red', 'Scotch Curly'
Taro (*Colocasia esculenta* 'Black Night')
Wahlenbergia 'Overshelf Gold'
Woodland tobacco (*Nicotiana sylvestris*)
Zonal geraniums *(Pelargonium* x *hortorum)*

ANNUALS FOR SHADE

Shade is often viewed as a problem, but for the gardener who grows annuals, it's a delightful opportunity. Shade lets us weave wondrous webs of colorful foliage emphasizing varied forms and textures. Large leaves that scorch or discolor in full sun develop their fullest potential in shade, and dozens of flowers bloom long and hard in shady settings. Given the right kind of shade, we can drape a shady arbor with trailing vines, surround a water feature with a luxuriance of glossy foliage, and create vivid tapestries of bloom, starting with primroses and baby blue eyes in spring and continuing steadily into autumn, when sweet violet cress spills its haunting fragrance. Dappled, airy shade is ideal, offering plenty of light and air but blocking the fiercest rays of the summer sun. Dense, dank, or bone-dry shade makes it challenging for most plants to grow well, but in such situations, raised beds, pots, and containers provide ample planting space.

Woodland understory annuals like forget-me-nots will thrive in filtered shade, especially where there is plenty of reflected light from house walls or nearby walkways. Damp shade makes streamside annuals from all over the world feel at home, from native monkeyflowers to tropical begonias and fuchsias.

However, be wary of beautiful thugs like giant Himalayan balsam *(Impatiens glandulifera),* which rises in exotic-looking thickets where damp ground provides constant moisture, scenting the air with flowers like wild orchids. This brazen beauty should never be planted near running water or anywhere that it can migrate into waterways, where it will force out less-determined natives.

Even moderately dry soil is harder to plant well, but a handful of tough annuals will make the attempt. Cheerful poached egg flower, baby blue eyes, and foxgloves will tolerate dry shade if given a periodic boost with supplemental watering. Hydrophyllic polymers (water-holding gels) will also improve moisture content in dry soils, enabling a wider range of plants to flourish. A deep mulch of compost and aged manure will improve the soil even more, enabling plants to settle in quickly.

Planting in pots and containers removes any difficulties of soil and allows playful exploration of ever-changing arrangements and combinations. Set pots of night-fragrant tobacco and mignonette near your seating area, and natural aromatherapy will help you relax after work. Sophisticated color combinations such as near-black 'Solar Eclipse' coleus with the coppery, tubular-flowered fuchsia 'Gartenmeister Bonstedt', and hot orange 'Non-Stop' begonias provide potent but pleasing color shocks.

If you prefer pastels, mingle 'African Orchid' impatiens in gentle pinks and pale purples with starry 'Amethyst' browallias. For a tropical foliage effect, mix silver-splashed elephant ears with rex begonias, 'Ruffled Raspberry' coleus, and towers of woodland tobacco. Where shade gives way to fuller light, all kinds of climbing and trailing annuals bolster the plant palette. A tremendous range of annuals grow beautifully in partial shade (which is often an apt description of the coastal Northwest), so don't hesitate to experiment with plants you enjoy, even if they are not strictly considered to be shade lovers.

SHADE ANNUALS

American browallia	*Browallia americana*
Amethyst flower	*Browallia speciosa*
Baby blue eyes	*Nemophila menziesii*
Begonia	many
Busy Lizzy	*Impatiens wallerana*
Coleus	Day-neutral series
Elephant's-ear	*Colocasia* species
Flowering tobacco	*Nicotiana alata* 'Fragrant Cloud'
Foxglove	*Digitalis purpurea* 'Foxy'
Fried egg flower	*Limnanthes douglasii*
	Impatiens 'African Orchid'
Madagascar periwinkle	*Catharanthus roseus*
Mignonette	*Reseda odorata*
Monkey flower	*Mimulus* x *hybridus*
New Guinea impatiens	*Impatiens* New Guinea hybrids
Primrose	*Primula* x *polyantha*
Variegated monkey flower	*Mimulus* x *hybridus* 'Variegata'
Violet cress	*Ionopsidium acaule*
Wishbone flower	*Torenia fournieri*, Clown series
Woodland tobacco	*Nicotiana sylvestris*

ANNUALS FOR COOL NORTHERN GARDENS

In the northernmost parts of the Northwest, cool summers are the norm. Anywhere along the coast, cool nights, foggy days, and sea breezes can make Northwest gardens challenging for plants that appreciate accumulated heat. Deep mulches of compost and aged manure help insulate warmth into the soil, making nighttime blankets for chilly flowers. There are also quite a few annuals that grow and flower well despite a lack of summer heat and sunny skies.

ANNUALS FOR COOL SUMMERS

Annual phlox	*Phlox drummondii* 'Phlox of Sheep'
Begonias	many hybrids
	Bidens 'Golden Goddess'
Black-eyed Susan vine	*Thunbergia alata*
Blue lace flower	*Didiscus coerulea*
Browallia	*Browallia speciosa* and hybrids
	Bupleurum griffithii 'Green Gold'
Butterfly orchid	*Schizanthus x wisetonensis*
Calla lily	*Calla* hybrids
Cape daisy	*Dimorphotheca sinuata*
China pink	*Dianthus chinensis*
Dahlia	*Dahlia* hybrids
English daisy	*Bellis perennis*
Fairy snapdragon	*Linaria maroccana*
Farewell to spring	*Clarkia* hybrids
Field poppy	*Papaver rhoeas*
Flowering cabbage and kale	*Brassica* species
Forget-me-not	*Myosotis sylvatica*
Foxglove	*Digitalis* 'Foxy'
Fuschia	*Fuchsia* hybrids
Iceland poppy	*Papaver nudicaule*
Larkspur	*Consolida ambigua*
Lobelia	*Lobelia erinus*
Mignonette	*Reseda odorata*
Monkey flower	*Mimulus x hybridus*
Nasturtium	*Tropaeolum majus*
New Guinea impatiens	*Impatiens* New Guinea hybrids
Painted tongue	*Salpiglossis sinuata*
Pansy	*Viola x wittrockiana*
Pouch flower	*Nemesia strumosa*
Primrose	*Primula x polyantha* and others
Stock	*Matthiola incana*
Swan River daisy	*Brachycome* hybrids
Sweet William	*Dianthus barbatus*
Viola	*Viola cornuta*
Wallflower	*Chieranthus cheiri*

In cool maritime gardens, calender flower (Calendula officinalis) *may be in flower all year long. Easy to please and drought tolerant, it does best in full sun.*

If you have a hot, dry place nothing much will grow in, try California poppies. Newer selections flower in delicious shades of pink, copper, apricot, and pale lemon, providing months of blossom without demanding anything from the gardener.

ANNUALS FOR HOT SPOTS

The Northwest is not famous for hot summers, but there are plenty of places where temperatures can climb in sunny summers. In cities, the streets, sidewalks, and nearby buildings can cast reflected heat and light, creating hot-spot microclimates. Water can also bounce light, making many waterfront gardens warmer than their neighbors a few blocks away. The presence of water tempers climate in other ways as well, holding heat at night and reducing frost effects in winter.

A lot of annuals can be persuaded to take the heat as long as their particular needs are met. Generally, humus-enriched, well-drained soil and plenty of water will do the trick, but sometimes one supplement is enough. Calendulas and baby's breath, geraniums and dusty miller perform brilliantly in hot spots where the soil is lean and poor if given ample and regular watering. Prairie plants like blanket flower and tickseed can tolerate an amazing amount of heat and drought when they are growing in deep, rich soils. Garden verbenas and the colorful amaranth known as Joseph's coat do best with both great soil and frequent watering.

Certain stalwart annuals are troupers that can be counted on to cover a difficult area neatly without much fussing. To find these effortlessly rewarding plants, take a look in lowlier surroundings. The annuals that enliven urban alleys and empty lots are invariably tough, adaptable, and easygoing. Before you take seeds or seedlings home, however, double-check to see just how easygoing they are. Some ardent annuals make themselves all too readily at home. Others, like rose moss, ice plant, and California poppy, simply do their job well, growing nicely in demanding sites without crowding out choicer plants or spreading too rapidly and taking over more than their allotted space.

LONG-BLOOMING ANNUALS

Lots of annuals will bloom for months so long as you keep them deadheaded, but will stop flowering if allowed to set seed. When you can't always be on hand, consider growing a selection of everlastings. These are sold by the boxcar load for cut flowers and dried arrangements. However, few people think about using everlasting annuals in pots, where they remain lovely for months on end.

*Dainty, cheerful fried egg flower
(*Limnanthes douglassii) *is a tough
little native that blooms exuberantly
in sun or shade.*

Borage relative Cerinthe major *offers
summer-sky blue flowers over a very
long period. A self-sowing annual, it
prefers good drainage and at least half
a day of sun.*

HEAT-LOVING ANNUALS

	Arctotis (several species)
Baby's breath	*Gypsophila elegans*
Blanket flower	*Gaillardia pulchella*
Burning bush	*Kochia scoparia*
Bush marigold	*Tagetes lemmonii*
	Calendula officinalis 'Pacific Beauty'
California poppy	*Eschscholzia californica* 'Thai Silk'
Cigar plant	*Cuphea ignea*
Clary sage	*Salvia sclarea*
Crested cockscomb	*Celosia cristata*
Cypress vine	*Ipomoea quamoclit*
Dusty miller	*Senecio cineraria* 'Cirrus'
Garden verbena	*Verbena* x *hybrida*
	Gazania 'Silver Leaf', *G.* 'Talent'
Geranium	*Pelargonium* x *hortorum*
Globe amaranth	*Gomphrena globosa*
Ice plant	*Mesembryanthemum* species
Joseph's coat	*Amaranthus tricolor*
Mexican creeping zinnia	*Sanvitalia procumbens*
Mexican zinnia	*Zinnia elegans* 'Red Pulcino', *Z. e.* 'Terra Cotta'
Moss rose	*Portulaca grandiflora* 'Sundance'
Pepperpot	*Capsicum annuum*
Periwinkle	*Catharanthus* 'Peppermint Cooler'
	Petunia hybrids
Rock daisy	*Melampodium* species
Statice	*Limonium sinuatum*
Sweet alyssum	*Lobularia maritima*
Tickseed	*Coreopsis tinctoria*
Transvaal daisy	*Gerbera* hybrids

Globe amaranth *(Gomphrena globosa)* produces plump little balls or spiky thimble flowers in a tumble of jewel colors, from white to apricot and pink, rose and maroon. Choose single colors like 'Amber Glow' and 'Lavender Lady' or blended color mixtures. Some wheat celosias look like brains or curly cock's combs, but my favorite is silvery pink 'Flamingo Feathers', which looks like the silkiest of plumes. Try it with cut-leaf dusty miller and the buttery miniature rose called 'Popcorn'.

Statice (2 to 3 feet) is ever popular with the flower-craft crowd, who value the staying power of its fizzy flower clusters. Many single-color strains can be found, from 'Apricot Shades' to 'Purple Majesty' and 'Iceberg'. A new Japanese blend called *Statice sinuatum* 'Pastel Shades'

LONG-BLOOMING ANNUALS FOR CUTTING

African marigold	*Tagetes* hybrids
Annual aster	*Callistephus* species
Baby's breath	*Gypsophila muralis* 'Gypsy'
Bachelor's button	*Centaurea cyanus* 'Florence Violet'
Bells of Ireland	*Moluccella laevis*
Blanket flower	*Gaillardia* 'Sunshine Mix'
Black-eyed Susan	*Rudbeckia hirta* 'Irish Eyes', *R. h.* 'Nutmeg'
Bupleurum	*Bupleurum griffithii* 'Green Gold'
Bush marigold	*Tagetes lemonii*
Butterfly flower	*Schizanthus* 'Disco', *S.* 'Sweet Lips'
Butterfly orchid	*Salpiglossis sinuata* 'Envy'
Butterfly weed	*Asclepias curassavica* 'Red Butterfly', *A. c.* 'Silky Gold'
Calendula	*Calendula officinalis* 'Prince Yellow'
Calla lily	*Zantedeschia* 'Apricot'
Cape daisy	*Dimorphotheca sinuata* 'Apricot Queen'
Clary sage	*Salvia sclarea*, *S. horminum* 'Claryssa'
Cockscomb	*Celosia cristata* 'Chief Carmine', *C. c.* 'Chief Gold'
Cosmos	*Cosmos bipinnatus* 'Seashells Mixed'
Dahlia	*Dahlia* (many species)
Everlasting	*Salpiglossis sinuata* 'Grandiflora Mixed'
Floss flower	*Ageratum houstonianum* 'Blue Horizon', *A. h.* 'White Bouquet'
Flowering tobacco	*Nicotiana alata*
Forget-me-not	*Myosotis sylvatica*
Geranium	*Pelargonium* x *hortorum*
Green lace plant	*Ammi visagna* 'Green Mist'
'Italian White' sunflower	*Helianthus annuus* 'Italian White'
Joseph's coat	*Amaranthus tricolor*
Larkspur	*Consolida ambigua* 'Blue Spire', *C. a.* 'Salmon Beauty'
Love-in-a-mist	*Nigella damascena* 'Oxford Blue', *N. d.* 'Red Jewel'
Mexican sunflower	*Tithonia rotundifolia*
Painted daisy	*Chrysanthemum carinatum* 'Court Jesters'
Pansy	*Viola cornuta* 'Swiss Giants'
Penstemon	*Penstemon barbatus*
Phlox	*Phlox drummondii* 'Phlox of Sheep'
Pincushion flower	*Scabiosa atropurpurea* 'Ace of Spades'
Plumed cockscomb	*Celosia plumosa* 'Sparkler Cream', *C. p.* 'Sparkler Red')
Poppy	many species
Queen Anne's lace	*Ammi majus* 'Queen of Africa'
Salvia	*Salvia horminum* 'White Swan'
Snapdragon	*Antirrhinum majus*
Snow-on-the-mountain	*Euphorbia marginata* 'Kilimanjaro'
South African daisy	*Venidium fastuosum* 'Monarch of the Veldt', *V. f.* 'Zulu Prince'
Spider flower	*Cleome hasslerana* 'Helen Campbell', *C. h.* 'Violet Queen'
Stock	*Matthiola incana*
Sweet pea	*Lathyrus odoratus* 'Antique Fantasy'
Sweet William	*Dianthus barbatus*
Wheat celosia	*Celosia spicata* 'Flamingo Feather', *C. s.* 'Flamingo Purple'
Zinnia	*Zinnia* 'Oklahoma Mix', *Z.* 'Red Spider'

Annual black-eyed Susan, Rudbeckia *'Nutmeg' makes a splendid cut flower and is at home in a mixed border as any perennial.*

LONG-BLOOMING ANNUALS WITH DRYABLE FLOWERS

Bells of Ireland	*Moluccella laevis* 'Green Bells'
Blue lace flower	*Didiscus coeruleus* 'Blue Lace', *D. c.* 'Madonna White'
Carmel daisy	*Scabiosa prolifera*
Globe amaranth	*Gomphrena globosa* 'Pink', *G. g.* 'Strawberry Red'
Moonweed	*Lunaria annuua* 'Variegata'
Paper drumsticks	*Scabiosa stellata*
Red broom corn	*Sorghum vulgare*
Russian statice	*Statice suworowii* 'Rose Rat Tail'
Shoo-fly plant	*Nicandra physaloides*
Spanish love-in-a-mist	*Nigella hispanica*
Statice	*Limonium sinuatum* 'Fortress Apricot', 'Lavender'
Strawflower	*Helichrysum bracteatum* 'Bright Bikinis'
Sunflower	*Helianthus annuus*
Sweet wormwood	*Artemisia annua* 'Sweet Annie'
Winged everlasting	*Amobium alatum* 'Bikini'

offers a soft, cloudy mass of delicate tints from palest pink to slate blue. If you prefer zippy brights, look for Thompson & Morgan's 'T & M Mixed', which includes citrus yellows and oranges, warm blues, strong pinks, and clean white.

South African daisies are a related group of annuals that includes magnificent forms of *Venidium fastuosum,* a sturdy plant that likes nothing better than plenty of sun. The regal, flame orange 'Monarch of the Veldt' has snapping black eyes and thick, fuzzy gray-green leaves, a standout in any hot-colored combination and a great partner for the bushy California native marigold *(Tagetes lemonii),* covered with small, bitingly fragrant citrus-orange flowers. 'Zulu Prince' is even more striking, its creamy white petals surrounding burgundy black eyes above silver plush foliage. This one needs sophisticated company like tall 'Italian White' sunflowers *(Helianthus annuus)* and frothy, black and white 'Pennie Black' baby blue eyes *(Nemophila menziesii).*

Bells of Ireland is an oddball annual, easily overlooked when not in bloom. Once given ground space, it sends up spires of flaring green bells, emerald netted with sage and tinted with olive. Dramatic and shapely, these robust spikes are favorites for dried arrangements, but they can have considerable garden impact as well, providing pleasing contrast of form beside foamy baby's breath, cascades of roses, or sheaves of glittering grasses.

ANNUALS FOR FRAGRANCE

Annuals offer some of the most potent perfumes in nature, from honey-scented sweet alyssum to the smoky, alluring night-scented phlox. A host of night bloomers like moon vine and woodland tobacco will scent the evening air with mysterious scents, while day bloomers can be combined to create living perfumes.

Green-flowered *Reseda odora* has whiskery, insignificant-looking flowers that release the bewitching fragrance known as mignonette. Warm air makes the scent especially potent, so tuck this unobtrusive plant into a gaudy container bouquet near the picnic table and plant a few in the border near the hammock. Beloved of Empress Josephine, this frumpy little green flower exudes one of the world's most delectable scents. A slow starter, it comes into its own in midsummer.

Heliotrope 'Marine' is an outstandingly fragrant annual with long-lasting clusters of deep-sea-blue flowers. A friend puts 'Marine' heliotrope near her giant sea kale *(Crambe cordifolia),* where its sweetness masks the rank sweaty-sock smell of the crambe amazingly well. 'Black Prince' has the same lovely scent, but its flowers are midnight blue, the foliage an inky green that turns almost black in full sun.

Flowering tobaccos are famous for their perfume, especially 'Fragrant Cloud'. The same species has produced well-known mixtures like 'Domino', 'Nikki', and 'Sensation', all of which bloom in shades of dusty rose and mauve, rich purples and muted reds. The tall woodland tobacco stands 3 to 5 or more feet tall and blooms well in sun or partial shade. This beauty boasts great, dangling clusters of white trumpet flowers, which breathe out their gentle fragrance on the evening air. With wrist-thick stalks and large, heart-shaped leaves, it looks too substantial to be an annual, and indeed, it may resprout from its thick roots after a mild winter, though it is much more apt to regenerate from its abundant seed.

FRAGRANT ANNUALS

Almond flower	*Schizopetalon walkeri*
Angel's trumpet	*Brugmansia* and *Datura* species
Flowering tobacco	*Nicotiana alata* 'Fragrant Cloud'
Heliotrope	*Heliotrope* 'Black Prince', *H.* 'Marine'
Honeybells	*Hermmania verticillata*
Mignonette	*Reseda odora*
Moon vine	*Calonyction aculeatum*
Night-scented phlox	*Zaluzianskya capensis*
Night-scented stock	*Matthiola bicornis*
Stock 'Ten Weeks Mixed'	*Matthiola x hybridus*
Sweet alyssum	*Lobularia maritima*
Sweet pea	*Lathyrus odorata* 'Antique Fantasy', *L. o.* 'Fragrantissima'
Sweet William	*Dianthus barbatus*
Sweet wormwood	*Artemisia annua* 'Sweet Annie'
Wallflower	*Chieranthus cheiri*
Woodland tobacco	*Nicotiana sylvestris*

Sweet alyssum makes a foamy mass of tiny, honey-scented flowers in spreading mats just a few inches high. Drop a few seeds at the edges of big containers, and alyssum will spill down the sides in scented curtains all summer. Choose white, pink, lavender, rose, or purple or the new peach and apricot shades.

Sweet peas are often bred for size and color rather than scent these days. The 'Antique Fantasy' strain smells intoxicatingly sweet, as does 'Fragrantissima'. Both produce clouds of perfumed flowers in watercolor shades of pink and blue, rose and cream, lavender and purple. They need a trellis insert in your pot to climb on, or wrap a nearby gutter pipe with plastic netting for them to scramble up.

Don't try to pronounce night-scented phlox's real name (*Zaluzianskya capensis*), but do grow some. The feathery white flowers smell more like play-dough than perfume early in the evening, but as the night wears on, the fragrance matures with increasing beauty, just as women do.

BUYING ANNUALS

When you shop for annuals, be very picky. Shop-worn perennials are often well worth buying, since they may spring back to health over the winter. Annuals, which live only a single season, do best when their life is uncomplicated by health problems. Before you buy, visit several nurseries and garden centers to get an idea of what's available. Look for wide selections of healthy, attractive plants that are well rooted and vigorous.

It's usually most lastingly rewarding to buy the very best, but inexpensive mass-market annuals can offer genuinely good value if you shop wisely. If local stores offer terrific prices on spring bedding annuals, ask the sales clerks when new shipments of annuals are expected, and be on hand to pick out the cream of the crop. In every case, select the best specimens to take home, giving preference to those that look obviously healthy and boast plentiful new growth.

Don't buy annuals whose foliage is either limp or brittle (both are signs of distress). Avoid plants with withered new growth or puckered or discolored mature leaves, which are also indicators of stress or disease. Discoloration can be harder to detect in variegated plants such as coleus, so check the overall appearance and buy only plants that appear to be in sturdy good health. Healthy plants stand upright on strong stems and are held firmly in their pots. Plants with damaged root systems will tilt or flop over, and their anchor roots may be partially exposed above the soil level. Choose compact, sturdy plants over larger but lanky or floppy-looking ones.

Check the bottom of each pot to inspect root growth. A few small roots poking from the drainage holes usually indicate that the plant is growing strongly, but to make sure, give the pot a gentle squeeze. If there's some give, the plants is probably a fine choice. If it feels like you're squeezing a rock, turn the plant carefully out of its pot and take a look. Ideally, the roots will make a solid web through which you can still detect some soil. A solid mass of tightly wound roots means the plant has been waiting too long.

Rootbound annuals should generally be avoided, but if the whole plant looks great, it's probably not too late. When you plant, simply slice a crisscross to cut the roots apart, then tease them open before planting. Healthy, vigorous plants will respond quickly to this minor surgery, bouncing back in days with renewed growth.

ANNUAL PLUGS

Until recently, annuals grown in plugs were available only to wholesale buyers. These days, many nurseries are offering small but sturdy annual starts grown in wedge-shaped blocks of spongy, semirigid material called plant plugs. Marigolds, dusty miller, and similar bedders are often available as mini-plugs about an inch long. Vegetatively propagated and tropical "annuals" like coleus, double nasturtiums, and marguerites are frequently grown as cuttings stuck into larger plugs.

The nursery industry prefers plug starts because they eliminate or reduce root trauma during transplanting. Plug starts can be popped out of their growth trays and set into 4-inch pots with a minimum of disturbance, so they never stop active growth. Plant plugs should be packed in plastic bags at the nursery to avoid moisture loss on the way home, where they must be transplanted immediately.

TIP PINCHING

Nursery stock is often smothered with bloom that captivates the eye but may overstress the plant's resources once pampered greenhouse conditions are left behind. To reduce transplant shock, pinch off all mature flowers (float them in a bowl to reduce your own pangs of loss) before planting. Out-of-season bloom should also be removed to encourage stronger rebloom later. For instance, when buying chrysanthemum starts in spring, pinch off every last flower, along with all buds. You'll be glad you did, since their roots will redirect their energy into making big, bushy plants that will bloom even more abundantly at the right time.

PLANTING OUT AND TRANSPLANTING

As you learned in Chapter 3, making great soil is the first step to a thriving garden. Next comes proper plant placement. Like all plants, annuals grow best when arranged so that their foliage barely overlaps that of their neighbors. The leafy tapestry acts like a living mulch, conserving soil moisture and encouraging beneficial soil bacteria that help plants take up nutrients. Too much crowding, on the other hand, can lead to fungal and mildew problems. Unless the annuals you buy or transplant are already fully grown, you'll need to allow room for their natural expansion. Consult the seed packet or plant tag for mature size (which may be given as height only) and spacing recommendations (these may read "plant on 18-inch centers," or "use six plants per square yard").

For a generous look, you can opt to space young plants a little more closely, but over time, crowded plants tend to be leggy rather than well furnished. Annuals benefit from generous planting practices, so heed folk wisdom and dig a gallon hole for a 4-inch pot. In new beds, blend the sandy loam and manure with a potful of compost or good potting soil (a gallon-sized plant receives a gallon of soil, and so on).

In an established bed, blend the removed soil with an equal amount of compost or aged manure. Fill the planting hole halfway up with blended compost and potting soil, making a slight depression in the center. If the roots are tightly wound or densely filling the pot, gently loosen them with your fingers or a garden knife to stimulate new root growth. Most annuals have relatively fragile root systems that don't benefit from extensive fussing, so it's best to simply ruffle up the outer roots, leaving the rootball as intact as possible.

Set the plant in place, making sure that its crown remains at soil level (just as it was in its pot). Fill in the planting hole with compost and potting soil, firming it in gently as you work. Water well and fluff up or renew the mulch or top-dressing around it.

RESOURCES

CHAPTER 3: DELICIOUS DIRT

PROBIOTICS

For information on BLEND, LASE, and soil tests that evaluate the soil food web, contact:

SOIL FOODWEB, INC.
980 NW Circle Boulevard
Corvallis, OR 97330
541-752-5066
Website: www.soilfoodweb.com
E-mail: info@soilfoodweb.com

Both retail and wholesale quantities of LASE and BLEND can be obtained from the folks at

ADVANCED AGRITECH
Toll-free: 888-547-3163
In Oregon, call: 509-547-3163
Fax: 509-545-6508

Aerobic compost tea brewers are available from the following sources:

GROWING SOLUTIONS
1150 Darlene Lane
Eugene, OR 97401
541-343-8727
Fax: 541-343-8374
Website: www.growingsolutions.com
E-mail: info@growingsolutions.com

SOILSOUP
9792 Edmonds Way, No. 247
Edmonds, WA 98020
206-542-9304
Toll-free: 877-711-7687
Fax: 206-533-0748
Website: www.soilsoup.com
E-mail: info@soilsoup.com

ACTIVATED CHARCOAL

Activated charcoal is sold in 40-pound bags and can be difficult to find. If your garden center wants to order some, the nearest wholesaler is probably Wilber-Ellis in

Portland, Oregon. Tell the buyer to ask for Paul Collins; the phone number is 503-227-3525.

CHAPTER 4: NORTHWESTERN LAWNS

ECO-LAWN SEED MIXTURES

NICHOLS GARDEN NURSERY
1190 N Pacific Highway
Albany, OR 97321
541-928-9280
Website: www.nicholsgardennursery.com

NATURAL LAWN CARE COMPANIES IN SEATTLE

EARTHGUARD INC.
425-885-3002
Toll-free: 800-895-5100

IN HARMONY ORGANIC BASED LANDSCAPE SERVICES

425-486-2180
Website: www.inharmony.com

PUBLICATIONS ON LAWN CARE AND VEGETATION MANAGEMENT

The handbook *Ecologically Sound Lawn Care for the Pacific Northwest* can be downloaded in PDF format from the Seattle Public Utilities website under the Natural Lawn Care heading: www.ci.seattle.wa.us/util/rescons.

For copies of the handbooks *Vegetation Management: A Guide for Puget Sound Bluff Property Owners, Slope Stabilization and Erosion Control Using Vegetation: A Manual of Practice for Coastal Property Owners,* and *Surface Water and Groundwater on Coastal Bluffs*, write to:

WASHINGTON STATE DEPARTMENT OF ECOLOGY
Shorelands & Coastal Zone Management Program
PO Box 47600
Olympia, WA 98504-7600
Website: www.ecy.wa.gov/

Your city government's water management program may also have similar material available.

CHAPTER 5: MAINTAINING THE SUSTAINABLE GARDEN

PLANT AMNESTY

For more information on Plant Amnesty and a complete list of available educational material, contact:

PLANT AMNESTY
PO Box 15377
Seattle, WA 98115-0377
206-783-9813
Website: www.plantamnesty.org

CHAPTER 6: NATURAL PLANT CARE

LASE AND BLEND

Retail and wholesale quantities of LASE and BLEND are available from:

ADVANCED AGRITECH
Toll-free: 888-547-3163
In Oregon, call: 509-547-3163
Fax: 509-545-6508

CHAPTER 13: VINES AND CLIMBERS

CLEMATIS

For information about joining the Pacific Northwest Clematis Society, write to the following address:

THE PACIFIC NORTHWEST CLEMATIS SOCIETY
1145 SE Linn Street
Portland, OR 97202

Twelve monthly newsletters and membership cost $25 per year.

INDEX

PAGE NUMBERS IN **BOLD**
DENOTE SIDENOTES.